The English School

The English School
its architecture and organization 1370 - 1870

Malcolm Seaborne

University of Toronto Press

First published 1971 in Canada
and the United States of America
by University of Toronto Press
Toronto and Buffalo

ISBN 0-8020-1784-3

Printed in Great Britain

Contents

List of figures in the text

The author is very grateful to the architects, noted below, who lent plans on which many of the figures have been based. Those marked R.C.H.M. are reproduced by permission of the Royal Commission on Historical Monuments (England) and are Crown Copyright.

List of plates

The plates are reproduced together after the main body of the text for convenience of reference, and are arranged broadly according to the order in which they are referred to in the text. (Occasionally the order has been slightly varied to achieve a coherent layout or to make some visual point.)

The captions have been kept brief, since virtually all of the plates are fully discussed in the text, where numbers in bold type indicate references to the plates.

The author and publishers are very grateful to the holders of copyright (noted in parentheses in the list below) who have given permission for reproductions to be made. Plates attributed to N.M.R. are reproduced by permission of the National Monuments Record and those to R.C.H.M. by permission of the Royal Commission on Historical Monuments (England) and are Crown Copyright. Those attributed to B.M. are reproduced by courtesy of the Trustees of the British Museum and those to *The Builder* by courtesy of the R.I.B.A. Library and the Editor of *Building*. In the list below L. = Left and R. = Right.

Bibliographical note and abbreviations

Information has been drawn from a wide variety of sources, all of which are acknowledged in the notes to be found at the end of each chapter. Little purpose would be served by providing a separate bibliography, since the books written specifically on the subject of school architecture before 1870 are very few and are fully discussed in the text. In citing books, however, full bibliographical details have been given, and these have where necessary been repeated so that the note '*op. cit.*' in every case refers to a work mentioned in the notes relating to that particular chapter. The place of publication is London unless otherwise stated. The notes not only cite authorities directly used, but also contain further references for the use of readers who wish to follow up particular points. The following abbreviations have been used:

B.J.E.S.	*British Journal of Educational Studies* (Faber & Faber).
B.M.	British Museum.
C.C.R.	*Charity Commissioners' Reports* (H.M.S.O., 1819–40).
C.R.O.	County Record Office.
Carlisle	N. Carlisle, *A concise description of the endowed grammar schools in England and Wales* (2 vols., Baldwin, Cradock and Joy, 1818).
D.E.S.	Department of Education and Science.
G.L.C.	Greater London Council.
H.M.S.O.	Her Majesty's Stationery Office.
N.M.R.	National Monuments Record.
Pevsner	N. Pevsner, *The buildings of England* series (Penguin Books, 1951 f.).
R.C.H.M.	Royal Commission on Historical Monuments (England) (Inventories published by H.M.S.O.).
R.I.B.A.	Royal Institute of British Architects.
S.I.C.	*Schools Inquiry Commission Report* (H.M.S.O., 1868).
U.P.	University Press.
V.C.H.	*The Victoria History of the Counties of England* (now published by the University of London, Institute of Historical Research).

Preface

There is in this country a rich heritage of school buildings of various dates from the later Middle Ages onwards. Many of them are of architectural merit, and to that extent have begun to attract the attention of the architectural historian. But no-one has looked at these buildings from the educational as well as from the architectural point of view. They have considerable interest as the reflection of changing ideas about how children should be educated and organized for teaching purposes. Even those schools with little or no architectural merit are often important from the educational and sociological points of view. Furthermore, the documentary material relating to the history of education is often fragmentary, so that surviving buildings frequently constitute a valuable source of knowledge about the development of particular schools, and sometimes of general educational history.

This book begins with the background to the founding of Winchester College in 1382 and ends with the major legislative changes of 1868–70. It is intended not only as a contribution to architectural history but also, and indeed primarily, as a study of the development of educational ideas and practices over five centuries. It is hoped to cover the period from 1870 to 1970 in a subsequent volume.

The starting-point at every stage of my inquiry has been the architectural evidence, especially school buildings which may still be seen by the interested reader. Sir Nikolaus Pevsner's *The Buildings of England* series has been invaluable for helping to locate surviving school buildings, as, in the smaller area they cover, have been the published inventories of the Royal Commission on Historical Monuments. Some use has also been made of the Ministry of Housing and Local Government's lists of buildings of special architectural or historic interest. I owe a particular debt of gratitude to the National Buildings Record (now part of the National Monuments Record), with its extensive collection of photographs and ever-helpful staff. For the historical and educational background, I made much use of the local history collection in Leicester University Library, and especially of the resources of the School of Education Library, to whose staff my warmest thanks are due. That I was able to visit many of the schools mentioned

I owe to the co-operation of the heads of schools and to the Research Board of Leicester University, which gave me financial assistance for this purpose. I am also very grateful to Mrs B. Starkey, who typed my manuscript, to Mr G. Rigby, who redrew most of the plans, and to Mr B. Burch, who helped to read the proofs and compiled the index.

Other acknowledgements are made in the notes at the end of each chapter. So many headmasters, architects, librarians, archivists and others have helped me in the preparation of this work that I apologize in advance for any chance omissions of those to whom I owe my sincerest thanks. In covering so much detailed (and hitherto largely unexplored) ground, I cannot hope to have avoided errors or to have included all points of importance. I should be glad to receive further information from any reader who cares to get in touch with the publisher.

M. S.

One

The legacy of the Middle Ages

The physical remains of medieval schooling are, with a few notable exceptions, extremely scanty. Many of the buildings used for school purposes were not designed as schools and in many cases were not adapted for educational use until the Reformation had released on to the property market a large number of surplus ecclesiastical buildings.

The earliest schools were relatively undifferentiated as to curriculum and organization, and virtually no record remains of their internal organization. One of the most recent writers on the subject suggests that in schools before the fourteenth century the curriculum was graded neither according to the difficulty of the subject nor according to the age of those being taught (cf. pl. **1**).[1]* Before the invention of printing, books were comparatively scarce: it is probable that only the teachers possessed them, and that they read out passages from the books over and over again until the pupils had them by heart. Very few manuscript drawings of the fourteenth century seem to show boys as well as masters holding books, but books are more commonly shown being used by children in the fifteenth century and later (pls. **3** and **4**). Even so, it is likely that the teaching methods used were still essentially oral: the child was mainly dependent on the teacher for information, and the days of private study and 'home-work' were still in the future. To what extent the pupils wrote their exercises (instead of merely reciting them from memory) is not clear. A recent writer states that the medieval schoolboy 'had no permanent record of his exercises'.[2] The excavation of a fourteenth-century school at Lübeck in Germany last century provides evidence of wax tablets used by the boys, who seem to have used styluses to write on them,[3] as was common in Roman times: they are probably wax tablets bound together with straps rather than books which the boys are holding in some of the manuscript pictures of schools which have survived from this period (e.g. pl. **2**). Certainly by the late fifteenth century (and probably associated with the spread of printing and the greater availability of paper) written exercises seem to have become more usual. Erasmus, who was at school in Deventer in

*The notes appear at ends of chapters throughout.

1475, tells us that the grammatical text was dictated slowly by the master, so that the boys could take down every word.[4] We also have visual evidence, such as the brass monument at Little Ilford (Essex), which commemorates Tom Heron, who died in 1512, aged fourteen, and shows him with penner and inkhorn hanging from his girdle.[5]

Nevertheless, it is clear that the oral method of instruction persisted for many years, even after the introduction of printed text-books and written exercises in paper-books during the sixteenth century. Roger Ascham, who was born in Yorkshire in about 1515, wrote of the boys in his local grammar school 'always learning, and little profiting; learning without book, everything; understanding within the book, little or nothing: their whole knowledge, by learning without the book, was tied only to their tongue and lips and never ascended up to the brain and head and therefore was soon spit out of the mouth again'.[6] Such methods of rote-learning again became widespread (if indeed they ever died out at all) in the nineteenth century, when even cheap printed books were scarce in schools for the very poor.

What evidence we have, therefore, about methods of teaching schoolchildren in the Middle Ages indicates that very little special provision was needed by way of equipment or buildings. The internal organization of the schools was similarly of the most rudimentary kind. The first development of importance, leading to a somewhat more complex organization of schools, has been attributed to the emergence of colleges in the fourteenth and fifteenth centuries.[7] Colleges frequently included educational provision as an integral part of their organization, and it is fortunate that we have in Winchester (founded 1382) and Eton (founded 1440) two important surviving examples of this kind of institution. Both were to have considerable influence in effecting the transition to modern forms of school organization and buildings.

Colleges, with their tightly-organized structure, reflected a reaction against the often ill-disciplined and undifferentiated character of earlier schooling. The scholars were subjected to a carefully laid-down régime, and were now grouped more according to age. The specifically educational activities performed by the scholars on the foundation were only a part—and in most cases a subordinate part—of the total activities for which the colleges were responsible. Even at Winchester, where the educational activities were particularly stressed, the full establishment consisted of a warden at the head, with ten fellows, three chaplains and sixteen choristers, in addition to the master, usher (assistant master) and seventy scholars.[8] At Eton, similarly, the provost took precedence over the headmaster, and the original foundation included ten fellows, four clerks, six choristers, twenty-five poor and disabled men and twenty-five scholars to learn grammar (later increased to seventy, as at Winchester).[9] It is also interesting to note that the original schoolrooms at both Winchester and Eton occupied an architecturally subordinate position in the total complex of buildings. At Winchester, the school, now called Seventh Chamber, was not a separate building but was beneath the hall and flanked by the chapel and kitchen, which themselves formed part of an inner courtyard (fig. 1 and pl. **5**). At Eton, the original school, now called Lower School, was

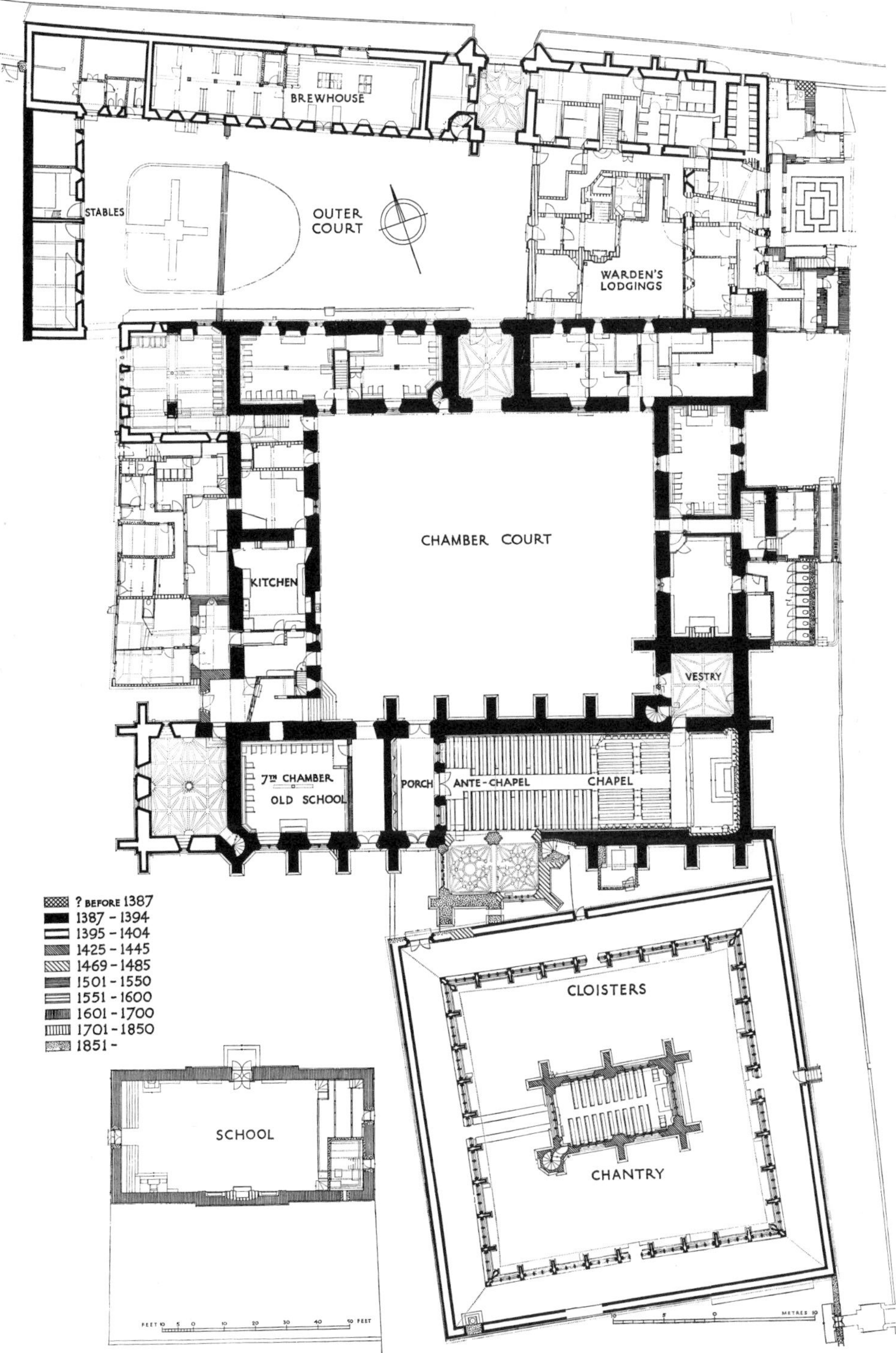

Figure 1 Winchester College, ground plan showing dates of work and state of buildings in 1954.

architecturally somewhat less integrated with the rest of the college. It was on the ground floor of a separate wing opposite the chapel, and the courtyard so formed was not fully enclosed until the late seventeenth century, when Upper School was built (fig. 2).

The school at Winchester, the prototype of many subsequent foundations, needs to be considered in more detail.[10] The scholars attended services in the chapel with the rest of the community, and dined in hall with the warden and fellows. They slept eleven or twelve to a room on the ground floor of a block of chambers (the word commonly used for bedrooms at this date) built on each side of Middle Gate; above them slept the fellows, three to a room, with the warden's chamber over Middle Gate and the master, usher and tenth fellow in another room on the first floor.[11] The schoolroom itself was completed in 1394, and is therefore 'the only ancient school building of the fourteenth century now existing'.[12] It consisted of a room 45 feet 6 inches long, 29 feet wide and 15 feet high. (In 1687 it was reduced in size by the construction of a passage, and from 1701 it became known as 'Seventh Chamber', because it was then used as a bedroom, a new schoolroom having been built in 1683–7.) The only clue we have concerning the internal organization of the school at Winchester comes from a passage in the revised statutes of 1400:

> In each of the lower [i.e. scholars'] chambers let there be at least three scholars of good repute more advanced than the rest in age, sense and learning to superintend the studies of their chamber-fellows and diligently oversee them, and when called upon truly to certify and inform the Warden, Sub-Warden and Master Teacher of their morals, behaviour and advancement in learning from time to time as often as may be necessary; or bound by their oath, so that such scholars who are under any defect in morals, are negligent or lazy in their studies may receive due and sufficient chastisement, correction and punishment according to their faults.[13]

There was in fact nothing really new in this arrangement: a similar provision was made for the sister college at Oxford (New College), whose statutes were themselves based on those of Merton College (1274) and Oriel College (1329), where, however, they applied to somewhat older scholars than those on the foundation at Winchester. The role of the prepositors or prefects (as they were called) was merely to inform the master of misdemeanours, and they had at this date no power to impose punishments themselves.

The only structural features to be remarked upon in the original schoolroom at Winchester are the stone benches in each of the three windows (two of which are unaltered) in the south wall (pl. **6**). A poem written by Robert Mathew in *c.* 1647 (and not in the sixteenth century, as earlier authorities state) mentions that there was no fireplace in the room (one was inserted at a later date) and that the window benches were 'for the 18 prefects [i.e. three from each of the six chambers], raised high that they may

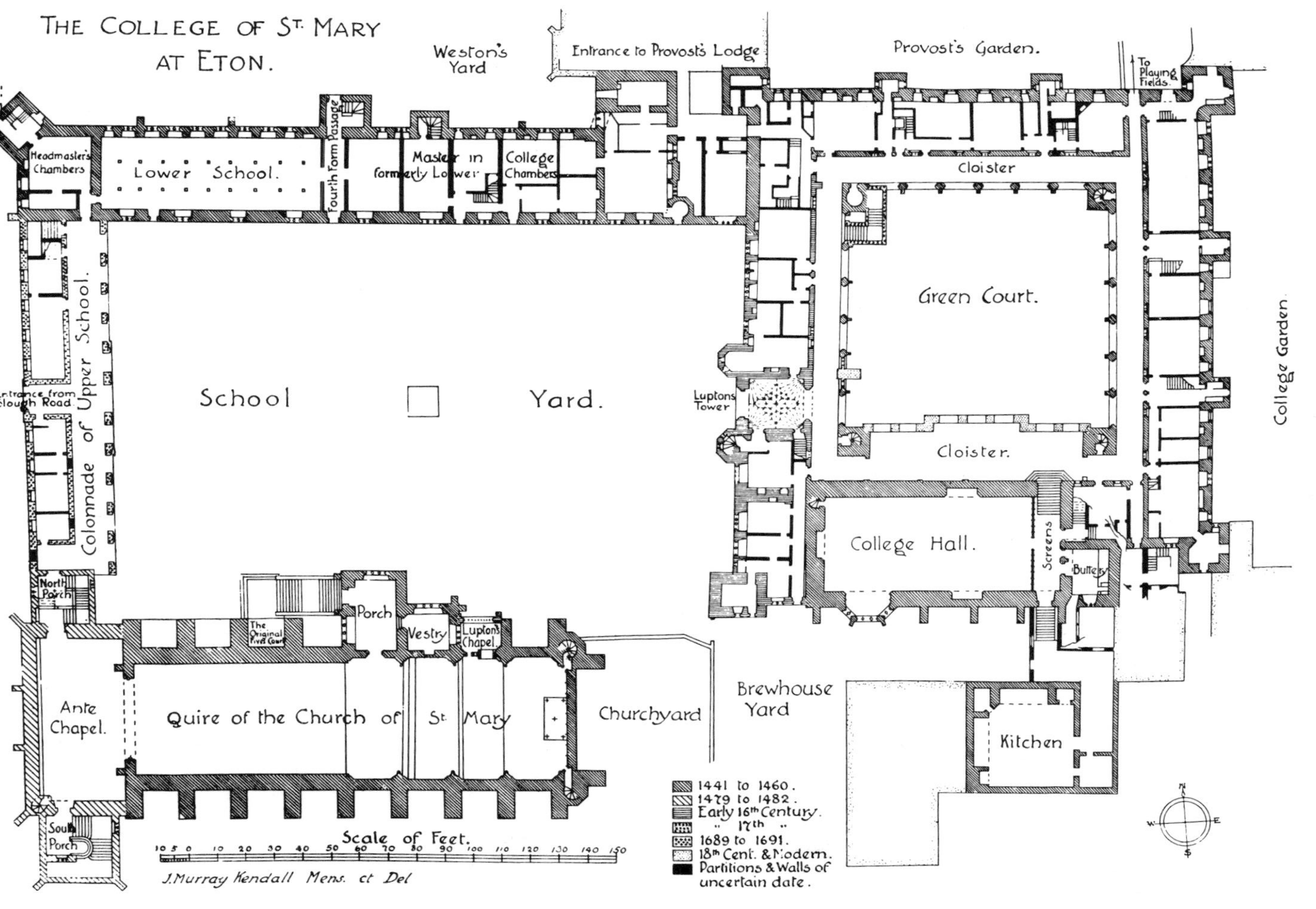

Figure 2 Eton College, ground plan showing dates of building.

watch over (*praevideant*) the others'. From this it seems likely that the prefects had duties in the schoolroom as well as in the dormitories. Mathew does not say where the headmaster's chair was or how the boys were arranged inside the room. A. F. Leach infers that the master's chair was in the same position in the original school as in the new school which replaced the old in 1687, viz. in the corner furthest from the door, with the usher in the opposite corner on the same side, so that together they commanded the whole room, but this is conjectural.[14]

At Eton also the original schoolroom now called Lower School and measuring about 76 by 24 feet, has survived virtually unchanged. The character of the room was, however, altered by the addition of substantial wooden pillars in the early seventeenth century, probably to help support Long Chamber above it (pl. **7**).[15] Whereas at Winchester the scholars slept in six chambers, as already described, at Eton they were all accommodated in one long room above the school, and in fact continued to use this room until the nineteenth century. By that date the lack of supervision had resulted in scandalous conditions, which led to the dividing up of Long Chamber into separate rooms, though drawings of Long Chamber before it was subdivided still exist.[16]

Virtually nothing is known about the internal organization of the school at Eton until the middle of the sixteenth century. A description of Eton customs in 1560 (the *Consuetudinarium*) shows that there were eighteen *praepositi* chosen from among the senior boys, as at Winchester. Four were employed in the schoolroom and had to report absentees, four exercised supervision in the dormitory, four on the playing fields, two in the chapel, and one in the hall; two others were responsible for supervising the commoners (fee-payers not on the foundation) and the eighteenth enforced cleanliness among the boys.[17]

A few other colleges with school buildings have survived down to the present day. At Higham Ferrers (Northants.) Henry Chichele, Archbishop of Canterbury, founded a college, including a school, in 1422. He did not establish a separate chapel for his college, but made use of the existing church, alongside which the original school building, measuring about 37 by 16 feet, still stands (pl. **8**). Nearby he built a college for clerks and an almshouse (which also survive, the former, however, in only fragmentary form). Another great founder of the fifteenth century was William Waynflete, who, when Bishop of Winchester, founded Magdalen College at Oxford and attached to it two grammar schools, one at Oxford and the other at Wainfleet in Lincolnshire. Magdalen School, Oxford, was part of the college buildings, but the surviving structure, now called the Old Grammar Hall, dates from a rebuilding of about 1614.[18] His school at Wainfleet (built in 1484) is an impressive brick building which has survived in virtually its original state. It is a two-storey structure which appears to have been designed originally with only two rooms, one on each floor. The top floor was used as a chapel and the ground floor as a school, but by 1818 the chapel had become the schoolroom and the ground floor had been converted into the master's house.[19]

There are a number of other fifteenth-century school buildings which have been preserved down to our own time and illustrate other types of grammar school foundations. An outstanding example is the school at Stratford-upon-Avon (pl. **9**), which was built in 1427 and can claim to have remained longer in continuous use as a schoolroom than any other school in the country—right down, indeed, to the present day. The accounts for the building have survived and record the amounts paid to the carpenter and the plasterers for erecting this half-timbered structure. The accounts are headed 'for j Scholehows with j chambre to be made over it', and they include a reference to earth and mud for the 'floryíng' and payment for making benches (*scamma*) for the schoolhouse.[20] There is no suggestion, at least by this date, that pupils sat on the floor, though some manuscript drawings of the period seem to show this.[21] The school was established by the Gild of Holy Cross, which also maintained a chapel and priests as part of the foundation. (The present chapel adjoining the school was built in 1496, and the school itself is at first-floor level, i.e. presumably the 'chambre' referred to in the accounts.)

Another remarkable example of continuity in school architecture is the school at Ewelme (Oxon.), built in 1437, this time of brick (pl. **10**). The school itself (measuring about 38 by 18 feet) occupied only a subsidiary position in a complex of buildings established for charitable purposes by William de la Pole and his wife, Alice.[22] Close to the magnificent Perpendicular church at Ewelme is a delightful group of almshouses planned like a small college, and nearby are the schoolmaster's house and the schoolroom. There was originally a large room over the schoolroom, which was probably intended as a dormitory for the boys, but the internal arrangements were altered when the school later became an elementary day-school.[23]

Other fifteenth-century grammar school buildings which may be mentioned are those at Westminster, Grantham (Lincs.) and King's Norton (originally in Worcestershire, but now a suburb of Birmingham). At Westminster the boys in the school attached to the Benedictine monastery moved in 1461 to part of the abbey next to the cellarer's building, where they occupied a room built in the late fourteenth century and measuring 48 by 20 feet on the east side of what is now Dean's Yard.[24] In somewhat altered form, it is still part of Westminster School. At Grantham a school associated with a local chantry was rebuilt in 1497 by Richard Fox (Bishop of Winchester, 1501–28) and his crest, a pelican, decorates the gable top. The school is still in use, and is a rectangular, single-storey structure near the parish church. The outside wall has recently had added to it by the Royal Society a plaque commemorating the school's most famous pupil, Isaac Newton. Fox also rebuilt the Grammar School at Taunton (Som.) in 1522 and placed his initials and crest over the entrance door. This building was acquired by the Corporation in 1886 and survives as part of the municipal buildings in Corporation Street, Taunton.[25] At King's Norton there was a school associated with a chantry, and its fine two-storey building with half-timbering of fifteenth-century date still survives there in virtually its original state (pl. **11**). Little is known about the origin of this school, but a school with a priest as master and a layman as usher, who together were teaching 120 scholars, is mentioned in the reign of Edward VI, so it seems to have been one of some importance at that date.[26] It had declined to elementary school status by the eighteenth century, and this building ceased to be used as a school towards the end of the nineteenth.

All the schools so far mentioned were founded as grammar schools. As such, they concentrated upon teaching Latin grammar, though English was the medium of instruction, at any rate by the fifteenth century.[27] It also appears that, certainly by the early sixteenth century, some grammar schools were admitting 'petties', or little boys who were taught to read before being admitted to the full grammar-school course.[28] Side by side with the grammar schools were the song schools, which were intended principally for training choristers. The song schools at important religious centres were highly specialized institutions which taught the complicated music used in cathedral and other major churches. But in other places the song schools were usually small parish schools where a local priest taught children (probably in the church building itself) to read the Psalter and to make the responses used in the ordinary Latin services. They were not elementary schools in the modern sense, since in general it appears that the children were taught to read Latin rather than the vernacular.[29]

The only architectural remains of song schools are in some of the cathedrals and other major centres. For example, at Lincoln there is a two-storeyed building, erected in the thirteenth century, adjoining the west corner of the south-east transept, the lower storey of which is a vestry and the upper the choristers' song school. It is thought that this part of the Cathedral has been in continuous use as a song school since before the Reformation. The choristers' house, where the boys were boarded, was situated in the Close, though the existing building dates from 1616.[30] At Windsor evidence has recently come to light that in *c.* 1480 the choir-school of St George's Chapel occupied a room in the block of chambers at the end of the Great Hall in the lower ward of the castle: wall paintings, including musical notation of that period, have been retained in the now restored chamber.[31] There is some architectural evidence of two other song schools of the fifteenth century. At Ottery St Mary (Devon) the singing school (later the King's School, demolished in 1884) measured 60 by 20 feet and was flanked by the dormitories of the choristers and 'secondaries', i.e. youths on the college staff, and at Wells (Som.) there are remains of the singing school over part of the West Walk of the cloisters, the school having originally been attached to the organist's house.[32] The only surviving example I know of a grammar school and song school associated architecturally is at Durham, where, however, the existing schools on the Palace Green date from a rebuilding of 1666.

So far we have been considering only those school buildings which were specifically designed as schools. But there are many other medieval buildings which were originally intended for other purposes, but came to be used as schools, particularly after the Reformation. When one recalls the rudimentary architectural requirements of schools at this date and the large number of ecclesiastical buildings thrown onto the market as a result of the dissolution of the monasteries and friaries in the reign of Henry VIII, and of the chantries, hospitals and other smaller buildings in Edward VI's reign, this is hardly surprising. The number of such adaptations to school use are too numerous to list in full, but some of the more significant and interesting examples which have survived to the present day may be mentioned.

Architecturally, the most impressive schools are those which used buildings derived in whole or in part from the former monastic houses. At Canterbury the grammar school was reorganized as the King's School in 1541 and from 1573 to 1859 occupied the almonry buildings, as well as having the use of other parts of the Cathedral.[33] At Chester, the school occupied part of the monks' refectory, and at Gloucester the monastic library was converted for school use when a new bishopric was set up there in Henry VIII's reign. Later in the sixteenth century the school at Westminster also came to occupy important parts of the monastic buildings: the huge dormitory of the monks (built *c.* 1090) became the room in which all teaching took place between 1602 and 1884 (pl. **12**). Although it was severely damaged by bombing during the Second World War, and subsequently restored, some eleventh-century work is still visible in the walls.[34] Another school which came to occupy previously monastic buildings was Sherborne School (Dorset). After its refoundation in 1550, it was housed in the cloister range, while the master's house occupied parts of the Lady Chapel and the Chapel of St Mary le Bow. Other parts of the abbey building were later taken over by the school.[35] Another impressive survival is the Great Gate at St Albans (Herts.), though it was not used by the school until 1871, when the former monastic church (including the Lady Chapel, which the school had occupied from the reign of Edward VI) became a Cathedral and the boys were moved out. Priory buildings also formed part of the school at Repton (Derbs.), founded in 1557.

Smaller ecclesiastical buildings were converted to school use on a nation-wide scale: in particular, former hospital buildings were commonly used, probably because their halls were of a convenient size, as at Abingdon, Buckingham, Coventry, Exeter, High Wycombe, Huntingdon, Reading and many other places. Some of these buildings incorporated early medieval features, as at Buckingham, where the Royal Latin School occupied a chapel with a twelfth-century door,[36] and Huntingdon, where the hall of St John's Hospital (built *c.* 1160) was occupied by a school from the middle of the sixteenth century.[37] (This building was restored in 1878, and is now the Cromwell Museum—Cromwell was himself a pupil at this school.) Among the more unusual religious buildings taken over by schools in the Tudor period may be mentioned the Carnary at Norwich, previously used to store the bones of the dead (pl. **13**).[38] Also numerous were former parish churches taken over as schools in the sixteenth century, as at Northampton and Stamford.[39]

Minor secular buildings of medieval date were also occupied by schools, though on a smaller scale. Surviving examples include the fourteenth-century hall in Mill Street, Ludlow, in Shropshire (occupied by a grammar school in 1553)[40] and Cradley in Herefordshire, where a fifteenth-century hall near the church was later used as a schoolroom.[41] Shrewsbury School, as we shall see, also began its modern career in a number of converted medieval houses.

In this way the marked expansion of education which took place after about 1550 found expression in the adaptation of many ecclesiastical buildings and endowments which the Reformation had made redundant. One further example will suffice to illustrate the new spirit: at Leicester, the grammar school of 1573 (which still exists) was built with the timber, stone and lead of the old St Peter's Church nearby, and the new school statutes were written in English on the reverse side of the pages of an old Latin service-book.[42] We must now turn to consider this new spirit at work in the schools of the New Learning.

Notes

1 Ariès, P., *Centuries of childhood*, Cape, 1962, 145f.
2 Charlton, K., *Education in Renaissance England*, Routledge & Kegan Paul, 1965, 15–16.
3 Illustrated in Alt, R., *Bilderatlas zur Schul-und Erziehungsgeschichte*, Berlin, 1960, I, 196. These however probably relate to a writing school rather than a grammar school. Cf. Adamson, J. W., *A short history of education*, Cambridge U.P., 1922, 78.
4 Allen, P. S., *The age of Erasmus*, Oxford: Clarendon Press, 1914, 33–6.
5 Illustrated in Seaborne, M., *Education*, Studio Vista, 1966, pl. 25. Cf. Lawson, J., *A town grammar school through six centuries*, Oxford U.P., 1963, 37.
6 Ascham, R., *The Scholemaster*, 1570, ed. by Mayor, J. E. B., Bell and Daldy, 1863, 94.
7 Ariès, *op. cit.*, 155f.
8 Leach, A. F., *A history of Winchester College*, Duckworth, 1899, 68.
9 Lyte, H. C. Maxwell, *A history of Eton College*, Macmillan, 1877, 7. The almshouse was suppressed before the end of Henry VI's reign.
10 For details of recent restoration work, see the article on 'Winchester College' by Harvey, J. H., in the *Journal of the Archaeological Association*, 3rd Series, Vol. XXVIII, 1965. I am indebted to Mr Harvey for further information about the buildings.
11 Leach, *op. cit.*, 114–15.
12 *Ibid.*, 121.
13 Quoted in Leach, *op. cit.*, 174–5.
14 Leach, *op. cit.*, 121–6, but see Cook, A. K., *About Winchester College*, Macmillan, 1917, 3–10.
15 Lyte, *op. cit.*, 224. For the buildings at Eton generally, see R.C.H.M., *Buckinghamshire*, I, 1912, 142–52, and Hussey, C., *Eton College*, Country Life, 1922.
16 See for example, Lyte, *op. cit.*, facing p. 144 (Long Chamber, A.D. 1844).
17 Lyte, *op. cit.*, 143.
18 Illustrated in R.C.H.M., *The City of Oxford*, 1939, pl. 132 (*a*) and plan, p. 72. The school moved to its present site in 1928 (Stanier, R. S., *A History of Magdalen College School*, 2nd ed. Oxford: Blackwell, 1958, 189).
19 Carlisle, I, 854. Illustrated in Pevsner, N., and Harris, J., *Lincolnshire*, 1964, pl. 38.
20 *V.C.H.*, *Warwickshire*, II, 1908, 330.

21 Ariès, *op. cit.*, 153, suggests that benches were not introduced until the fourteenth century.
22 Plan and description of Ewelme buildings in Godfrey, W. H., *The English almshouse*, Faber & Faber, 1955, 44–5. See also *Country Life*, 22 March 1941.
23 Carlisle, *op. cit.*, II, 304.
24 See historical ground plan of Westminster Abbey in R.C.H.M., *London*, I, 1924, at end.
25 *V.C.H., Somerset*, II, 1911, 444.
26 *V.C.H., Worcestershire*, IV, 1924, 474.
27 See, for example, Nelson, W. (ed), *A fifteenth-century school book*, Oxford, 1956. English replaced French in the law courts in 1362 and in the schools by 1377 (Armytage, W. H. G., *The French influence on English education*, Routledge & Kegan Paul, 1968, 5).
28 Adamson, J. W., *The illiterate Anglo-Saxon and other essays*, Cambridge U.P., 1946, 54.
29 In a few places, as at Rotherham (Yorks.) in 1483, a 'writing master' was employed to prepare boys for lay occupations. See Leach, A. F., *Educational charters and documents*, Cambridge U.P., 1911, 425.
30 Pevsner, N., and Harris, J., *op. cit.*, 126 and 138. (The description of the song school given here is not entirely accurate.) I am indebted to Canon H. F. Riches, Librarian of Lincoln Cathedral, for further information about the song school.
31 See article by Curnow, P. E., on 'Royal lodgings of the 13th century' in the *Report of the Society of the Friends of St George's*, 1965, 218–28 (including plans and photos).
32 See Dalton, J. N., *The Collegiate Church of Ottery St Mary*, Cambridge U.P., 1917, p. 75 and pl. XXVII, and Parker, J. H., *The architectural antiquities of the City of Wells*, Oxford: Parker, 1866, p. 22 and pl. XXII. Cf. Pevsner, *North Somerset*, 1958, 312.
33 Edwards, D. L., *A history of King's School, Canterbury*, Faber & Faber, 1957, 70, 80.
34 For the school buildings at Westminster see Carleton, J., *Westminster School*, Rupert Hart-Davis, 1965, ch. 9.
35 See plan in R.C.H.M., *Dorset*, I, 1952, 200. Further details in Gourlay, A. B., *A history of Sherborne School*, Winchester: Warren, 1951, ch. 2.
36 Illustrated in R.C.H.M., *Buckinghamshire*, II, 1913, facing p. 24.
37 Illustrated in R.C.H.M., *Huntingdonshire*, 1926, 156.
38 Conjectural plan and elevation in Saunders, H. W., *Norwich Grammar School*, Norwich: Jarrold, 1932, 6–7.
39 At Stamford the school chapel is what remains of the parish church of St Paul. For Northampton School, which met in the church of St Gregory from 1557 (now demolished), see Buckler, J. C., *Sixty views of endowed grammar schools*, Hurst, 1827.
40 Pevsner, *Shropshire*, 1958. The hall was heightened in *c.* 1600 to house a dormitory (photo. in N.M.R., A45/1137).
41 See R.C.H.M., *Herefordshire*, II, 1932, 62 (including plan).
42 Cross, M. C., *The Free Grammar School of Leicester*, Leicester U.P., 1953, 13. The original statutes are in the Archives Dept. of Leicester City Museum. The building, in High-cross Street, Leicester, was converted to offices in 1966, but the main walls have been retained.

Two

The new schools of the sixteenth century

I

The prototype of the schools of the New Learning was St Paul's School in London, where the ancient cathedral school was replaced by a new foundation by John Colet, Dean of St Paul's, in 1509. Colet was himself a leading exponent of the humanist ideas of the Renaissance, and his school included many new features, not least in its organization and arrangement of the scholars. The statutes of 1518[1] laid down that there should be 'taught in the school children of all nations and countries indifferently to the number of 153' (this was the number of the miraculous draught of fishes recorded in John, xxi. 11). The government of the school was placed, not in the hands of the dean and chapter, but of the lay Company of Mercers, while the first headmaster was a married layman. In these and other ways the break with the past was emphasized.

The new school building was completed in 1512. Little is known of its external appearance: a map of London in 1591 shows the school with a central portion of one storey and houses of several storeys at each end,[2] but this building was destroyed in the Great Fire of London in 1666. We are more fortunate in the information available about the internal arrangement of the school, for Erasmus, in a letter to Justus Jonas, gave the following detailed description:

> He [i.e. Colet] divided the school into four apartments. The first, namely the porch and entrance, is for catechumens, or the children to be instructed in the principles of religion, where no child is to be admitted but what can read and write. The second apartment is for the lower boys to be taught by the second master or usher. The third [is] for the upper forms under the head master: which two parts of the school are divided by a curtain to be drawn at pleasure. . . . The fourth or last apartment is a little chapel for divine service. The school has no corners or hiding places; nothing like a cell or closet. The boys have their distinct forms or benches, one above the other. Every form holds sixteen, and he that is head or captain of each form has a little kind of desk by way of pre-eminence.[3]

Some of these details are confirmed by the statutes of 1518, which tell us more of Colet's intentions. No child was to be admitted unless 'he can read and write competently' and 'in every form one principal child shall be placed in the chair, president of that form'. As for the hours of attendance, the statutes laid down that

> the children shall come unto the school in the morning at seven of the clock, both winter and summer, and tarry there until eleven, and return again at one of the clock and depart at five. And thrice in the day, prostrate they shall say the prayers with due tract [i.e. protraction] and pausing as they be contained in a table [i.e. on a board] in the school, that is to say in the morning and at noon and at evening.

In providing a boy-president for each form, Colet was following the precedent of Winchester and Eton, where, as we saw in the previous chapter, prefects were appointed from the beginning. But the division into distinct forms was more clear-cut at St Paul's than appears to have been the case in the older schools. Since there were sixteen boys and a head boy in each form and there were 153 places in the school, there must have been nine forms in all, and not eight, as is frequently asserted. There is evidence that the subdivision of schools into forms was going on elsewhere at this date, which probably indicates that the grammar-school curriculum was becoming more systematic and progressive. The endowment deed of the school at Saffron Walden (Essex) in 1525 required that the school should follow the 'order and use of teaching grammar in the schools of Winchester and Eton'. The details are set out in a document of 1530 which shows that there were seven forms at both Winchester and Eton at this date. The classical authors studied in the various forms are also listed.[4]

Another innovation at St Paul's was that the status of the masters seems to have been enhanced in comparison with earlier schools. The statutes laid down that the principal master, called the 'high master' (still so called at St Paul's), should be 'a wedded man, a single man, or a priest that hath no benefice with cure nor service that may let [i.e. hinder] the due business in the school'. This last provision was clearly meant to distinguish the high master from the type of chantry-schoolmaster who taught boys as a subsidiary part of his ecclesiastical office. The second master, called the 'surmaster' in the statutes, was similarly to give his whole time to the school. In addition there was to be a chaplain who, if the high master so decided, could 'help to teach in the school'. He was to 'teach the children the catechism and instruction of the articles of the faith and the ten commandments in English' and was also to give all his time to the school.

At Winchester and Eton the teaching staff, as we have seen, were members of a religious community, and at Winchester there was no separate living accommodation for the masters immediately adjoining the school. In this respect Colet's arrangements for St Paul's marked a notable change. The children and masters themselves formed a distinct community and the staff were housed next to the schoolroom. To summarize the evidence available from a number of sixteenth-century sources, there were separate houses for the high master and surmaster immediately adjoining the school. The high master's house had on the ground floor a hall, kitchen and buttery with a vestibule leading into the school. On the first floor was a dining-room, another buttery and two more rooms. He also had the use of the attics on the third floor. Colet expressly excluded the rooms on the second floor from the high master's personal use; by 1584 at least one of them was being used by boarders, while another was used as a 'posing chamber' for the annual examination of the scholars. The surmaster's house consisted of a hall, kitchen and study next to the school, with chambers above. The chaplain also was accommodated nearby.[5]

This description of the high master's house indicates that his office was one of substance. The prestige attached to the post was further emphasized by a provision in the statutes that he should be formally admitted by the mercers, who were to 'stall him in his seat in the school and show him his lodging'. Similar ceremonies were performed elsewhere in this period. Thus at Newark-on-Trent (Notts.) the ordinances of 1531 declared that the vicar and aldermen were to 'put the said grammar school-master in possession of the school there by setting of him in his chair'.[6] Clearly, the master's chair had become the symbol of his office and his possession of it a mark of his increasing authority. The master's chair now features prominently in contemporary illustrations (see, for example, pl. **14**). The schoolmaster's powers of corporal punishment, which had traditionally belonged to him, seem likewise to have assumed a greater significance at this time, and Tudor pictures of schoolmasters invariably show them with rod or birch (see pl. **15** and **16**). It may not be altogether fanciful to see in the growing authoritarianism of the Tudor schoolmaster an analogy with the increasing importance of the J.P. sitting in petty and quarter sessions. Similarly, the provision of separate accommodation for the master and usher may be compared with contemporary developments in domestic architecture, where one finds that rooms were becoming more specialized in function, with the head of the household and his wife increasingly using a parlour and chambers separate from the hall, where traditionally the whole household had lived together without distinction of rank or status.[7]

One ought not, however, to exaggerate the novelty of the arrangements made by Colet at St Paul's. Although the control of the school was placed in the hands of laymen, the close connection between education and religion was as firm as ever—indeed, this was to remain so in all the new grammar schools of the sixteenth century. It has also been suggested that 'Colet's belief in the virtues of the classics was somewhat half-hearted', since, although he shared the humanists' scorn for medieval Latin, the books he prescribed for St Paul's were mainly Christian poets of late classical times, rather than the earlier, pagan writers.[8] A similarly somewhat indecisive break with tradition was made by Cardinal Wolsey, who, in founding a new school at Ipswich (Suffolk) in 1528, based the curriculum on wholly classical authors, but followed the precedent of Winchester and Eton in

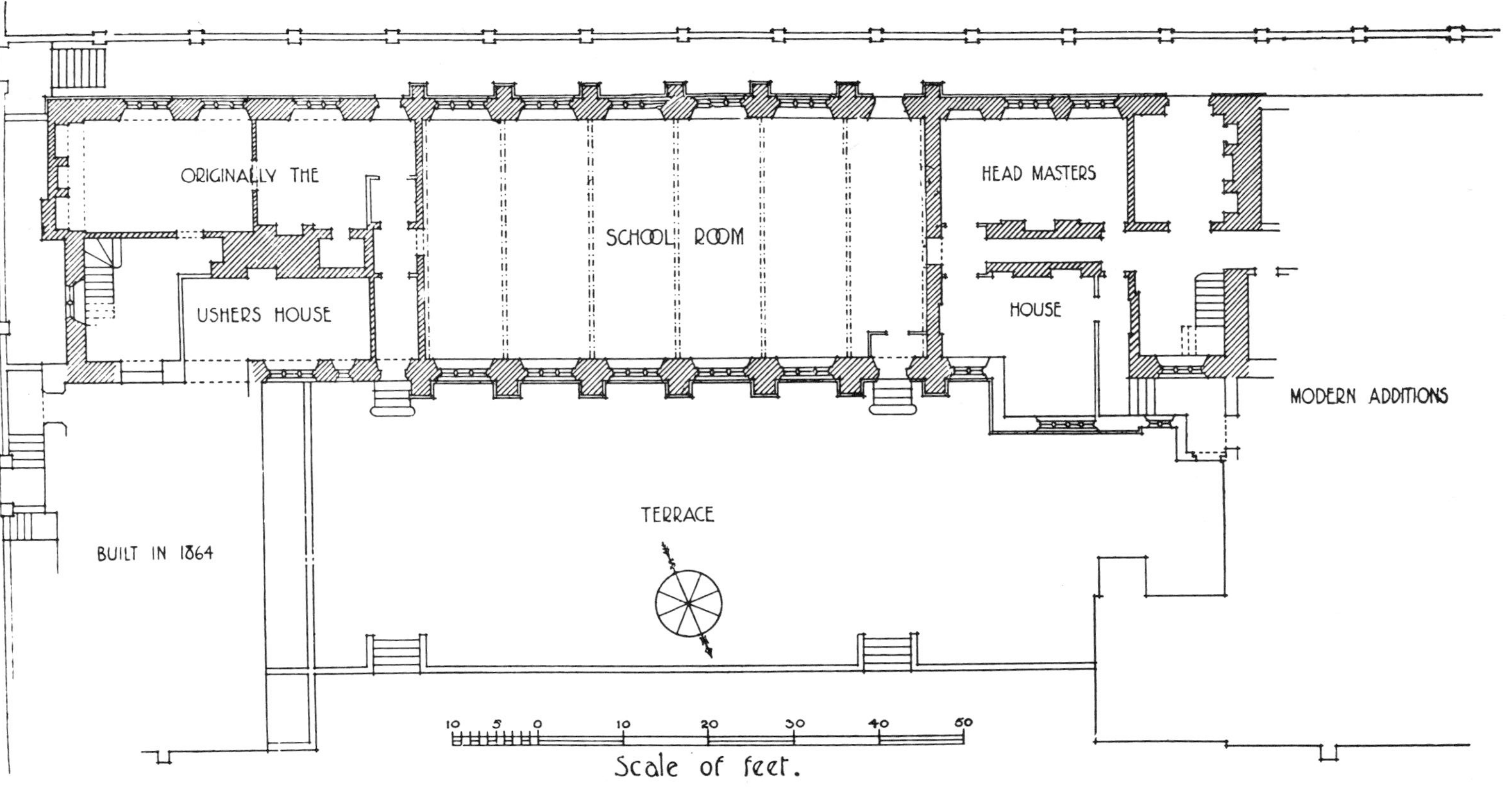

Figure 3 Berkhamsted School, *c.* 1541, ground plan.

making the school part of a college. 'Cardinal's College' was to consist of a dean, twelve fellows, eight clerks, eight choristers and twelve poor men, besides the grammar school master, usher and fifty scholars.[9] Wolsey had ambitious plans for extensive buildings in Caen stone, but his fall from power in 1530 came when they were only half-built: the unfinished buildings were then demolished and only a minor gateway, built in brick and now known as Wolsey's Gate, survives (pl. **17**). The foundation-stone was discovered built into a wall in Ipswich in the eighteenth century, and is now at Christ Church, Oxford,[10] Wolsey's other foundation, which survived his downfall in somewhat altered form.

Henry VIII's establishment of cathedrals of the New Foundation,[11] with schools founded or refounded in association with them, further encouraged the movement towards the reformed classical curriculum of the humanists. But, in terms of buildings, there was less opportunity for innovation, because the schools (as we saw at Canterbury and elsewhere in the previous chapter) were accommodated in various parts of the existing monastic buildings. Probably the earliest surviving school building of the post-Reformation period which incorporates architecturally the new ideas of the reformers is at Berkhamsted in Hertfordshire (pl. **18**). We may trace a direct link with St Paul's School, since the founder, John Incent, was also a Dean of St Paul's, so must himself have been familiar with its school buildings and organization. Incent was a successful ecclesiastical lawyer who skilfully anticipated the fall of the gilds by obtaining letters patent in 1541 re-establishing the chantry school in his native town. The school consisted of a master, usher and 144 children, and Incent, with the help of the townspeople, provided a new building which is of considerable interest from our point of view. Architecturally it has been described as 'an interesting example of work of mid sixteenth-century date, but of late fifteenth-century style';[12] from the educational point of view it is outstanding as one of the earliest—if not the earliest—surviving example of a school distinct from a college with separate but closely integrated accommodation for the teaching staff (see plan, fig. 3). The arms and initials of the founder are over the north doorway and the whole of the original building is covered with a single roof. The schoolroom is in the centre, with an open timber roof, and at each end is a block of two storeys for master and usher. When the building was complete, Incent assembled the chief men of the town in the school and, calling the master, 'placed him in his seat there made for the schoolmaster'—the link with the town and the vesting of authority in the master were no doubt in direct imitation of St Paul's School. A description of the school written in *c.* 1560 states:

> The dean, not without the help of the town and county, built with all speed a fair school large and great all of brick very sumptuously with a lodging for the schoolmaster joining to the west end of the same . . . and at the east end of the said school there are two lodgings, one for the usher and the other for the chaplain or chantry priest. The whole building is so strong and fair that

the like grammar school for that point is not to be seen in the whole realm of England.[13]

II

The radical reorganization of the Church which took place during the reigns of Henry VIII and Edward VI resulted in widespread changes in the organization of schools and, once Elizabeth had secured more settled conditions, the rate of school-building accelerated rapidly. The rebuilding of schools takes its place alongside the renaissance of vernacular architecture which began during the sixteenth century. Perhaps the most significant change was the decisive way in which groups of townspeople and merchants now entered the field of school-building. The individual benefactor by no means disappears, but his endowments, though important, are rarely on the grand scale. Major schemes on the model of Wykeham or Wolsey are no longer characteristic. Instead, the largest foundations are group enterprises, dominated by laymen. We may select as notable examples of this genre two Elizabethan schools whose buildings have survived down to the present comparatively unaltered, those at Guildford (Surrey) and Ashbourne (Derbs.).

The school at Guildford (pl. **19**) is of particular interest because it marked a distinct advance in ideas about the planning of schools. Its preservation down to the present day makes possible a detailed examination (see plan, fig. 4) and there is also good documentary evidence relating to the original building.[14] A manuscript of 1607 states that 'the mayor and approved men of Guildford . . . did in 1557 begin at their own costs and charges to build and rear the large room now used for the school house, with the great chamber and garret over the same'. In 1569 John Austen, former Mayor of Guildford and a Merchant Adventurer, began to build a three-storey west wing for the accommodation of the master, and two years later William Hamond, also a former Mayor, began an east wing for the usher and a gallery connecting it with the master's house. This had the effect of forming a small central quadrangle, and the total

Name of school	*Size of schoolroom, feet*	*Designed for*	*Square feet per pupil*
Winchester	45 × 29	70 scholars and 10 commoners	16
Eton	76 × 24	70 scholars and 20 commoners	20
Berkhamsted	70 × 27	144 maximum	13
Guildford	65 × 21	100 maximum	14

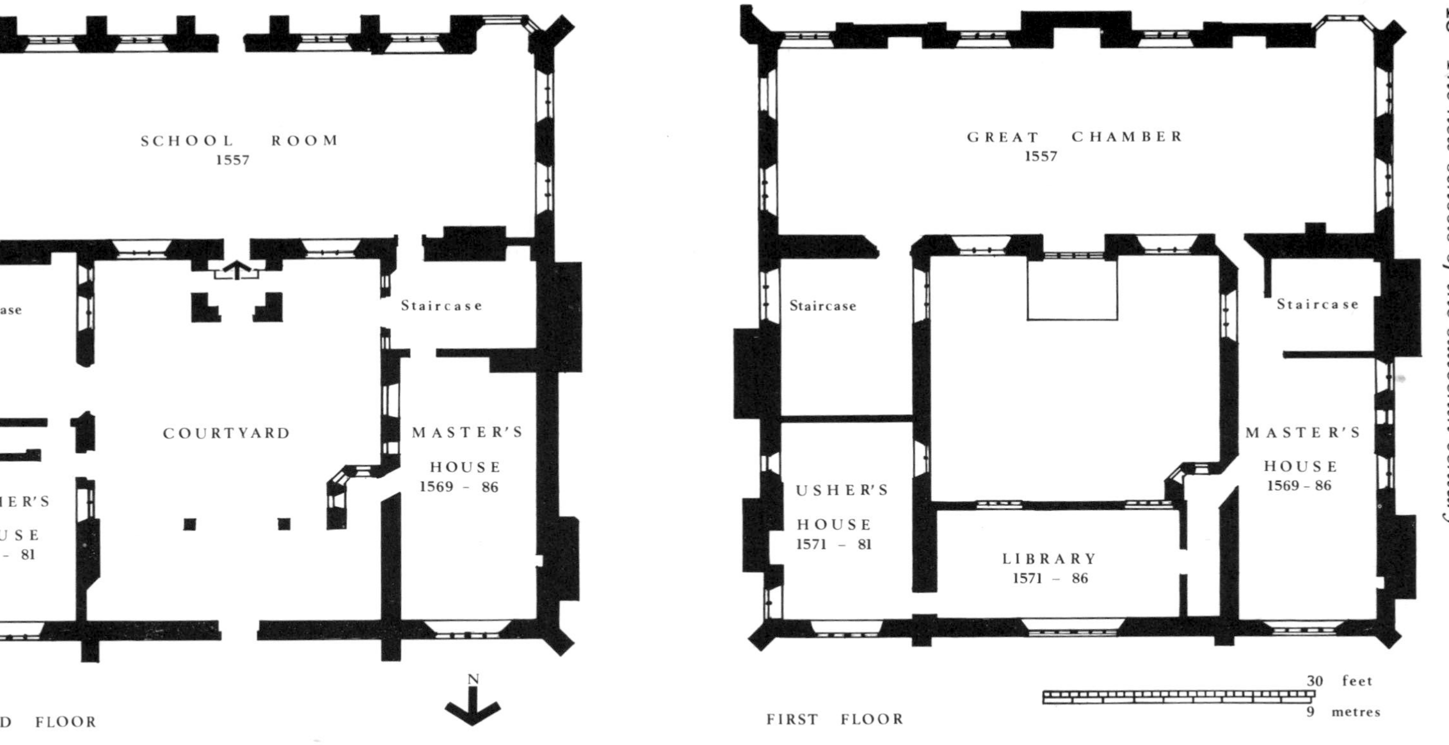

Figure 4 Guildford School, 1557—86, ground and first-floor plans. (So far as possible, only original work has been shown. Minor alterations have been made since the sixteenth century, e.g. there may have been a fireplace in the schoolroom, where there is now a rear entrance.)

complex has been called 'a particularly good example of a tightly-planned town grammar school'.[15] It may be noted that the schoolroom was somewhat larger than that at Winchester, but smaller than those at Eton and Berkhamsted: it was not particularly large in relation to the number of pupils to be accommodated (see table above).

The accommodation for the master and usher at Guildford was relatively generous and their houses communicated with each other via the gallery, but not with the school. The statutes of 1608 fixed the maximum number of pupils at 100, but throw no light on whether this number included boarders. Nor is it certain how the chamber and garrets over the schoolroom were used. The manuscript of 1607 quoted above implies that all the boys were taught in the ground-floor room, but it is conceivable that the usher (whose duties were becoming more clearly defined in most of the larger schools) took the lower forms in the great chamber above the main schoolroom. The great chamber has three original stone fireplaces, whereas the schoolroom has none. The garrets may have been intended as dormitories for boarders. Equally, however, the chamber and garrets may have been intended for other municipal purposes, as we shall see was the case in the contemporary school building at Enfield.

In 1586 George Austen (the son of John) adapted the gallery for the purposes of a library (pl. **20**) to house the books bequeathed to the school by John Parkhurst, Bishop of Norwich. This is one of the earliest mentions anywhere of a school library and is the only known example of a chained library belonging to a school (there was one at Bolton School, but the books belonged to the parish church, not the school).[16] The books given by Bishop Parkhurst are of some interest, since they consisted largely of commentaries on the Bible by Lutheran and Calvinist reformers (he had been a Marian exile).[17] Other books were added to this nucleus and in 1648 new book-shelves were provided. Some 484 volumes have survived, but how far they were used by the boys at the school is not known. Most grammar schools at this date merely had one or two dictionaries for the boys to use. Thus at Boston (Lincs.) in 1578 it was decided 'that a dictionary shall be bought for the scholars of the Free School, and the same book to be tied to a chain and set upon a desk in the school, whereunto any scholar may have access as occasion shall serve'.[18] Similarly, at Cheltenham (Glos.) in 1586 it was laid down that the master should buy with the money paid in entrance fees 'such Latin and Greek books as shall be most necessary for the public use of the said scholars, to be tied fast with little chains of iron'.[19]

At Ashbourne a substantial school building (fig. 5 and pl. **21**) was also erected by co-operative effort. A charter to establish the school was obtained from the Crown in 1585, but building seems to have been going on as late as 1603. In that year, a surviving minute book records donations from various London merchants and a gift of a staircase by Sir James Lancaster, Grocer and Merchant Adventurer, who also helped to endow a grammar school at Basingstoke (Hants.). Stow in his *Survey of London* (1598) states that 'diverse well-disposed citizens of London desirous as yet not to be named, being born in or near Ashbourne in the Peak in the county of Derby,

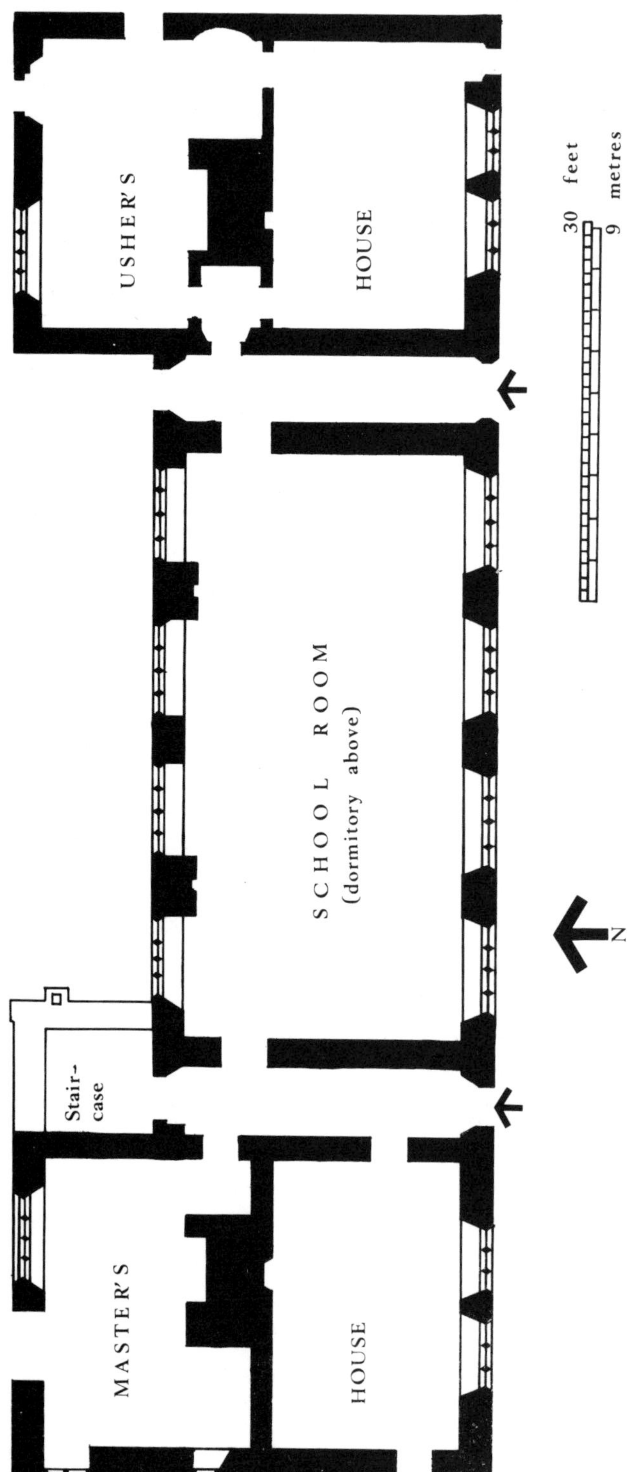

Figure 5 Ashbourne School, 1585–1603, ground plan.

combining their loving benevolence together, have builded there a fair schoolhouse with convenient lodgings for a master and liberal maintenance allowed thereto'.[20] The schoolroom, measuring 46 by 22 feet, was in the centre, with chamber and attics (probably used as dormitories) above, surmounted by four small gables. The master occupied a house on the west and the usher a similar one on the east, each house being surmounted by a gable. The gables and regularly-spaced windows give the whole design an attractive unity. The original building in Church Street is now used as a boarding house by the school, which moved to its present site in 1909. The original schoolroom is now used for dining, and the chamber and garrets as dormitories.

The outstanding Elizabethan example of municipal enterprise in school provision was at Shrewsbury, but buildings specially designed for educational purposes were not completed until the seventeenth century, and will be dealt with in a later chapter. It may be mentioned here that a charter to establish the school was granted in 1552 'at the humble petition as well of the bailiffs and burgesses and inhabitants of the town . . . as of very many other our subjects of our whole neighbouring country there'. By 1562 there were 266 boys arranged in seven (later nine) forms and divided between *oppidani* (those from the town) and *alieni* (those from away). By 1581 the number had risen to 360, and five years later Camden called it 'the largest school in all England'. Because of the large numbers, four masters were employed—three taking the 'higher schools' (i.e. in grammar) and one the 'accidence school' (i.e. the preparatory department for the petties). The remarkable fact is that for the first fifty years of its life this large and successful school was accommodated in a number of ordinary houses bought and adapted for school use. The *alieni* were boarded by householders in the town, possibly in return for domestic services to the families who 'tabled' them. There was no attempt at this date to provide boarding houses as part of the school organization.[21]

While the Elizabethan period was notable for the major schools established by co-operative effort, there were also many smaller schools founded by individuals, both lay and ecclesiastical. Among the best surviving examples of the former may be chosen those at Felsted (Essex) and Enfield (Middx.) and among the latter those at Uppingham (Rutland) and Hawkshead (Lancs.).

Felsted School (pl. **23**) was established in 1564 with funds bequeathed by Richard, Lord Rich, formerly Chancellor of the Court of Augmentations. The master was given a separate house, but the usher was accommodated at one end of the school, which consisted of the upper storey of a long, low, timber-framed building situated along the edge of the churchyard. The lower storey was let out as a dwelling and two shops: there was certainly no attempt to isolate the school from the everyday life of the town, and many other examples could be given of schools sited amid the hurly-burly of busy commercial centres (perhaps the outstanding example of this was Christ's Hospital, which will be mentioned later in this chapter). Surviving accounts relating to Felsted School show that in 1601 seven books were bought, including works by Livy, Xenophon and Erasmus and a dictionary 'for the use of the scholars perpetually to remain in the school'.[22] Here again we have the beginnings of a school library.

The school at Enfield (pl. **22**) has a front elevation similar in some respects to Guildford School already described, but it is on a more modest scale (internal dimensions, 52 by 22 feet) with two and a half instead of three and a half storeys; it is also without wings or gallery. In 1586 a certain William Garrett left £50 to build a school, but it is likely that other local people helped to finance it, since the cost of building schools at this time seems to have varied from about £100 to £300.[23] A deed of 1621 shows that both elementary- and grammar-school subjects were taught, with, it seems, an emphasis on the non-classical side, for it instructs the master to 'teach the children of all the inhabitants of Enfield the cross-row or alphabet letters, and the arts of writing, grammar and arithmetic'. The same deed states that the chamber and garret over the schoolroom were to be reserved for such uses as the vestry should direct. The master lived in a house near the school, and it seems likely that this was a purely local school without boarders.[24]

Uppingham School (pl. **25**) was founded in 1584 by the Rev. Robert Johnson, Rector of North Luffenham in Rutland and Archdeacon of Leicester. The building, which is still in use, is a simple rectangle in plan, without upper storeys or internal divisions, and the only external features of interest are a number of inscriptions in Hebrew, Greek and Latin (pl. **26**). In its modest scale, it is typical of many country schools founded in Elizabethan and early Stuart times. It was, however, only part of Johnson's foundation, for a similar school (altered in the eighteenth century) was built at Oakham, as well as a hospital or almshouse for fourteen old people in each place.[25] In medieval times schools were often associated with almshouses (as we saw at Ewelme) and this practice was continued after the Reformation at Uppingham and elsewhere. Our other example of an ecclesiastical foundation—again on a fairly small scale, as one would expect in an area of sparse population—is the delightful school at Hawkshead (pl. **27**), founded in 1585 by Edwin Sandys, Archbishop of York and a native of the parish. The master lived in a separate house, and it is not known whether the upper floor of the school was used by the usher or for boarders.[26] This was the school attended by Wordsworth as a boy and a quotation from his *Personal Talk* on the subject of books has been painted around the walls inside: 'Round these with tendrils strong as flesh and blood our pastime and our happiness will grow' (pl. **28**). The school is now open to the public at limited times, and contains a small Wordsworth exhibition and a library dating in part from 1669.[27]

III

The Elizabethan period also saw (no doubt reflecting the increasing interest in school-building and organization) the first more or less systematic treatment of the subject in Richard Mulcaster's *Positions* (1581). He has much to say which is relevant to our theme and this section of his book is therefore worth examining in some detail.[28]

Mulcaster begins by distinguishing clearly between education at home ('private places') and education in a school ('public places'). 'Private places, where every parent hath his children taught within his doors, have but small interest in this place [i.e. book]', he writes, though his mention of them indicates that education at home by parents or private tutors was still an important factor in English education. With regard to public places, Mulcaster subdivides them into 'elementary', 'grammatical' and 'collegiate' (i.e. mainly university). He dismisses the elementary schools fairly briefly:

> The elementary places admit no great counsel, because such as enter the young ones do provide the rooms of themselves and the little people be not as yet capable of any great exercise: so that there is no more to be said herein but this, that the elementary teachers provide their rooms as large as they may, and that the parents domestical care supply, where the master's provision is not sufficient.

He stresses that elementary education 'for the petty ones' was a matter for parents and teachers jointly and was normally 'upon private charge', i.e. provided privately on a fee-paying basis. 'But', he adds, 'if any well disposed wealthy man . . . would begin some building even for the little young ones . . . all they would pray for him.' In fact, so far as the evidence of surviving buildings goes, it was not until the following century that public elementary schools (in Mulcaster's sense of charitable endowments) began to be founded in any significant number.

This, however, is not entirely the end of the matter. He advocates that for children who intend to go on from the elementary to the grammar stage of education 'elementary entrances' should be done in the grammar school itself, since they 'will hardly be kept if they be posted over to private practising at home'. He therefore suggests that the grammar schools should be of two storeys, with 'a fair school house above . . . for the tongues [i.e. the classical languages] and another beneath for other points of learning, and perfecting or continuing the elementary entrances'. He adds that the Latin school should be on the first rather than the ground floor, to protect the scholars from 'too great noise if the place be . . . enclosed with other building'. It should also be a large room 'for as reading and things of that motion do require small elbow room, so writing and her appendents [i.e. appendages] may not be straited'—an interesting reflection of the movement from wholly oral to part-oral and part-written exercises which was taking place in the grammar schools of this period.[29] He also points out that a large room had the advantage that, where the total number of children was limited, the same room could be used by both the elementary and grammar pupils.

These remarks throw some additional light on the way in which the buildings so far considered in this chapter were used. Mulcaster admits, in effect, that it was not always possible to confine entry into the grammar school to those who had already learnt to read and write. Many Elizabethan grammar schools were in fact admitting petties,[30] and in some schools in the London area (notably at St Olave's, Southwark, in 1571)[31] the elementary school curriculum was extended to include the casting of accounts as well as reading and writing, with the implication that an 'English' education need not merely be the preliminary to the study of Latin grammar. Although it is not now usually possible to determine with certainty the use to which the various rooms were put in the schools which we have been discussing, we cannot discount the possibility that the larger grammar schools, like those at Guildford and Ashbourne, had a considerable number of petties who may have been taught in a different room in the same building. In other places (as in Leicester in *c.* 1575)[32] the petties were taught in a room separate from the grammar-school building, though the more general practice, especially in the smaller schools, was to teach the elementary and classical subjects in the same room. The school seal of Uppingham (pl. **29**) appears to show two petties in addition to four older children being taught by the master.[33] Similarly, the same room at Alleyne's School, Stevenage, in Hertfordshire, was for over 300 years from 1572 used by both the grammar school and the petties' school in the town and survives as part of the present school.[34] Mulcaster also makes it clear that there were separate elementary schools run by private teachers. Manuals of guidance were published to help teachers in petty or 'English' schools. The illustration from Edmund Coote's *The English schoolmaster* (first published in 1596) appears to show a girl being taught in an 'English' school (pl. **30**), though there is very little evidence that girls were admitted to the grammar schools.[35]

Mulcaster's advice on the building of schools also reflected the best contemporary practice in its insistence that the master and his family should be 'conveniently well lodged'. It is clear from what Mulcaster says on the subject that some masters were taking boarders, as was sometimes specifically allowed in school statutes; but in general he was not in favour of this practice, and certainly there was no conception of boarding as a valuable educational experience in itself, which is a much later development. His objections were mainly, though not wholly, of a practical nature:

> And sure to set down my resolution, methinks it enough for the master to take upon him the train[ing] alone. . . . If parents dwell not near the school, let some neighbours be hosts and deliver the master of the parents' care [for] . . . they be distinct offices, to be a parent and a master. . . . Boarding, that is the undertaking of both a father's and a master's charge requireth many circumstances of convenience in place, of provision for necessities, of trusty and diligent servants, and a number more. . . . The master's charge is great of itself, but this composition of a double office is a marvellous matter.

Certainly, as we have seen, his advice was followed by those responsible for running the largest of Elizabethan schools, that at Shrewsbury.

Finally, Mulcaster has something of interest to say about the location of schools, and his views mark a reaction against the traditional practice, which we noticed at Felsted, of permitting schools to be placed immediately adjoining shops and houses. Here is his description of an ideal grammar-school building:

> As the elementaries [i.e. elementary school pupils] of force must be near unto their parents because of their youth, and therefore are not to be denied the middle of cities and towns, so I could wish that grammar schools were planted in the [out]skirts and suburbs of towns,[36] near to the fields, where partly by enclosure of some private ground, for the closer exercises . . . [and] partly for the benefit of the open fields for exercises of more range, there might not be much want of room, if there were any at all.

In addition, there should be an airy, two-storeyed school building, ample accommodation for the master and his family, and a covered playground for the children to use in wet weather. All this, as Mulcaster admits, 'will require a good mind and no mean purse'; yet he adds that 'there is wealth enough in private possession, if there were will enough to public education'. In fact, we find that an increasing number of schools were beginning to approximate to this ideal, and Mulcaster was able to boast (with, however, some degree of exaggeration) that 'we have no great cause to complain for number of schools and founders. For during the time of her Majesty's most fortunate reign already, there hath been more schools erected than all the rest be that were before her time in the whole realm'.

We are still some distance from the period when architects were employed to design schools. But an interesting 'plan of a school' dating from about 1590 has survived among the archives of Harrow School. The plan (fig. 6 (*a*)) shows a schoolroom measuring internally 56 by 20 feet and well lit by windows on both sides and in the gable end. The walls inside are 'benched round with a wainscot back' and the master's seat is in the centre of the rear wall facing the entrance, with the usher's seat in the corner immediately to the left of the entrance. There is an entrance vestibule, flanked by the master's study and chamber on the south side, with the same for the usher on the north. (The plan may not be accurate at this point: quite possibly the studies were on the ground floor, with the chambers above, for the two stairs are labelled 'to the schoolmaster's chamber' and 'to the usher's chamber', the word 'chamber' usually meaning bedroom at this date.) An outside latrine ('house of office') is shown on the north-east corner of the building. Chimneys indicate that there were intended to be fireplaces in the masters' rooms and possibly in the schoolroom. It may be that those responsible for building Harrow School were considering various plans in the 1590s, though the school actually built at Harrow in 1615 was, as we shall see, somewhat different. However, schools on this plan were being built in Elizabethan times—for example, the plan of the grammar school at Thame in Oxfordshire (fig. 6 (*b*)) built between 1559 and 1575 is almost identical, with its schoolroom measuring 50 by 20 feet and the master's and usher's rooms at one end. (This school had William Lenthall and John

Hampden among its pupils in the following century.) A similar plan in a surviving school may be found at what is now Ilminster Girls' Grammar School in Somerset (*c*. 1584), where the original schoolroom measured 36 by 16 feet.[37]

We may compare these plans with the drawing of Pate's Grammar School, Cheltenham (Glos.), in 1586, which shows both the outside and inside of the school (pl. **31**). The exterior view shows the entrance door in the front wall and there are windows at first-floor level, though it is not clear whether these lit garrets above the schoolroom or merely provided additional light to the schoolroom. The chimneys billowing smoke indicate that fireplaces were provided. The drawing of the interior shows the master in his chair reading a book with Latin on one page and Greek on the other. There is a birch lying on the floor, with what may be a bowl or dish beside it. The boys, dressed in long robes, sit on benches around the walls with books resting on their

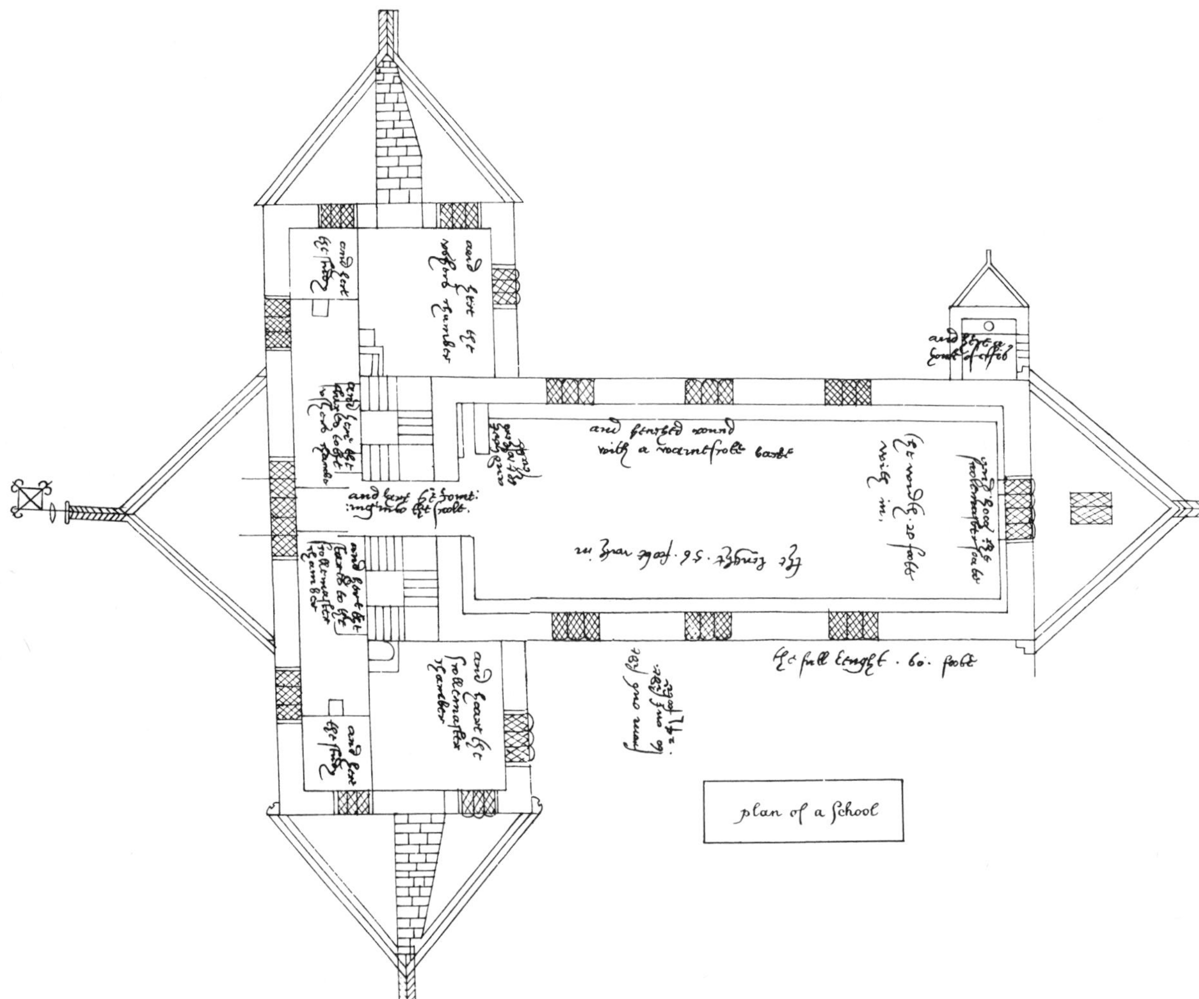

Figure 6 (*a*) Plan of a school *c*. 1590.

knees. Another boy (perhaps older, since his dress is different) is carrying to the master what looks like a scroll of parchment or a small log of wood. This could be a baton used as a pass, giving a boy permission to leave the room, such as is known to have been used in schools at this time.[38]

No other furniture is shown in the room. It may well be that, although written exercises were becoming more common, the majority of schools followed the practice of Bury School (Lancs.), where the statutes state that 'when they [i.e. the pupils] have to write, let them use their knees for a table'.[39] On the other hand, there is a record of 1582 showing that at Ipswich Grammar School three deal boards and four trestles were provided to serve as 'a table in the midst of the grammar school for the children to write upon'.[40] But there is very little evidence that desks were regularly provided for grammar-school pupils in the sixteenth century. Although some manual skill was

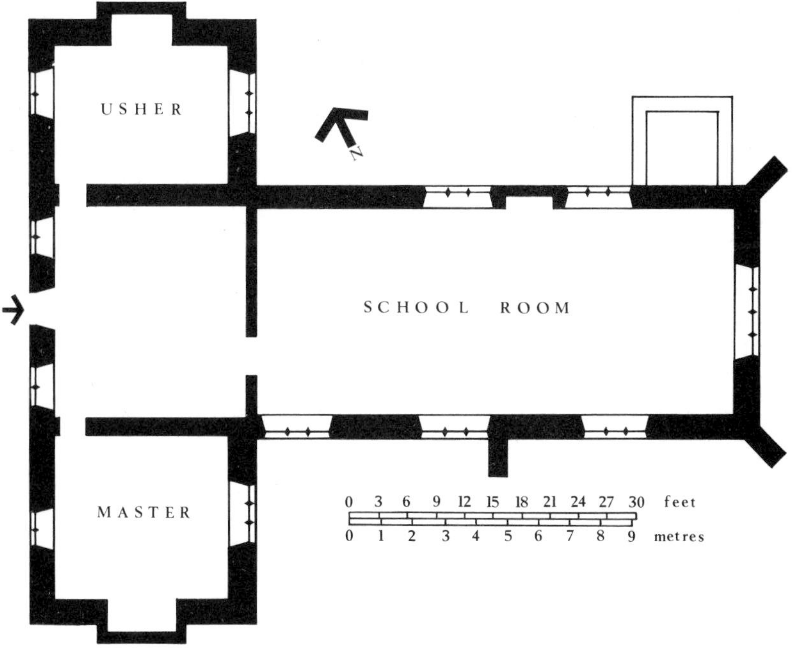

Figure 6 (*b*) Thame School, built between 1559 and 1575, ground plan.

needed to complete written exercises in 'paper-books' of the kind suggested, for example, by Roger Ascham in *The Scholemaster* (1570), the art of writing was not regarded at this date as the concern of the grammar schools as such, and it was usually practised only during holiday periods.[41]

For fuller instruction in 'writing', a term which often included calligraphy, arithmetic and other practical skills, a child would have to be placed with a 'writing master'. There was during Elizabeth's reign growing interest in this subject (or, rather, group of subjects), especially in London, where a commercial education was needed for the clerical and accountancy work which supported the activities of the merchant class. Writing in its wider sense was usually taught by private masters and at first made comparatively little impact upon the ordinary elementary and grammar schools (what Mulcaster called the 'public places').[42] There is, however, an outstanding exception to this general statement, that of Christ's Hospital, which began in 1552 when Edward VI granted to the City of London for charitable purposes the site and buildings previously occupied by the Grey Friars. The institution, or more accurately complex of institutions, which developed on this site began as something between a school and a foundling hospital. Orphan children of both sexes and of all ages from a few days to fourteen or fifteen years old were admitted. The babes in arms were boarded out to nurses, and the older children received what today might broadly be called a technical or commercial education. During its first year there were some 280 children of teachable age and a teaching staff of seven, viz. a grammar master, an usher under him, a writing master, two elementary teachers (for the petties), a music master and a matron for the 'maiden-children'. In the course of the late sixteenth and early seventeenth centuries a number of different 'schools' emerged, all within the same foundation. An upper and lower grammar school were organized by the master and usher, a writing school was endowed in about 1577 and a music school in about 1609. A reading school developed under the petty masters, while the girls were taught in a separate 'maidens' school'.[43]

The friary buildings were considerably damaged in the Great Fire of London and much rebuilding, as we shall later see, then took place. But a plan of about 1660 has survived which gives some impression of what the buildings were like before the Fire (fig. 7). The plan shows an astonishing mass of small rooms carved out of the friary buildings. The 'Garden Plot' was the former cloister, and on the east side was the grammar school. On the north side were the maidens' school (with a cellar on one side of it and a coalhouse on the other) and the writing schools, situated between the 'morterhouse' (? mortuary) and what look like latrines. The 'Town Ditch' was originally the open sewer of the City, but it had been covered over in 1553. Even so, this part of the site must have been far from salubrious. The rest of the site was occupied by a congeries of rooms (many let out to tenants not connected with the foundation), together with numerous yards, small garden plots, etc. Some of the rooms were used for the children's sleeping and eating quarters and others were occupied by the teaching

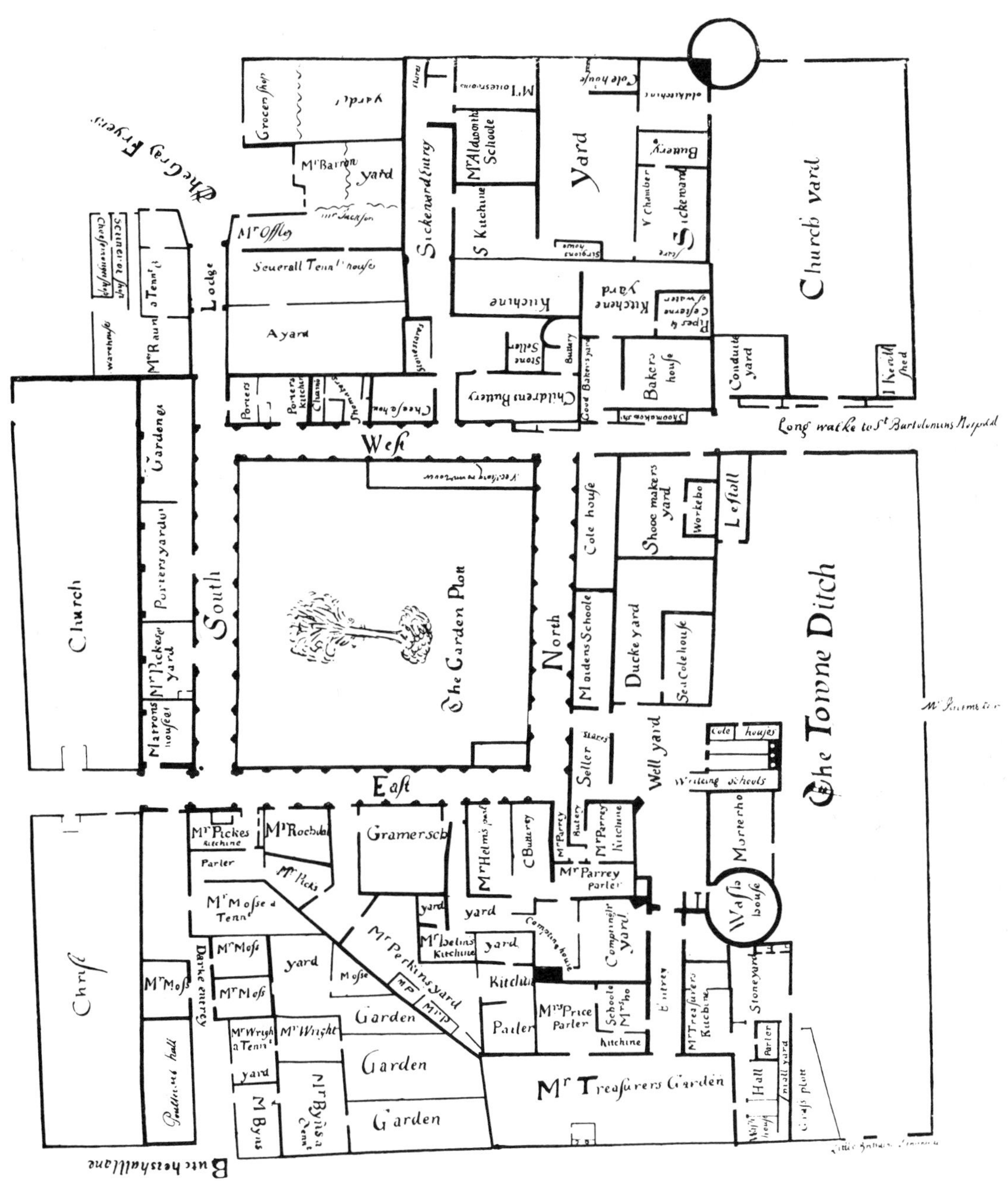

Figure 7 Christ's Hospital, London, ground plan, *c.* 1660.

and nursing staff. A close study of the plan impels one to comment that the Great Fire was by no means an unrelieved disaster so far as Christ's Hospital was concerned.

Christ's Hospital was in many respects a unique institution. But because it gave expression to a number of new educational ideas and provided the necessary buildings at public expense, its example was of great importance. In particular, its inclusion of commercial subjects and its provision for orphans' and girls' education were to influence subsequent founders of schools to broaden the scope of their foundations. Even in the sixteenth century it had its imitators in the provinces. Probably the best surviving example is the original Bablake School in Hill Street, Coventry, which began in 1560 as a hospital school for twenty-one boys.[44] They were accommodated in a long, two-storey building dating from about 1500 (pl. **24**), which is now used as the offices of the Clerk to the Governors of Bablake School. The schoolroom (which was also used for dining) occupied half of the ground floor, with dormitories above. This building forms the eastern side of a quadrangle, with Bond's Hospital (which still accommodates twenty-one old men) on the north side and further buildings on the west side occupying the site of an extension to the school built in 1832 and destroyed in the blitz of 1940. The boys wore blue tunics and yellow stockings, no doubt in direct imitation of Christ's Hospital in London. Other schools, as we shall see, were to take up some of the new ideas associated with this famous London school.

Notes

1 Printed in Carlisle, II, 71f.
2 McDonnell, M. F. J., *A history of St Paul's School*, Chapman & Hall, 1909, 67.
3 Quoted in Carlisle, II, 82.
4 Leach, A. F., *Educational charters and documents*, Cambridge U. P., 1911, 448–50.
5 McDonnell, *op. cit.*, 64–6.
6 Jackson, N. G., *Newark Magnus*, Nottingham: Bell, 1964, 274.
7 See, for example, Barley, M. W., *The house and home*, Studio Vista, 1963, 40, and Hoskins, W. G., *Provincial England*, Macmillan, 1963, 144. (The rebuilding of schools clearly takes its place alongside the 'Great Rebuilding' of houses during this period.)
8 Clarke, M. L., *Classical education in Britain*, Cambridge U.P., 1959, 5–6.
9 Gray, I. E., and Potter, W. E., *Ipswich School*, Ipswich: Harrison, 1950, 19.
10 *Ibid.*, 21.
11 At Canterbury, Carlisle, Durham, Ely, Norwich, Rochester, Winchester and Worcester the monks were replaced by secular canons; and six new bishoprics were established at Bristol, Chester, Gloucester, Oxford, Peterborough and Westminster.
12 R.C.H.M., *Hertfordshire*, 1910, 100.
13 Quoted in *V.C.H., Hertfordshire*, II, 1908, 72–4.
14 *V.C.H., Surrey*, II, 1905, 164–70, and Williamson, G. C., *Royal Grammar School, Guildford*, Bell, 1929, 27f. I am much indebted to Mr D. M. Sturley, Senior History Master

at the school, for further information and for showing me the building.

15 Pevsner, N., and Nairn, I., *Surrey*, 1962, 237. Summerson, J., *Architecture in Britain, 1530–1830*, Penguin, 4th ed., 1963, remarks on the Guildford school plan as 'somewhat resembling a Tudor type of large town-house, with the great schoolroom in place of the hall'.

16 For a full description of the library at Guildford see Williamson, *op. cit.*, 96f.

17 See Garrett, C. H., *The Marian exiles*, Cambridge, U.P., 1938, 224–5.

18 *V.C.H., Lincolnshire*, II, 1906, 456.

19 *V.C.H., Gloucestershire*, II, 1907, 425.

20 *V.C.H., Derbyshire*, II, 1907, 254–65, and Frangopulo, N. J., 'History of Queen Elizabeth's Grammar School, Ashbourne', M.Ed. thesis, Leeds, 1937. The latter (pp. 1–8) effectively disposes of Leach's argument in the *V.C.H.* that this was merely an old school refurbished. I am indebted to the Headmaster, Mr D. A. Kimmins, for showing me around the building.

21 Oldham, J. B., *History of Shrewsbury School*, Oxford: Blackwell, 1952, 4–17. The medieval house bought by the bailiffs in 1552 and the Elizabethan part-rebuilding in timber have been fully recorded by Mr J. Smith of the R.C.H.M.

22 *V.C.H., Essex*, II, 1907, 531–3. See also R.C.H.M., *Essex*, II, 1921, 77, and Craze, M., *A history of Felsted School*, Ipswich: Cowell, 1955, ch. 2, and interior illustrated facing p. 49.

23 The cost of building Elizabethan grammar schools seems to have varied between £100 and £300 (Brown, J. H., *Elizabethan schooldays*, Oxford: Blackwell, 1933, 17). The school at Ashbourne was estimated to cost £400 (Frangopulo, *op. cit.*, 19).

24 Marshall, L. B., *Brief history of Enfield Grammar School*, Richmond: Dimbleby, 1958, 15, 22–3. Plan of the school in R.C.H.M., *Middlesex*, 1937, 23.

25 Carlisle, II, 335. The inscriptions on the schoolroom at Uppingham are from Prov. xxii. 6 (in Hebrew), Mark x. 14 (in Greek), and Eccles. xii. 1 (in Latin).

26 *V.C.H., Lancashire*, II, 1908, 608.

27 Ex inf. Librarian, Public Library, Kendal.

28 Quotations from the edition by Quick, R. H., Longmans, 1888, 222–31. Spelling modernized.

29 The grammar-school curriculum is described in Charlton, K., *Education in Renaissance England*, Routledge & Kegan Paul, 1965, 105f.

30 *Ibid.*, 98f.

31 *V.C.H., Surrey*, II, 1905, 183. The usher, who taught writing and ciphering, received the same salary as the grammar master.

32 Cross, M. C., *The Free Grammar School of Leicester*, Leicester U.P., 1953, 18.

33 Adamson, J. W., *The illiterate Anglo-Saxon and other essays*, Cambridge U.P., 1946, 60, suggests that the two children in long dresses are girls, but such dresses were commonly worn by small boys during this period (see Cunnington, P., and Buck, A., *Children's costume in England*, A. & C. Black, 1965, 37, 39, 42, 72).

34 *V.C.H., Hertfordshire*, II, 1908, 70–1.

35 The illustration appeared in the 1662 edition of *The English schoolmaster*, but the style of dress belongs to an earlier period. The long train and coiled hair suggest that the child in the foreground is a girl. On girls in the grammar schools see Adamson, J. W., *op. cit.*, 59–61.

36 The schools at Guildford, Ashbourne and (later) Shrewsbury were all built near the old town boundaries. (At Guildford the former town boundary actually ran along the side of the school.)

37 I owe this reference to Mr Robert Taylor. The original building survives at Thame as a warehouse owned by Messrs Pursers Ltd.

38 Brown, *op. cit.*, 115. Cf. the 'remedy ring' at Winchester (Cook, A. K., *About Winchester College*, Macmillan, 1917, 21, 338–9). Pate's Grammar School at Cheltenham survived until 1888. An old photograph (reproduced as pl. 7 in Hart, Gwen, *A history of Cheltenham*, Leicester U.P., 1965) shows a two-storey building with a door at one end: it closely resembles the drawing on the indenture of 1586.

39 Brown, *op. cit.*, 20 (this was as late as *c.* 1625).

40 Gray and Potter, *op. cit.*, 46.

41 Charlton, *op. cit.*, 99.

42 Cf. Charlton, *op. cit.*, 105: 'the aim [of the grammar school] always was to get on with the real business of the day, the study of Latin grammar'. For a somewhat different emphasis, see Simon, J., *Education and society in Tudor England*, Cambridge U.P., 1966, 377 and *passim*.

43 Pearce, E. H., *Annals of Christ's Hospital*, Methuen, 1901, 26, 137, 146.

44 *V.C.H., Warwickshire*, II, 1908, 329. See also article on 'Bablake School' in Humberstone, F. W., *Contributions to the Coventry newspapers* (privately printed, 1924; copy in present school library) and Poole, B., *Coventry: its history and antiquities*, Smith, 1870, 266–9. Surprisingly, there is no published history of this interesting school, which is now a direct-grant grammar school. It moved to its present site in the 1880s. I am indebted to Mr R. H. Pogson, Clerk to the Governors, and to Mr R. Mann, Senior History Master, for showing me around the school building.

Three

Town and village schools 1600-60

I

The first half of the seventeenth century may be regarded as in many respects the golden age of the English grammar school—and not of the grammar school alone. There is growing evidence to support the view that during this period something approaching a national system of schools of varying types was established, or at any rate that by 1660 a whole network of schools had been set up, covering not only the principal towns, but many villages and hamlets as well.

The most eloquent propounder of this general thesis, the American historian, Professor W. K. Jordan,[1] has been criticized on a number of grounds: as, for example, that he underestimates the medieval contribution to the provision of schools,[2] and also that he does not sufficiently recognize that the poorest members of the community were on the whole still outside the system of formal education.[3] But the many details which he gives of philanthropic activity, particularly by the merchants of London during the reigns of the first two Stuarts, are impressive. He has attempted to calculate the exact amounts donated or bequeathed for education and other benevolent purposes in ten English counties (Bristol, Buckinghamshire, Hampshire, Kent, Lancashire, Middlesex (including London), Norfolk, Somerset, Worcestershire and Yorkshire) in the period 1480 to 1660. He explains the formidable difficulties involved in making this compilation, and admits that he has not attempted to take account of changes (very marked during this period) in the purchasing power of money. Even so, the significance of the early seventeenth century in the progress of school provision seems to be clear. Donations and bequests for schools in the ten counties had averaged about £20,000 in each of the last three decades of the sixteenth century and rose to over £30,000 in the first decade of the seventeenth. This was followed by a quite remarkable rise in the period 1611–20, to nearly £100,000, after which there was a decline, followed by a partial recovery. The detailed figures given by Jordan are set out in the following table:[4]

Period	*Gifts to schools*	*Total gifts to education (including colleges, libraries, etc.)*
	£	£
1601–10	30,314	60,791
1611–20	97,774	133,092
1621–30	63,118	116,238
1631–40	29,391	73,471
1641–50	33,345	53,548
1651–60	55,387	75,749

That the early seventeenth century was a 'peak period' for school provision is indirectly supported by Professor Lawrence Stone's recent work on the Tudor and Stuart universities, for the great expansion which took place at both Oxford and Cambridge was itself a reflection of the growth of schools. He shows that the first wave of expansion at Oxford and Cambridge began in the 1560s, rose to a climax in about 1583 and then, after a short lull, a second great movement began which lasted until the outbreak of the Civil War, by which date the number of entrants had reached a peak not again exceeded until after 1860.[5]

Another valuable piece of evidence which appears to support the view that there was a rapid growth of schools in the first half of the seventeenth century is that adduced by Professor and Mrs Simon in their study of Leicestershire schools in the period 1625–40.[6] By examining the subscription books in which schoolmasters were obliged by law to enter their names, and other contemporary records, including the admission registers of some of the Oxford and Cambridge colleges, they show not only that there were during this period established schools in the market towns, but also that in many of the rural parishes a curate or schoolmaster taught on a more casual basis. Where permanent schools were established, they were often supported out of the town estates or from the parish rates.

These changes provide the background against which to study the development of school architecture at this time, and certainly it is during this period that surviving school buildings begin to become more numerous. Thus, for example, in the two adjoining Midland counties of Leicestershire and Northamptonshire the number of surviving school buildings of the sixteenth century or earlier is very small—in Leicestershire the only pre-1600 school building known to me is that of the town grammar school in Leicester itself, built in 1573 in Highcross Street, subsequently altered, and now used as offices. In Northamptonshire, apart from Chichele's School at Higham Ferrers (1422), there is, so far as I know, only the former school building north of the church at Finedon (1595). But between 1600 and 1660 the following have survived, although none is still used as a school:

Leicestershire

1614. Market Harborough (the old grammar school in the Market Place, restored in 1868 and used as a school until 1892).

1637. Wymondham (school founded by Sir John Sedley near the church; now a parish room).

1650. Billesdon (used as a school until 1876, and used occasionally since as an 'overflow' for the local church school).

c. 1650. Medbourne (the north transept of the parish church adapted as a schoolroom and so used until 1868).

Northamptonshire

1600. Daventry (the old grammar school in New Street, restored in 1857 and now the Catholic church of Our Lady of Charity and St Augustine).

1617. Wellingborough (the former grammar and English school near the churchyard, used until 1903).

1622. Burton Latimer (the old grammar school in Church Street; now closed).

1624. Weekley (a small English school, now the Boughton Estate Office).

1642. Abthorpe (enlarged in 1866 and then occupied by the National school; closed 1959).

1651. Cottesbrooke (erected by Sir John Langham, together with almshouses which have been recently restored).

II

When one begins to look in detail at these buildings, and others of similar date elsewhere in England, one is faced with the problem of categorization and classification. From the point of view of architectural style and type of building material, the only safe generalization is that these schools normally reflect local vernacular styles, which varied widely in different parts of the country. There is a real sense in which one feels that the schools of this period grew out of local needs and aspirations, without the imposition of architectural styles or methods of construction foreign to the localities they were designed to serve. As with vernacular domestic buildings of this period, there is no question of architects having been employed, and there can be no doubt that these schools were built by local craftsmen employing traditional techniques. An exception to this—which perhaps proves the rule—is Peacock's School in the High Street at Rye, Sussex, built in 1636 as a grammar school, but closed as a school in 1907 and now used as a Conservative Men's Club. The plan of the building, which consisted simply of two large rooms, one over the other, with attics in the roof space, was traditional, but the style of building employed has attracted the attention of architectural historians, because of its interesting use of brick and its very early use of Dutch gables and giant pilasters (pl. **32**).[7]

These small school buildings—often consisting simply of one room—which we are now considering were not merely built by local craftsmen, but were often financed by the parishioners themselves. There is ample documentary evidence of this, and we may cite two Yorkshire examples. At Otley a presentment was made in 1614 to the Archbishop of York, who was the Lord of the Manor. It was signed by twenty freeholders, only one of whom added 'gent' after his name, and seven of whom were able only to make their mark:

> We present that there is a piece of waste ground adjoining upon the hall garth in Otley upon part whereof there is a common town fold or pound now standing, which said parcel of waste ground containeth about forty-five yards in length and twelve yards in breadth and that the same is a very fit and convenient place for the building of a school house and not prejudicial or hurtful to any freeholder or other tenant in Otley. And all we of the jury and the rest of the freeholders in Otley are agreed and very willing that a house for a free grammar school shall be there builded. And we humbly pray that it would please his Grace to grant the same piece of waste ground to the free school for the purpose aforesaid.[8]

The school at Otley had benefited from a bequest of £250 made in 1603 by Thomas Cave, a chapman or itinerant merchant, whose gift was conditional upon the parishioners raising an equal sum among themselves. This they did, as well as later providing the building. The original school survives as a private house, but it was considerably altered when an upper storey was placed on it in 1790; it was abandoned as a school in 1874.[9]

In the case of our other Yorkshire example, that of Ilkley, the original building of 1637 has survived virtually unchanged (pl. **36**). As in many other places of which there is documentary evidence, boys (and it seems girls as well) were being taught at this period in the church itself. Then the Town Book records that from 1616 onwards a number of small donations were made towards the building of a separate school house for the children. In 1636, the following statement was signed by fourteen of the parishioners, five of whom could only make their mark:

> By general consent of the inhabitants of Ilkley, we, whose names are here subscribed, do undertake to pay our proportion towards the erection of a school house and do think fit that whereas, by a late unavoidable casualty, the sum of money given to this charitable use is impaired, that the remainder of the sum being £89, be put into the hands of Reginald Heber and Christopher Baynton gents [they are among the signatories] and by them improved [i.e. invested] until by the interest thereof the sum be made up to one hundred pounds; and that in the meantime such of the parishioners as send their children to school shall pay such sums as they and the schoolmaster shall agree upon.[10]

Soon after this the small school building on the Skipton road was built of local stone in the traditional style. It may be noted that an early pupil at this school recorded that in 1662 'I learnt English with Mr Nicholls, who then was minister and schoolmaster to the church and school of Ilkley. I heard no exceptions about either English or Latin. Then Mr Coates [taught me] who also usually without any objections taught the same . . . teaching any—English, Latin, Greek, Hebrew.'[11] Thus we have a picture of a small local school, typical of many others up and down the country, teaching any of the recognized school subjects according to the ability of the schoolmaster. It would indeed be wrong to make artificial distinctions at this period, particularly in the smaller schools, between 'grammar' and 'elementary' or classical and English teaching. But we will return to this theme later in the chapter.

Another general point of interest which arises from the Ilkley example is the effort that was made by the parishioners to move the children out of the church into a separate school building, albeit a humble one. This was not, of course, an indication of anticlerical feeling: at Ilkley the schoolmaster seems to have been the incumbent, and in many other places the incumbent or his curate taught in the local school, a practice which was already established before the Reformation.[12] The moving of the children out of the church was mainly a matter of convenience; yet it also probably reflected contemporary changes in liturgical practice, which were laying greater stress on the church as a sacred building to be reserved for devotional purposes.[13] It is interesting to note that most founders of grammar schools during this period insisted that the scholars should attend the parish church on Sundays, but always under the strict supervision of the master and the senior boys. Some of the wealthier founders built galleries in the church for the scholars' use (as at Chigwell, Essex, and Wolverhampton),[14] so that the close link with the church building remained, but under discipline.

Whether a village school was able to move out of the church into its own building was mainly a question of finance. The school at Medbourne, Leicestershire (pl. **34**), met in the parish church from at least the middle of the seventeenth century until 1868. It is significant that this school was unendowed until 1761 and was never well financed.[15] But at least a definite part of the church building was allocated to the school and minimal alterations made, for in about 1650 the north transept was separated from the body of the church by a lath-and-plaster partition and in the space so formed a fireplace and additional door were inserted. We may add on this general point that when a school did move into a separate building, it was usually built very close to the church, often on the edge of the churchyard itself. An early surviving example of this is the school at Wymondham, also in Leicestershire, 1637 (pl. **33**). This architectural association of church and school remained a characteristic feature of parish schools until the end of the nineteenth century.

We may choose four other examples from this numerous class of early seventeenth-century schools consisting of a single room in order to illustrate regional architectural styles. Typical of this type is the school at Uffington, Berkshire (pl. **35**), built of the local chalk close to the parish church. The origin of this school is obscure: it was probably founded under the will of one Thomas Saunders, but the building has three dates carved on it—1617, 1634, and 1637—perhaps recording other gifts of which no other record survives. It appears that the master received the rents of small pieces of land and cottages in Uffington for which, at any rate by the early nineteenth century, he was teaching the three Rs to twelve boys from Uffington and six from the neighbouring village of Woolstone.[16] Another country school built in the local stone, in this case limestone rubble with ashlar dressings, is the delightful building, now unfortunately derelict, at Burton Latimer, Northamptonshire (pl. **43**). It consists of a single room measuring 44 by 16 feet and bears the inscription: 'This house was built in 1622. The Freeschoole was founded by Thomas Burbanke and Margaret his wife 1587.' The names of those who financed the building are carved on the window lintels, again with the date 1622.[17]

In a different vernacular building tradition are the schools at Market Harborough, Leicestershire, and Weobley, Herefordshire, both of which originally consisted of a single room with attics in the roof-space. The school at Market Harborough (pl. **37**) was erected in 1614 under the will of Robert Smyth, a native of the town who had later become a merchant tailor in London. He gave very detailed instructions for the building, which explain its unusual design. He directed that it should 'stand upon posts or columns over a part of the market place to keep the market people dry in time of foul weather', and further instructed 'those who shall survey and direct the building . . . to be careful that it be strong and plain and that the main bearing posts be set upon stone somewhat above the ground and the windows all clear storeys. It is conceived that 36 foot for the length and 18 foot for the breadth will be a sufficient proportion.' He also directed that Biblical texts should be painted around all four sides of the school, and renewed when they became faded.[18] The building was of half-timbered construction, though when it was restored in 1868 it was faced with imitation timbering and decorative plaster-work.[19] Also in half-timbering, though this time wholly original, is the school at Weobley (pl. **38**). It was founded by the will of William Crowther in 1653. He also was a native of the place and had prospered as a London haberdasher.[20]

Some of these schools were founded as grammar schools, and in the case of Market Harborough it is known that pupils were sent from the school to Oxford and Cambridge colleges, which is further evidence that Latin was taught there, at least in the seventeenth century. No doubt a prestige element was involved in bequeathing money for the study of the classical languages, but we find that the school at Weobley, though founded to teach Latin and Greek, was very soon teaching purely English subjects and apprenticing the boys to husbandry. Apart from the terms of an endowment—and these were often vague—a great deal depended on how much money it produced, the qualifications of the master and the nature of the local demand. Moreover, some early seventeenth-century schools were never intended for the teaching of Latin. These are of particular interest because they show that some benefactors were now taking up the point which we saw was made by Mulcaster in Elizabeth's reign, viz. that elementary as well as grammar schools were worthy of endowment by 'well-disposed wealthy men'. Perhaps this was inevitable in areas where the provision of Latin schools appeared to be sufficient, but there was also, as we shall shortly see, a new interest at this date in the promotion of a purely English education.

Surviving buildings in this category and dating from the early seventeenth century seem to be rare, but I know of three examples, at Tiverton (Devon), Weekley (Northants.) and Great Marlow (Bucks.). At Tiverton there is a small stone building in St Peter Street, now used as a local museum, consisting of one room open to the roof. At the lower end of the schoolroom is a transverse passage leading from the street to a small courtyard and what was formerly the master's house behind the school. This passage resembles the screens-passage of a medieval house and above it is a gallery.[21] (There is a similar arrangement at the old Magnus Grammar School at Newark, Nottinghamshire, which dates from 1531.) Above the door (pl. **39**) is the inscription: 'Robert Comin al[ia]s Chilcot borne in this towne founde[d] this free English schoole and indow[ed] it with maintenanc[e] for ever. Anno D[omi]ni 1611.'

Our other two examples both date from 1624. The school at Weekley (pl. **40**) is the only original building to survive of four similar schools founded by Nicholas Latham, Rector of Barnwell St Andrew's in Northamptonshire, who settled land upon trust for schools at Barnwell St Andrew's, Brigstock, Luddington and Weekley.[22] The school at Weekley is a single-storey building of local limestone. A small wing was added to it in the same material during the nineteenth century, when it was still in use as an elementary school. It is now the Boughton Estate Office, the school having been supported for most of its later history by the Duke of Buccleuch. Over the school doorway is the well-preserved inscription: 'A free schoole for Weekley and Werckton [i.e. Warkton] founded by Nicolas Latham, clerke, parson of Barnewell St Andrew to teach theire children to write and reade Anno Domini 1624.' It will be noted that writing is mentioned before reading, perhaps because reading, unlike writing, was commonly taught at home or in private (dame) schools. Also, the reference to 'children' may well indicate that Latham had in mind the education of girls as well as boys.

Finally, at Marlow in Buckinghamshire is the school built in 1624 by Sir William Borlase, whose will provided that

> twelve pounds a year shall be allowed a schoolmaster to teach twenty four poor children to write, read and cast accounts. [They are] to be taken into the said school between the age of ten and fourteen, and after any of them can read, write and cast accounts, which I conceive in two years, they will be ready to do [i.e. work].

There were further provisions for binding the boys as apprentices, as well as for building alongside the school a 'work house and house of correction', which was also to be used for the teaching of 'twenty-four poor women children . . . to make bone lace, to spin or to knit'.[23] This workhouse has long since been demolished, but the boys' school survives as part of the present Sir William Borlase's School, which became a secondary school in 1880. The original school (pl. **41**) is of fairly ambitious design in flint and brick, with a dominating central porch. The main doorway was originally where the ground-floor window of the porch now is, and above it is an inscription to Sir William's son, in whose memory the school was built. Originally the front elevation was symmetrical, the portion on the right of the photograph having been added later. There are two inscribed panels on each side of the porch: over the west window, 'In the sweate of thy face shalt thou eate bread, Genesis 3, 19', and over the east window, 'If any will not worke neither shall hee eate, 2 Thessa. 3, 10'. The strong Puritan spirit which inspired the good works of so many of these early seventeenth-century founders of schools could hardly be stated in more uncompromising a fashion. The original plan of the school is difficult to reconstruct, but it probably consisted of two rooms on the ground floor (one used as the schoolroom and the other possibly as the master's living-room) with two rooms on the first floor and attics above.[24]

Two other schools of this period which have since become well known had a similar origin to those mentioned above, although their original buildings have not survived. The first is the Latymer School founded at Hammersmith by the will of Edward Latymer (1624), which provided for 'eight poor boys to be put to some petty school to the end that they may learn to read English and to be so kept at school until they shall attain the age of thirteen years, thereby to keep them from idle and vagrant courses and also to instruct them in some part of God's true religion'.[25] They were to be clothed in doublets with a red cross, the colour also chosen for the girls of the Red Maids' School at Bristol founded in 1634 by Alderman John Whitson, who bequeathed property to maintain a hospital (i.e. boarding) school in which 'one grave, painful and modest woman' was to teach forty 'poor women children'.[26] In these schools, and some of those mentioned earlier, we may discern the influence of the ideas which were embodied in Christ's Hospital in London, and we also have virtually all the elements which are more usually associated with the so-called charity-school movement of the following century—the recruitment of poor children, the limited curriculum, the stress on work and religion and the provision of school uniforms. More particularly, we have this architectural and other evidence that an English education was now being publicly provided (in Mulcaster's sense of the word 'public'), not merely as a preliminary to the study of Latin, but as a type of education justifiable in its own right and the most appropriate for at least some children.

Many of the schools which we have so far been considering in this chapter were taught by the local incumbent or his curate, or were not well enough endowed to provide accommodation for a schoolmaster, let alone an usher as well. But from the beginning of the seventeenth century we find an increasing number of schools, usually endowed by local gentlemen or merchants, where specific provision was made for the schoolmaster's living accommodation, frequently under the same roof as the schoolroom and as an integral part of the design. We saw in the previous chapter that in some of the major schools of the sixteenth century—as at Berkhamsted,

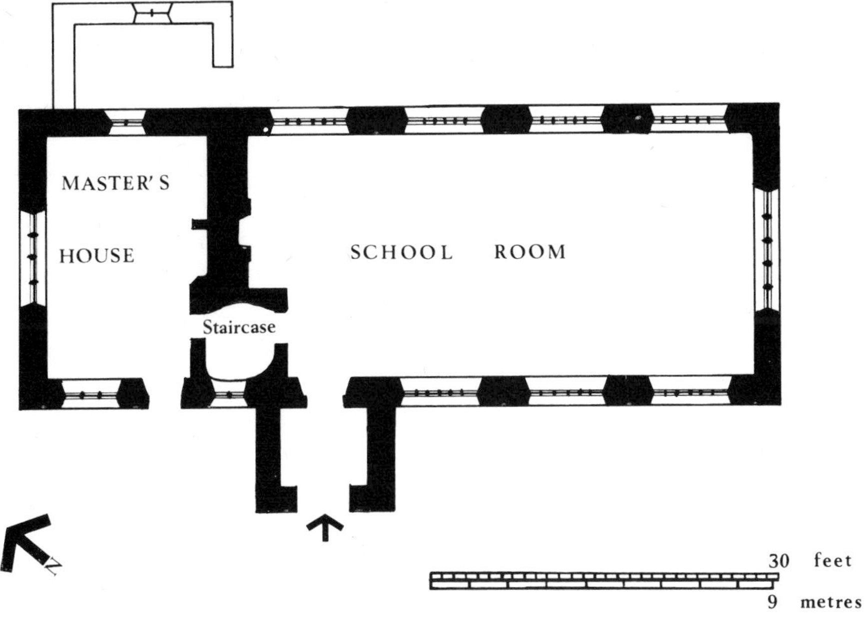

Figure 8 (*a*) Burnsall School, *c*. 1605, ground plan. (The whole of the first floor was occupied by bedrooms.)

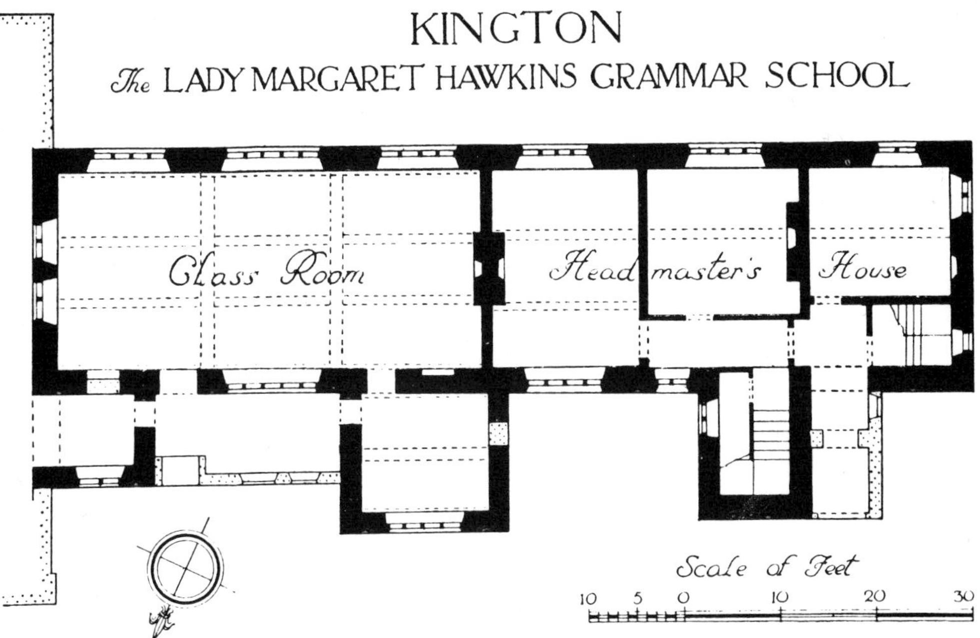

Figure 8 (*b*) Kington School, 1622, ground plan. (Originally the master and usher occupied the area marked 'Headmaster's House'.)

Guildford and Ashbourne—provision had been made for the teaching staff. Now we find schools, sometimes in remote places and small enough to require only one schoolmaster, where relatively generous staff accommodation was built. We may illustrate this category of school by again taking four typical examples drawn from different parts of the country.

Taking them in date order, we have first the school at Burnsall, beautifully situated in the Yorkshire dales (pl. **42**). There are indeed a number of seventeenth-century stone-built schools in this delightful area around Grassington—Threshfield (1674) and Malham (1682) as well as Burnsall. The school at Burnsall was founded in 1605 by Sir William Craven, Alderman of London.[27] The plan (fig. 8(*a*)) shows that most of the building was taken up with the schoolroom, measuring 43 by 20 feet, above which were three rooms probably used as dormitories, since in this area of sparse population some of the boys must have boarded. The wall dividing the school from the master's house contains the chimney-flue, which served fireplaces in the schoolroom and in the master's house. There were originally two small bedrooms for the master and his family directly above the living-room. It is pleasant to record that this building is still in use as a school and that it has recently been sympathetically restored and extended (at the rear) by the architect and surveyor to the archdeaconry.[28]

Our next two schools both belong to the 1620s: Kington in Herefordshire and Stanwell in Middlesex. The former was founded in 1622 under the will of Lady Margaret Hawkins, widow of Sir John Hawkins, Treasurer of the Navy in Queen Elizabeth's reign. Her reason for founding the school links up with what was said earlier about Ilkley School: 'I discern it very convenient to have a schoolhouse built there, otherwise they must be forced to teach the scholars in the parish church.' She provided for both a schoolmaster and usher, and we find that half of the total accommodation was taken up by the masters' rooms (see fig. 8(*b*)).[29] At Stanwell the school was built in 1624 under the will of Sir Thomas Knyvett, Lord of the Manor (pl. **44**). It is in Bedfont Road at the east end of the old village and consists of the master's house and schoolroom in a single rectangular building of red brick with tiled roof. The master's accommodation (on the right of the photograph) was of two storeys, while the schoolroom on the left is a single-storey room lit by tall windows. The doorway leading into the schoolroom and the windows were somewhat altered in the nineteenth century. In the centre of the front elevation is a cartouche of the founder's arms, with an inscription to his memory. Over the school door is a text from Proverbs xxii. 6: 'Train up a child in the way he should go.' This building also is still in use as a school.[30] Our final example is the flint-and-brick school built in 1631 under the will of Sir John Leman at Beccles in Suffolk (pl. **45**). It is now in use as a private school (a new grammar school building having been opened in 1914) and it is difficult to reconstruct the original plan. It seems likely, however, that the schoolroom was in the centre with the master and usher accommodated at each end, on the model of Berkhamsted in the previous century.[31]

We may summarize our conclusions about these various types of early seventeenth-century school buildings by saying that, although of modest size and unpretentious appearance, they nevertheless reflect an educational movement of great importance—the penetration of formal education not only into the towns, but into the countryside, with an emphasis not only on the classical subjects, but also on what may for the first time truly be called 'the three Rs'.

Notes

1 Jordan, W. K., *Philanthropy in England 1480—1660*, George Allen & Unwin, 1959, and later books.

2 Tate, W. E., in *St Anthony's Hall Publications*, No. 23 (1963), 37—9.

3 Simon, Joan, *Education and society in Tudor England*, Cambridge U.P., 1966, 370, 398.

4 Jordan, *op. cit.*, 373.

5 Stone, L., 'The educational revolution in England, 1560—1640', in *Past and present*, XXVIII (July 1964), 50—1.

6 Simon, B., 'Leicestershire schools, 1625—40', in *British Journal of Educational Studies*, III, No. 1 (1954), 42—59. See also Simon, B. (ed.), *Education in Leicestershire 1540—1940*, Leicester U.P., 1968, ch. 1, and Carter, E. H., *The Norwich subscription books*, Nelson, 1937. The subscription books appear to provide evidence of a highly mobile body of schoolmasters, and of curates who taught part-time, rather than of established schools, a point I owe to Mr Brian Burch.

7 For the history of Rye Grammar School see *V.C.H., Sussex*, II, 1907, 425—6; also L. A. Vidler's article in the school magazine (1940) and *Sussex Archaeological Collections*, Vol. LXVIII. (I owe these references to Mr G. S. Bagley of the Rye Museum Association.) For the architectural features see Pevsner, *Sussex*, 1965, 598, and Lloyd, N., *A History of English brickwork*, Montgomery, 1925, 71, 85, 90, 98, 181, 273, 300, 418 (called 'Pocock's school' here).

8 Cobley, F., *Chronicles of the Free Grammar School at Otley*, Otley: Walker, 1923, 75.

9 *Ibid.*, 74. There is a photograph of the school in the N.M.R. (ref. A42/2643).

10 Quoted in Salmon, N., *Ilkley Grammar School 1607—1957*, the School, n.d., 14.

11 *Ibid.*, 15.

12 Cf. Purvis, J. S., *Educational records*, York: St Anthony's Press, 1959, 2 and 4, where it is pointed out that the schoolmaster was frequently the incumbent, especially before 1640; later the parish clerk tended to act as schoolmaster.

13 See Addleshaw, G. W. O., and Etchells, F., *The architectural setting of Anglican worship*, Faber & Faber, 1948, especially ch. IV. When children were taught in a church, they sometimes left their mark, e.g. the *graffiti* on the screen at Salthouse, Norfolk (photos. in N.M.R.). On the use of churches for schools in the Middle Ages and later see Davies, J. G., *The secular use of Church buildings*, S.C.M. Press, 1968, 76—7, 188—91. Note also the multiplication tables and scholars' initials carved on some of the pillars in the Lady Chapel of Long Melford (Suffolk), which was used as a school for 200 years.

14 For the gallery at Chigwell (erected *c*. 1620 and demolished 1886) see Stott, G., *A history of Chigwell School*, Ipswich: Cowell, 1960, 178 and pl. 6. For the gallery at Wolverhampton (erected 1610) see Mander, G., *The history of the Wolverhampton Grammar School*, Wolverhampton: Steens, 1913, 83–7 and plate between pp. 88 and 89.

15 *V.C.H., Leicestershire*, V, 1964, 239–40.

16 *Ibid., Berkshire*, II, 1907, 281.

17 Plan in N.M.R. by Surridge, R., 1906.

18 Stocks, J. E., ed., *Market Harborough Parish Records 1531–1837*, Oxford U.P., 1926, 487–8. Inscriptions on schoolhouse from Matt. vi. 33; Ps cxxii. 1; Ephes. ii. 8–9; Ps. cxxii. 1; 1 Sam. xvi. 7. On contemporary market halls built above arcades, see Barley, M. W., *The English farmhouse and cottage*, R.K.P., 1961, 10.

19 *V.C.H., Leicestershire*, V, 1964, 137.

20 Salt, A. E. W., *The Borough and Honour of Weobley*, Hereford: Thurston, 1954, 39–40. See also R.C.H.M., *Herefordshire*, III, 1934, 202.

21 I am indebted to Mr A. W. Everett for information about this building.

22 *V.C.H., Northamptonshire*, II, 1906, 283.

23 Davies, J. C., *A history of Borlase School*, Aylesbury: Fraine, 1932, 9–10. See also *V.C.H., Buckinghamshire*, II, 1908, 214–15.

24 For details of the building at Marlow see R.C.H.M., *Buckinghamshire*, I, 1912, 253–4. I am also grateful to the Headmaster, Mr E. M. Hazelton, for further information.

25 Quoted in Wheatley W., *The history of Edward Latymer and his foundations*, Cambridge U.P., 1936, 126.

26 *V.C.H., Gloucestershire*, II, 1907, 384.

27 *V.C.H., Yorkshire*, I, 1907, 481. See also the school nearby, built on to the west end of Halton Gill chapel (1626), described in Raistrick, A., *Old Yorkshire dales*, Newton Abbot: David and Charles, 1967, ch. 10.

28 I am indebted to Mrs Mary Wales, F.R.I.B.A., for a plan and other information about Burnsall School.

29 Parry, R., *The history of Kington*, Kington: Humphreys, 1845, 163. This is one of the earliest schools where the architect's name is recorded—John Abel, 1577–1674 (Ware, D., *Short dictionary of British architects*, George Allen & Unwin, 1967, 19). See also R.C.H.M., *Herefordshire*, III, 1934, 91. (Photo. in N.M.R. shows a much-altered building.)

30 *V.C.H., Middlesex*, III, 1962, 34 and 49. Also R.C.H.M., *Middlesex*, 1937, 117.

31 *V.C.H., Suffolk*, II, 1907, 337–8, and information from the Headmaster, Mr S. G. Standing.

Four

The changing grammar school 1600-60

I

A good deal of the history of formal education in England could be written by collating the subsequent histories of the numerous schools founded in the late sixteenth and early seventeenth centuries, only a fraction of which have been mentioned above. Many declined during the eighteenth and nineteenth centuries and some have completely disappeared from view. Others have remained small country schools down to our own time. Others again—for a variety of reasons, such as the growth of population, increases in the endowments, or the work of outstanding headmasters—have developed into major public and grammar schools.

If we look generally at the founding or refounding of schools in the period 1600 to 1660, we find that comparatively few of them began as large schools. Nevertheless, a small number of major school buildings of this period have survived and need to be considered for the light they throw on the further development of ideas particularly about the organization of grammar-school education. The conception of a grammar-school education during this period has sometimes been regarded as static and unchanging,[1] whereas in fact a number of new ideas were introduced which had their effects on school architecture and organization. Notable changes of emphasis occurred because of several new pressures, the most important of which were the Puritan spirit, which appeared in such works as Brinsley's *Ludus literarius, or, The grammar schoole* (1612) and the new scientific ideas of men like Bacon.

Probably the most famous school established during the reign of James I was that founded by Thomas Sutton in 1611 at the Charterhouse. He made provision for the education and maintenance of forty scholars (also called 'gown boys') and eighty old men (also called 'brothers' or 'pensioners'). The proposal to found the school met with some opposition, however, notably from Bacon. In *c.* 1612 he wrote a lengthy letter to the King, which included the following passage:

Concerning the advancement of learning, I do subscribe to the opinion . . . that

> for grammar schools there are already too many, and therefore no providence to add, where there is excess. For the great number of schools which are in your Highnesses realm doth cause a want and likewise an overthrow; both of them inconvenient and one of them dangerous; for by means thereof they find want in the country and towns, both of servants for husbandry and apprentices for trade; and on the other side, there being more scholars bred than the state can prefer and imploy, . . . it must needs fall out that many persons will be bred unfit for other vocations and unprofitable for that in which they were bred up, which fills the realm full of indigent, idle and wanton people which are but 'materia rerum novarum'.[2]

Bacon went on to suggest (unsuccessfully as it turned out) that the funds made available by Sutton would be better used to promote the study of 'science, philosophy, arts of speech and the mathematicks' at the universities. In the event, a compromise of a sort was agreed upon: the master was to teach only Latin and Greek, but the usher was 'to teach the scholars to cypher and cast an account, especially those that are less capable of learning, and fittest to be put to trades'.[3] It may be added that the vital role played by education as a leaven among members of the parliamentary opposition to the Crown, and the need for the advanced study of science which eventually resulted in the formation of the Royal Society, are both themes which have attracted the attention of recent historians; and the indirect influence of Bacon and his followers on the content and methods of school-teaching were to be considerable.

The buildings of Charterhouse School form an interesting contrast to Christ's Hospital and the other schools which took over former religious houses. The site and buildings of the Carthusian monastery had been bought in 1545 by Sir Edward North and were sold by his son to the Duke of Norfolk twenty years later. He adapted and extended the monastic buildings for use as a town mansion, called Howard House. This was in turn sold to Thomas Sutton and further adapted for the charitable purposes he had in mind. The surviving buildings and the site of the old monastic cells are shown in fig. 9. Howard House had been built around two courtyards, which now came to be known as Master's Court and Wash House Court. Immediately to the east of Master's Court was the former monastic church, which became the chapel of Sutton's hospital. On the northern side of Master's Court is the Great Hall, formerly used by the pensioners for dining. Adjoining the Great Hall to the north is a room (probably the former frater), now called the Brothers' Library, but formerly used as the gown boys' dining-hall (pl. **46**). In this room is an early seventeenth-century fireplace above which are the arms of Sutton. The doorway is also elaborately carved and the ceiling beams are supported by a row of four round oak columns. Some of the original tables and stools, with a fixed bench along the wall, have also survived. A separate schoolroom for the boys, with dormitories above, was built in 1612 further north, on the site of the cells marked D and E on the plan. This building was demolished soon after the school moved from

Charterhouse Square to Godalming in Surrey in 1872, but the school door, with its inscribed stones, was re-erected at Godalming.[4]

The architectural history of the Charterhouse School is not easy to disentangle because of the varying uses made of the buildings at different times, but the contrast with the earlier Christ's Hospital is apparent: the latter, as we saw, also settled around a monastic cloister, but in much more haphazard fashion. Practical writers on education were also becoming more systematic, and in Brinsley's *Ludus literarius* we have the

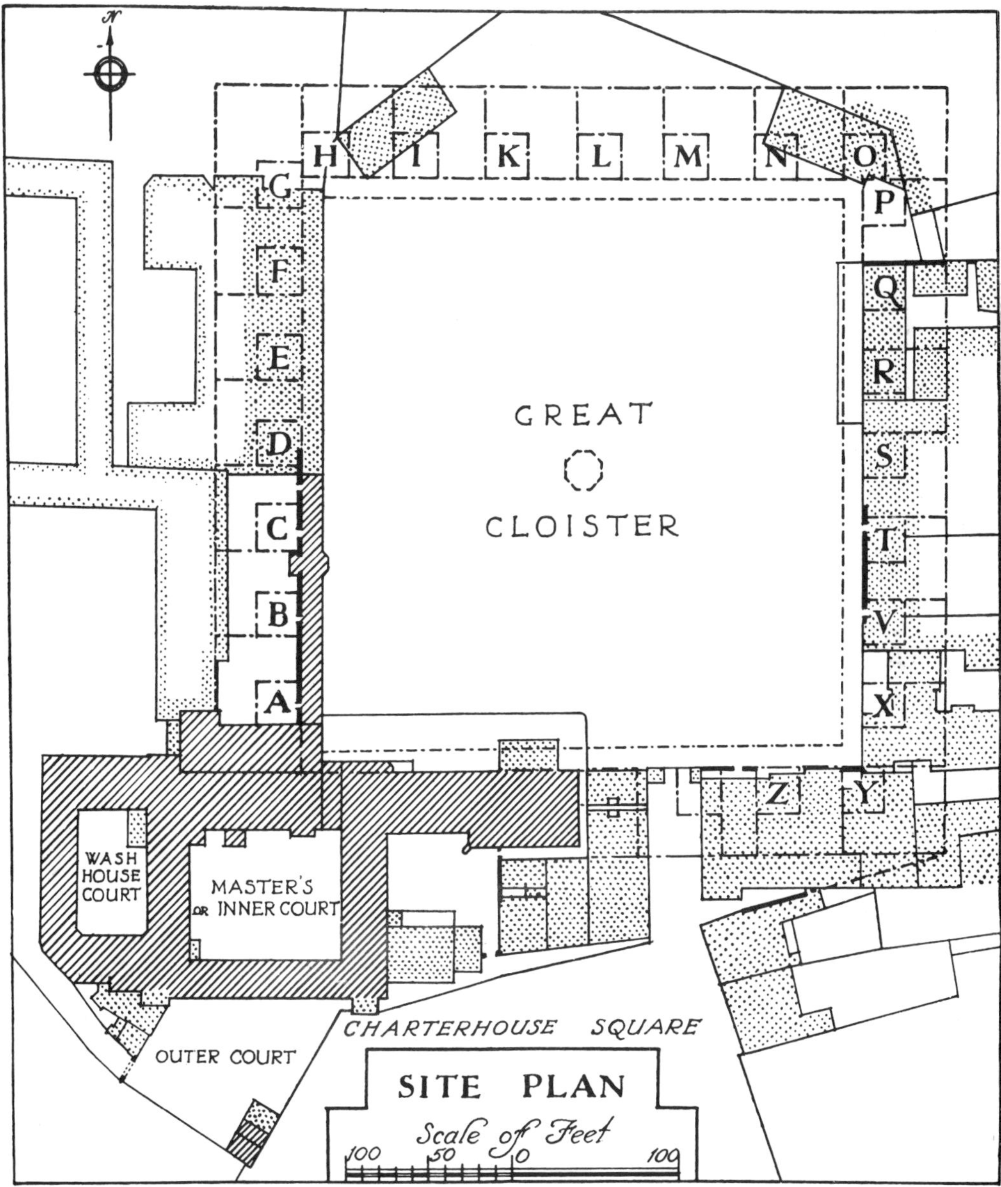

Figure 9 Charterhouse, site plan.

first really detailed treatment of grammar-school organization and teaching methods.[5] His influence on schools was more direct and immediate than that of Bacon and his followers, probably because his book was based on his own actual experience as a schoolmaster. He was a man of strong Puritan sympathies, and helped to promote new ideas about school organization which, as we shall see, influenced the planning particularly of the larger schools of this period.

Ludus literarius is written in the form of a dialogue between two schoolmasters, Spoudeus and Philoponus, the former representing the 'average' grammar-school master and the latter his more progressive but still highly practical colleague. Their discussion of the question of teaching English in the grammar schools (ch. 3) is particularly relevant to our present purpose. Spoudeus complains 'that the grammar schools should be troubled with teaching A.B.C.', and Philoponus agrees, 'for it were much to be wished that none might be admitted to the grammar schools until they were able to read English: as namely that they could read the New Testament perfectly and that they were in their Accidences [i.e. elementary grammar] or meet to enter into them'. 'Yet notwithstanding', he adds, 'where it cannot be redressed, it must be borne with wisdom and patience.'[6] He therefore goes on to give detailed advice on how best to teach the reading of English. Spoudeus then raises the thorny problem of how far the teaching of English should be kept up in the later years of the grammar-school course, when the emphasis was traditionally on the learning of Latin. The reply given by Philoponus is interesting:

> But to tell you what I think, wherein there seems unto me to be a very main want in all our grammar schools generally, or in the most of them; whereof I have heard some great learned men to complain; that there is no care had in respect to train up scholars so as they may be able to express their minds purely and readily in our own tongue, and to increase in the practice of it, as well as in the Latin or Greek; whereas our chief endeavour should be for it, and that for these reasons. 1. Because that language which all sorts and conditions of men amongst us are to have most use of, both in speech and writing, is our own native tongue. 2. The purity and elegance of our own language is to be esteemed a chief part of the honour of our nation, which all ought to advance as much as in us lieth. . . . 3. Because of those which are for a time trained up in schools, there are very few which proceed in learning, in comparison of them which follow other callings.[7]

He therefore advocates that English and Latin should be taught side by side throughout the grammar-school course, and to this end he recommends that written as well as oral exercises should be practised in the schools.

In the following chapter (ch. 4) Spoudeus raises the question of writing skills. He says that with his own pupils he has 'daily set them copies' to make, but has found this very laborious; and he refers to the common practice of using travelling scriveners to teach writing, 'whereof we find no small inconveniences'. Philoponus proceeds to give very detailed instructions on the teaching of writing, stressing the need to have 'all necessaries belonging thereunto; as pen, ink, paper, ruler, plummet, ruling-pen, pen-knife etc.'. Writing should be practised every day, and copy-books used. We also find the first mention of a chalk-board, for Philoponus says that 'when the young scholar cannot frame his hand to fashion any letter . . . some do use to draw before them the proportion of their letters with a piece of chalk upon a board or table, or with a piece of blacklead upon a paper'.[8]

Subsequent chapters give equally detailed advice about the teaching of Latin grammar, but these early chapters on the value of English, both written and oral, show how important Brinsley regarded it. The early Stuart grammar school was not obsessed with Latin to the extent which is oft… he skills of reading and writing in English a… ctised in them. The training of the younger… s as well) in these basic skills assumed suc… w beginning to be made for it, particularly i… any grammar schools was also making it es… tiation in planning the main components c…

This pr… lved, at the important school founded in 16… . Sutton had been a childless widower and … plain the scale of their foundations. Blund… ation of no less than 150 boys, to be taught b… alary of £50 a year) and an usher. The ori… -houses, still survives and is owned by the … 599 gave minute instructions about the buil… y large sum of £2,400:

> I will tha… house to contain for the place for … nd in breadth four and twenty fo… ient space and bigness to be joined … ne . . . all the windows well and s… and well covered, the floor of th… ak . . . with so many strong settles and… rd to the bigness of the same scho… therein, and to be divided on or near … oot in height or thereabout… tted round about and the same wains… above the settles or forms. . . .[9]

The plan of the school (fig. 10) shows that one long building was divided up into higher and lower schools, separated from each other by screens, with the masters' rooms at one end. The interior (pl. **49**) shows how the two schools were visually connected,

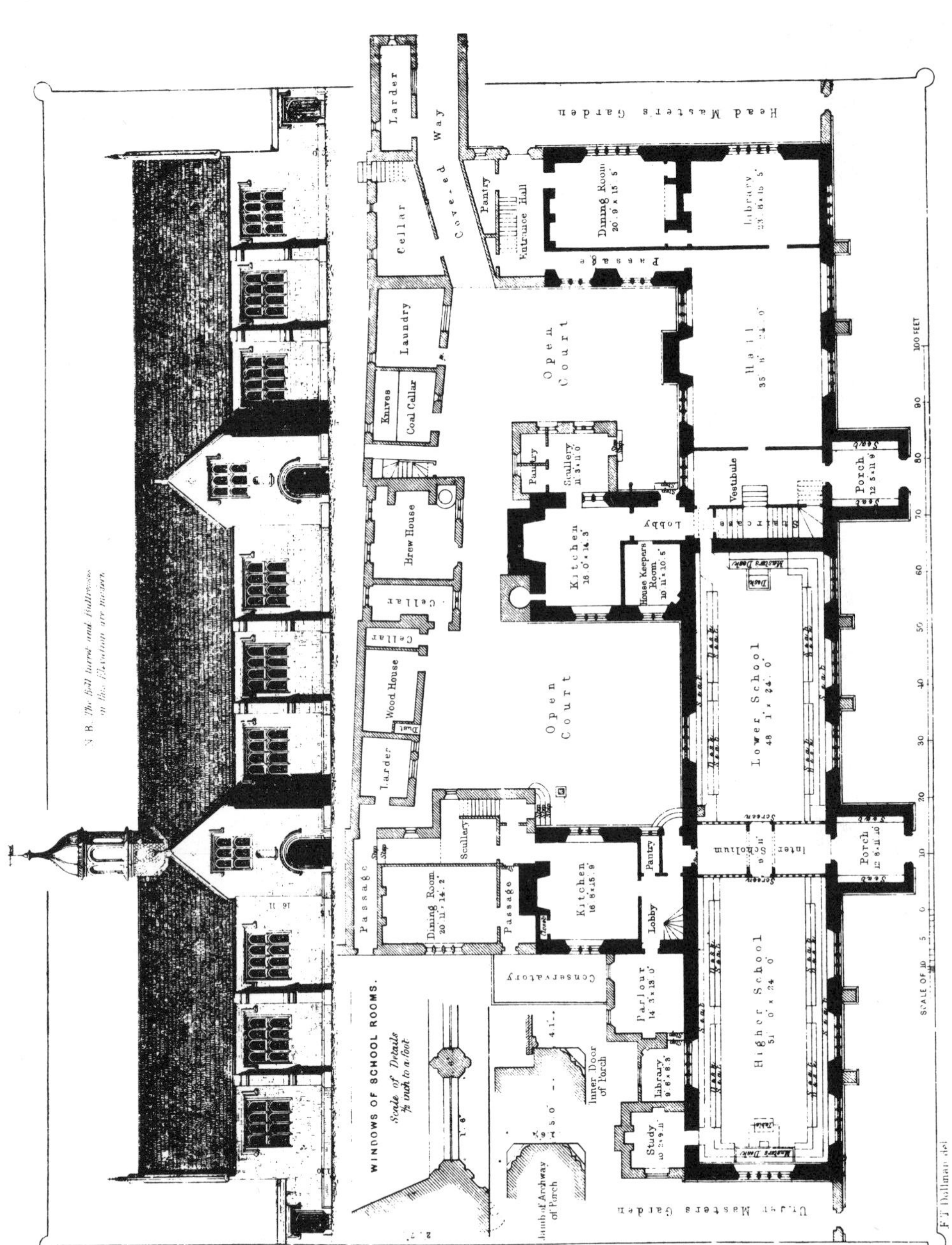

Figure 10 Tiverton, Blundell's School, 1604, plan and elevation.

so that, although the specialization of function, which had been developing in the course of the sixteenth century between the master teaching the upper forms and the usher teaching the lower, was taken a stage further, the old idea of one large schoolroom containing all the pupils was not wholly abandoned. The boys' seats were arranged along the side walls facing each other, as we saw in more rudimentary form in Pate's School, Cheltenham (pl. **31**). The masters' accommodation was also very generous by the standards of the day.

The plan of Blundell's School was followed on a more modest scale by Archbishop Harsnett when he established a school, or, more correctly, two schools, at Chigwell in Essex in 1629. The foundation deed provided for the erection of 'two fair and large schoolhouses' so that in the one the local children might be taught 'to read, write, cypher, and cast accounts and to learn their accidence' and in the other 'the Latin and Greek tongues'.[10] Both schools were housed under the same roof, and there is no architectural evidence to support the view of the latest historian of the school that the English school may have been added to the Latin school building at a later stage.[11] It is true that only the Latin master was given accommodation within the same building (the usher's house being quite separate), but there is no sign of jointing in the side-walls, and the original English school seems to have been much the same size as the Latin school (see plan, fig. 11). It will be noted from the exterior view of the building made in the early nineteenth century (pl. **47**) that there were originally two doors, alongside each other, which can only have been to give separate entrances to the respective schools. (These two doors were replaced by the present porch in Victorian times, but the lintels of the original doors may still be seen in the exterior wall on both sides of the porch.) The present partition is modern and it is likely that there was originally a screen, or some other demarcating line, a little further to the west, roughly in line with the present opening. The wing built at right angles to the Latin master's house was added in the eighteenth century.

How far the English school at Chigwell was regarded merely as the preparatory department for the Latin school, or as providing a different type of education for a different kind of pupil, it is impossible to say, but the wording of the foundation deed quoted above perhaps suggests that some of the English school pupils, having been grounded in the accidence, would have proceeded to the Latin school, while others would have continued their education in the English school, possibly concentrating on writing and cyphering as a preparation for careers in commerce (for London was not far away). At any rate, the growing importance of the teaching of English, not only in the petty schools, but among older children as well, is sufficiently clear.

The most elaborate expression of developing ideas about school organization was at Shrewsbury. As we saw in an earlier chapter, the school there had been carried on in a number of ordinary houses, but it had always been the intention of the burgesses to provide new school buildings as soon as the funds would allow. Extensive accommodation was built between 1595 and 1630, which survives today as the Public Library

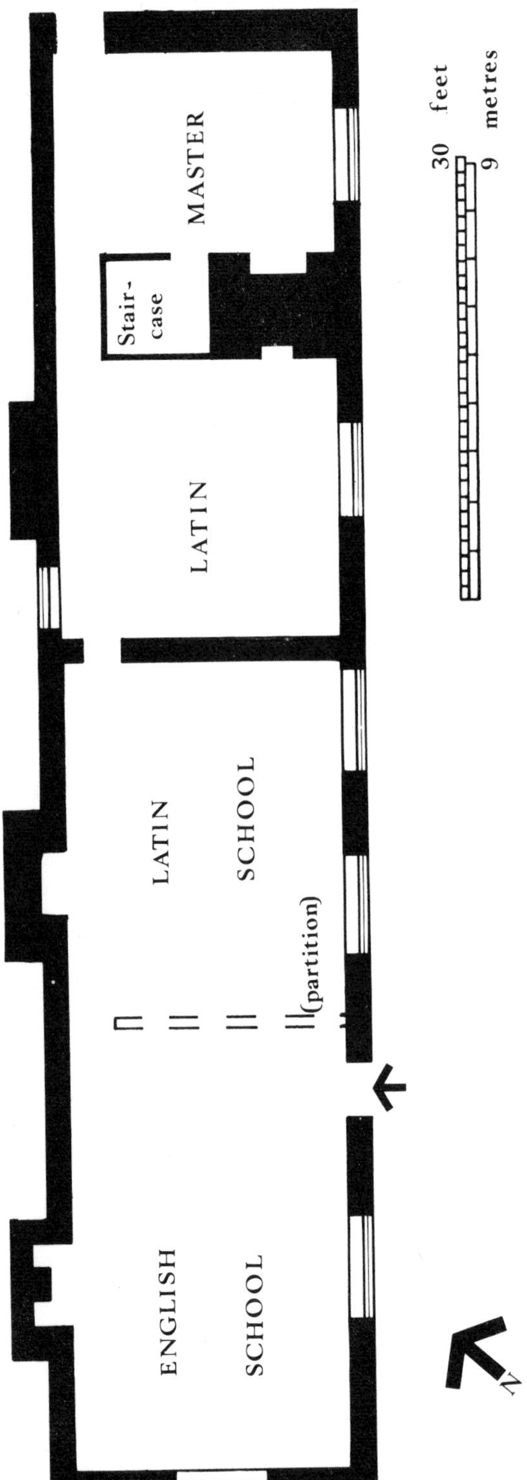

Figure 11 Chigwell School, 1629, ground plan. (The partition dividing the English and Latin schools is modern. The Victorian porch and eighteenth-century wing on the east side are omitted.)

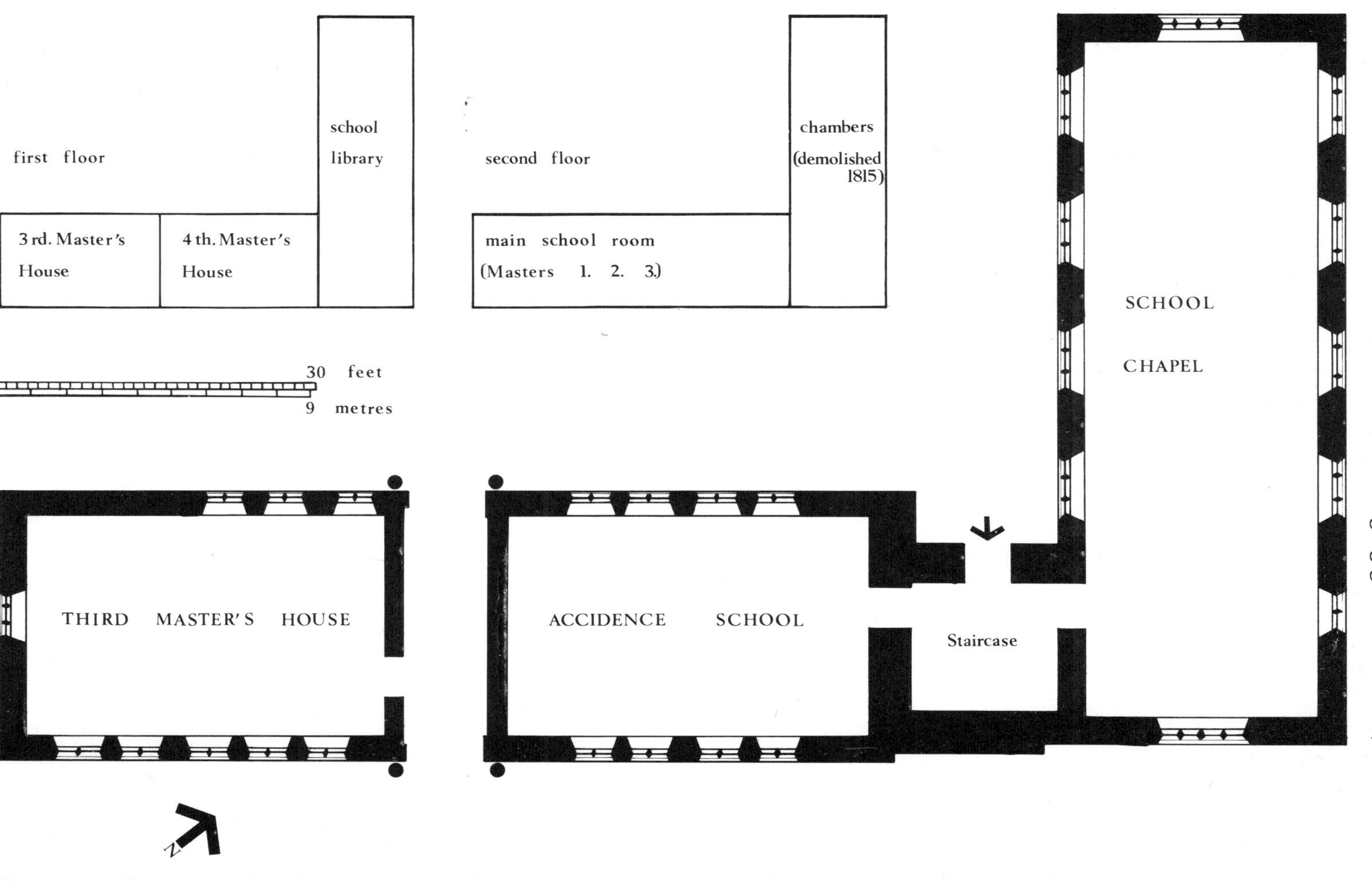

Figure 12 Shrewsbury School, 1595–1630, plan. (The Headmaster and Second Master were accommodated in houses nearby.)

and Museum (pl. **50**), the school having moved to its present site at Kingsland in 1882.[12] There were two main phases of building. The first began in 1595 (as recorded in the school accounts and on a carved stone built into the library wall, which reads '1595, David Lloyd and Thomas Lewis Gentlemen then Baylives') and provided for a building of Grinshill stone with a cellar or basement, a ground floor and two floors above. The accounts show that building work continued until 1605, and that the ground-floor room was fitted out as a school chapel in the years 1608–17. On the first floor was the school library with a gallery and attics above. About this time, also, a tower block was added to contain the stairs leading to the library. In 1815 the attics were removed and the present Gothic windows inserted in order to increase the height of the library. What was the school chapel is now the Public Lending Library, and the former school library is now an art gallery (see plan, fig. 12).

The second phase of building was completed in 1630, with a new block built at right angles to the chapel and library. This was also of Grinshill stone and of three storeys, and was designed to provide all the teaching accommodation required, together with rooms for the third and fourth masters. (The headmaster and second master were accommodated in separate houses nearby.) There is some difficulty in determining exactly how this new block was used. A legal brief of 1636 stated:

> The school hath three rooms above stairs for teaching and one below. He that is below in the Accidence School can teach but petties. The three rooms above are distinguished one from the other and none of them [i.e. the three Latin masters] teach but in their own school. And if the headmaster be absent he himself always placeth a substitute till his return; the others use not nor will not meddle in the head school.[13]

There is no doubt that the first, second and third masters taught on the top floor in one long room measuring about 78 by 21 feet (see plan), but they were separated from each other by wooden screens. These screens have now been removed, but their former positions are clearly marked by the tie-beams which still exist in the room now used as a natural history museum. There is also a Victorian photograph (pl. **51**) showing one of the screens still *in situ*. The side benches used by the pupils also remain in their original positions.

As for the layout of the rooms on the ground and first floors, a writer of 1779 tells us:

> The whole of the attic storey contains the three upper schools. . . . [On] the ground floor is the accidence school on one side of the gateway [i.e. archway], and the third master's house on the other. The middle storey contains the upper rooms in the third master's house, and the accidence master's apartment, which has for many years been used as a writing school.[14]

Unfortunately, this does not make clear whether the accidence school was on the east or west side of the archway. Until forty years ago, the Borough Librarian lived in the western half of the building, which was fitted out as a house,[15] so it seems reasonable to suppose that the third master originally lived there, in what is now the juvenile library. The plan here reproduced shows the layout of the various rooms, based on this assumption.

The main point which emerges from the architectural evidence is that, because of the large number of pupils and the further development of ideas on school organization, there were in effect four (later five) schools at Shrewsbury, but the three upper schools were housed under the same roof and visual contact maintained between them (as at Tiverton and probably at Chigwell) by the use of screens. The accidence school was quite separate, but still in the same building. Subsequently a writing school seems to have been established in the fourth master's rooms, though the history of this is obscure. (A writing master is mentioned early in the school's history and the post remained in being until 1882.)[16] The school was primarily concerned with the teaching of the classics, as the Greek inscription over the archway indicates: 'If thou love learning, thou shall be well learned',[17] with the figure of a schoolboy on one side and a university graduate on the other (pl. **52**). But the layout of the school shows that the English subjects were far from neglected. The building of a separate library also indicates that the classical curriculum was itself being widened and enriched through the use of a growing number of printed books on a wide variety of subjects.[18] Few schools at this date could afford a separate library, but contemporary pictures show the schoolmaster not only with his traditional birch, but also with at least a shelf full of books (pl. **53**).

II

Information about the internal organization of schools also becomes more plentiful after 1600. We have seen that in the sixteenth century there were seven forms at Winchester and Eton, nine at St Paul's and seven (increased to nine in 1564) at Shrewsbury. The lower forms were, in general, taken by the usher, and the upper forms by the master. Brinsley recommended 'that the whole school be divided into so few forms as may be, of so many [pupils] as can any way be fitted to go together, though they be sixteen or twenty, yes, forty in the form, it is not the worse'. The reasons he gives for this recommendation are, first, that 'it is almost the same labour to teach twenty as to teach two, as in reading all lectures and rules unto them [and] in examining all parts and lectures', and, second, that 'the fewer forms there are, the more time may be spent in each form and more labour may be bestowed in examining every tittle necessary'.[19] Clearly, in practice, much must have depended upon the total number of children to be taught in relation to the staff available, but there is some evidence to show that there was a tendency at this time to reduce the number of forms in the way Brinsley was suggesting.

In Mathew's poem about Winchester, written in the 1640s, only four forms are mentioned, with the master teaching the sixth and fifth, and the usher the fourth and 'second-fourth' forms. It seems that the lower forms at Winchester disappeared between 1565 and 1637, and that this may have been connected with the disappearance of the local day-boys who had formerly attended the college and who left when the usher was forced in 1629 to give up his post through marriage and started a school of his own in the town.[20] The seventh form at Eton disappeared some time before 1678, for it is absent from the Eton list (the first to survive) of that year.[21] It may be, however, that Winchester and Eton were exceptional and, because of their national standing, were able to recruit boys at a somewhat later age after they had received a grounding elsewhere. There is, in fact, very little evidence about the age-distribution of the various forms in the grammar schools at this period. Brinsley says that the usual age of entry was seven or eight, and suggests that boys should ideally begin at five. There is, however, an interesting list of forms among the records of Wolverhampton School dated 1609,[22] which gives the arrangement adopted in a school of sixty-nine pupils and two masters—not a small school by contemporary English standards. All the forms were taught in the same room, but it will be noted that more attention was given to the stage reached by the pupils in the curriculum than to their chronological age. The details are set out in the table opposite.

As for the furnishing and lay-out of a schoolroom of this period, the most detailed contemporary account is in Mathew's poem about Winchester.[23] The seats for the prefects in the south wall have already been mentioned; on the north wall was a map of the world and on the east the *Tabula Legum*, giving the school rules. On the west wall was the inscription '*Aut disce, aut discede, manet sors tertia caedi*', which has been loosely translated as 'Learn, leave, or be licked'. Above the words '*aut disce*' were the rewards of learning, a mitre and crozier; above '*aut discede*', the emblems of the alternative professions of the Army and the Law (a sword and inkhorn), and above the last phrase a rod. (This cryptic inscription was also written on the wall of the later schoolroom, see pl. **64**.) Below the inscription, says Mathew, stood a pulpit or rostrum from which the boys declaimed speeches as part of their grammatical exercises (a practice which Brinsley also refers to, and which continued until the nineteenth century in some schools).[24] There was no fireplace in the school at Winchester, since, as Mathew writes, 'in winter the sun keeps well to the south and gives our chilled frames all his warmth'.[25] (As we saw earlier, there was no fireplace in the school at Guildford, though most schools of this period seem to have provided one.)

Mathew also refers to the boys at Winchester being 'bound to [their] scobs as Prometheus was bound to his Caucasian rock'.[26] The word 'scob' comes from the Latin *scabellum*, the word for a cleric's seat. The word is first found in use at Winchester in 1580, and in 1620 a scholar was charged 3*s*. 6*d*. 'for a scobb to hold his books'.[27] They were probably smaller than the earliest surviving examples (see pl. **54**), but may be said to have been the forerunners of the modern locker-desks. The need for a writing

The arrangement of the Forms at Wolverhampton Grammar School in 1609

Name of form	*No. of boys*	*Average age*	*Comments*
Head form	2	17·5	One of 17 and one of 18
Second form	7	15·5	Age-range 14 to 17
The former part of the third form	11	13·5	12 to 14 with one of 9 and two of 17, just admitted.
The latter part of the third form	8	12·0	Age-range 11 to 13
Under the usher	15	10·6	10 to 12, with one of 8, one 9 and one 13
The second form*	15	9·7	8 to 11
The Accidence form*	11	8·8	Mainly 7 to 11, with one of 6 and one 13

* These, one assumes, were also under the usher.

surface and space to store the larger number of books now being used by the pupils no doubt brought the scob into being. At Felsted in 1606 the school accounts record the introduction of desks,[28] but many of the smaller schools seem to have managed simply with benches for the boys—they must have rested their books on their knees, or perhaps used a table placed in the middle of the room, as we saw was the practice at Ipswich in 1582. Schoolboys often continued to carry their inkhorns and pens around with them, a practice which persisted at Westminster until 1884.[29]

The actual appearance of an early seventeenth-century schoolroom is well preserved at Harrow. Here the original schoolroom (now called Fourth Form Room) has survived virtually unchanged as part of the existing Old Building (pl. **55**). This was opened in 1615, the school having been founded by John Lyon, yeoman, in 1571. The statutes of 1590 had given instructions for building 'meet and convenient rooms for the said schoolmaster and usher to inhabit and dwell in, as also a large and convenient school-house with a chimney in it'.[30] Early pictures of the school show a small two-storey building with cellars and attics, the schoolroom being on the ground floor and the masters' rooms above—'a building', as a writer of 1818 observed, 'little calculated to call forth the admiration of the casual spectator by any architectural embellishment'.[31] It was altered in 1819 by the addition of another block to correspond with the original building, but the plan of the existing old school building (fig. 13) makes the original layout clear.

The interior view of the schoolroom at Harrow (pl. **56**) shows the headmaster's chair at the north end, with a seventeenth-century fireplace in the middle of the west wall, and an oak muniment chest (as specified in the statutes) in front of it. The panelling, which extends to a height of 7 feet around the walls, is probably later than 1615. (As in most of the older schoolrooms which survive, it seems that the boys could not be prevented from making free with their penknives by carving their names and dates,

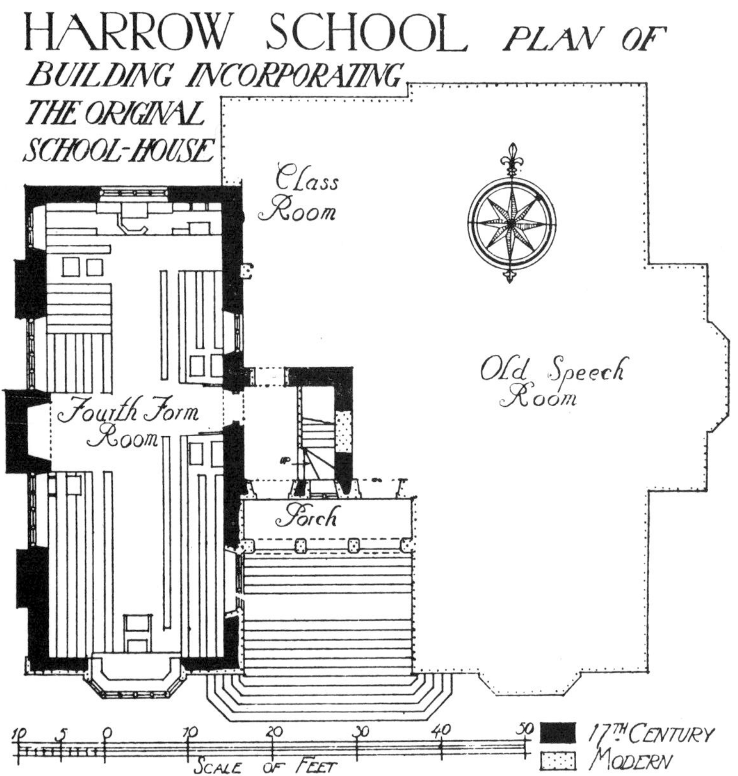

Figure 13 Harrow School, plan of building incorporating the original schoolhouse of 1615.

but the earliest date carved on the woodwork at Harrow is 1660.) The boys' forms are arranged along the side walls and the floor has shallow steps to which the forms are fastened.[32] The original rules at Harrow provided for five forms or classes (to use an alternative word now found in Brinsley),[33] in addition to the petties. Two monitors were appointed to report any misdemeanours by the boys, with a third monitor appointed secretly by the master 'to present the faults of the other two'[34]—a repulsive variant of the common practice in schools at this time of using a boy as 'custos' to spy on the rest.

Prefects or monitors with power to report on, but not to punish, the other boys were used, as we saw, at Winchester, Eton and a number of other grammar schools in the sixteenth century, and were commonly appointed in the seventeenth century also. How far the monitors also engaged in teaching the other boys is a matter of some uncertainty. At Westminster School the statutes of 1560 included references, not only to prefects on the Winchester model, but also to 'two of the highest form who have been appointed by the schoolmaster to teach the rest of the forms',[35] but at Winchester itself the earliest reference to senior boys teaching is in 1657.[36] Probably this practice developed in many schools in the course of the seventeenth century because the number of pupils was tending to increase, while the number of teachers in a school was fixed, usually at one or two, by the foundation statutes. Brinsley admits that the problem of effective teaching became acute 'if there should be 30 or 40 in form', and he recommends that in such circumstances the work of correcting the pupils' exercises should be done by 'some of the highest scholars and the number of faults noted'[37] (a procedure which was only possible because written exercises had become more common and which even today survives in a slightly different form where children mark each others' exercises).

Later in *Ludus literarius*, Brinsley elaborates his views on using senior boys in the teaching work of the school. He suggests that

> the two or four seniors in each form be as ushers in that form, for overseeing, directing, examining and fitting the rest every way before they come to say [i.e. recite what they have learnt to the master]. . . . Also in straight of time [i.e. if the master is himself too busy to do it] to stand forth before the rest and to hear them.

He further suggests that each form should nominate 'by voices' the two boys to act as seniors, who should then divide up the form between them, taking it in turn to choose their 'sides', 'even as gamesters will do at matches in shooting, bowling or the like'. Each pair of boys in the form should then test each other 'for the credit of their side'.[38] It seems that Brinsley's Puritanism was no impediment to making full use of the competitive spirit among the boys (if indeed this was not a reflection of it), but it should be added that Brinsley also laid great stress on the boys helping each other, and that he was opposed to the use of custodes as spies, as well as to excessive use of the birch.

In general, the teaching methods used during this period would seem to the modern teacher to have been rigid and uninspired, though they have not entirely disappeared from the schools even today. The master would have remained seated in his chair, reading out passages from the text-book, calling upon boys to translate or construe in turn, or calling them up to his desk to repeat what they had learnt. But at least in Brinsley one has more than a hint that the boys were being encouraged to understand what they had to learn, and to help each other to master the intricate rules upon which a sound knowledge of Latin seemed so much to depend.

Notes

1 E.g. Clarke, M. L., *Classical education in Britain*, Cambridge U.P., 1959, 34: 'The seventeenth century was on the whole a period of steady progress on the lines already laid down in the previous century.'

2 Quoted in Brown, W. H., *Charterhouse past and present*, Godalming: Stedman, 1879, 98–9.

3 Carlisle, II, 9.

4 For the buildings of Charterhouse, see R.C.H.M., *London*, II, 1925, 21–30, and Pevsner, *London*, 1952, ii., 121–4. The schoolroom of 1612 (re-fronted in the eighteenth century and now demolished) is illustrated in Brown, W. H., *op. cit.*, facing p. 89. This book also has a plan of the school buildings in 1872 before extensive rebuilding took place when the Merchant Taylors' school occupied the site, 1875–1933. Gown boys' hall and other parts of the former school buildings are illustrated in Barrett, C. R. B., *Charterhouse in pen and ink*, Bliss, 1895.

5 All quotations (spelling modernized) are from the 1627 edition, with notes by Campagnac E. T., Liverpool U.P., 1917. The date of this treatise devoted entirely to the education of children is significant. Cf. McLuhan, M., *The medium is the massage*, Allen Lane, 1967, 18: 'The "child" was an invention of the seventeenth century; he did not exist in, say, Shakespeare's day.'

6 Brinsley, *op cit.*, 12–13.

7 *Ibid.*, 21–2.

8 *Ibid.*, 28–9, 35. Pencils were just beginning to come into use, graphite having been discovered in Cumberland in 1565 (see Brown, J. H., *Elizabethan schooldays*, Oxford: Blackwell, 1933, 48).

9 Carlisle, I, 339.

10 Stott, G., *History of Chigwell School*, Ipswich: Cowell, 1960, 142.

11 *Ibid.*, 26–7. I am very grateful to the Headmaster, Mr D. H. Thompson, for information about Chigwell School and for allowing me to explore the buildings.

12 There is a good short description of the buildings at Shrewsbury in Carlisle, II, 385–7. See also Pevsner, *Shropshire*, 1958, 267 and pl. 46 (*a*), which is, however, wrongly captioned.

13 Hotchkiss MSS. 10, 309 (in Shrewsbury Reference Library).

14 Phillips, T., *History of Shrewsbury*, ed. by Hulbert, C., Shrewsbury: Wood, 1779, I, 127.

15 Ex inf. Borough Librarian. I am also grateful to the Borough Surveyor for further information about the old school buildings.

16 Oldham, J. B., *History of Shrewsbury School*, Oxford: Blackwell, 1952, 15.
17 A quotation from the *Colloquies* of Erasmus.
18 See further Watson, F., *Curriculum and textbooks of English schools in the first half of the 17th century*, Blades, 1903, and *The English grammar schools to 1660*, Cambridge U.P., 1908.
19 Brinsley, *op. cit.*, 48.
20 Cook, A. K., *About Winchester College*, Macmillan, 1917, 278—81.
21 Lyte, C. H. Maxwell, *History of Eton College*, Macmillan, 1877, 272. The first and second forms at Eton continued to exist until 1869. At Westminster also the lower forms continued until the nineteenth century (Sargeaunt, J., *Annals of Westminster School*, Methuen, 1898, 41).
22 Mander, G. P., *History of Wolverhampton Grammar School*, Wolverhampton: Steens, 1913, 373—5.
23 Cook, *op. cit.*, 17.
24 E.g. at King's School, Canterbury, 1845; see pl. **221**.
25 Cook, *op. cit.*, 19.
26 *Ibid.*, 17.
27 *Ibid.*, 224.
28 *V.C.H.*, *Essex*, II, 1907, 534.
29 A Westminster 'dip' is illustrated in Seaborne, M., *Education*, Studio Vista, 1966, pl. 26.
30 Laborde, E. D., *Harrow School*, Winchester Publications Ltd., 1948, 232.
31 Carlisle, II, 126. An illustration of the old school at Harrow before alteration is shown facing p. 24 in Warner, Rex, *English public schools*, Collins, 1946.
32 A full description of the old building is in Laborde, *op. cit.*, 67—85, and R.C.H.M., *Middlesex*, 1937, 67f. See also description of interior of seventeenth-century school at Sherborne in R.C.H.M., *Dorset*, I, 1952, 213—14.
33 Brinsley, *op. cit.*, 272: 'my school sorted into fourmes or *Classes*' (his italics). The *O.E.D.* gives 1656 for the use of the word 'class' as a division of a school. Perhaps the word in this context derived from the Puritan 'classes' of the period. On the Continent it seems that the word was first used by Erasmus in 1519, taken from a phrase in Quintilian (see Ariès, P., *Centuries of childhood*, Cape, 1962, 176—7).
34 Laborde, *op. cit.*, 239.
35 Leach, A. F., *Educational charters and documents*, Cambridge U.P., 1911, 515.
36 Cook, *op. cit.*, 87.
37 Brinsley, *op. cit.*, 201.
38 *Ibid.*, 272—4. The two seniors were to be 'chosen by election of the whole form' (cf. Puritan practice).

Five

Schools of the Restoration period 1660-1700

I

The consensus of scholarly opinion is that English educational institutions suffered comparatively little damage as a result of the disturbances of the Civil War period. Successive governments during the Commonwealth protected school endowments and in some places (notably in Wales) actively intervened to support or establish schools. If we accept the figures given by Professor Jordan for school endowments, it seems that the flow of charitable gifts had begun to abate even before the Civil War broke out: there was in fact, as we saw in ch. 3, a small increase in the total amount donated for schools in Jordan's ten counties during the 1640s and a further rise in the 1650s. This, however, was still not much more than half the total for 1611–20 and, so far as the evidence of surviving school buildings goes, it would seem that relatively few new buildings were put in hand during the Civil War period. It may indeed be the case that historians of education have underestimated the amount of dislocation caused, at least in some parts of the country, by the Civil War. In the West Riding of Yorkshire, for example, some schools were used as barracks (at Rotherham the boys themselves took part in the fighting) and others suffered through the imprisonment or death of governors, which sometimes resulted in the mismanagement of school estates.[1]

It is to the Civil War period, however, that we may trace the origin of many of the new ideas about educational theory and practice which were to have important effects on the subsequent design of schools. Charles Hoole, in *A new discovery of the old art of teaching schoole*, published in 1660 but written some years earlier, shows that he had been influenced not only by the writings of Mulcaster and Brinsley to which we have already referred, but also by those of Comenius and Dury. Comenius, the famous Czech educationist of this period, had urged the need for a great widening of education, both in content and in clientele. He wanted many more subjects added to the curriculum, and he argued that all children should be formally educated irrespective of sex or class. Hoole, who had been Master of Rotherham Grammar School and later of a private grammar school in London, was influenced by these ideas, as was John Dury, a Scot who had travelled widely in Europe and published his views in *The reformed school* of *c.* 1650.[2] In this pamphlet he outlined a scheme for a boarding school (accommodating fifty or sixty boys) in which scientific, linguistic and other studies would be pursued in addition to the usual course of English and Latin. He is particularly interesting on the attributes of the ideal school building:

> The rooms wherein the scholars should be at their exercises should be four: three lesser ones, for each usher and his peculiar scholars one; and one large one, or rather a gallery, which should be for common use unto all. The scholastic furniture and dressing of these rooms ought to be this. The large common room ought to be furnished with all manner of mathematical, natural, philosophical, historical, medicinal, hieroglyphical and other sort of pictures, maps, globes, instruments, models, engines, and whatsoever is an object of sense in reference to any art or science. These things are to be set in their order . . . that at the times appointed the ushers may lead their scholars into it to receive the lessons which they shall give them. . . . The lesser rooms each ought to be furnished with a high seat for the usher, that he may overlook all his scholars, and with twenty distinct places so ordered for the scholars to sit or stand in that their faces may be all towards him; and each in his place may have his own desk, to keep all his papers and other things to be used in good order. . . .[3]

A number of revolutionary new ideas about the planning of schools appear here. There is for the first time the idea of separate rooms for each class, while the school hall (which was all that most schools possessed at this date for all teaching purposes) has become what would now be called the school museum, art room and science laboratory. Also new was the proposed staff/pupil ratio of one to twenty and the recommendation that the pupils should face the teacher (instead of sitting along the sides of the room facing each other) and should each be provided with a locker desk.

Here, in a single stride, we are in the nineteenth century so far as the development of school planning is concerned. This was, of course, a purely theoretical, even Utopian, treatise, of the kind which could easily be dismissed at the time as a visionary's dream. Even so, it is interesting to note its influence on Charles Hoole, the practical schoolmaster, whose *New discovery*, like Brinsley's *Ludus literarius*, was to become a classic of educational literature.

A new discovery of the old art of teaching schoole (1660)[4] consists of four distinct treatises, entitled as follows:

1 A Petty-Schoole [separately paginated 1–41]
2 The Ushers Duty
3 The Masters Method
4 Scholastick Discipline } In a Grammar Schoole [pp. 1–309]

The treatise on the petty school owes much to previous writers, notably Coote and Brinsley, but it nevertheless marks a new stage of development. Hoole refers frankly to those 'children for whom the Latin tongue is thought to be unnecessary'—not in a tone of approval, but at least of one ready to accept realities—and he recommends that for such children even the elementary rules of Latin grammar (the Accidence) should be omitted, so that instead they may have time to read religious books, 'and afterwards in other delightful books of English history or poetry'. In addition, they should learn how to 'write a fair hand' and do arithmetical exercises.[5] Here we have the theoretical justification of the pursuit of a purely 'English' education in its own right, which we saw in an earlier chapter was already being adopted in actual practice.

The treatise on the petty school also marks an important change in the attitude towards using monitors as teachers, such as Brinsley had recommended and many schools had been forced to adopt. For Hoole writes:

> I conceive forty boys will be enough thoroughly to employ one man, to hear every one so often as is required . . . without making use of any of his scholars to teach the rest, which . . . occasioneth too much noise and disorder and is no whit so acceptable to parents or pleasing to the children, be the work never so well done. And therefore I advise that in a place where a great concourse of children may be had, there be more masters than one employed according to the spaciousness of the room and the number of boys to be taught, so that every forty scholars may have one to teach them . . . [and that there may be] as many masters as there are forms.[6]

Turning to grammar-school organization, Hoole deals with the duties of the usher in teaching forms 1, 2 and 3, and with the methods of the master, who takes forms 4, 5 and 6, the total number of forms having by this date crystallized at six in many schools, a number which they have retained to this day, though the age-range has altered. As in Brinsley, it is clear that English is to be taught alongside the Latin, and in particular Hoole stresses the importance of having a wide variety of books for the pupils to consult. The younger boys should use the *Orbis sensualium pictus* of Comenius (which Hoole had himself translated into English in 1659) while the older boys should read books on 'languages, oratory and poetry as well as grammar'. Indeed, he recommends that every grammar school should have a library, a practice which we saw beginning in Elizabethan and early Stuart times and which was followed in several of the larger schools, especially in the second half of the seventeenth century. Thus, for example, Busby's library at Westminster was built in the period 1655–60, while a separate library building was attached to the grammar school at Leeds in 1692.[7]

Particularly relevant from our point of view are Hoole's views on the building of schools, given in his final treatise on scholastic discipline. This contains a judicious mixture of the writings of Mulcaster and Dury, but also draws on his own experience in Yorkshire and London. He begins by pointing out that in most grammar schools 'there is but one, two, or three ushers besides a master, employed in teaching . . . together in one room, to six or seven forms of scholars, who by reason of the noise of one another (not to mention the clamour of children) . . . do both over-tire themselves and many times leave things to the halves'. His ideal school building would overcome these difficulties, and would also provide for a much wider syllabus. The building itself should be situated 'about the middle of the outside of a town', so that the towns-people would be able to 'entertain tablers', i.e. take in boarders, while at the same time the school would be 'not far from the fields where it may stand in good air and be free from all annoyances'. There should be a paved court around the school, part of which should be 'shedded or cloistered over' to enable the scholars to play outside in wet weather. All this follows Mulcaster and Dury, but in his description of the internal arrangements of his ideal school building he goes in some respects beyond them both:

> This schoolhouse should be built three storeys high whereof the middle-most . . . should be so spacious that it may contain (at least) 500 scholars together, without thronging one another. It should be so contrived with folding doors made betwixt every form as that upon occasion it may be all laid open into one room, or parted into six, for more privacy or hearing every form without noise or hindrance one of another. There should be seats made in the school, with desks before them, whereon every scholar may write and lay his book. . . . The ushers' pews should be set at the head ends of every form so as they may best see and hear every particular boy. And the master's chair should be so raised at the upper end of the school as that he may be able to have every scholar in his eye and to be heard of all when he hath occasion to give any common charge or instruction. There may be shelves made about the school and boxes for every scholar to put his books in and pins whereon they may hang their hats. . . . Likewise every form should have a repository near unto it wherein to lay such subsidiary books as are most proper for its use.

He goes on to recommend that in the lowest storey there should be several rooms, including one to be used as a writing school, another for 'such languages as are to be taught at spare hours' and a third as a petty school 'for such children as cannot read English perfectly'. The uppermost storey should contain 'a fair pleasant gallery wherein to hang maps and set globes and to lay up such rarities as can be gotten in presses or drawers that the scholars may know them'. There should also be 'a school library and the rest may be made use of as lodging rooms for ushers and scholars'. There should also be a 'house of office' for the sanitary needs of the scholars and a large house for the headmaster close to the school.[8]

Clearly Hoole is letting his imagination take wing. Yet there were a few schools already—notably Shrewsbury—which approximated to this ideal, and there were to be others, as we shall shortly see, which in the last decades of the seventeenth century incorporated some of the features here suggested by Hoole. The period 1660–1700 was in fact a time of marked advance in the construction of schools. Jordan's calculations of charitable gifts do not go beyond 1660, and this is the date which is usually accepted as marking the end of the greatest period of the English grammar school. 'There is no doubt', writes Foster Watson, 'as to the decadence of the grammar schools from 1660 onwards.'[9] Yet this statement is hard to reconcile with the impressive record of school buildings of the Restoration period and with the evidence they provide of continued development in school planning. It is true that the grammar schools were on the defensive, and had been so, perhaps, since Bacon's famous attack at the time of Sutton's foundation. Milton and others had also freely criticized the narrow classicism of some of the schools. As late as 1678 Christopher Wase, in his *Considerations concerning free-schools*, referred specifically to Bacon's opinions and repeated most of the traditional arguments in defence of the schools. But, so far as school architecture is concerned, it would seem that 'decadence' is far too strong a word to use for the period now under consideration.

There are obvious dangers in laying too much stress on the evidence of school buildings of the period 1660–1700 which happen to have survived down to our own day. It can, however, be hypothesized that, if the period of the Civil War and Commonwealth may have seen a falling off in the number of new school buildings, the Restoration saw a renewed impetus which lasted until the end of the seventeenth century and, as we shall see, continued into the early decades of the eighteenth. Only a detailed survey, county by county, taking account not only of those buildings which still survive, but also of those which are known to have been built at this time though later demolished, could prove or disprove this hypothesis.[10] It may suffice for our present purpose to note that, for example, in the two Midland counties previously referred to (Northamptonshire and Leicestershire) the building of schools seems to have continued at a good rate after 1660. And if we examine the adjoining county of Nottinghamshire, we find that, whereas only one pre-Restoration school building appears to have survived (the Magnus School at Newark-on-Trent, 1531) a number of new school buildings may now be located. The following list gives only the briefest details, but some of these schools will be described in more detail later in this chapter:

Northamptonshire	*Leicestershire*	*Nottinghamshire*
1667, Clipston*	1670, Osgathorpe*	1667, Bulwell
1668, Guilsborough	1691, Woodhouse	1669, Tuxford
1671, Aynho	1697, Appleby	1692, Haughton
1680, Courteenhall		1700, Bunny*

* An asterisk indicates that the school is architecturally associated with almshouses.

If we look more generally at surviving post-Restoration schools, it may be said that the style of building now comes to rely somewhat less on vernacular traditions, and that certain well-defined plans begin to establish themselves. We also find that full-time architects are beginning to be employed on the design of schools. All this, of course, is related to the general emergence of an architectural profession and to the triumph of classical forms in contemporary architecture as a whole.

Two of the best-defined types of post-Restoration planning may be illustrated from the schools at Witney (Oxon.) and Guilsborough (Northants.). The school at Witney (pl. **57** and fig. 14 (*a*)) was founded by Henry Box, a prominent member of the Grocers'

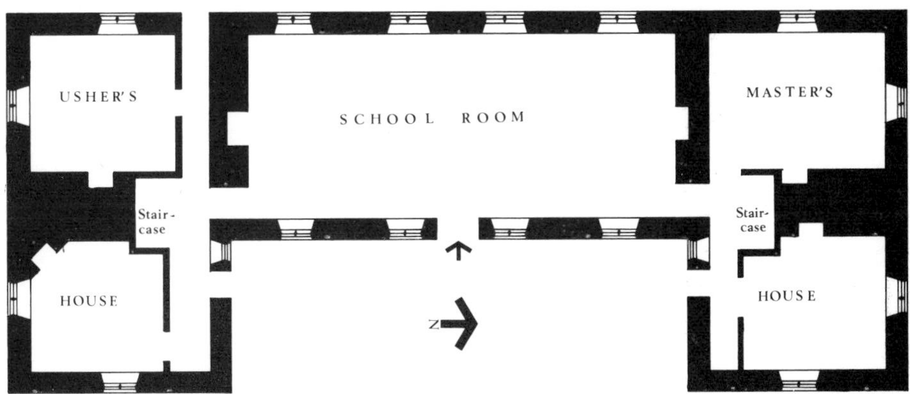

Figure 14 (*a*) Witney School, 1660, ground plan.

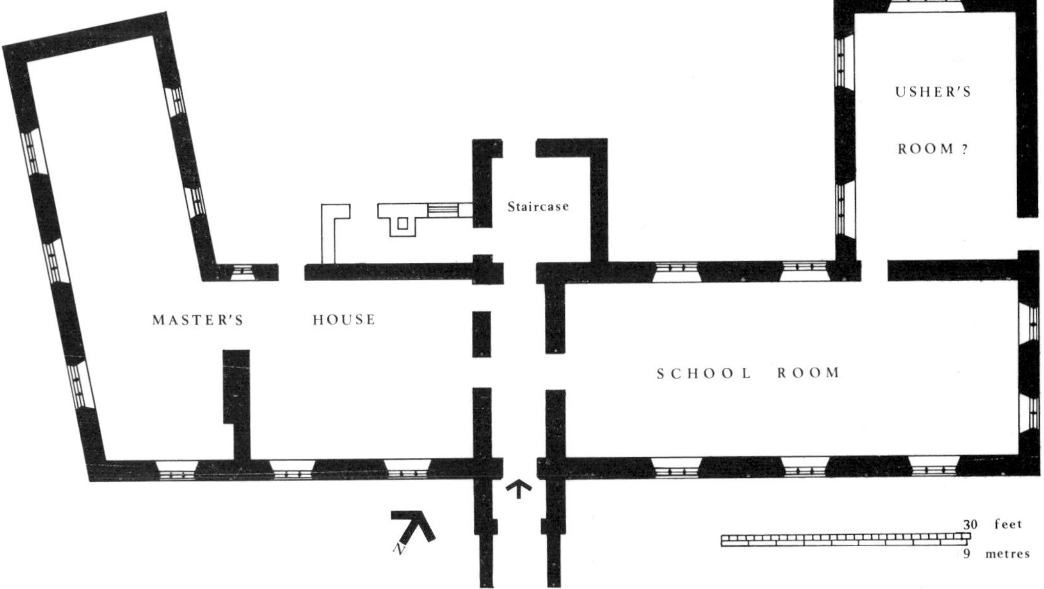

Figure 14 (*b*) Guilsborough School, 1668, ground plan.

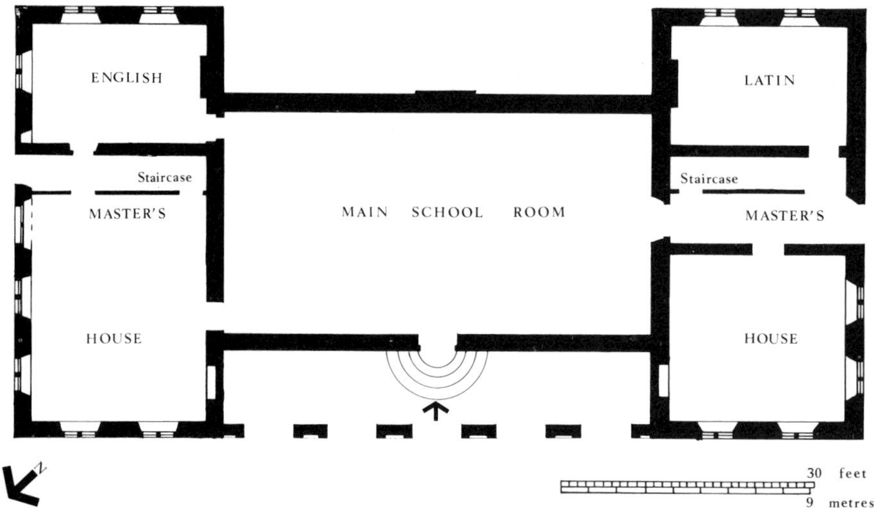

Figure 14 (c) Appleby Magna, Sir John Moore's School 1693–7, ground plan.

Company, who in 1661 bequeathed a house which he had lately built for a free school and £50 a year with which to endow it. There were to be a master and usher to teach thirty boys Latin and Greek, and in 1670 a writing master was also added to the staff.[11] The building consists of a central schoolroom of one storey (open to the roof) and measuring 50 by 22 feet, with two-storey accommodation for the master and usher in each wing. This is a development of the plan of Berkhamsted, Guildford and Ashbourne, but the design is more compact and the accommodation for the master and usher more clearly defined. The total effect is extremely pleasing in its well-balanced symmetry. The school at Guilsborough (pl. **58** and fig. 14 (*b*)) is, by contrast, more traditional in style, though the scale is impressive. It was founded in 1668 by Sir John Langham, who was also a London Grocer, having made his fortune trading with Turkey. The master's house and the school accommodation (consisting of a schoolroom measuring 54 by 20 feet, with bedrooms above) were placed next to each other, and there is complete architectural unity of style. The school was built to accommodate 50 pupils from Guilsborough, Cottesbrooke, Cold Ashby and other parishes within four miles of the school, who were to be taught Latin, Greek and Hebrew. During the first half of the eighteenth century it developed into a fee-paying boarding school, no doubt because the local demand for the classical languages was limited. Its subsequent decline was probably due partly to the rise in importance of the grammar school in the nearby town of Rugby and partly to the popularity of a writing school in Guilsborough (founded 1609), which was an additional factor preventing Langham's School from developing an English curriculum.[12] The building was empty and in a very poor state of repair in 1969 (the photograph was taken in 1945 before decay set in).

Two other schools of considerable architectural merit may be taken to illustrate the new style of post-Restoration building. They were both founded by Charles Read,

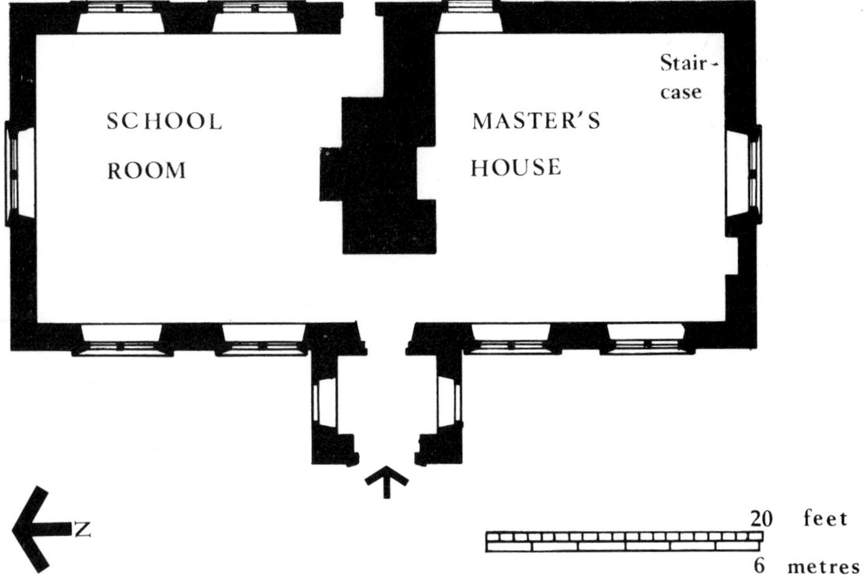

Figure 15 (*a*) Corby Glen, Read's School, 1668–69, ground plan.

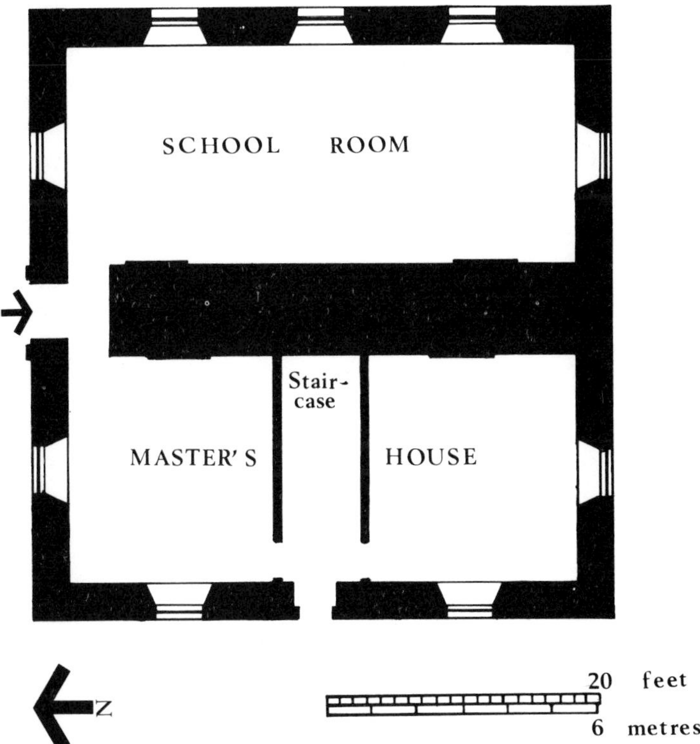

Figure 15 (*b*) Crudwell School, 1670, ground plan.

the one (of brick) at Tuxford in Nottinghamshire (pl. **59**) and the other (of stone) at Corby Glen in Lincolnshire (pl. **60** and fig. 15 (*a*)). They were both built in 1668–9 and endowed by Read's will of 1671, which provided for a schoolmaster in each place 'to instruct the children of the inhabitants in reading, writing and casting accounts, and in Latin as occasion should require'—in fact, they seem to have developed as English schools.[13] At both places provision was made for boarding four poor boys, so it is reasonable to conclude that (as the plans also suggest) the masters were accommodated in the school buildings, a practice which was by this date firmly established. So much was this accepted practice that the schoolroom at Courteenhall, Northamptonshire, for example, was built alongside two farm-houses which were adapted to accommodate the master and usher respectively (1680). Another variant is the school at Crudwell, Wiltshire, built in 1670 (fig. 15 (*b*)), and now converted into cottages. It is pleasant to record that the school at Corby Glen has recently been restored and adapted as a library, reading-room and art gallery by Lord Ancaster, while the school at Tuxford is now used as a branch of the County Library.

Sir John Langham, besides building the school at Guilsborough, also founded almshouses nearby at Cottesbrooke (1651) to which a small school was attached. As we have seen in a previous chapter, it was traditional practice for charitable bequests to associate schools and almshouses together—as at Ewelme, Uppingham and elsewhere. But in the post-Restoration period the association becomes architectural as well as constitutional, and we invariably find schools and almshouses which are combined in one design. The school at Cottesbrooke is merely added on to the end of the row of almshouses (the end nearest the road) and consists simply of one small single-storey room. A more varied effect was achieved in other places, often by placing the school at right angles to the almshouses. We may instance Osgathorpe in Leicestershire (1670), a pleasant building of local granite, now the Parish Hall, Arksey near Doncaster in Yorkshire (1683), still in use as a primary school, and Corsham in Wiltshire (1668), which is especially rich in architectural detail (see pl. **61**).[14] Another arrangement was to place the school in the centre of the composition, as at Farley, Wiltshire (1681), where the almshouses form a wing on each side of the school,[15] and Great Linford, Buckinghamshire (1700).[16] Similarly, the almshouses on the Palace Green at Durham are flanked on the one side by a grammar school and on the other by a school for writing and plain-song (an interesting late example of a choristers' school). This building was erected by Bishop Cosin in 1666 on the site of the medieval grammar and song schools.[17] But the most ingenious combination of school and almshouse of this period known to me is that at Clipston, Northamptonshire (pl. **62**). This was founded in 1667 by Sir George Buswell, and provided for the maintenance of twelve poor persons and a schoolmaster, who was to teach the local children reading, writing, grammar and Latin (i.e. a typical 'mixed' curriculum, depending on local demand).[18] The building was in 1926 adapted for use wholly as a primary school (which it still is), but a plan of the building was made before alteration (fig. 16) and shows how skilfully the old people were provided for, while leaving sufficient room for the master and for a large schoolroom on the first floor.

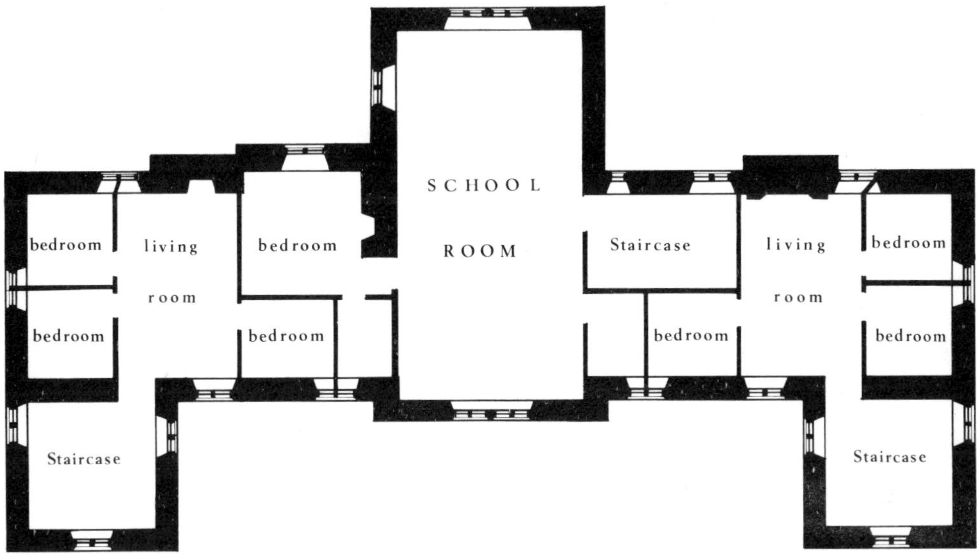

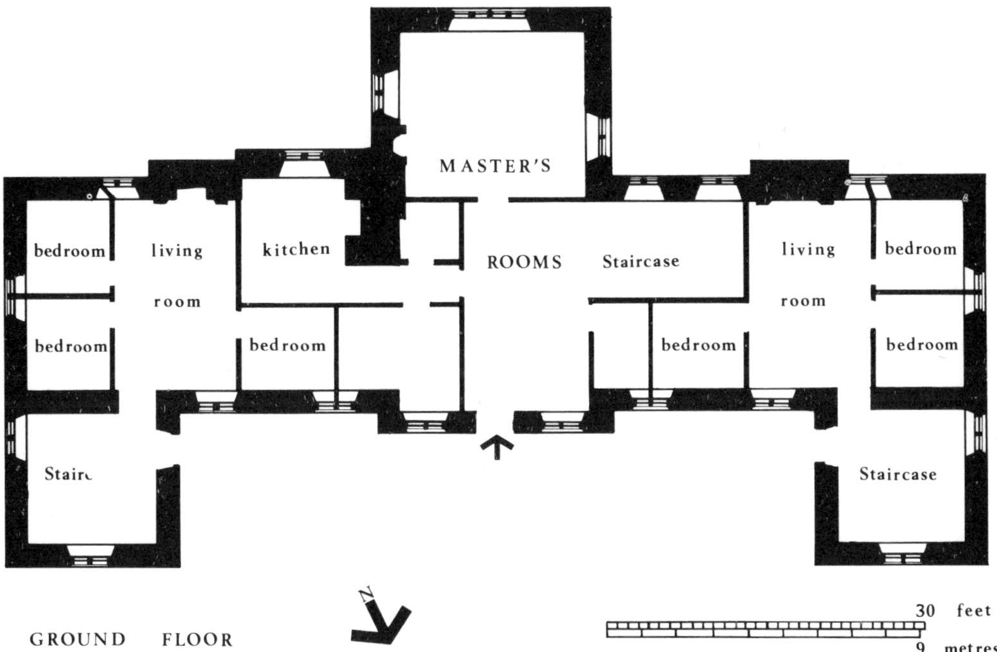

Figure 16 Clipston School and Hospital (i.e. almshouses), 1667, ground and first-floor plans. (There was originally a fireplace in the schoolroom opposite the staircase.)

II

The searching out of country schools of the immediate post-Restoration period is a fascinating pursuit, but we have probably given enough examples to illustrate the main types. For school buildings on a grander scale we must turn to Winchester and Eton and to the buildings financed by wealthy London merchants, with which Sir Christopher Wren was associated.

In the case of Winchester and Eton, the reasons for new buildings at this time are clear. Little mention has so far been made of the commoners (*commensales*) at these schools. Wykeham's rubric had permitted 'sons of noble and powerful persons, special friends of the said college, to the number of ten' to be instructed 'without charge to the college'. The number of commoners, which was twenty-six in 1653, had risen to fifty-three by 1679, which, with the seventy scholars, brought the total number of boys in the school to over 120. Two years later the number of commoners rose to seventy-nine, so outnumbering the scholars on the foundation. Leach suggests that the frequent visits of the Court attracted aristocratic pupils to the school, and Cook that the appointment of a young headmaster in 1679 may have led to the increase.[19] Another possible factor was the additional income derived from fee-paying pupils. But, whatever the reasons, it rapidly became clear that the existing teaching accommodation was too small, and in 1683–7 a new schoolroom was built to the south of Chamber Court, at a cost of £2,600, possibly to the design of Wren (pl. **63**).[20] The new school was twice as large as the old (measuring 2,700 as compared with 1,300 square feet), but the internal fittings (pl. **64**) were modelled on the old school, as already described. There had been no fireplace in the old school, and none was put in the new; but as the new school was lit mainly from the north, it received less sunlight than had the old school—an interesting comment on the triumph of traditionalism over considerations of the pupils' comfort. (A fireplace was eventually inserted in 1784.)

At Eton the aristocratic character of the school emerged earlier and more strongly than at Winchester. The Eton statutes authorized the admission of up to twenty sons of nobles (later called 'gentlemen commoners') and an unspecified number of 'another class of commensals who shall dine at the third table in hall with the scholars and choristers': the high table was reserved for the provost, fellows and headmaster, and the second table for the chaplain, usher, upper clerks and richer commensals. The number of commoners increased considerably soon after the dissolution of the monasteries—possibly relating to the fact that the sons of the nobility could no longer be sent to complete their education in abbots' households. The commoners had their meals in college, but usually slept at dames' houses in the town of Eton, from which they came to be called 'Oppidans'. The charges for taking commons in college (and also for teaching for which a charge was made, in spite of instructions to the contrary in the statutes) rose rapidly during the sixteenth century and clearly constituted an important source of additional income for the headmaster and usher. By 1613 there were over forty commoners, and in 1635 it was reported that the school was 'very much thronged with young nobility'. During the Commonwealth period many of the commoners began to board as well as lodge at dames' houses and by 1678, while the number of collegers (i.e. scholars) remained at seventy-eight, little more than the statutory minimum, the number of commoners had risen to 129, so bringing the total number of boys in the school to over 200.[21]

Clearly, this increase, taken with the similar rise at Winchester and a few other schools (notably Westminster under Busby), reflected an important change in aristocratic habits and a growth in the practice of sending the sons of the nobility away to school instead of having them educated by private tutors at home. The immediate solution to the problem of accommodation at Eton, as at Winchester, was solved by building another schoolroom—the long range known as Upper School, which completed the quadrangle opposite to Lupton's Tower (pl. **65**). The existing building (repaired after war damage in 1941) was designed by Wren and built in the years 1688–91 at a cost of £2,300. A somewhat similar building had been erected a few years before by Provost Allestree, but it was badly constructed and had to be pulled down and replaced. The present building has a number of features characteristic of Wren, notably the balustrade and the arcade towards the quadrangle, which closely resembles Trinity College library at Cambridge. Inside, the room was furnished with masters' thrones and pupils' benches along the sides in the traditional manner (pl. **66**).[22]

Wren was also closely associated with the rebuilding of Christ's Hospital, which had been seriously damaged in the Great Fire of London. In 1672 Erasmus Smith pointed out to the Governors of the hospital that the children were 'scattered we scarce know where to the number of 140 and have no other benefit of this great charity but to be kept alive'. He gave £500 towards the cost of a new school, which was built in 1672, though none too soundly, since it had to be replaced, owing to structural weaknesses, in 1790. In any event, it proved to be too small for the total requirements of the hospital, especially as in 1673 a mathematical school had been established with royal support to encourage the training of boys for the Navy and the Mercantile Marine. There was also a demand for increased provision for the teaching of writing in order to supply clerks for the London merchant offices. As a result, the hospital was almost completely rebuilt around the original cloister-garth, principally at the expense of two wealthy merchants, Sir Robert Clayton and Sir John Moore.[23] Clayton's block, facing Newgate Street, was designed by Sir Christopher Wren and opened in 1682. It was demolished when the school moved to Horsham in 1902 and the site is now occupied by the G.P.O. building. A small part of this building was re-erected at Horsham, but no plan of it has survived. There is, however, a contemporary drawing which gives a good impression of its magnificence (pl. **67**).[24] In addition, Sir John Moore financed, and Wren designed, a new writing school at the north-west corner of the cloister (pl. **68**). It was completed in 1695 at a cost of over £4,000, and consisted of a long room, sufficient to accommodate

300 boys (pl. **69**), with an arcade below. A statue of the founder, carved by Grinling Gibbons, was placed inside the room and later moved to the front of the building. A writing master's house was also provided alongside.[25]

Wren was also associated in lesser degree with two important schools in the provinces which both had connections—the one direct, the other indirect—with Christ's Hospital. In about 1650 the Governors of the hospital had decided to transfer some of the younger children (both boys and girls) to the three neighbouring towns of Hertford, Ware and Hoddesdon. The Hertford premises were practically rebuilt in 1691–5 and it is 'safe to ascribe the scheme to Sir Christopher Wren, the execution being in the hands of John Oliver, his deputy at St Paul's'.[26] These buildings now form part of Christ's Hospital Girls' School in Fore Street, Hertford, and consist of the gateway in Fore Street with later lead figures of Bluecoat boys (1721), and, at the end of an avenue of trees, the steward's house and the school hall, refaced in the present century, but retaining its original ceiling inside.

Of much more ambitious design is the school at Appleby Magna, Leicestershire (pl. **71**), whose association with Christ's Hospital derives from its founder, Sir John Moore, who took a very close interest in the design of the school and showed that he was influenced by the wider curriculum and extensive rebuilding of the London school. The design also shows that the ideas of Hoole had made some impact on the planning of schools. Wren himself made a drawing of the proposed building, but this was somewhat modified by the architect finally employed, William Wilson. It seems that Wilson consulted Wren about the final plan: 'Sir Christopher Wren remains in the background, but it is fundamentally his scheme', writes a modern authority on Wren.[27]

The school at Appleby was built during the years 1693–7 at a total cost of £2,800. Wren's design (pl. **70**) was for a two-storey building consisting of a schoolroom on the ground floor measuring 62 by 28 feet, with rooms in the wings for master and usher. Above the hall were rooms for boarders. Wilson's plan (fig. 14 (*c*) on p. 68) is basically similar, but it provided for a building of three instead of two storeys. The hall measures 51 by 26 feet, but it is higher than Wren's would have been, and is also provided with a gallery. Cloisters are not shown on Wren's design, but he had, of course, made use of them at Eton and elsewhere. (There was originally a cloister at the back as well as the front of the school at Appleby, but it was taken down in 1786 when a dining- or sitting-room for the boys, with a study for the headmaster, were erected in its place.) Wilson also carved the statue of Sir John Moore inside the schoolroom (pl. **72**) and claimed £125 for the work, with a further £125 for his services as architect, but he was actually paid only £126 in all.[28]

Wilson's plan followed the tradition of one large schoolroom with wings, but Thomas Moore, nephew of Sir John, wrote to his uncle while the school was being built and confirmed that 'the first [i.e. ground?] floor of the Under-Master's end . . . is intended for an English and Writing Schoole'.[29] It is therefore clear that Moore did not wish to provide only for classical teaching, and eighteenth-century accounts show that an English master and a writing master were employed, in addition to a Latin master.[30] Of particular interest is the generous provision for boarders. We noticed in an earlier chapter that, although a small number of 'foreigners', i.e. non-local boys, were no doubt being boarded with the masters, particularly in remote country areas, it was not a policy recommended by Mulcaster, nor was provision for boarders initially made at Shrewsbury, where the *alieni* were 'tabled' in the town, a course of action also recommended by Hoole. But by the time that Christopher Wase was writing (1678) certain new factors had clearly emerged. He deplored the low stipends commonly paid to schoolmasters, and pointed out that such stipends were frequently fixed by foundation statutes, even though the number of pupils and the cost of living continued to rise. He referred, for instance, to the stipend of a typical master of an old foundation, and pointed out that 'what was well sufficient in the time of donors, though faithfully dispensed by feoffees, in fact is now become incompetent for his reasonable maintenance'. This was even more of a problem in 'towns populous, well traded and replenished with youth, where the number of scholars cannot be well taught without an assistant, when the stipend already appointed is but tolerable living for one man'.[31] The days when the use of monitors could be considered an adequate solution to the problem were over, but Wase could only suggest that fresh endowments should be made to increase those which were insufficient.

The answer actually found to this problem had already been foreshadowed at Winchester and Eton, where (as we have seen) the number of fee-paying commoners increased rapidly after the Restoration. It was for the schoolmaster to limit the number of free scholars to the minimum laid down in the statutes and to increase his income by admitting fee-paying 'foreigners'. Sir Christopher Wren, in a letter to Sir John Moore in 1693 concerning the design for the school at Appleby, summarized very clearly the issues here being discussed:

> If you have room for boarders it is no great addition of charge, in regard it is but a floor over the hall, and it is certainly better for the boys to be always under their master's eye than to board at a distance in the village, and I should think that a less salary with advantage of room for boarders is more considerable than a large allowance without it, and to have gentlemen's sons well accommodated is that will bring reputation to the school and a good interest to the master, for which reason you will always have choice of worthy men to succeed in the school, because it will be more desirable to any person than a mere salary.[32]

Here was an important new factor which was to change the educational and architectural character of many schools in the course of the following century.

We may conclude this chapter with a brief reference to the internal furnishing of post-Restoration schoolrooms. Hoole's translation of the *Orbis sensualium pictus* (1672 edition) includes a picture of a contemporary schoolroom (pl. **74**),[33] the caption to which runs as follows, the figures referring to the numbers printed on the picture:

> A school (1) is a shop in which young wits are fashioned to virtue, and it is distinguished into forms. The master (2) sitteth in a chair (3), the scholars (4) in forms (5). He teacheth, they learn. Some things are writ down before them with chalk on a table (6). Some sit at a table and write (7). He mendeth (8) their faults. Some stand and rehearse things committed to memory (9). Some talk together (10) and behave themselves wantonly and carelessly; these are chastised with a ferula (11) and a rod (12).

The only other point to remark on is that desks as well as benches were now regularly provided for the pupils (not, however, free-standing, except at Winchester, where, as we noted, 'scobs' were used). Original desks of this period may still be seen at Clipston, Courteenhall (pl. **75**), Corsham and other schools. The master's chair or desk continued to occupy a prominent position, and at Corsham the master, who also acted as warden to the almshouse, was provided with both a chair and a pulpit, the latter fitted with a wooden hand to hold a candle.[34] It may also be noted that at Corsham a gallery was constructed at the end opposite to the master, as at Appleby. The exact purpose for which galleries such as these were designed is not easy to determine. Possibly they were provided in imitation of the college halls at Oxford and Cambridge and were included mainly for reasons of prestige—but they were not of the elaborate kind recommended by Dury and Hoole.

It is clear that the period from 1660 to 1700 was one of considerable building activity so far as schools were concerned. And in those places where wealthy endowments were available or where important London merchants gave their support, schools of impressive size and novel design were being built.

Notes

1 See 'State intervention and school education in the West Riding during the Interregnum', an M.Ed. thesis by Stephens, J. E., Leeds, 1963, *passim*. See also his article, 'Investment and intervention in education during the Interregnum', in *British Journal of Educational Studies*, Vol. XV, No. 3 (1967).

2 Reprinted with an Introduction by Knox, H. M., (Liverpool University Press, 1958). Many of Dury's ideas about school buildings were based on Comenius: see Sadler, J. E., *J. A. Comenius and the concept of universal education*, Allen & Unwin, 1966, 259.

3 *Ibid.*, 58.

4 All quotations are from the facsimile reprint edited by Campagnac, E. T. (Liverpool University Press, 1913). Spelling and punctuation modernized.

5 *Ibid.*, 23, 26, 27.

6 *Ibid.*, 39.

7 The Busby Library was bombed in 1940, but has since been restored (Carleton, J., *Westminster School*, Rupert Hart-Davis, 1965, 122–3). For the library at Leeds (now demolished, but photo. in Leeds reference library) see Carlisle, II, 842. On grammar-school libraries generally at this time see Hoole, *op. cit.*, 289–92, and Wase, C., *Considerations concerning free-schools*, Oxford: The Theater, 1678, 97–106. See also Yeats-Edwards, P., *Catalogue of the Select Library, King Edward VI School, Southampton*, the School, 1967. This library was established in the period 1691–1710.

8 Hoole, *op. cit.*, 218–25.

9 Watson, Foster, *The old grammar schools*, Cambridge U.P., 1916, 128.

10 Since this chapter was written, *Education in Leicestershire, 1540–1940* (ed. B. Simon, Leicester University Press, 1968) has appeared. The second chapter, on 'Post-Restoration developments', by Joan Simon, lends ample support to the contention that the period 1660–1700 was one of continued development in educational provision, including the building or re-building of schools.

11 *V.C.H., Oxfordshire*, I, 1939, 478–82.

12 *V.C.H., Northamptonshire*, II, 1906, 278. Also *C.C.R.*, III, 1825, and Renton, E. L., *Records of Guilsborough*, Kettering, 1929, 95–100.

13 *V.C.H., Nottinghamshire*, II, 1910, 250–1, and *Lincolnshire*, II, 1906, 488. Read also founded a school at Drax (Yorkshire). The school at Corby Glen has been restored by Mr Lawrence Bond, F.S.A., L.R.I.B.A., to whom I am grateful for further information. The school at Tuxford (external dimensions 62 by 21 feet) has a very similar plan to that of Corby Glen (54 by 24 feet).

14 See also the article on 'The Warden's House, Corsham' by Fyleman, R., in *Country Life*, 8 January 1938.

15 Godfrey, W. H. *The English almshouse*, Faber & Faber, 1955, 80–1 (with plan) and pl. 44 (*a*). The inscription on the building makes clear that the warden's house was also used as a school (as at Corsham).

16 R.C.H.M., *Buckinghamshire*, II, 1913, 127–8 and plate, p. 61.

17 *V.C.H., Durham*, I, 1905, 381. Illustrated in Seaborne, M., *Education*, Studio Vista, 1966, pl. 3.

18 Isham, G., *The story of Clipston Grammar School*, Market Harborough: Green, 1956, 14. The school/hospital was designed and built by Matthew Cole, who described himself as a carpenter. He died a poor man and his widow herself lived in the hospital (*ibid.*, 18–19).

19 Leach, A. F., *History of Winchester College*, Duckworth, 1899, 96, 363; and Cook, A. K., *About Winchester College*, Macmillan, 1917, 225–6.

20 Pevsner (*Hampshire*, 1967, 704) states roundly that 'the attribution to Wren has no authority', but there are stylistic and other pointers to Wren possibly having had a hand in the design (see Harvey, J. H., article on Winchester College in *Journal of the Archaeological Association*, XXVIII, 1965, 108n.). See also Cook, *op. cit.*, 234–5.

21 Lyte, H. C. Maxwell, *Eton College*, Macmillan, 1877, 159, 160, 204, 227, 239, 272.

22 The Upper School building at Eton is fully described in R.C.H.M., *Buckinghamshire*, I, 1912, 150, and in Vol. XIX of the Wren Society, Oxford, 1942, 108–110. See also Lyte, *op. cit.*, 266–7, 281–2. Allestree's Upper School, which had to be rebuilt, is shown in Loggan's well-known engraving of Eton in *Cantabrigia illustrata* (1690).

23 Pearce, E. H., *Annals of Christ's Hospital*, Methuen, 1901, 51–5. St Paul's School was also destroyed in the Fire and rebuilt on ambitious lines (1670). See McDonnell, M. F. J., *History of St Paul's School*, Chapman & Hall, 1909, 234–7, including picture. Merchant Taylors' School was also rebuilt in 1670–5 and continued in use until 1875 (see, further, in ch. 9).

24 See Vol. XI of the Wren Society, Oxford, 1934, 60–80 and pl. XLVI (elevation by A. E.

Richardson, 1900).

25 *Ibid.*, 61. The statue of Moore is now at Horsham. See also Summerson, J., *Architecture in Britain, 1530–1830*, Penguin, 4th ed., 1963, 160, where Hawksmoor's hand is also detected.

26 *Ibid.*, 61, 81–3. On John Oliver see Ware, D., *Short dictionary of British architects*, George Allen & Unwin, 1967, 171.

27 Wren Society, XI, 84–107, 108–13, for biographical note on Wilson (he was the son of a baker).

28 *Ibid.* The information about the rear cloister is from Nichols, J., *Leicestershire*, Vol. IV, Part II, Nichols, Son & Bentley, 1811, 441, where, however, the dimensions of the school-room are wrongly given as 100 by 50 feet. I am indebted to the Leicestershire County Architect for providing a plan of the Appleby school and to the Headmaster, Mr J. Smith, for showing me around the building.

29 Wren Society, XI, 97.

30 Nichols, *op. cit.*, 441. According to him, there was accommodation for fifty boarders.

31 Wase, *op. cit.*, 111, 68.

32 Wren Society, XI, 88 (spelling modernized).

33 This engraving may well be of Continental origin, and therefore not necessarily typical of the interior of an English school.

34 The Corsham building is described and illustrated in *Country Life*: see note 14, above.

Six

Public and private schools in the eighteenth century

I

The term 'public places' had been used, as we saw, by Mulcaster in the sixteenth century to describe schools founded for general or public use, especially those which provided education free of charge. Much the same definition was used by the schoolmaster-author, John Clarke, when he wrote in 1730 that 'by what I call *public* I mean an education in a school, where all comers are admitted; and by a *private* one, an education in the house and under the eye of a parent, or in a boarding-school, where none but boarders are received'.[1] But in the course of the eighteenth century we find that a small number of schools emerged from the general run of old-established grammar schools and increased greatly in size and importance owing to the admission of fee-paying boarders on an unprecedented scale. It was to this select group that Gibbon and others, writing later in the century, seem to be referring when they use the term 'the public schools'.[2]

What distinguished Winchester, Eton and Westminster and gave them the status of the 'great schools' *par excellence* in the eighteenth century was their size and their aristocratic clientele. The growth of the boarding element (which we saw beginning in the previous century) seems in fact to have been a general development in many types of school in the eighteenth century. In particular, as Wren had so clearly realized when writing to Sir John Moore about the school at Appleby Magna, it was only by increasing the number of fee-paying boarders that many grammar-school masters could hope to improve their financial position, and we now find that this device was very widely adopted. Another very important factor was that it was much easier to introduce non-classical subjects when there was a substantial number of fee-payers not on the foundation, since it could be argued that the education offered to such pupils was not legally confined to the curriculum laid down in the foundation statutes.

Most of the evidence at present available points to a decline of the grammar schools during the eighteenth century. Similarly, admissions to Oxford and Cambridge remained at a relatively low level throughout this period,[3] and the decline of many of the older schools is usually seen as merely a further reflection of the general decay of established institutions and the growing slackness of public life which is often said to have characterized the period of the Whig oligarchy. Yet this picture of gradual decline and obsolescence does not do justice to the emergence of public schools in something like the modern sense of this phrase, nor to those endowed schools, especially in commercial centres, which managed to adapt themselves to changing conditions. Moreover, in many places where the local grammar school went into decline, private schools emerged to supply the deficiency.

At Winchester, Eton and Westminster, which had from their beginnings enjoyed a national reputation and recruited on a national basis, the number of commoners increased remarkably and soon far exceeded the number of foundation scholars. Winchester changed least in respect of numbers, and was indeed hidebound by its constitution as part of a collegiate body which grew increasingly selfish and slack. In 1678 there were 127 boys at Winchester (about fifty of whom were commoners). The total number on the roll built up to 181 by 1732, after which there was a decline, followed by another peak of 186 in 1778 and then another decline. At Eton the increase was even more striking. There had been a total of 207 boys in 1678, but by 1725 this had grown to 378. After a decline during the 1730s and 1740s numbers again increased to reach a peak of 522 in 1765. Thereafter the number of boys began to drop until the nadir was reached with 246 in 1775; but again this was followed by a revival, reaching another peak with 477 boys on the roll in 1793. At Westminster the number of 'town boys' had been growing since Busby's time and greatly outnumbered the forty scholars on the foundation (as early as 1655 there were 241 boys in the school). The peak was reached in 1728 with a total of 434 boys, after which there was a decline, with numbers varying between 250 and 300 during the second half of the century—still, however, a very large school by contemporary English standards, and second only to Eton.[4]

The fluctuating numbers at these schools should not be allowed to blind us to the fact that the really big school had made its appearance for the first time in English education. Now we have schools which approached the size which Hoole at his most visionary had considered ideal—for his perfect school, it will be recalled, was designed for 500 children; and for the first time there was at least a handful of schools which could match some of the leading schools on the Continent. The implications for the development of ideas about school organization were immense, and have not attracted the attention they deserve. How, in fact, were these very large groups of boys organized for teaching and other purposes? What new procedures were devised, and could they be imitated in other schools, perhaps smaller in size?

The internal organization of a number of schools in eighteenth-century France has recently been examined by a leading French demographer and social historian. He shows that the idea of a homogeneous form or class developed very slowly and that small regard was paid to classifying pupils according to chronological age.[5] We saw the embryo of some of these developments in the internal organization of Wolverhampton School as early as 1609, where we noticed the very wide age-range of boys in each of the seven forms in the school. We also noted the contribution to educational theory underlying school organization and buildings made by Brinsley and Hoole, among others. Now in the eighteenth century we are able to trace in some detail the day-to-day organization of much larger schools than ever before. At Eton, for example, the school rolls from 1678 onwards have been collected together and published, and much valuable work has been done on the antecedents, school careers and subsequent occupations of the boys at the school after 1753. These two sources of information are referred to below as the *Eton College Lists* and the *Eton College Register* respectively.[6]

Let us therefore consider the position at Eton in 1775—the year in which, it is true, numbers reached their lowest point, but still sufficiently large for us to observe some of the essential characteristics of its internal organization. The 246 boys were divided into an upper and lower school in separate buildings and were organized into six forms and a remove. They were further divided (though not for teaching purposes) into scholars or collegers (seventy-two, pretty well the statutory number, though mainly in the upper school) and commoners or oppidans (174). It will be seen from Table I that the size of the forms varied considerably, and that several were very large by modern standards.

Table I Boys at Eton in 1775

Form	*Scholars (Collegers)*	*Commoners (Oppidans)*	*Totals*
Upper school			
Sixth	13	7	20
Fifth	31	41	72
Remove	1	13	14
Fourth	11	46	57
Lower school			
Third	13	31	44
Second	3	10	13
First	—	23	23
Unplaced	—	3	3
Totals	72	174	246

When we come to examine the age-distribution of the boys in the various forms we are in slightly greater difficulty. It is not always possible to relate the names given in the *Lists* with absolute certainty to the names in the *Register*, e.g. sometimes no record of any kind has been discovered about some of the boys apart from the names on the college lists. Sometimes, also, it is not possible to distinguish particular boys with a common surname from others with the same name or from relatives who also went to Eton at about the same time. Nevertheless, it has proved possible to obtain a reasonably accurate idea of the ages of all but ninety-nine of the 246 boys on the 1775 list, using either the known date of birth or the date of baptism (which in the great majority of cases followed birth within a month). The results of this analysis are set out in Table II, and show very clearly the wide age-range in each form and the considerable overlapping of ages between forms.

Table II Age and form distribution at Eton in 1775

Probable age	*Forms (and number of boys)*								
*in 1775**	*6*	*5*	*R†*	*4*	*3*	*2*	*1*	*U‡*	*Totals*
18	7								7
17	9	7							16
16	3	18		1					22
15		12	1	5	1				19
14		11	6	5					22
13		2	2	5	1				10
12		2	2	3	6	2			15
11		1		8	4				13
10				1	7	1			9
9					4	1	1		6
8						1	2		3
7					2	1	1		4
6							1		1
Uncertain	1	19	3	29	19	7	18	3	99
Totals	20	72	14	57	44	13	23	3	246

* Based on dates of birth or baptism.

† Remove.

‡ Unplaced.

It has also been possible to trace the school careers of all the boys who were in the Sixth Form at Eton in 1775 (Table III), and this shows that it was usual for boys to spend two, three or even four years in one form. Clearly, the whole system of progression must have depended on the stage reached in the (by now well-established) classical course. The exact age of the individual boy was regarded as of less importance than this knowledge of the set books, nor was there any idea of annual promotion from one form to the next, as is usual today.

Table III School careers of Sixth Form at Eton in 1775

Name of pupil	*Form in which pupil placed at given date*														*Probable age*	
	1764	*65*	*66*	*67*	*68*	*69*	*70*	*71*	*72*	*73*	*74*	*75*	*76*	*77*	*Began*	*Left*
Hayes				3	3	4	R	5	5	5*	5	6			9	17
Luxmore						4*	R	5	5	5	5	6			12	18
Emley						?*	4	R	5	5	5	6			11	17
Dampier	1	1	2	3	3	3	4	R	5	5*	5	6	6		6†	18
Norbury		?	2	3	3	3	4	R	5	5*	5	6	6		6†	17
Hatch		1	2	3	3	3	4	R*	5	5	5	6			8	18
Butler				2	3*	3	4	R	5	5	5	6	6		9	18
Oliver					3	3	4	R	5*	5	5	6			11	18
Anstey									5	5*	5	6	6		15	19
Bernard						3	4	4	5	5*	5	6	6		11	18
Amyatt						3	4	4	5*	5	5	6			11	17
Mitchell					?*	3	4	4	5	5	5	6	6	6	9	18
Calvert							4	4	5	5	5	6			12	17
Hayes (2)							4	4	5*	5	5	6	6	6	12	19
Baker								4	R	5	5	6			14	18
Willmot						3	4	4	R	5	5	6	6		12	19
Grenville							3	4	R	5	5	6	6		11	17
Dupuis								4	R	5	5	6	6		14	19
Mason								4	4	5	5	6	6		13	18
White								4	4	5	5	6	6		?	?

* Elected King's Scholar.

† Dampier was the son of the lower master and Norbury of an assistant at Eton, i.e. it was exceptional to begin as young as six.

R indicates the Remove.

Perhaps the main impression left by a detailed study of the Eton *Lists* and *Register* is that of the fluidity of the internal school organization (which must have also been affected by the great fluctuations in total size from year to year). Table III shows the variation in the number of years spent at Eton by the Sixth Form of 1775. In fact, only a minority of boys went on to the Sixth Form at all: many began late and left early—to such an extent, indeed, that one feels bound to conclude that the classical course, though presented as a single unity in school time-tables, was in practice fragmented and incomplete for most of the boys. Many must have left with only a smattering of classical learning; others—like the sixteen-year-old boy in the Fourth Form at Eton in 1775, who left in the following year[7]—may well have had as much of the classics as they could absorb.

The criterion of classical knowledge was in many ways a draconian one to employ in organizing a school. Thus in 1775 we find four brothers newly arrived at Eton and all placed in the First Form, since presumably none of them knew any classics (all but one of these boys left after two years).[8] In a situation such as this, one can begin to see the significance of one of the points made by Philippe Ariès, viz. that the traditional idea that all boys at school were 'children' (even the seventeen-year-olds) was increasingly coming into conflict with something approaching the modern idea of adolescence.[9] Thus, all the boys at Eton were subject to the same punishment of flogging, and there is some evidence to show that it was the resentment of this form of punishment on the part of the older boys which contributed to the serious disturbances which took place at Eton and elsewhere towards the end of the eighteenth century. It was perhaps in the attitude of mind which characterized a system of universal flogging, rather than in the influence of French revolutionary ideas, that we should see the real cause of the rebellions of boys against masters which took place in several of the major schools towards the end of the century and the beginning of the next.[10]

The increased size of schools also had important effects on staffing and teaching methods. At Winchester assistant masters (known as 'tutors') are first mentioned in 1738 and there were three of them by the end of the century.[11] At Eton additional masters are first recorded in 1698 and by 1718 there were eight.[12] The *List* of 1774 (when there were 267 boys) gives the names of four upper school assistants and three lower school assistants, besides the upper and lower masters, who were alone recognized as part of the foundation.[13] It also seems that the number of hours actually spent in the school-room was substantially reduced in the course of the century, for the assistants also acted as tutors on a private fee-paying basis, tutoring individual boys who went to the masters' own rooms for the purpose.[14] Indeed, this was the assistants' principal source of income, since they received no official stipends. A similar system was in operation at Westminster also, and, as we shall see, spread to other schools.

From the point of view of school architecture, the most remarkable feature of the rapid expansion in the number of pupils mentioned above was that it did not result in a radical reconstruction or extension of the school buildings. At Winchester and Eton the colleges were an architectural unity and major alterations to their already venerable buildings were no doubt unthinkable; at Westminster, on the other hand, where the school had developed on the edge of the former monastic buildings, there was somewhat greater scope for alterations. In all three places, however, the old schoolrooms were retained and architectural changes took place in a somewhat haphazard manner.

At Winchester the increasing number of commoners led the master in 1742 to build 'Commoners' College', now demolished, but described as 'a spacious quadrangular building' in which all the commoners were lodged under the second master.[15] At Eton in the years 1726–9 the cloisters on the south side of Green Court (see fig. 2) were completely rebuilt in order to construct a new library, which still occupies the first floor above the south cloister. No attempt was made to imitate the original architectural style of the college—a matter of regret to Victorian writers, though a recent authority has called the library 'perhaps the finest [room] in the college, except for the chapel' (see pl. **76** for interior view).[16] Further alterations were made in Green Court in 1759, when an attic storey of stone was added to the northern and eastern sides of the cloister above the original brickwork.

At Westminster the architectural changes of this period were greater. The scholars' dormitory (which was in the former granary of the monks) had fallen into disrepair, and was replaced by a magnificent new building on the west side of the college garden. Wren made plans for the proposed building, but a legal dispute between the school and the chapter led to delays and the building finally constructed (in 1722) was to the design of Lord Burlington. The ground floor was originally an open cloister, but this was enclosed in 1847 to make studies. The dormitory itself consisted of one big room (pl. **79**), which was partitioned into cubicles in 1860. This building was badly damaged during the Second World War, but was restored in the original style in 1947. The best view is from the garden, which is not normally open to the public (but see pl. **78**).[17] Burlington also probably designed the school gate (1734), which has since acquired many initials carved by the boys. Of greater topographical importance was the clearing away of a congeries of old buildings (begun during the Headmastership of William Markham, 1753–64) to form what is now Little Dean's Yard (pl. **77**). Six houses were built on a terrace at the south end of the yard and helped to solve the pressing problem of boarding boys coming from a distance. There were dames' houses in a number of streets near the school and an usher was established in each house, where he could undertake private tuition.[18] This dual control of houses by dames and ushers lasted into the nineteenth century, and there are clear analogies here with the system which was operating at Eton during this period.

The employment of assistant masters and the development of boarding houses did not solve all the problems brought by the unprecedentedly large number of boys attending these schools. The masters' incomes were subject to considerable variation as the number of boys fluctuated. Nor in most cases were the assistants in a position to exercise disciplinary powers over the boys[19] or to introduce changes in the traditional classical curriculum—though here we may note that there was less demand for the introduction of modern subjects from members of the leisured classes.[20] The prefects, who, as we saw in an earlier chapter, had from the beginning certain supervisory duties, now began to acquire the power to punish boys themselves, and it was during the eighteenth century that the 'fagging' system made its appearance. Partly no doubt as a result of the older boys' acquisition of the right to give corporal punishment, they began to challenge the masters' authority, and open rebellion against the staff occurred on a considerable scale.

Nevertheless, many features which we have noticed at Winchester, Eton and Westminster spread to other schools, and it was during the eighteenth century that Rugby and Harrow really emerged as major public schools. They had both originated as small local grammar schools, and their rise to fame was due to a chance combination of factors: lack of outside clerical control, endowments of land in London which subsequently increased enormously in value, and the good fortune of having a number of very able headmasters. Let us therefore examine briefly the rise of these two schools and the effect of the increase in the number of boys on the school buildings and organization.

At Harrow the number of boys had risen to 235 by 1770, then dropped slowly to 119 in 1791, but rose again to 200 in 1799. The schoolroom of 1615, which we examined in some detail in an earlier chapter, remained in use throughout the century, though the rooms above it, which were originally designed to accommodate the master and usher, were taken over by the boys. The additional boarders at the school were largely accommodated in private houses nearby.[21] At Rugby, however, the changing character of the school was reflected in somewhat more radical architectural changes, which themselves showed how educational ideas were developing.

Lawrence Sheriffe, the Elizabethan founder of Rugby School, had provided a house for the master and funds to build a school, which consisted of the usual large room.[22] The buildings fell into disrepair during the Civil War period, but there was a revival after the Restoration, and in 1676 two chambers were built over the schoolroom to accommodate a growing number of boarders.[23] During the headship of Holyoake (1688–1731) the number of boys increased to about 100. The trustees raised Holyoake's salary to £70 and also allowed him to take a nearby rectory, to which he was able to appoint a curate, using the greater part of the profits to employ a number of assistant masters, who supplemented their income by giving private tuition. In 1750 a new school was built, consisting, like the old, of a schoolroom with chambers above, which were used as dormitories.[24] Under Thomas James (Headmaster from 1778 to 1794) the number of boys at Rugby rose very rapidly—from eighty in 1777 to 240 in 1790. He was himself an Etonian and introduced the Eton system of dames' houses and private tutors. But he went beyond the Eton system in building separate classrooms (still called 'schools', however) for Forms 1, 2 and 3, and by fitting up as classrooms a number of barns and outhouses.[25] Drawing as Rugby did on a less aristocratic clientele, James was also able to introduce some non-classical subjects—French, English history, modern geography and some mathematics. The rebellions which took place at Rugby at the turn of the century may be seen not so much as evidence of decline as of the need for new methods of gaining the co-operation of boys whose greater numbers and organizing capacities were themselves a measure of the school's success.

II

The development of these major schools does not, of course, complete the story of grammar-school building in the eighteenth century. An examination of surviving buildings of the period tends on the whole, however, to confirm the general picture we have of the declining importance of the grammar schools—though it would be wrong to underestimate the continuing work of the schools already established.[26] Northamptonshire, for example, was already, as we have seen, well provided with grammar schools in the seventeenth century and not a single grammar-school building survives from the eighteenth. There are examples in other counties of old schools being rebuilt, particularly in the earlier part of the century, but it seems that this building activity, such as it was, recorded the high-water mark of a period of prosperity which had begun after the Restoration and was now coming to an end. We may illustrate this point from the schools at Sedbergh (West Riding) and Kibworth Beauchamp (Leics.).

At Sedbergh the school founded in the early sixteenth century expanded during the headship of Posthumous Wharton (1674–1706). In about 1681 he bought a house for himself and extended it to accommodate boarders. By 1705 there were 120 boys on the roll and the school also possessed a library containing almost all the books recommended by Hoole. A new school was built on the site of the old in 1716, but the number of boys now began to decline, and the reputation of the school really dates from its revival in the nineteenth century.[27] The school of 1716 (pl. **85**) was used for teaching until 1879, and survives today as the library of the present greatly enlarged school, the interior of the original building having recently been remodelled to designs by Sir Albert Richardson.

Similar factors seem to have operated at Kibworth Beauchamp, where the school was rebuilt in 1725 (pl. **81**). It consisted of a large schoolroom, with a commodious master's house attached to it, clearly designed to accommodate boarders (plan, fig. 17). The rebuilding came at the end of a long period of dispute between the Anglicans and Dissenters of Kibworth over the control of the governing body (1708–24), which ended in the victory of the Anglican party. It was, however, a pyrrhic victory: numbers fell and the school was only kept going by the appointment of an usher in 1758 to teach elementary subjects. (It was not until 1836 that a partition wall was erected in the schoolroom to separate in decisive fashion the work of the usher teaching the free scholars from that of the master teaching the fee-payers.)[28] Another school which

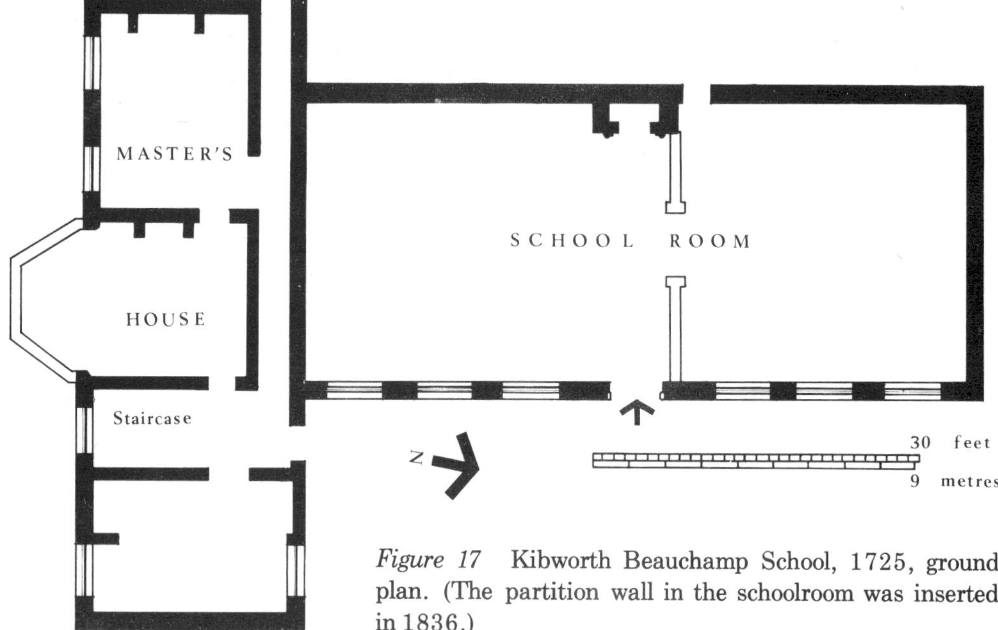

Figure 17 Kibworth Beauchamp School, 1725, ground plan. (The partition wall in the schoolroom was inserted in 1836.)

provided ample accommodation for the master and his boarders during this period may be seen at Scorton (N. Yorks.), illustrated on pl. **80**.

There were some new grammar-school foundations during the eighteenth century, but surviving buildings are by no means common. They show that, in response to the social and economic changes already mentioned, accommodation for boarders had become usual. They also show that even in the grammar schools the importance of teaching English and writing (including arithmetic), which we saw developing throughout the seventeenth century, was now fully recognized—indeed, we find, in a few places at least, that provision came to be made for what by eighteenth-century standards was almost a comprehensive type of education. The changing character of the schools did not, however, result in fundamental changes in layout, but more usually in a certain spaciousness of design, including generous provision for the master, who was now expected to spend much of his time looking after the boarders. Yet all too often the spacious rooms were not filled, and in one or two cases magnificent new buildings seem to have been little more than expensive white elephants which never fulfilled the grandiose plans of their founders.

Perhaps the outstanding surviving example of the last-mentioned feature is the former school (now called the Old Hall and used partly as a private house and partly as a depository) at Kirkleatham, near Redcar in the North Riding of Yorkshire. The school was founded by Sir William Turner in 1692, but not built until 1709 (by his great-nephew, Cholmley Turner, who enlarged the adjoining hospital or almshouses, also on a grand scale). The founder stipulated that the master should be an M.A.

and the usher a B.A., and that both should be 'skilled and expert in Latin and Greek'; thus, he clearly had in mind the setting up of a grammar school of the traditional type. There were to be thirty free scholars from the locality and an unspecified number of fee-paying boarders. The building (shown on pl. **82**) was of splendid proportions and included apartments for the master and usher as well as the schoolroom and accommodation for boarders. The school was endowed with an excellent library and the school estate amounted to no less than 553 acres. Yet it never seems to have been a success. The Charity Commissioners, who visited it in 1823, reported that

> it is understood that the schoolhouse, after its completion, was applied for its intended purpose for a very short space of time only; that it was afterwards used as a place of residence by Mr William Turner, who succeeded Mr Cholmley Turner in the manor and estate at Kirkleatham; and it has since been occasionally vacant and unoccupied, and at other times inhabited by persons placed in it by the lords of the manor for the time being, for the accommodation of such persons, or in order that they might take care of the premises.

It seems likely that the relatively remote geographical situation of the school prevented it from attracting many boarders, and that the narrow classical curriculum which it offered held little attraction for local parents. The Charity Commissioners also reported (with ponderous thoroughness) that

> according to the traditional account which prevails, Mr Cholmley Turner, either because the school and scholars, from being placed too near to his mansion house and adjoining property at Kirkleatham, were found to disturb him in the enjoyment thereof, or because the school did not sufficiently answer in its intended purpose, or for some other reason not well known, or now forgotten, used his endeavours to discourage the resort of scholars, and to prevent the continuance of the establishment in a state of activity, and in consequence the school declined.

As a result, the offices of master and usher (worth £100 and £50 respectively) became sinecures held by the land agent and the Vicar. Later in the nineteenth century the endowments were reformed and are now enjoyed by the Sir William Turner's Grammar School at Redcar.[29]

Almost as ambitious, but this time much more successful, was the school founded and endowed in 1708 by Sir John Pierrepont at Lucton, near Leominster in Herefordshire, and still in existence as an independent school. Pierrepont was a citizen and vintner of London, and showed that he was fully aware of the need for a broadly-based curriculum catering for a wide range of social classes. The rules which he approved for the school stated that

> this school shall be for the instruction of children in religion, grammar

> learning, writing, arithmetic and mensuration, of such poor parents as are not able to bear the charge of training up their children, so as to be fit for the university or to be put out apprentices, services or other employment.

The emphasis on religion and apprenticing showed that Pierrepont had been influenced by the work of the S.P.C.K. (to which further reference will be made in our next chapter), but it was also possible for children to learn the classics with a view to going on to the university. It was also Pierrepont's intention to provide for children of more than one social class, for he stipulated that 'the boys to be admitted into this school shall be of two sorts'—the first to be children of parents 'of the meaner sort of people, whether labourers or freeholders who shall not have in their own right lands or tenements above the yearly value of £20' (these were not to exceed fifty at any one time); and the second sort, to a maximum of thirty, to be children whose parents held property worth between £20 and £50 p.a. (they were charged an annual fee of 10*s*.). Both these categories of children were to be drawn from the locality, but in

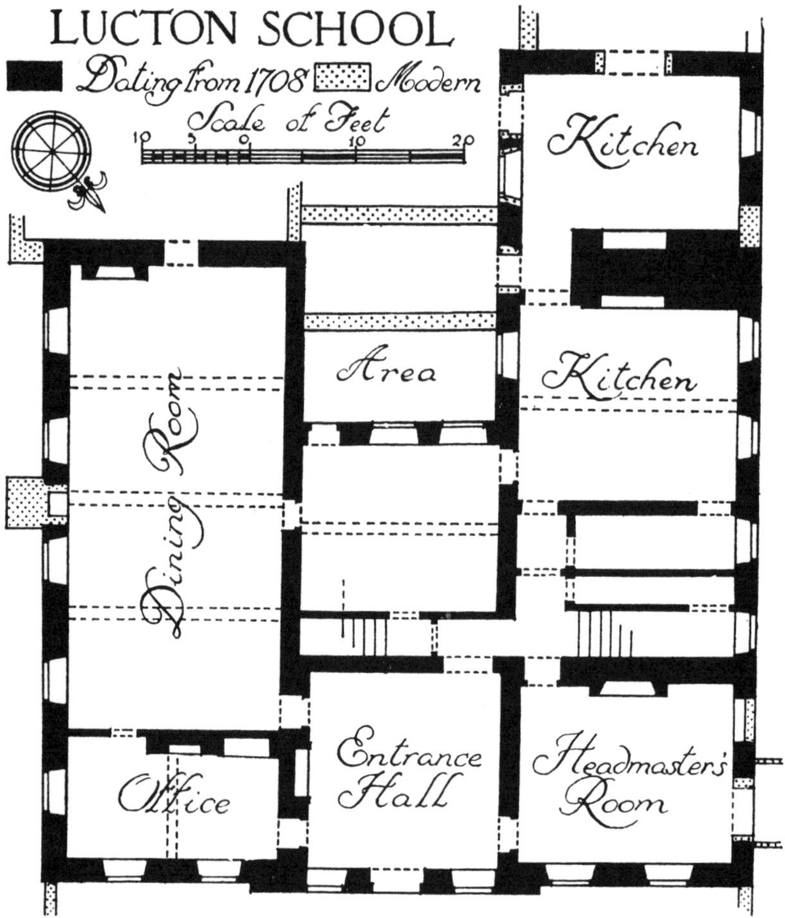

Figure 18 Lucton School, 1708, plan. (The schoolroom was where the dining-room now is.)

addition the master was permitted to admit from elsewhere up to ten 'sons of gentlemen' with property worth more than £50 p.a. and they were to be charged an annual fee of £20; clearly they were to be boarders.

The school building itself (pl. **83**) is an outstanding example of the Queen Anne style of architecture, a beautifully-proportioned house of red brick with stone dressings and a central pediment, and a statue of the founder in a recess above the front door. The original clock bears the date 1708. The plan (fig. 18) shows that the master was well accommodated. The usher was also to live in the school and the upper floors were doubtless designed for the boarders. There was one large schoolroom (now a dining-room), which seems to indicate that, although the social classes were carefully differentiated, all the boys were taught in the same room—indeed, so traditional does Pierrepont seem to have been in his provision for the schoolroom that, as at Winchester in 1687, no fireplace was included, which, according to a contemporary account, was a 'great discouragement' to regular attendance. Nevertheless, the numbers at the school remained at between fifty and seventy for most of the eighteenth century.[30]

An equally broad provision was made in some other places, but more usually in separate buildings. An excellent surviving example is the interesting group of buildings at Risley (Derbs.) facing the main Nottingham–Derby road (see fig. 19). The original school, dated 1706, was built close to the parish church by Elizabeth Gray, who had inherited a large fortune from her grandfather, Sir Henry Willoughby. An indenture of 1718 stated that she had erected 'a convenient schoolhouse in the town of Risley for a schoolmaster and usher'. The master was to teach grammar and the

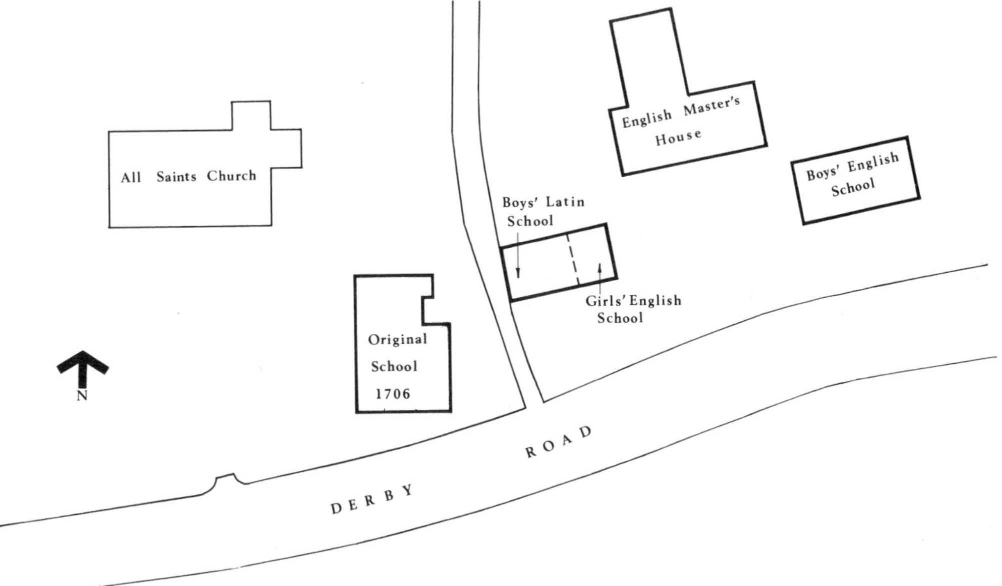

Figure 19 Risley, sketch-map showing position of schools.

classics 'to such as should be qualified and desirous' to learn them, while the usher was to teach 'spelling, writing, arithmetic and the church catechism'. Thus a mixed curriculum was to be followed within the same building, which, it appears, was also to accommodate the master and usher. The indenture also mentioned the possibility that in the future a separate house might be built for the usher, and that the school building might be extended so that a mistress could teach girls 'to knit, sew and do other things proper for their education'—in fact, Elizabeth Gray's will of 1720 bequeathed money for the building of a separate school for the girls, who were also to be taught to write and cast accounts.

Taken together, therefore, the various provisions made by Elizabeth Gray were on an unusually generous scale. When the Charity Commissioners visited Risley in 1827, they found (as the modern visitor will find) no less than four separate buildings. First, there was the 'original school house' (i.e. that of 1706), occupied in 1827 by the local incumbent. Pevsner describes this building as 'one of the best of its time in the county', and it has a particularly fine entrance (pl. **84**). Alongside it to the east were two school buildings, separated by the English master's house. The school nearest to the original school of 1706 was divided into two: the western half of one storey with panelled walls inside and the master's chair at one end was used as the Latin school, and the eastern half, of two storeys, consisted in 1827 of the girls' school on the ground floor with the mistress's rooms above (this part is now occupied by the Clerk to the Trustees and his family). The other school further to the east was an English school for boys, with a large playground in front of it. It consists of one large room, now used for an infants' class by the local primary school, which rents it from the Trustees. The *Victoria County History* states that the Latin and girls' schools seem to have been built in 1724, the English school in 1753 and the English master's house in 1771, but the architectural evidence suggests that the Latin and English schools were built at about the same time, probably soon after 1720. Since the Latin Master was also the incumbent during the eighteenth century, it appears that, once the various other buildings on this site had been erected, the original school of 1706 became the private house of the incumbent, who seems to have taken in boarders and taught them with the local boys in the adjoining Latin school.[31]

It is clear that founders of eighteenth-century grammar schools were in general well aware of the need for providing an English as well as a classical education. There was, indeed, a declining demand for Latin, which was no longer the universal language of scholarship and diplomacy. French was rapidly becoming the language of diplomacy and culture and the need to teach more utilitarian subjects was making itself felt more strongly than ever, especially among the middle classes. It could, of course, be argued that many of the older grammar schools were limited by their statutes to teaching Latin and Greek, and, since the office of schoolmaster had in many places come to be regarded as a freehold tenable by the master as of right, it was often difficult to effect a change. But these were arguments in defence of the established order more commonly invoked at the beginning of the nineteenth century, when sinecures were under widespread attack. There are several eighteenth-century examples of grammar schools which ignored or circumvented the instructions of the founders, and in other cases the original terms of the foundation were changed by decree of Chancery or by private Act of Parliament.

At Hull, for example—where there were in fact no statutes at all for the town school—the Corporation on the whole maintained the school efficiently and allowed a notably progressive Headmaster (John Clarke, 1716–32) to modernize the Latin course and introduce a certain amount of history, geography and divinity.[32] (The last-named subject was important, for in the older foundations religious instruction was often neglected, while at Eton there was 'an entire absence of religious teaching'.)[33] Similarly, at Manchester, where scientific subjects are known to have been taught in the grammar school in the early eighteenth century, it was found possible to include mathematics in the curriculum by making use of two adjoining private schools. The school was rebuilt in 1776—'itself in some measure', says the historian of the school, 'a recognition of the fact that a new order of things had arisen with new needs'.[34] It was only the decline of the Corporation (which came to represent the local landed interest, rather than the commercial classes in the town itself) which led to the decline of the school later in the century. So, too, at Macclesfield in Cheshire, which was the centre of an expanding textile industry, the Governors built a new schoolhouse early in the reign of George III and obtained an Act of Parliament authorizing the teaching of children 'not only in grammar and classical learning, but also in writing, arithmetic, geography, navigation, mathematics, the modern languages, and such branches of literature and education as shall from time to time in the judgment of the governors be [thought] proper and necessary'.[35] This school continued to flourish, with, it seems, strong Nonconformist support.

Perhaps the outstanding surviving example of a publicly-provided school teaching commercial subjects is the Corporation's Academy at Berwick-on-Tweed (pl. **87**). This academy was set up in 1798 and was modelled upon the more progressive burgh schools of Scotland. It was erected by the Corporation on a playground belonging to the town's grammar school trust. It charged no fees and the pupils came from all walks of life: 'side by side may be found the children of fishermen, tradespeople and professional persons'. Its internal planning was much in advance of most contemporary English schools, for the building contained six rooms, one devoted to sewing under the charge of a mistress and five consisting of classrooms each with its own master (used respectively by the writing master, the headmaster, the English master, the mathematical master and the master in charge of the juniors).[36]

III

These changes in curriculum and buildings occurred relatively late in the eighteenth century and took place mainly in important commercial centres. The more general picture of grammar schools when, for example, John Clarke, the master of Hull School, was writing, was far from satisfactory from the point of view of middle-class parents, and especially the Dissenters. Clarke, who was the product of a private academy and Edinburgh University and was himself apparently an occasionally conforming Dissenter, outlined his views in his *Essay on the education of youth in grammar schools* (1720, enlarged edition 1730). He refers in scathing terms to the general run of small grammar schools, of which 'we have many scattered here and there in obscure parts of the country, which are generally little more than houses of correction for the boys of the neighbourhood'. As for the larger schools in the major towns, a boy attending such a school will find himself

> in a promiscuous, numerous herd of rude, wild boys, many of them very vicious (for it is impossible it should be otherwise in a great school, especially in a populous place) where if he escapes without the loss of his innocence, or without a strong infection from the foulest of vices, it must be next to a miracle.[37]

In these opinions, and in his views on the need for reforming the classical curriculum, Clarke was closely following Locke, who in his *Thoughts concerning education* (1693) had recommended that the son of a gentleman should be educated, not in a school, but by a private tutor at home. Clarke, however, reaches a somewhat different conclusion. He points out that even education at home is not free from the risk of corruption by servants and visitors from outside, quite apart from the disadvantages to the child of lack of contact with other children of his own age. He therefore recommends that private boarding schools, each with about twenty pupils and under the continuous supervision of the master, should be set up, since in such schools not only would the children's morals be safeguarded, but there would be no legal or traditional impediments to the introduction of non-classical subjects of more immediate use in commercial life. And, indeed, we now find that many more private schools—both boarding and day—came to be set up.[38]

Ideas of this kind seem to have been most vigorously taken up in some of the Nonconformist private schools of the eighteenth century. The practice of educating their children in boarding schools was partly a matter of necessity where the members of a Nonconformist body were thinly scattered over various parts of the country; but chiefly it was devised as a method of preventing the children of the faithful from being contaminated by outside influences. This element was very apparent in the schools established by the Moravians soon after they started work in England in 1738. The educational work of the Moravians was from 1753 concentrated (as it still is) at Fulneck, near Pudsey in the West Riding, and the boys' school there was, according to its modern historian,

> not so much a school as an orphanage. It was not that the boys had no parents; as a rule the reverse would be true. But it is of an orphanage that one is strongly reminded when one first realizes on what lines the school was managed. . . . Parents who were rich enough paid fees; the rest were relieved of all pecuniary obligations by the [Moravian] Church; but in either case the care of their children was taken entirely out of their hands.[39]

Parents were discouraged from visiting their children, who were kept under the direct and continuous supervision of the staff both night and day. Usually the headmaster placed boys in suitable occupations at the end of their schooling, or they were sent to a theological college in Germany to read for the Moravian ministry. Here, perhaps for the first time in England since Winchester was founded to train boys for the priesthood, we find a system of boarding education which was both theoretically justified and actively practised on purely moral grounds, and not merely for the convenience of the parents or the financial advantage of the school.

John Wesley was clearly influenced by Moravian practice in his plans for a boys' boarding school at Kingswood, near Bristol. Whitefield had already (in 1739) founded an elementary school for the children of the colliers whom he had converted to Methodism, but Wesley's own foundation (1748) in the same place was essentially a fee-paying boarding school for the more affluent sympathizers with Methodism. There was thus a greater degree of social-class differentiation at Kingswood than at Fulneck, and the curriculum advocated by Wesley also took more account of the teaching of non-classical subjects. But the moral basis of Wesley's school was strikingly similar to that of Fulneck: it also was set up in a relatively isolated spot, the pupils were continuously supervised and their time-table was worked out in the minutest detail. Wesley's plan for the school may be read in his *Short account of the school in Kingswood, near Bristol*, published in 1768.[40] It begins as follows:

> Our design is, with God's assistance, to train up children in every branch of useful learning. We teach none but boarders. These are taken in, being between the years of six and twelve, in order to be taught reading, writing, arithmetic, English, French, Latin, Greek, Hebrew, history, geography, chronology, rhetoric, logic, ethics, geometry, algebra, physics [and] music.

The very wide range of subjects to be taught is noteworthy, but the 'general rules of the house' given later in the *Short account* are even more remarkable for their narrow insistence on the most rigid discipline. The boys had to get up at 4 a.m., winter and summer, and spend an hour in private reading and prayer. Then followed an hour spent all together and an hour of work before breakfast at 7 a.m. School work followed until 11 o'clock, when the pupils could 'walk or work' until dinner at noon. More school work followed from 1 to 5 p.m., when there was an hour of private prayer. This was followed by supper at about 6, a public service at 7 and bed at 8 p.m. A lamp burned in the dormitory all night and a master slept at each end of the room. Wesley adds that there were eight classes in the school, supervised by three masters, and 'an usher chiefly to be with the children out of school'. Teaching went on every day except Sundays throughout the year and 'neither do we allow any time for play on any day'.

Kingswood School first opened in 1748, and the original building provided accommodation for fifty children, besides masters and servants. It consisted of a dining-hall and schoolroom on the ground floor, a large dormitory on the first floor and attics above. Games were forbidden, but gardening was encouraged—in fact, early prints of the school show that the garden was divided into as many small plots for cultivation as there were boys in the school.[41] The daily services for the boys (which seem to have taken place in the nearby elementary schoolroom, also used as a public chapel) further emphasized the religious character of the school and provided a new feature which was to be widely imitated by middle-class schools of all denominations in the following century. One is not surprised to learn that, although the school attracted a good number of pupils, the rigours of the discipline were too great for many, and the school after about 1796 admitted only the sons of Methodist ministers. In this form it prospered, and was rebuilt near Bath in 1852.

The Society of Friends had similar educational problems to face, but their efforts may most appropriately be described in our next chapter on schools for the poor. It was the Kingswood School which had perhaps the greatest influence on the middle-class schools, supported by parents of all religious persuasions, that were set up in increasing numbers during the second half of the eighteenth century.

The private schools of this period have been examined by Dr Hans in his book *New trends in education in the eighteenth century* (1951).[42] He shows that, although there were such schools from at least the middle of the seventeenth century (or earlier if we include the 'dame schools'), they seem to have increased in number mainly from 1750 onwards, and particularly in the London area. He distinguishes between the private academies in which mathematical, scientific and vocational subjects were taught, and the private classical schools, usually kept by Anglican clergymen, which combined a more modern approach to classical teaching with close personal supervision of the pupils' behaviour. Hans' main concern is with the interesting curricular developments which took place in these institutions, as revealed in the published writings of the masters of some of the principal schools. Comparatively little information is available, either in Hans' book or, it seems, in the sources he used, about the school buildings and internal organization. Although it is unwise to generalize when the evidence about most of these schools is extremely scanty, it appears that the great majority (particularly of the classical schools) were quite small, and usually met in the masters' private houses or in rooms hired for the purpose. There seems to have been a considerable boarding element, but nothing on the scale of the public schools examined earlier in this chapter—indeed, it was in reaction against such schools that many of the new private schools derived their impetus.

Typical of the sources available for the study of eighteenth-century private schools is *The plan of education at Mr Elphinston's academy, Kensington* (c. 1764).[43] After a characteristic reference to the former dominance of Latin and Greek—which Elphinston describes as 'the attempt of raising the dead in order to smother the living'—a plea is made for the study of idiomatic English and French, 'the general tongue of Europe'. The classical languages are not dismissed from the curriculum, but are made to occupy a subordinate position. Writing and arithmetic are both considered to be absolutely essential and a large number of new subjects is suggested—history, geography, logic, ethics, metaphysics, pneumatology (now called psychology), physics and mathematics. There should also be specific instruction in the Scriptures and in good manners. Physical education is seen to be of great importance, since 'bodily exercise invigorates also the mind' (a theory much in vogue in the following century). Elphinston believed that 'though the head and then the heart claim the first attention, the very hands and feet must not be forgotten'—hence he advocates the teaching of dancing, fencing, gardening and drawing. All this is summarized in a school time-table which even by modern standards would appear to have made for a well-balanced curriculum. But he has very little to say about the kind of building in which such activities would take place. He vaguely remarks that 'the situation and accommodations are in every respect as peculiar [in the eighteenth-century sense] as the higher parts of the plan'. It does appear, however, that the school had extensive grounds, a good library and a garden with allotments for each boy, after the manner of Kingswood School (much of Elphinston's curriculum is in fact similar to Wesley's, with the excessive religious exercises omitted).

Gardening was also encouraged at Cheam School (Surrey), a private school which had originated in the seventeenth century, but flourished especially under William Gilpin, who took it over in 1752. Gilpin practised in his school a system of internal self-government which anticipated in an interesting way some of the ideas of radical thinkers of the nineteenth and twentieth centuries. For example, the 'twenty or thirty little plots' into which the school garden was divided could be legally conveyed from one boy to another and left by will when a boy left the school; they could also be grouped in 'estates' and let out to 'tenants'. Gilpin's methods of enforcing discipline are reminiscent of the school 'councils' and 'parliaments' of some modern progressive schools:

> Instead of presiding over it [i.e. the school] in a magisterial manner, as is generally practised in schools, he formed a code of laws with punishments annexed to each transgression. . . . He observed them strictly himself. . . . In all doubtful cases where the law was not obvious, or the offence not sufficiently proved, a jury of twelve boys was impanelled.[44]

Various kinds of buildings were used as private schools. At Bristol, there was a mathematical academy in the library building in King Street (1769); at Newcastle, Charles Hutton built his own mathematical schoolhouse in Westgate Street (*c.* 1770); at Highclere in Hampshire, the Rev. Isaac Mills had a school in his Rectory and in 1794 built new outhouses to accommodate boarders.[45] An illustration of what was in part a purpose-built private school of considerable size, with the master's house alongside it, appears in the prospectus of Mr Emblin's Academy at Leyton, Essex, in 1785 (pl. **88**). He claimed to teach the whole range of classical and modern subjects, and his picture also illustrates the spaciousness of the school grounds and the health-giving properties of a rural situation.[46]

Matters of health began to attract rather more attention towards the end of the century, especially in connection with the design and equipment of boarding schools for girls. In 1792 the Misses Parker bought a house with extensive grounds at Ashbourne (Derbs.) for use as a girls' school and went for advice to Erasmus Darwin, a doctor of medicine and Fellow of the Royal Society. In 1797 he wrote *A plan for the conduct of female education in boarding schools*,[47] a treatise in which his medical training is very apparent. He makes detailed recommendations about the best height and slope for the school desks (so as to prevent the pupils from acquiring bad postures),[48] and he also stresses the need for the girls to practise suitable exercises, such as 'swinging as they sit on cord or cushion', and 'frequent drawing up of a weight by a cord over a pulley' (to extend the spine and strengthen the muscles of the chest and arms).[49] He also has a section on the importance of proper ventilation, with such specific advice as the desirability of sawing off an inch from the top of every door and letting down the upper sashes of windows to improve the flow of air.[50] Most of Darwin's suggestions for improving posture seem to be sensible, but they were carried to excess in some girls' schools of the period. The satirical painting by Edward Bunney (1760–1848) called 'The school of deportment: an elegant establishment for young ladies' (pl. **89**) shows a great variety of activities going on—all, it may be noted, in the same room, since specialized rooms for specialized activities were still in the future.

Much work remains to be done on the smaller and more ephemeral private schools of the later eighteenth century, details of which are often given in the advertisements which appeared in provincial newspapers. For example, an examination of the pages of the *Leicester and Nottingham Journal* in the 1780s shows that there were at least ten such schools active at this time.[51] There was Mrs Loseby's school for girls and little boys in High Street, Leicester, and Mr Carrick's school in Silver Street, which in 1784 he advertised as occupying his whole house, 'properly fitted up for the accommodation of young gentlemen'. Then there was the school of William Daniel, who advertised himself as a 'writing master and accomptant' and taught 'everything requisite to form a tradesman'. Mathematical and commercial subjects were also taught by J. Watson, 'professor of penmanship from the academy in Hoxton Square, London'. There was also a boarding school run by the Rev. W. C. Newton, and one for young ladies by a Mrs Linwood, which gave attention 'not only in the plain and useful but elegant parts of education'. Another schoolmaster described his school as being 'in a very pleasant healthy situation, stand[ing] open to the fields'; another as being held in 'a commodious room . . . at the house of Mr Daniel, baker'; another as being able to accommodate a small number of boarders 'in an apartment unconnected with the public school'; and another, who 'took boarders and employed assistants', as capable of taking both boys and girls, who, he was careful to point out, would be accommodated separately.

It is clear that the great majority of private schools were too small and short-lived to pay much heed to new ways of designing and organizing schools. They provided, however, for Nonconformists as well as Anglicans, girls as well as boys, and, by offering a much wider range of subjects and introducing or reintroducing ideas such as the importance of moral training and physical education, they foreshadowed many subsequent developments in educational theory and practice. When the ideas of eighteenth-century private schoolmasters came to be 'writ large' in the following century, a radical remodelling of school buildings and internal organization came in their train.

Notes

1 Clarke, J., *Essay on the education of youth in grammar schools*, 2nd ed., Bettesworth, 1730, 190.

2 Cf. Mack, E. C., *Public schools and British opinion 1780 to 1860*, Methuen, 1938, xiiin., 52.

3 See the 'Graphic chart showing the provision of living accommodation in the colleges in relation to the number of students in Cambridge from 1550 to 1850' in R.C.H.M., *City of Cambridge*, 1959, illustrating the steep decline in the number of matriculations after 1670 and continuing at a low level throughout the eighteenth century, with a corresponding decrease in provision of new accommodation.

4 There is a useful 'Table of numbers at Eton, Winchester, Harrow and Rugby' in Austen Leigh, R. A., *Eton College Lists 1678–1790*, Eton College, 1907, 367–8.

5 Ariès, P., *Centuries of childhood*, Cape, 1962, ch. 3 ('The origins of the school class') and 4 ('The pupil's age').

6 Austen Leigh, R. A., *Eton College Lists 1678–1790, op. cit.*, and *The Eton College Register 1753–90*, Eton, 1921. I am much indebted to Mr Patrick Strong, Keeper of College Library and Collections at Eton, for further information, and permission to view the Library.

7 This was Sir John Lade, b. 1759, baronet from birth, matriculated at Oxford 1776, aged seventeen; a well-known sportsman and a friend of the Prince Regent, from whom he received a pension of £300 a year; d. 1838, having squandered all his fortune (Austen Leigh, *Register, op. cit.*, 318).

8 These were the Fraser brothers, *maximus, major, minor* and *minimus* (Austen Leigh, *Register, op. cit.*, 207).

9 Ariès, *op. cit.*, ch. 5 ('The progress of discipline').

10 Cf. Warner, Rex, *English public schools*, Collins, 1946, 18: 'These rebellions were, no doubt, largely caused by the political ferment at home and especially on the Continent; indeed in some of them the tricolour was adopted as standard: but they are remarkable too as showing how entirely at variance had become the organization of boys from the masters.' See also Mack, *op. cit.*, 79.

11 Cook, A. K., *About Winchester College*, Macmillan, 1917, 89–91.

12 Lyte, H. C. Maxwell, *Eton College*, Macmillan, 1870, 289.

13 Austen Leigh, *Lists, op. cit.*, 175.

14 Lyte, *op. cit.*, 312. The same system ruled at Eton in the early nineteenth century; see Carlisle, I, 60f.

15 Cook, *op. cit.*, 78, 507–8, 567–9.

16 Pevsner, *Buckinghamshire*, 1960, 128. Contrast Lyte, *op. cit.*, 309–10. See also R.C.H.M., *Buckinghamshire*, I, 1912, 142f.

17 For the dormitory at Westminster, see Pevsner, *London*, Penguin, 2nd ed., 1962, I, 439–40, and Carleton, J., *Westminster School*, Rupert Hart-Davis, 1965, 119–22.

18 Sargeaunt, J., *Annals of Westminster School*, Methuen, 1898, 158–9 and 190–1.

19 Cf. Mack, *op. cit.*, 34: 'By the middle of the eighteenth century the masters in most schools tacitly ceased to concern themselves with anything but instruction and permitted the moral character of the boys to develop by itself.'

20 The classical curriculum became even more 'impractical' during the eighteenth century at Eton and elsewhere; there was a general neglect of prose in favour of poetry (see Clarke, M. L., *Classical education in Britain*, Cambridge U.P., 1959, 51–7).

21 Laborde, E. D., *Harrow School*, Winchester Publications, 1948, 38–43, 69. The system of boarding was regularized in 1767 when 'dames' houses' were instituted, a system which grew out of the earlier practice of employing six dames in the town to teach elementary subjects to the younger boys at the school (p. 32).

22 The original schoolroom is fully described in Rouse, W. H. D., *A history of Rugby School*, Duckworth, 1898, 32–3.

23 *Ibid.*, 86.

24 *Ibid.*, 110.

25 *Ibid.*, 131–4.

26 Hans, N., *New trends in education in the eighteenth century*, Routledge & Kegan Paul, 1951, 18, analyses the educational careers of 3,500 men born between 1685 and 1785 whose names appear in the *Dictionary of National Biography*, and shows that 47 per cent. of them were educated at grammar schools (including the nine major schools as defined in 1864). The remaining 53 per cent. was made up as follows: educated at home or by private tutors, 27 per cent.; at private schools, 9 per cent.; at Dissenting schools and academies, 8 per cent.; at Catholic colleges, 4 per cent.; at Scottish parish schools, 4 per cent.; and 1 per cent. elsewhere.

27 Clarke, H.W., and Weech, W.N., *History of Sedbergh School*, Sedbergh, 1925, 57–8. See also *V.C.H., Yorkshire*, I, 1907, 466–71. The sixty-two books in Sedbergh School library in 1707 are listed in *Early Yorkshire Schools*, ed. Leach, A.F., Yorks. Archaeological Society, XXXIII, 1903, 438–9. See also Fulford, R., 'The Sedbergh School Library' in *Country Life*, 10 July 1958. I am indebted to the present School Librarian for further information.

28 Elliott, B., *History of Kibworth Beauchamp Grammar School* (1957), 33–6, 40. See also *V.C.H., Leicestershire*, V, 1964, 175–7, which states that the two lower storeys of the headmaster's house are original, but a third storey and new south front were added in *c.* 1836. This school is now a 'Leicestershire Plan' High School, the grammar school having moved to Oadby, near Leicester, in 1964.

29 *C.C.R.*, VIII, 1823, 743–4. See also *V.C.H.*, *Yorkshire, North Riding*, II, 1923, 372, where the frontage is given as 94 feet, with the wings 50 feet apart, projecting 4 feet in front, but much more at the back, so making an H plan. Pevsner, *North Riding*, 1966, calls it an 'extraordinarily generous building'. See also *Catalogue of the interesting Library of the Free School of Kirkleatham*, Christie, Manson & Woods sale, November 1948. I am grateful to the Headmaster of the Sir William Turner School at Redcar and to the County Archivist, Northallerton, for further information.

30 *C.C.R.*, XXXII, 1837, 239–52. See also Little, B., *The Story of Lucton School*, Bristol: Arrowsmith, 1958, 7–19, and R.C.H.M., *Herefordshire*, III, 1934, 137–8. I am grateful to the Headmaster, Mr T. K. Vivian, for further details.

31 *C.C.R.*, XVII, 1827, 223–31. See also *V.C.H.*, *Derbyshire*, II, 1907, 267–9, and Pevsner, *Derbyshire*, 1953, 209. I am grateful to the Derbyshire County Archivist for further information, to the Clerk to the Trustees for permission to view the buildings and to Dr P. Eden for drawing my attention to them.

32 Lawson, J., *A town grammar school through six centuries*, Oxford U.P., 1963, 144–54.

33 Lyte, *op. cit.*, 370.

34 Mumford, A. A., *The Manchester Grammar School*, Longmans, 1919, 206 and *passim*.

35 Quoted in Robson, D., *Some aspects of education in Cheshire in the eighteenth century*, Manchester: Chetham Society, 1966, 55.

36 *Report of the Schools Inquiry Commission*, 1868, VIII, 290–1. At this date French and German were also being taught. It is possible that division into classrooms was also a later feature.

37 Clarke, *op. cit.*, 188, 193.

38 *Ibid.*, 204–7. He also wrote prophetically of private boarding schools: 'If such schools should once become fashionable, we should soon see a numerous race of tutors start up in the world.'

39 Waugh, W. T., *A history of Fulneck School*, Leeds: Jackson, 1909, 19. A school time-table of 1782 shows that there were two forms in the boys' school: the upper form learnt Latin, Greek, German, ancient history, geography and Euclid; the lower form Latin, but no Greek or German (*ibid.*, 25).

40 Reprinted in Pritchard, F. C., *Methodist secondary education*, Epworth Press, 1949, 324–8. Pritchard notes (p. 59) that the curriculum at Kingswood 'reveals a closer affinity to Dissenting academies than to the public and grammar schools'. The Dissenting academies are excluded from the present study because they normally recruited at fifteen, sixteen or seventeen, i.e. they overlapped with the top forms of the grammar schools, but were mainly institutions of university type. (See McLachlan, H., *English education under the Test Acts*, Manchester U.P., 1931, 26.) Wesley himself had gone to school at Charterhouse.

41 The best account of the original buildings is in *The history of Kingswood School* by Three Old Boys, Kelly, 1898, 18–23 (picture facing p. 20). Wesley's school was called 'New House' to distinguish it from the elementary school, which lasted from 1739 to 1803.

42 Published by Routledge & Kegan Paul, 2nd impression, 1966.

43 There is an undated copy (no publisher given) in the library of Birmingham University School of Education. Quotations are from pp. 4, 7, 22, 23, and 29 of this copy.

44 From 'An Account of the Rev. Mr Gilpin', in Gilpin, W., *Memoirs of Dr Richard Gilpin*, Quaritch, 1879, quoted in Templeman, W. D., *The life and work of William Gilpin*, Urbana, Illinois, 1939, 61. See also Stewart, W. A. C., and McCann, W. P., *The educational innovators 1750–1880*, Macmillan, 1967, 3–23.

45 Hans, *op. cit.*, 100, 109, 133.

46 See the two articles on this building by Miss M. L. Savell in *The Walthamstow Guardian* (2 and 9 July 1965). She shows that the 'Academy' occupied a house first leased to a schoolmaster in 1765; it continued as a school until 1821 and was demolished in 1928. In his advertisement of 1785 Mr Emblin stated: 'The School and dancing-rooms (designedly built for those purpose[s]) are spacious and well-constructed, the bed-rooms are numerous, large and airy, the gardens and fields are well inclosed, and the play-ground extensive and dry; in short, neither pains nor expence have been spared to render the whole as commodious and compleat as possible.'

47 Quotations are from the first edition published by J. Drewry, Derby, 1797.

48 *Ibid.*, 15–16. The desks should be 16 inches broad, with a $3\frac{1}{2}$-inch slope, and stand 2 feet 8 inches from the floor.

49 *Ibid.*, 68–70.

50 Ibid., 70–5.

51 I owe the details in this paragraph to Mr E. J. W. Venable, 'Education in Leicester 1780–1816' (unpublished M.Ed. thesis, Leicester, 1969), 99f.

Seven

Schools for the poor in the eighteenth century

I

The eighteenth century has been characterized as the era of the 'charity school movement'.[1] In fact, there is considerable ambiguity in this phrase, since schools of many types and periods were in a sense charity schools, while the principle of public subscription in order to finance a school was not an invention of the eighteenth century,[2] nor were other features of 'charity schools', such as the practice of providing clothes for the children or apprenticing them when they left school. There is also evidence to suggest that the S.P.C.K., which popularized the phrase 'charity school'—and gave it a special meaning—early in the eighteenth century, included in their lists of schools many which had originated at an earlier date, or which were not of the catechetical type which they advocated.[3] The customary view of the early eighteenth century as the first great period of elementary-school expansion does not take sufficiently into account the earlier rise of the parish schools, referred to in an earlier chapter, and many of these schools continued throughout the seventeenth century and into the eighteenth.

There can, however, be no doubt that the eighteenth century—particularly the first quarter of it—saw a renewed interest in the elementary education of the poor and a marked expansion of the funds available to it—an expansion which also found expression in new endowments for such traditional purposes as providing bread, clothing and money for the poor and almshouses for the aged.[4] So far as education was concerned, there was after 1700 a declining demand for instruction in the classical languages and there were also, as we shall see, pressing economic and social reasons for concentrating on making extra provision for the elementary education of the poor, particularly in the large towns. Certainly, when we turn to examine the new school buildings of the eighteenth century, we find that most surviving examples are in fact English or elementary schools, rather than grammar schools of the traditional type, though it will be recalled that even during the seventeenth century many local schools were teaching English as well as classical subjects.

If, for example, we consider the school buildings of the eighteenth century which survive in Northamptonshire we find that, while no grammar-school building of this

Date	*Place*	*Description*
1705	Ashton, near Oundle	Small room attached to church, now a vestry; former schoolroom of Creed's Charity; fifteen children taught reading, writing and knitting.
1714	Finedon, Church Street	Founded by subscription. About twenty girls educated, maintained and clothed, partly from the profits of spinning. Now a private house of seven bays and two storeys.
1717–25	Lowick, Drayton Road	For twenty poor children, by will of Sir J. Germain and deed of Lady E. Germain. (Coat of arms over door.) Not in Pevsner.
1749	King's Cliffe, Bridge Street (north side)	Master's house, boys' school and almshouses. (Described later in chapter.)
1752–4	King's Cliffe, Bridge Street (south side)	Mistress's house (including girls' school) and almshouses. (Described later in chapter; not in Pevsner.)
1752	Ecton	Small cottage with inscription: 'A School for Poor Children built by John Palmer MDCCLII.' Not in *C.C.R.* (not endowed?).
1775	Hanging Houghton, near Lamport	Three-bay, two-storeyed cottage, now occupied by the teacher of the village school. Inscription over door reads: 'This Charity School founded & endowed by the will of Sir Edmund Isham Bart. for the Boys and Girls of Lamport & Houghton. MDCCLXXV.' Originally housed the master, mistress and about thirty children.
1792?	Yelvertoft	Brick schoolroom with teacher's house attached. Sun-dial has date 1792. Presumably the free school for twenty children established by subscription in 1713–20. Not in Pevsner.
1795	Culworth	Founded by deed of M. and F. Rich, 1795. About seventy children of poor inhabitants were attending in 1825. Five bays with four upper windows and a cupola.

date exists, there are a number of elementary schools built for the poor of the neighbourhood, as shown in the list on the opposite page.[5]

Before looking more generally at surviving elementary-school buildings of this period, it is necessary to give a brief outline of the important social and economic changes which stimulated interest in the education of the poor. New economic pressures were strongest in the large towns, but to some extent they affected the country as a whole. In London it has been shown that the problem of poverty received particular attention in the late seventeenth and early eighteenth centuries, for this was a time of rapid physical expansion, the growth of service industries and much shifting of occupations.[6] Orphans and foundlings were so numerous that special measures had to be adopted, and indeed we find that educational provision and the relief of poverty were very much bound up with each other. Several of the 'charity schools' of this period were classed with workhouses in contemporary lists, and there was a renewed emphasis, not only on preparing children for apprenticeships, but also on the provision of boarding education in 'hospital' schools. The motive force was a mixture of piety, fear and self-interest and found expression in what has aptly been called the 'old philanthropy, inherited by the early eighteenth century from the seventeenth' and 'dominated by fears of starvation and vagrancy. . . . Its ideal was the child who was self-supporting and inured to labour at the earliest possible age.'[7] It was not until later in the eighteenth century, under the influence of Methodism and Whig-Utilitarianism that a new philanthropy was born, more suited to the new economic conditions which industrial changes were bringing about.[8]

The outlook of the 'old philanthropy' in relation to education is well illustrated in *An account of the methods whereby the charity-schools have been erected and managed*, issued by the S.P.C.K. in 1705.[9] This publication was chiefly intended to encourage further gifts for the founding of schools of a special type. It begins as follows:

> It is manifest that a Christian and useful education of the children of the poor is absolutely necessary to their piety, virtue and honest livelihood. It is also plain and evident that piety, virtue and an honest way of living are not only of absolute necessity to their happiness both here and hereafter, but are necessary also to the ease and security of all other people whatsoever: in as much as there is no body but may stand in need of their help or be liable to receive injuries from them.

It goes on to define a charity school as one designed 'for the education of poor children in the knowledge and practice of the Christian religion, as professed and taught in the Church of England'. Accordingly, the 'chief business' of the master of such a school must be 'to instruct the children . . . in the church catechism',[10] and particular attention should be paid to 'the manners and behaviour of the poor children'. As for the subjects of instruction, the boys should be taught reading, writing and arithmetic 'to fit them for services or apprentices', while the girls should learn to read and 'generally to knit their stockings and gloves, to mark, sew, make and mend their clothes', with some of them learning to write and spin. There is also a reference to the desirability of employing the children on paid work, such as making shoes, knitting and spinning, so that their earnings could pay for their food and lodging, especially in hospital (i.e. boarding) schools; indeed, it is recommended that the pauper children from the workhouse should where possible join with the charity-school children for this purpose. While in general such attempts to combine education and manual employment—imitated in many provincial schools as well as in London—were not successful,[11] the attempts themselves illustrate the whole rationale which underlay the setting up of these schools.

Another striking feature of the eighteenth-century schools for the poor was the greater social class differentiation which they reflected.[12] The parish schools, which earlier seem in some places to have taught the children of the squire as well as the ploughman, were now less often regarded as preparatory to the local grammar school, and in many places they appear to have concentrated on teaching a very limited elementary curriculum to the poorer classes.[13] The separation of the children of the poor was strikingly illustrated in the arrangements which were frequently made for their attendance at church on Sundays. At Lucton School, referred to in our previous chapter, the founder, though providing for all social classes in his school, was also anxious to maintain social distinctions in their public worship. His will of 1711 gave the most elaborate instructions about the seats to be erected in the adjoining Anglican chapel. There must be, he stated,

> one pew or seat of five feet broad and six feet deep for the schoolmaster . . . and his family; one other pew or seat of about three feet broad and six feet deep for the usher and writing master . . .; one other pew or seat adjoining to it six feet square for boarders and gentlemen's children . . .; and at the west end of the chapel another pew of six feet and six inches deep, with three seats therein for all the charity and other children of the said parish of Lucton to sit in.[14]

Pews were a source of income, and in many churches of this period those who could not afford sittings were 'relegated to galleries, or either sat on stools or stood in the aisles', write the leading authorities on the arrangement of church interiors.[15] They add that 'the period [i.e. the eighteenth century] was not good in its provision for seats for children. Usually they were placed in aisles or galleries, or else if there was no Communion in the chancel.' They give a number of examples of seating arrangements for children, often from the local school, which show that religious conformity was certainly insisted on, but that the children of the poor invariably occupied a separate and subordinate position.[16] Sometimes the figure of a schoolchild was placed near the poor-box in the church to encourage donations to a local school (there are surviving examples in St Nicholas's Church at Newbury in Berkshire, and at Maidstone Museum in Kent).[17] It may also be noted that there is some evidence to suggest that during this period fresh efforts were made to prevent day schools from being held in church buildings,[18] a practice of considerable antiquity to which reference was made in ch. 3.

One other general feature worthy of comment is the increased provision made for the elementary education of girls, though it is likely that they had been admitted to the parish schools in the previous century. Again, there was a greater degree of differentiation in that separate schoolrooms seem to have been provided for them wherever the numbers were sufficient (for an example of 1747, cf. pl. **101**).[19] Separate provision for girls had, it is true, been made earlier, as we saw, for example, at Red Maids' School, Bristol (1634), and at Christ's Hospital, but the separation now often became more complete. Thus it will be recalled that the younger boys and girls of Christ's Hospital had been transferred to three towns in Hertfordshire towards the end of the seventeenth century and that the Hertford premises had been rebuilt in 1695. The older girls, who remained in London, dined in their own quarters after 1703 and no longer attended the boys' writing school after 1710. Then in 1776 all the girls were transferred to Hertford, though the younger boys continued to use the school there until 1902. The long brick building which now faces Fore Street in Hertford is the new girls' school of 1778, and it still contains its original figures of Bluecoat girls (pl. **102**).[20]

II

A number of important charity-school buildings of this period have survived in London, and are well worth examining for the further light which they throw on the organization of schools of this type. A good early example is the Blue Coat School in Caxton Street, Westminster (in the parish of St Margaret's), which was established by voluntary subscriptions in 1688 and met in hired premises until it moved to a specially-designed building in 1709. The number of pupils for whom the school was originally built is uncertain but in 1819 there were fifty-two boys and thirty-four girls aged from seven to fourteen. An additional twenty children were taught in the school from the proceeds of a separate charity. All were taught reading, writing and the first four rules of arithmetic, and in addition the girls learnt knitting, needlework and household work. The children were examined every Sunday evening in the presence of the governors and the general public. The master and mistress had the rent-free use of a house and were paid extra for teaching psalmody, collecting subscriptions and cutting out the children's clothes.[21]

The school building of 1709 (pl. **90**) has been described as 'an historic record of great value in a quarter of London where relatively few structures of its age remain'.[22] It is built of brick, and each elevation is divided into three vertical divisions by pilasters. Above the entrance doorway in Caxton Street is the figure of a scholar in the dress of the period, while on the south side is a painting of a scholar in a recessed niche. The top windows do not light an upper floor, as one might expect, but provide clerestory lighting to the main room, which is built over a basement floor. The school is in fact a one-apartment structure measuring internally 42 by 30 feet and about 19 feet high. The interior view (pl. **91**) shows that the walls are panelled to a height of 7 feet and that a wooden entablature runs round the room at two-thirds of its height. About 4 feet from the north wall are four fluted wooden columns which support the original clock chamber. A modern (architectural) authority describes the interior as 'beautifully proportioned and in every way attractive and suited to the purposes for which it was built'.[23] While agreeing with the first part of this statement, one wonders whether, from the purely educational point of view, this room was as suitable as this writer suggests. Do we not have here a notable example of 'prestige building' designed to show off the wealth and standing of the patrons, rather than being adapted to the needs of children? This building was still in use as a school (part of the Christchurch, Caxton Street, public elementary school) in 1926. It later ceased to be used for educational purposes and was purchased by the National Trust in 1954. In the following year, it was opened to the public as the membership department of the Trust.[24]

When it was intended to board children as well as teach them, a more elaborate building was required, and a good surviving example is the Grey Coat Hospital School, also in St Margaret's parish, Westminster, and now a girls' secondary school. The building was erected early in the eighteenth century in what is now Greycoat Place, but it was considerably damaged in the Second World War; it was restored in 'a twentieth-century version of the Queen Anne style',[25] though the two wooden statues of a charity boy and girl on the front are original (pl. **92**). Fortunately, pre-war architectural evidence is available[26] and a good deal is also known about the original layout of the building, for the school is exceptionally well provided with documentary records.[27] It began as a day school in a rented house in 1698, and the reasons for establishing it were set out in the first minute book as follows:

> Several of the inhabitants of the parish of St Margaret, Westminster, having taken into their serious consideration the great misery that the poor children of the said parish do generally suffer, by reason of their idle and licentious education; their nurses, or those that provide for them, generally suffering, if not encouraging, them to wander about and beg, by which means and the evil customs and habits they contract thereby, they become (for the most part) the curse and trouble of all places where they live, and often by their wicked actions are brought to shameful untimely death and destruction. To prevent the like miseries for the future . . . the persons hereafter named . . . did think it proper and convenient to erect a free school in the said parish, where 40 of the greatest objects of charity they could find should from time to time be educated in sober and virtuous principles and instructed in the Christian religion. . . . [Six of the eight men who signed this were Westminster tradesmen.][28]

The scheme for the school stated that 'it is absolutely necessary that the scholars be kept under good discipline and due obedience and subjection'; they were to be taught from 6 to 11 a.m. and 1 to 6 p.m. in summer and 8 to 11 a.m. and 1 to 4 p.m. in winter and were obliged to attend church twice on Sundays as well as joining in daily prayers in the schoolroom, where special attention was also to be given to learning the Catechism.[29] Three years later it was decided to move to a new building where the children could be boarded. The idea of a hospital or boarding school was not, of course, a new one: several earlier examples have already been mentioned and there were others during the seventeenth century, as, for example, Bruton Hospital School, Somerset (1638) and Chetham's Hospital, Manchester (1651). But there were special reasons for adopting this type of education in Westminster in the early eighteenth century, for it was soon found to be impossible to ensure regular attendance without making provision for boarding. Accordingly, the Trustees agreed to take over the Elizabethan workhouse in Tothills Field, which had become redundant when a new workhouse was opened in 1700,

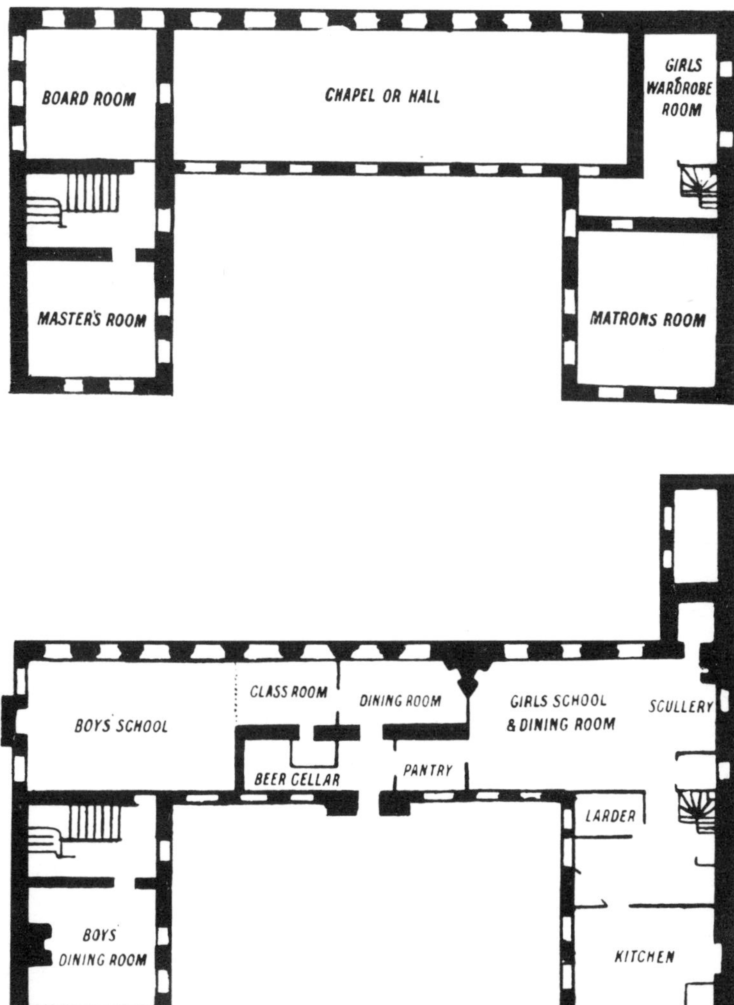

Figure 20 Grey Coat Hospital, Westminster, 1701, ground and first-floor plans. (The second floor consisted entirely of dormitories.)

and to fit it out as a 'hospital' for seventy children, twenty of whom should be nominated by the overseers of the poor.[30] The children were 'set on work', but the elementary subjects were also taught, and later the practical work element disappeared. The old workhouse was virtually rebuilt in 1701 and the hospital school was granted a charter by Queen Anne in 1706; a mathematical school, which trained boys for the sea, was added in 1739. By 1785 there were sixty boys and thirty girls on the roll and by 1819, owing to continued benefactions, the school had an annual income of over £2,000.[31]

The original Queen Anne building was added to during the nineteenth century and restored after the Second World War, but the original plan has been reconstructed (see fig. 20). This shows a half-H-shaped building, with separate schoolrooms and dining-rooms for the boys and girls on the ground floor. The master and matron were accommodated on the first floor, where there were also the Governors' board-room and a large room called the 'Hall-Room', which occupied the whole of the middle block and extended to the roof. In 1738 this room was furnished with 'two Brass Chandeliers, a large Bible and Common Prayer Book, and small Bible in the Boy's [? Boys'] Desk, [and] four long Tables with Benches round them'. This room was used only for prayers until early in the nineteenth century, when it came to be used also as a refectory, the boys' dining-room having been converted into a wash-place (the children had previously washed in a trough in front of the building).[32] By 1911, when the photograph reproduced as pl. **93** was taken, the hall seems to have been used for ordinary teaching purposes. The rest of the original accommodation consisted of the children's dormitories (called 'wards', as in medical hospitals) in the wings on the second floor.

Three other London schools merit a brief mention, and two of them furnish early evidence of the tendency for the providers of schools in London—because of the shortage of land in some parts—to 'build upwards'. The first of these, the charity school at Kensington, was built in 1713, but was demolished to make way for Kensington Town Hall in 1878. A water-colour painting of 1871 has, however, survived (pl. **94**), showing a three-and-a-half-storey building with statues of a charity boy and girl placed, unusually, on the corners of the central projection. The architect was Nicholas Hawksmoor, who at that time was Clerk of Works at Kensington Palace (some early sources mistakenly attribute it to Vanbrugh). In 1734 there were fifty day-pupils at the school (thirty boys and twenty girls) but in 1786 it was converted into a hospital school for twenty boys and ten girls. In 1809 it became a day school once more, and a few years later two public houses near the school were converted, so that in 1819 there were no less than 130 boys and 100 girls in attendance. A new school was built in 1875 and continues today as St Mary Abbots School, a voluntary primary school under the Inner London Education Authority.[33] Although the building with which we are here concerned has disappeared, the figures of the boy and girl are preserved on the present school building. A sketch plan of the 1713 building also survives and is reproduced as pl. **95**. The ground floor consisted of a number of rooms of unknown purpose (perhaps originally for the master and mistress, who, however, moved into a house next to the school in 1721). The girls' schoolroom (an interior sketch of which, showing an elaborate mantel-piece with small figures of charity children, has also been preserved) was presumably on the first floor, with the boys' schoolroom above.

Our second example, which still survives, is the charity school in St Mary's Church Street, Rotherhithe, the inscription on which reads: 'Free school founded by Peter Hill and Robert Bell 1613. Charity school instituted 1742. Removed here 1797. Supported by voluntary contributions.' The building itself (pl. **96**) was almost certainly built as a private house earlier in the eighteenth century, and the figures of charity children on the front were probably removed from the earlier charity school.[34] (They were taken down during the Second World War for safe-keeping and close-up photographs were taken which are reproduced as pls. **97** and **98**.) In 1820 there were 200 children attending the school, but it ceased to be used as a school many years ago.

The only other surviving charity-school building in London of the early eighteenth century known to me is also a large one. This is St Andrew's School in Hatton Garden, Holborn, founded by subscription in 1696.[35] A partially-constructed chapel was given to the school by the Bishop of Ely in about 1721, and the building was completed as a school by subscription (pl. **99**).[36] In 1819 it housed ninety-five boys and ninety-five girls, eighteen of whom were boarders. Its interior was gutted in the Second World War, and the building was purchased by a private firm in about 1950 and is used for storage purposes.

Outside London, charity-school buildings on the scale of those described above seem to have been comparatively rare. A notable exception is the Blue Coat School at Liverpool, which survives today in altered form as Bluecoat Chambers. Somewhat similar social and economic factors were operating in Liverpool at the beginning of the eighteenth century as in contemporary London, for the Blue Coat School was founded in 1708 when Liverpool was just coming into prominence as a major port.[37] As in the case of the Grey Coat School at Westminster, the Liverpool school began as a day school, with fifty children taught and clothed by the charity, but fed and housed by their parents. But when in 1714 Bryan Blundell, a retired master mariner, was elected Treasurer, he soon realized that boarding was essential. He wrote:

> In a little time, I saw some of the children begging about the streets, their parents being so poor as not to have bread for them, which gave me great concern, insomuch that I thought to use my best endeavours to make provision for them, so as to take them wholly from their parents, which I hoped might be promoted by a subscription. I therefore got an instrument drawn out for that purpose on parchment, went about with it to most persons of ability and many subscribed handsomely. On the strength of which I went to work and got the present charity school built, which has cost between two and three thousand pounds and was finished in 1718, at which time I gave for the encouragement of the charity £750, being a tenth part of what it pleased God to bless me with.[38]

The parchment about which Blundell writes[39] was based on the standard S.P.C.K. form of subscription and makes the usual reference to the 'profaneness and debauchery' of 'the poorer sort', arising from their 'gross ignorance of the Christian religion'; it claims that 'the charity schools erected in the several parts of this kingdom have abundantly improved the morals of poor children'. Hence the need for funds 'for finding them with meat, drink, apparel and lodging, and teaching poor children in the said school to read and write, and arithmetic, and instructing them in the knowledge and practice of the Christian religion as professed and taught in the Church of England'. The foundation stone of the new buildings had been laid in 1716; they were opened in 1717 and completed in 1725. At first the number of boys and girls boarded at the school was about fifty, but later the building was extended so that the number on roll rose to 200 by 1763 and 280 by 1790.[40] Architecturally, the result was impressive (see pl. **100**), and followed the half-H-shaped plan adopted at the Grey Coat Hospital.

The subsequent history of the Liverpool Bluecoat building is an interesting one. The school moved in 1906 to larger premises in Wavertree, where it continues today as a voluntary aided school for boys. The original building was bought by Lord Leverhulme, who planned to make it a centre for the arts, but this plan failed on his death in 1925. Two years later, as a result of a public appeal, the building was purchased for a newly-formed Bluecoat Society of Arts. The building was severely damaged by bombing in 1941, but was restored and reopened in 1951. Bluecoat Chambers, as it is now called, houses some twenty working artists, ten cultural societies and four firms of architects.[41]

There is one other feature of the original scheme for the Liverpool school which is worthy of comment, since it well illustrates the shift of emphasis which took place in the education of poor children towards the end of the eighteenth century. It is clear that the children were engaged in manual labour for part of their time, and in 1765 the trustees arranged for the boys to work in a stocking manufactory near the school; this was given up in 1789, but in the following year 200 of the children were engaged in pin-making, which lasted until 1802, when it was stopped because it was deemed to be detrimental to their health. From that date onwards the whole of the children's time was given over to the usual elementary-school subjects.[42] The historian of the English poor in the eighteenth century has noted that after about 1775 a new sympathy for the poor became apparent and 'by the end of the century a complete revolution had taken place in men's thoughts with regard to the poor'.[43] Similarly, in London 'the spirit of the time was changed since the founders of the charity-schools . . . had been intent on giving children a carefully limited training which should fit them for menial services'.[44]

These changes in attitude were foreshadowed in the educational work of the Society of Friends, some of whose schools of eighteenth-century origin have survived down to our own time. The oldest Quaker foundation is the school at Saffron Walden (Essex), which began as a workhouse-school in Clerkenwell, London, in 1702 (it moved to Islington in 1786, to Croydon in 1825 and to its present site in Saffron Walden in 1879).[45] The founders of the school were very much aware of the contemporary problem of poverty to which reference has already been made. In 1695 John Bellers, the principal Quaker behind the setting up of the school, published *Proposals for raising a colledge of industry of all useful trades and husbandry* which suggested that colonies of poor people (men, women and children) should be founded all over England to relieve the pressing problems of poverty. In 1702 the Friends obtained a lease of a workhouse in Clerkenwell, the buildings of which formed three sides of a quadrangle—a favourite plan both for workhouses and hospital schools, as we have seen at the Grey Coat Hospital at Westminster and the Blue Coat School at Liverpool. (The same plan was followed by Thomas Coram for his foundling hospital in London in 1739[46] and later for the foundling hospital at Ackworth.) By 1739 there were in the Clerkenwell building eighteen old men and women, forty boys and twenty girls. Only two hours' schooling a day were given to the children, who spent most of their time on trade occupations (for, as Bellers said, 'The body requires more hands and legs to provide and support it, than heads to direct it').[47]

After 1774, however, a new approach was adopted. There was greater stress on book-learning, and the need was seen for a genuine technical education which related manual occupations more closely to the careers likely to be taken up by the children, rather than merely seeking to produce funds for the maintenance of the establishment. When in 1786 the move to Islington took place, the children were separated from the old people and more time was given to school-work, which was divided into the five activities of spelling, grammar, reading, arithmetic and writing.[48]

So too at the well-known Quaker school at Ackworth, near Pontefract (Yorks.), there was much less stress on manual work. In 1779 the Friends took over a foundling hospital which had been built in 1758 by the Governors of the London Foundling Hospital, who also established branch hospitals at Chester, Shrewsbury and Westerham (Kent).[49] The number of foundling children at Ackworth had at one time risen to 800, most of whom were employed in a woollen manufactory established in the hospital. These children were mainly brought from London, but later the children at Chester and Shrewsbury were transferred to Ackworth. (The foundling hospital at Shrewsbury was closed in 1773, but was taken over by Shrewsbury School in 1882, and still forms part of its buildings.)[50] Partly because of a possible improvement in social conditions and partly because of the economic failure of the working schools generally, the foundling hospital at Ackworth was itself closed, and it was at this point that the Society of Friends decided to make substantial provision for the children of its poorer members by adapting the premises for their use.

The buildings at Ackworth, which are still used by the school, were on a grand scale (see pl. **103**). In the words of a contemporary writer, 'the buildings were so strong and well constructed that they might be converted into a palace for a nabob or a barrack for a regiment'. They were advertised for sale with 127 acres of ground, and described as suitable for 'a convenient dwelling house for a very large family, an academy or manufactory'.[51] The plan made at this time (pl. **104**) shows the three main buildings joined by colonnades. The central block consisted of a hall in the middle (40 by 26 feet), with two long rooms on each side (70 by 24 feet); above was an attic storey 184 feet long, divided into three rooms, and behind was a row of eight smaller rooms, with cellars below and kitchens, laundry, cowhouse, barns, bakehouse, brewhouse and stables built around yards at each end. The west and east wings were each 140 feet long and 44 feet wide.

As in the case of the Moravian school at Fulneck and the Methodist school at Kingswood described in the last chapter, it was felt to be essential to concentrate Quaker children in a boarding school if they were to receive a true education according to the precepts of their parents' faith, and this applied particularly to the children of those 'not in affluence', for whom very few Quaker schools existed. The education provided at Ackworth was essentially an elementary one—Latin was not introduced until 1816[52]—and the intention was that the children should later go as apprentices to more affluent Quaker families. The girls were taught in the rooms in the west wing, and their dormitories were on the first floor above. The boys had their first schoolroom in the central block, where the boys' and girls' dining-rooms were also situated. The boys' dormitories were in the east wing over the ground-floor rooms, which also seem to have been used by the boys.[53] A *Report on the state of Ackworth school, 1780,* tells us that there were 190 boys and 119 girls at the school, taught by five schoolmasters and three schoolmistresses (a pupil/teacher ratio of 38/1).[54] In 1783 the total number of children was limited to 300 and the normal age of admission was raised to nine.

We can obtain some idea of the internal organization of the school from the regulations of 1785,[55] which stated that the boys should be divided into four classes under the care of four masters, two of whom taught reading and two writing and arithmetic. There were also twelve boys nominated as monitors 'to assist the masters in the business of the school'—a practice long established in the grammar schools, as we saw in a previous chapter, and probably followed in most of the larger elementary schools of the period. The girls were taught reading, sewing, knitting and spinning, and 'a proper number' of them were to be sent to one of the masters for instruction in writing and arithmetic. In this way a sound and (for the time) well-balanced elementary curriculum was taught, and it also appears that the excessive hardships suffered by some children in hospital schools during this period were avoided.[56]

III

Outside the large towns and the rather exceptional foundation at Ackworth, the schools for the poor in the eighteenth century were usually small in size and housed in modest buildings with few architectural embellishments. It may be that there was less stress on catechizing and discipline in the smaller country schools, but it still seems to be true that educational provision often formed only a part of a more general movement concerned with the problems of poverty. Thus, for example, the link between schools and almshouses for old people, which we have seen was a traditional one, now seems to have become more general, and the architectural integration which we noticed in a previous chapter becomes much more common. There are two excellent examples at Frome in Somerset, though only one of the original buildings has survived. These were the Blue Coat School with an almshouse for old women (now called 'Blue House', pl. **105**), described further below, and the Keyford Hospital, which was founded for forty girls and twenty old men by Richard Stevens, built in 1798–1803 and demolished only a few years ago (pl. **106**).[57] No plan of the Keyford Hospital exists, but it appears from the photograph that the girls occupied one half of the building (and had their own entrance), and the old men the other half.

The 'Blue House' at Frome was originally founded as an almshouse in 1644, but it

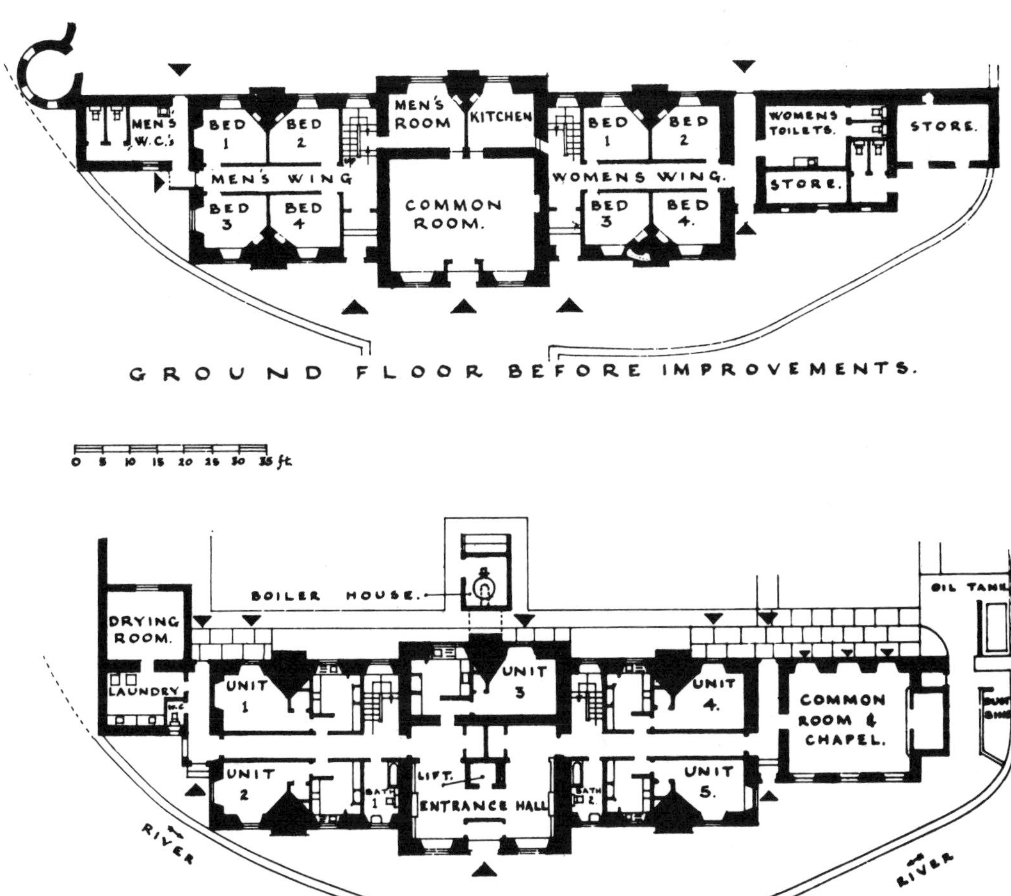

Figure 21 Frome, Bluecoat School and almshouses converted to old people's flats, before and after conversion. (The original schoolroom was in the centre, shown above as the common room, now the entrance hall.)

was rebuilt in 1728 to accommodate a charity school for twenty (later thirty-seven) boys in the central part, with a south wing occupied by fourteen old women, and a north wing, built later, for another seventeen old women. The dual purpose for which the building was designed is also apparent from the figure of a charity boy in the pediment over the door and the statue of a charity woman in a niche above. The boys' school was closed in 1921, and the whole of the building was used by old people, with men in one wing and women in the other. Then in 1964 the entire building was renovated (see fig. 21). The former schoolroom/common-room has been converted into an entrance hall, with a lift to the first and second floors, and a new common-room and chapel have been formed in the south wing. Each old person now occupies what were originally rooms for two, a practice recently adopted in several other places (e.g. in the almshouses at Cottesbrooke and King's Cliffe in Northamptonshire). It is indeed pleasing to see old buildings like this modernized to serve a present need, and one wholly in conformity with the spirit of the original foundation.[58]

An interesting complex of eighteenth-century buildings devoted to charitable purposes, including education, survives in Bridge Street (formerly School Hill) at King's Cliffe, Northamptonshire (see fig. 22). They owe their existence to the generosity of a Mrs Elizabeth Hutcheson and the Rev. William Law, the author of the classic devotional work, *A serious call to a devout and holy life* (1728), who in 1740 retired to the village

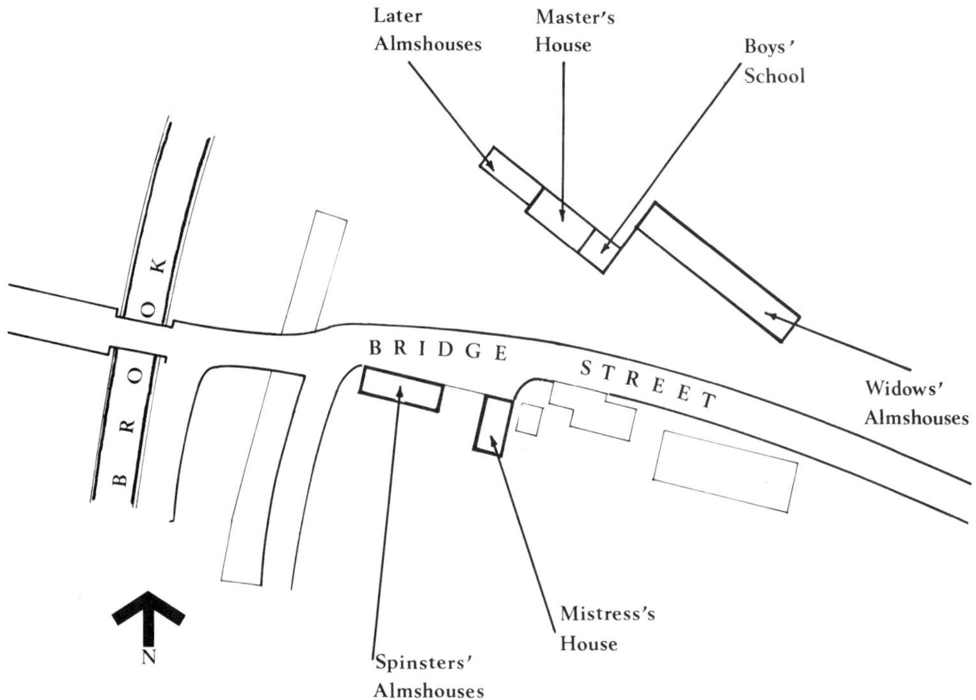

Figure 22 King's Cliffe, sketch-map showing position of buildings associated with William Law. (The girls' school was on the first floor of the mistress's house.)

where he was born.[59] Elizabeth Hutcheson, a wealthy disciple of William Law, purchased a house (probably built in the previous century) on the north side of what is now Bridge Street and converted it into a dwelling-house for the master of a school which she had founded for eighteen boys in 1745. Soon afterwards she built a separate school for them alongside the master's house and, adjoining the school to the east, a row of almshouses for four poor widows. Both the school and the almshouses have inscriptions dated 1749, and three years later the master was made responsible for looking after William Law's collection of books,[60] which was kept in the master's house. Pl. **107** shows the boys' school and the master's house, over the door of which is a sun-dial and the inscription: 'Books of Piety are here lent to any Persons of this or ye Neighbouring Towns' (pl. **108**). Law's library of books is still kept in the house, which continues to be occupied by a schoolmaster; the school itself is used only occasionally for meetings, though the interior still contains the master's desk and wall seats. The four almshouses have been converted into flats for two aged widows.

On the south side of Bridge Street are the buildings for which William Law was directly responsible. He had set up a school for fourteen poor girls in 1727, and in 1752 he erected a new building, with the inscription 'Charitati sacrum', to house both the girls and their mistress. The mistress was accommodated in two rooms on the ground floor, and the girls' schoolroom, measuring 20 by 12 feet, was on the first floor. Since the teacher occupied the same building as the girls, Law made a rule that only a single woman could occupy the position; she was not allowed to admit any other than foundation scholars and, while the girls were to be 'kept continually at some sort of work useful to them and their parents', he insisted that 'no spinning wheel is to be brought into the school' (for this was during the period when manual work was widely adopted in charity schools).[61] The original staircase and wall panelling in the schoolroom survive, though a new partition was inserted when the school was closed and the first floor converted into bedrooms towards the end of the last century. This building is still known as 'The Teacher's House' and is now occupied by two women teachers.[62] Immediately to the west of this building, Law built almshouses for use by two spinsters or widows (there is a Latin inscription on the building to this effect, dated 1754) and they are still so used. Law died in 1761 and Mrs Hutcheson in 1781, but the charitable trust which they founded has survived, and continues to serve a very useful purpose.

Apart from groups of buildings associating schools and almshouses, the most elaborate surviving charity-school buildings are in those places where an eighteenth-century school has been extended—sometimes several times—to keep pace with the growing school population. A good example, still in use as a school, is at Shinfield, Berkshire (pl. **110**). The original charity school was built in 1707 by Richard Piggott or Piggatt, citizen and cutler of London, for teaching twenty poor children 'reading, writing, accounts, singing psalms, the Church catechism and good manners'. It still stands on School Green, with an extension of 1860 to the north (on the right of the photograph) and another of 1889 to the south. Further buildings, including several prefabricated classrooms, have been added since the war, and in 1968 the school had 300 infants and juniors on the roll.[63]

Another interesting group of buildings, only recently abandoned as a school, is in Camp Road, Wimbledon, Surrey, on the edge of the Common. The school was supported entirely by voluntary subscriptions, and the subscribers, having noted 'the daily appearance of numerous poor children in the parish of Wimbledon', referred to the need

> for the instruction of these children in the first rudiments of reading and writing, so that they may be able to read the Bible or any other religious book and to understand any common written paper, or direction in writing, whereby it is hoped they may be more likely to become good Christians and useful members of the community, but by no means put above handicraft labour.[64]

The original school appears to date from between 1758 and 1773, and was for fifty boys and girls, who were accommodated in a building of unusual plan, viz. an octagon of two storeys (see fig. 23 and pl. **111**). This is the only school of this period of octagonal plan known to me, and the most common contemporary buildings with which it can perhaps be compared are the octagonal toll-houses of the type which survive, for example, at Thrapston in Northamptonshire and Todmorden in the West Riding of Yorkshire. It is possible that the design was influenced by octagonal church buildings of the time, and it may also be noted that Joseph Lancaster, writing in 1811, stated that 'I have seen a school built in an octagon shape', though he does not say where, and adds that 'the reason given for preferring this form was that shorter and consequently cheaper pieces of timber would come into use'.[65] The school at Wimbledon seems originally to have consisted of a two-storey building with a central chimney at the apex of the roof. Whether the wall which divides the octagon centrally on both floors is original is not certain, but there is no doubt that it was in existence before 1841, when the minutes record that half of the ground floor was used as the boys' schoolroom and the other half as the kitchen and scullery of the master and his wife. On the first floor, half of the space was taken up by the girls' school and the other half by bedrooms for the master and his family.[66]

In the early nineteenth century the school population in Wimbledon rose rapidly. A separate school for the infants was built a little distance away to the south-east of the original school in about 1834 and the original building was itself altered in 1841, from which date the boys and girls were completely separated, as was the accommodation for the master and mistress (who were no longer a married couple). The master's living accommodation and the boys' school now occupied the ground floor, and they were given a separate entrance on the east side. The mistress and the girls were accommodated on the first floor and used the original west entrance and staircase. Later still, the whole of the ground floor was given over to staff accommodation, the first floor became two classrooms and several new classrooms were built to the west and north, as shown on the plan. These buildings were used as a primary school until 1966, when a new school,

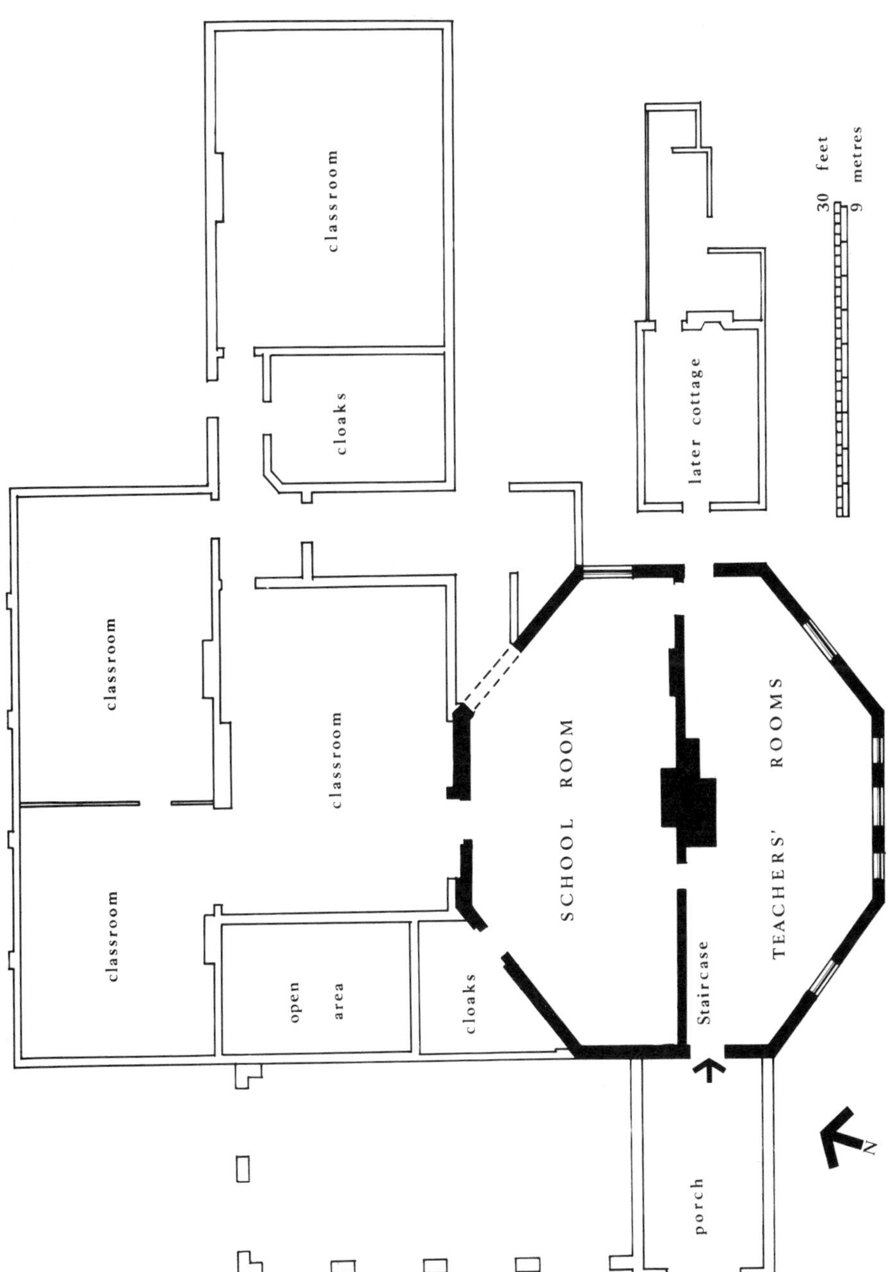

Figure 23 Wimbledon, plan of octagonal school, *c.* 1773, with later extensions. (The fenestration on the north side was probably like that on the south originally. The interior has been remodelled; whether the wall dividing the octagon is original or not is discussed in the text and notes.)

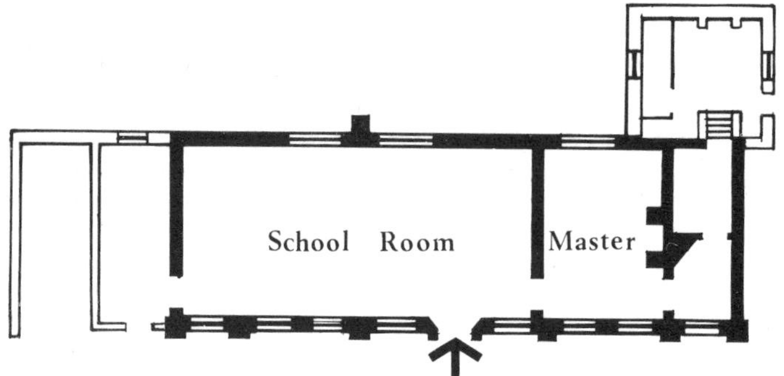

Figure 24 (*a*) Chippenham, Orford's School, *c*. 1714.

Figure 24 (*b*) Shrewsbury, Bowdler's School, 1724.

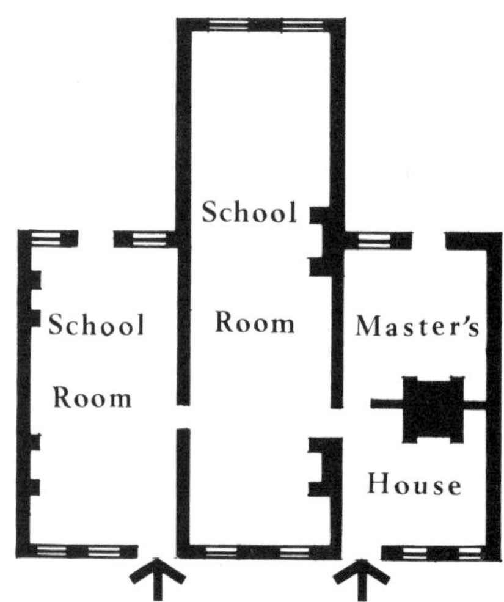

Figure 24 (*c*) Romford, Charity School, *c*. 1730.

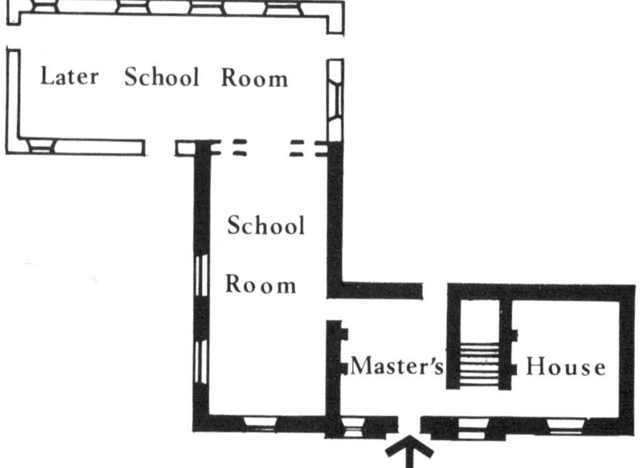

Plans of elementary schools, all to the same scale.

60

18 m

Figure 24 (*d*) Rotherham, Feoffees' School, 1776.

called Bishop Gilpin School, was built in Lake Road, Wimbledon. The buildings were then left empty and the possibility of demolishing them was under discussion in 1968.[67] (A workhouse, built near the school in 1752 and extended after the Poor Law Amendment Act of 1834, was later converted into almshouses, which were demolished in 1966 and have been replaced by old people's flats.)[68]

Looking more generally at the smaller schools which survive from the eighteenth century, we find that regional building styles persist to some extent (dictated largely by the continued use of local materials), but the plans follow a fairly regular pattern. Externally, the most usual embellishment is a date-stone, often with an inscription giving details of the foundation, and sometimes with the coat of arms of a local landed family who either founded the school or was a major contributor to its cost. Two of many such examples may be seen on the surviving school buildings at Lowick, Northamptonshire (pl. **109**) and Bunny, Nottinghamshire (pl. **112**), the latter built with an almshouse in 1700 by Sir Thomas Parkyns, an eccentric but benevolent land-owner whose monument is in the church nearby, with a long inscription giving details of his benefactions. An interesting example of the stress on piety and Bible-learning survives on an inscribed plaque of 1715 (set into a later school building) at Thurcaston, Leicestershire (pl. **113**).[69] Carved statues of charity children such as we noticed in London seem to have survived more rarely in the country schools. The figure of a girl taken from the school at Finedon, Northamptonshire (1714) is now in the parish church there; a similar example is the figure of a charity boy at Bottisham, Cambridgeshire, now in the parish church and formerly on the school building (1729), which was demolished a few years ago.[70] The original figures survive, however, on the school at Burrough Green, Cambridgeshire (1714), and other examples could no doubt be tracked down.

Most of the smaller schools, even those specially designed for educational use, differ little in appearance from the ordinary houses of their locality. This is hardly surprising, since these small elementary schools were still relatively unspecialized in their work. For the same reason, existing houses seem often to have been taken over for school use. In all but the humblest schools, the master or mistress was provided with accommodation, usually in the same, or an adjoining, building. Larger and somewhat

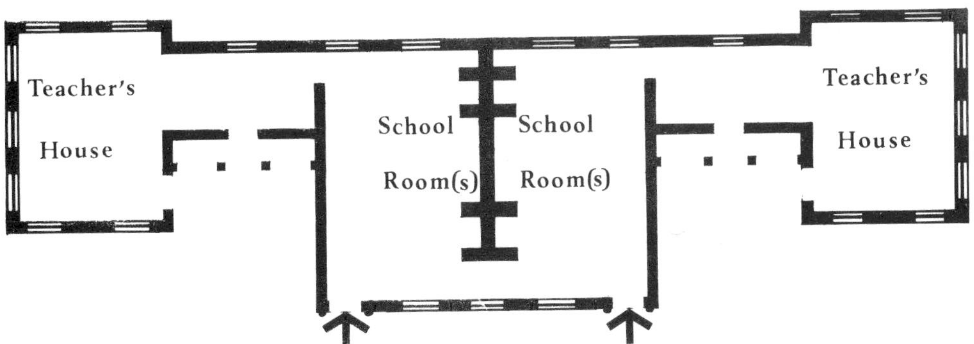

Figure 24 (*e*) Shrewsbury, Allatt's School, 1800.

more imposing schools were built where the numbers warranted the provision of separate rooms for boys and girls and separate living quarters for master and mistress (more commonly, however, they were man and wife living in one house). A selection of school plans of varying date and geographical location is shown in fig. 24, and further details are given below:

a Chippenham (Cambs.), founded by Lord Orford and opened in about 1714.[71] There were forty boys and girls in 1837. The schoolroom (which is still in use) measures 42 by 20 feet and is of single storey; the master occupied the north-west end of the building. See also pl. **114**.

b Shrewsbury (Salop), founded by Thomas Bowdler in 1724, in Beeches Lane, Town Walls.[72] It was closed in 1896 and is now an architect's office. It is possible that originally the boys were on the ground floor, with the girls above (or vice versa). The teacher may have been housed in the small rooms at the rear. See also pl. **115**.

c Romford (Essex), founded by subscription in about 1730 for forty-five boys and twenty girls, and built on the south side of the Market Place. There were two schoolrooms, the larger one presumably for the boys, with the teacher's house alongside (probably for a man and his wife). It has not been used as a school for some years and is due for demolition.[73]

d Rotherham (W. Yorks.), began by subscription in 1727, but the surviving building in the Crofts is dated 1776.[74] It was built on 'Quarry Hill' specifically because this was 'a spot . . . whereon stone for the purpose may be conveniently got'. There were twenty-eight boys and twenty girls in the school in 1827, and the layout of the building shows that they were either taught together in the one schoolroom measuring 35 by 16 feet; or (which seems less likely) the sexes were separated, use being made of the badly-lit attic floor above the schoolroom. Later in the nineteenth century, the number of children on the foundation was increased to forty boys and thirty girls and another schoolroom was built at right angles to the old. The school ceased to be maintained by the charity after 1892 and became a temporary Board school until 1897. It is now used as a garage by a private firm, the large schoolrooms being well suited for the purpose. (I have found several examples of old schools now used as garages; another common use is for storage.) See also pl. **116**.

e Shrewsbury (Salop), founded by John Allatt and built in Murivance, Town Walls, in 1800.[75] There were separate schoolrooms for boys and girls next to each other and separate houses for the master and mistress, one on each side of the school and connected to it by arcades. It was closed in 1927 and is now used by the town's health department. See also pl. **117**.

IV

Very little is now known about the working conditions for children and teachers in the elementary schools of the eighteenth century. An examination of trustees' minute and account books in the London area shows that furnishings and equipment were of the sparsest.[76] The walls of some schools had wainscoting around them, but most were left bare and white-washed from time to time. If anything was hung on the walls, it related directly to the disciplinary function which the schools were anxious to perform. Thus at St Anne's, Blackfriars, an account was displayed concerning the offences of a notorious pupil who had been expelled (1717); at St Andrew's, Holborn, a notice forbidding the children to climb the church steeple was put up on the schoolroom wall (1726); and at St Lawrence's, Lambeth, four Hogarth prints representing idleness and industry were displayed (1782). The trustees of the Isleworth Blue Coat school in 1752 ordered 'a writing form as plain as can be made and two forms to sit on', the latter to be constructed 'in as frugal a manner as possible'. In the following year it is recorded that there were two writing desks, five forms, two shelves and two rows of pegs for the forty pupils at this school. The fifty boys at St Dunstan in the West in 1773 had seven forms to sit on and forty-three books between them (thirteen spelling books, two psalters, twelve New Testaments, six Bibles and ten primers). In the same year, the fifty girls at St Giles, Red Cross Street, had two writing desks and four tables, and the only books were twelve Bibles.

In the hospital schools, strict economy was insisted upon. At the Grey Coat Hospital, there were forty-nine beds for about 100 children (it was common at this period—and later—for two or more children to sleep in one bed). In the 1770s there were reports of brutality, dishonesty and fraud; eight boys who could not endure the cruelty of the officers smashed the school windows to ensure an inquiry, and on another occasion the girls tried to set fire to the school because of the constant flogging and semi-starvation which they had to endure.[77] Trustees' minute books of several schools during this period refer to the lack of proper washing facilities, inadequate privies and poor ventilation (at St Marylebone in 1766 the girls actually broke their windows 'for the benefit of the air').[78]

It would probably be a mistake to generalize about school conditions from the large London schools. What evidence there is about the smaller schools in the countryside suggests that they were conscientiously and perhaps humanely administered, often by people who took a real interest in the affairs of the locality. Even so, there can be little doubt that the school equipment was of the simplest. The only authentic contemporary illustrations known to me of the interiors of elementary schools (possibly private rather than endowed schools) are reproduced as pls. **118** and **119**. They show bare walls and the minimum amount of furniture and (as was usual in the grammar schools also) the teacher is calling out the children in turn to go over their work, for the expository method of teaching the whole class at once was still largely in the future.

As for the internal organization of such schools, the ideals towards which many teachers worked were no doubt influenced by those outlined in what became a classic work in this field, James Talbott's *The Christian school-master: or the duty of those who are employ'd in the publick instruction of children, especially in charity-schools* (1707).[79] Talbott laid great emphasis on the need for teaching the church catechism; prayers were to be said at the beginning and end of each school day; and on Sundays the master was to take the children to church, where 'they should always sit together in some conspicuous part of the church, that so both the congregation and their master (who is to sit with or very near them) may more easily observe their deportment'. A careful order of seating was to be observed 'not only . . . in the school, where every one is to take [his] place according to his proficiency in learning; but likewise in the church, where the precedency may be given to such as have distinguished themselves by their piety'.[80] Talbott says that the children should be taught reading, writing and arithmetic, and should use the Prayer Book, the Psalter and the Bible, though 'it may not be amiss to sweeten their labours now and then by the choice of some pleasant but profitable book', such as Aesop's *Fables*.

Talbott also recommends that the school should be divided into four classes, as follows:

> The first, consisting of those that learn the alphabet, and the first rudiments of reading in the horn-book, primer and spelling-book.
> The second, of those that read the psalter and the New Testament.
> The third, of those that read the Bible, and such other useful books as the master or governors of the school shall appoint, and who do likewise learn to write.
> The fourth, of such as can write well and are fit to be instructed in arithmetic.[81]

In addition, Talbott urges that 'rules and orders' should be laid down to ensure good attendance, cleanliness and seemly behaviour, and there are suggestions on how best to organize the teaching when part of the class is engaged on manual employment.[82] How far all these recommendations were generally carried out is impossible to say, but, at the best, they would have made for what by modern standards would seem to have been an arduous training in the rudiments of literacy.[83]

In conclusion, it must be emphasized again that the very great majority of the schools for the poor at this period were for relatively small numbers of children, and that only in the major towns was anything like mass elementary education attempted. Such an attempt, stimulated by the ideas of the 'new philanthropy' and by the acceleration of economic and social changes, belongs mainly to the nineteenth century. We do, however, see the beginnings of a mass educational movement in the Sunday schools which began to spring up in some places after about 1780. Specially-designed buildings to cater for the new demand were not at first to be expected—indeed, the part-time nature of the education received and the fact that the Sunday schools were often attended by adults as well as children led supporters of the movement to advocate the use of rooms in ordinary houses; for, as a writer of 1785 argued, 'the persons who are grown up would not have any objection to come to such a room as this, whereas they could not, or would not, go to a place which is only fit for the reception of little children'.[84] The same writer described how in Leeds Sunday schools had been organized in every parish, so that there were twenty-eight schools, fifty-three masters and over 2,000 scholars. He says that 'the boys and girls are separated, unless very young, and no master, together with his assistant, teaches more than 40'. He adds that there were often 'several schools in one house, where upwards of 200 assemble, though in different rooms and under different masters'.

Here we are on the brink of a new form of organization for elementary education. It will be noted, however, that, while there might be several schoolrooms in one house, the idea of separate classrooms in one school has not yet emerged. It was also not until the following century that the mass elementary education of children and adults parted ways and found expression, as we shall see, in distinctive architectural forms.[85]

Notes

1 Jones, M. G., *The charity school movement*, Cambridge U.P., 1938.

2 Cf. Robson, D., *Some aspects of education in Cheshire in the eighteenth century*, Manchester: Chetham Society, 1966, 39. For the increased importance of 'associated philanthropy' in the eighteenth century, see Owen, D., *English philanthropy 1660–1960*, Harvard U.P., 1965, 3.

3 Simon, B. (ed.), *Education in Leicestershire 1540–1940*, Leicester U.P., 1968, ch. 3, 'Was there a charity school movement?', by Joan Simon.

4 Owen, *op. cit.*, 71–7, writes of 'the amazing outpouring of wealth for public purposes that marked the first four decades of the [eighteenth] century'. He points out that perpetual trusts were less common than subscriptions and cash legacies which have left no historical record; even so, 'the value of Britain's charitable endowments increased enormously in the course of the century' and 'as regards new endowments the eighteenth century was by no means a sterile period'. The purely financial evidence cited in Simon, *op. cit.*, ch. 3, seems to bear out Owen's statement.

5 All but three of the schools listed are mentioned in Pevsner, *Northamptonshire* (1961); further architectural details are contained in the Ministry of Housing and Local Government's lists of buildings of architectural or historic interest. Details of the charities of all but that at Ecton are in *C.C.R.*, 1825f. There is a useful summary covering the whole of England and Wales entitled *Digest of schools and charities for education as reported on by the commissioners of inquiry into charities* (1842). This lists for Northamptonshire sixteen grammar schools, all established before 1700, and sixty-five non-classical schools, thirty-six of which were established or endowed during the eighteenth century; not all of them may have had their own buildings, and others moved into new buildings in the nineteenth century.

6 George, M. D., *London life in the XVIIIth century*, Kegan Paul, 1930, Introduction.

7 *Ibid.*, 258–9. For an analysis of the complex elements of eighteenth-century philanthropy, see Owen, *op. cit.*, 13–15.

8 Owen, *op. cit.*, 91–6.

9 Quotations are from the copy in Reading University Institute of Education library (printed by Joseph Downing, London, 1705). Spelling modernized.

10 Catechizing was consistently stressed by Anglican writers during this period. Cf. *The nature and necessity of catechizing* (printed by J. Bentham, Cambridge, 1746).

11 Jones, *op. cit.*, 85f. The school at Finedon, Northants., mentioned above, was for a time a model spinning school (*ibid.*, 89 and 108). Cf. Owen, *op. cit.*, 28.

12 Cf. Dr Moss's *Sermon preach'd in the parish church of St Sepulchres, May 27, 1708* on the subject of 'The providential division of men into rich and poor'.

13 Cf. Robson, *op. cit.*, 113–15. Evidence about the elementary-school curriculum is hard to come by. Certainly some eighteenth-century schoolmasters taught a wider range of subjects (cf. Seaborne, M., *Education*, Studio Vista, 1966, pl. 86 and 87, and Simon, *op. cit.*, 86–7).

14 *C.C.R.*, XXXII, 1837/8, 239f.

15 Addleshaw, G. W. O., and Etchells, F., *The architectural setting of Anglican worship*, Faber & Faber, 1948, 92–3.

16 *Ibid.*, plans 14 (Chislehampton, Oxon., 1763), 22 (St Nicholas's, Newcastle-on-Tyne, 1785) and 23 (Witherslack, Westmorland, *c.* 1768). The old method of seating 'with so many pews in private hands . . . and the frequent relegation of the poor to the background' disappeared in favour of 'open seats free to all' during the Victorian period, largely as a result of the increase in population, *ibid.*, 97. (Cf. Inglis, K. S., *Churches and the working classes in Victorian England,* Routledge & Kegan Paul, 1963, 48–57, on 'Pews and the People'.) On school galleries in churches see also Clarke, B.F.L., *The building of the eighteenth-century church*, S.P.C.K., 1963, 31.

17 A Bluecoat school for twenty poor boys was established by the corporation in Newbury in 1707. The wooden effigy of a charity boy, now fixed to the wall of the north aisle of St Nicholas's Church, was originally set up in front of the poor box at the north entrance to the church, from whence it was removed in 1866. The wooden figure of a charity girl (*c.* 1711) now in Maidstone Museum is illustrated in Gardiner, D., *English girlhood at school*, Oxford U.P., 1929, facing p. 310. There is another example in Cirencester Parish Church (Glos.).

18 Simon, *op. cit.*, 86n., including a reference to Long Clawson, Leics. (1777): 'The Communion Table to be cleaned and all the ink stains taken out. No school-boys to be suffered again to write upon it, and the Door betwixt the chancel and the vestry to be kept locked so as to hinder the boys from getting into the Church, otherwise the vestry to be no longer used as a schoolroom.' Other eighteenth-century examples of the use (and misuse) of churches by schoolchildren are cited in Davies, J. G., *The secular use of church buildings*, S.C.M. Press, 1968, 189–90.

19 The wall tablet in All Saints' Church, Northampton (1747), relates to the charity school for thirty girls founded by deed of D. Beckett and A. Sargeant in 1735. The school was rebuilt in 1862 in Kingswell Street, Northampton, where it still stands (pl. **189**).

20 Pearce, E. H., *Annals of Christ's Hospital*, Methuen, 1901, 168–71.

21 *C.C.R.*, I, 1819, 177–8.
22 Cox, M. H., and Norman, P. (ed.), *Survey of London*, Vol. X, *The parish of St Margaret, Westminster, Part I*, L.C.C., 1926, 145. The building is fully described on pp. 144–7 and pls. 127–34. See also R.C.H.M., *London*, II, 1925, 137–8. Both have plans of the building.
23 Cox and Norman, *op. cit.*, 145.
24 The 'Blewcoat School' may be inspected on any weekday between 9.30 a.m. and 5.30 p.m. The National Trust has also issued a useful leaflet describing the present state of the building (by Carew Wallace, 1966).
25 Pevsner, *London*, I, 2nd ed. 1962, 604.
26 R.C.H.M., *London*, II, 1925, 137.
27 These were extensively used in Day, E. S., *An old Westminster endowment*, Hugh Rees, 1902, from which fig. 20 is reproduced. For the later history of the school, see Chetham-Strode, D. F., *History of the Grey Coat Hospital, Westminster* (the School, 1960).
28 Quoted Day, *op. cit.*, 3.
29 *Ibid.*, 8–9.
30 *Ibid.*, 29–34.
31 *C.C.R.*, I, 1819, 178.
32 Day, *op. cit.*, 105–6, 136.
33 For a short history of the school see Scott, J. D. G., *The story of St Mary Abbots, Kensington*, S.P.C.K., 1942, 109–25.
34 Pevsner, *London*, II, 1952, 63.
35 See also Pevsner, *op. cit.*, II, 211.
36 *The London Journal*, 23 December 1721. (I owe this reference to the Borough Librarian, Camden). The school is now no. 43 Hatton Garden, on the corner of St Cross street.
37 A 'Sketch of the history of Liverpool Blue Coat Hospital', by J. R. Hughes, was issued in three parts in *Transactions of the Historical Society of Lancashire and Cheshire*, XI (1858–9), 163–86, new series, I (1860–1), 71–102, and new series, IV (1863–4), 57–78. For a shorter history, based on Hughes, see Watcyn, G. C., *The Liverpool Blue Coat School 1708–1967* (published by the School, 1967).
38 Quoted in Hughes, *op. cit.*, XI, 175.
39 *Ibid.*
40 *Ibid.*, I, 76 (in 1790 there were 230 boys and fifty girls).
41 See the catalogue of an exhibition held in 1967 to celebrate the 250th anniversary of the opening of the building. I am indebted to Mr Watcyn, the present Headmaster, and to Mrs Van Mullen, Assistant Secretary of the Bluecoat Society of Arts, for further information about the building. See also MacCunn, W. S., *Bluecoat Chambers*, Liverpool U.P., 1956.
42 Hughes, *op. cit.*, 74–6. Manual work was given up in 1802 and not in 1783, as stated in Watcyn, *op. cit.*, 12.
43 Marshall, D., *The English poor in the eighteenth century*, Routledge, 1926, 55. For a less optimistic view see the essay on 'Man's economic status' by Jacob Viner in *Man versus society in 18th-century Britain*, ed. Clifford, J. L., Cambridge U.P., 1968, 22f. and commentary, 138–40.
44 George, *op. cit.*, 13.
45 See Bolam, D. W., *Unbroken community. The story of the Friends' School, Saffron Walden*, Cambridge: Heffer, 1952.
46 Coram's foundling hospital is illustrated (with plan) in Marshall, *op. cit.*, facing p. 144.
47 Quoted in Bolam, *op. cit.*, 14.
48 *Ibid.*, 64.

49 The following account is based on Thompson, H., *A history of Ackworth School*, S. Harris, 1879, which has the most detailed description of the early history of the school. There is a shorter account in Vipont, E., *Ackworth School*, Lutterworth Press, 1959.

50 See Oldham, J.B., *A history of Shrewsbury School*, Oxford: Blackwell, 1952, 130f. and plate facing p. 144.

51 Thompson, *op. cit.*, 22–3.

52 *Ibid.*, 135.

53 *Ibid.*, 37. I am indebted to the Bursar, Mr Kenneth Limb, for further information about the original layout of the buildings at Ackworth.

54 *Reports on the state of Ackworth School, 1780–1812.* (Copy in Leeds Institute of Education library, with plan.)

55 Quoted in Thompson, *op. cit.*, 40–2.

56 See, further, below. For the punishments at Ackworth at this time see Vipont, *op. cit.*, 44–5 ('Judging by the standards of the day, the punishments inflicted were not severe'.)

57 The two foundations are fully described in *C.C.R.*, III, 1820, 319–35, 337–41.

58 For an interesting description of the successful efforts to save the Bluecoat building at Frome, see the illustrated pamphlet, *The Blue House restored*, published by the Frome Charities Assoc., 1965. I am grateful to the Matron, Mrs Wait, for showing me round the building.

59 The best description of these charities is *A short account of the two charitable foundations at King's-Cliffe* (printed by F. Howgrave, Stamford, 1755; copy in Northants. County Library). See also Overton, J. H., *Life of William Law*, Longmans, 1881, ch. 13, and Moreton, G., *Memorials of the birthplace and residence of the Rev. William Law at King's Cliffe*, Guildford: London Printing Works, 1895.

60 The books given by Law are described in *A short account . . . , op. cit.*, 22. See also Central Council for the Care of Churches, report on *The parochial libraries of the Church of England*, with Introduction by N. R. Ker, 1959, 84. For a similar library at Ashby-de-la-Zouch (Leics.), founded in 1727, but later dispersed, see Fox, Levi, *A country grammar school*, Oxford U.P., 1967, 61–2. On clerical libraries generally at this date see Owen, *op. cit.*, 22.

61 *A short account . . . , op. cit.*, 9, 11, 21. Law also drew up a set of 'Rules to be observed by girls', quoted in Overton, *op. cit.*, 229–31. They included the provision that any girl found lying, cursing, swearing or stealing 'shall stand chained a whole morning to some particular part of the room by herself'.

62 I am grateful to Miss Joan Pilditch for showing me around the building and helping me to reconstruct the original layout. (The children were transferred to new premises in Park Street, King's Cliffe, in *c.* 1874.)

63 The original charity school building consisted of a schoolroom on the ground floor with the master's accommodation above. Later the whole building became the headmaster's house; it was converted to head's and secretary's offices and store-rooms in 1947. The Headmaster, Mr J. E. Jackson, to whom I owe this information, claims that the school is almost unique among primary schools in having a complete history of school-building on one site, with major extensions in 1830, 1860, 1889, 1953, 1958, 1960, 1966 and 1968. See also his interesting booklet, *Shinfield C.E. School* (published by the School, 1957).

64 Quoted in Arnold, C. T., *Wimbledon National Schools (now usually called Central Schools) on Wimbledon Common*, Wimbledon: Trim, 1912, 2. The date of this minute is 1773, but the school seems to have been started some years before. The exact date of the building is however obscure (Arnold, 1). The school is not recorded in the Charity Commissioners' reports because there was no endowment and the subscriptions were paid on an annual basis. I am grateful to Mr E. Daynes, who first drew my attention to this interesting school.

65 The toll-house at Todmorden is illustrated in Barley, M. W., *House and home*, Vista Books, 1963, pl. 154. In general, however, toll-houses were smaller than the school at Wimbledon (cf. Stephen, W. M., 'Toll-houses of the Greater Fife area', in *Industrial Archaeology*, Vol. 4, No. 3, August 1967). It may be noted that the Anglican chapel of St Mary's, Birmingham, erected in *c.* 1772, was of octagonal plan (Clarke, B. F. L., *op. cit.*, 44), as was the hospital chapel built in 1775 for the Duke of Norfolk at Sheffield (see Potts, J. D., *Platt of Rotherham*, Sheffield; the author, 1959, 14). An octagonal school was built at Clapham in 1809—10 for the education of boys on Dr Bell's system. (The quotation from Lancaster is from his *Hints and directions for building, fitting up and arranging school-rooms*, 1811, 16; see, further, ch. 8, below.)

66 This was how the building was arranged before 1841 (Arnold, *op. cit.*, 10). A drawing of 1810 (in Bartlett, W. A., *The history and antiquities of the parish of Wimbledon*, Marshall, 1865, extra-illustrated ed., opposite p. 128 of the copy in Wimbledon Reference Library) shows simply the octagonal building with central chimney. It is possible that originally the building consisted merely of two large, octagonal rooms, one over the other, for boys and girls respectively, or with the children on one floor and the teachers on the other. On the other hand, the fenestration would not have prevented the original builders from constructing a wall dividing the octagon into two, as it certainly was by 1841. Also, unless the rooms were heated by stoves (as in pl. **124**), there would have been a chimney flue in the centre of each room, which may suggest that the dividing wall was part of the original design.

67 Efforts to save the building were being made by the John Evelyn Society for maintaining the amenities of Wimbledon (see their annual report, 1967–8).

68 Ex inf. the Librarian, London Borough of Merton.

69 For details of the school at Thurcaston see Simon, *op. cit.*, 72–3. (The school was initially organized in five classes, viz. Primer, Battledore, Bible, Testament and Psalter.)

70 The original school building at Bottisham (now demolished) is illustrated in Jones, *op. cit.*, pl. IV.

71 *C.C.R.*, XXXI, 1837, 155–6. I am grateful to the present Headmistress, Mrs Dorothy O'Hara, for further information, including a reference to Barker, R. W., *An East Anglian village* (1897), which quotes a letter of 1708: 'My Lord Orford hath bought a house, which he designs very suddenly to fit up or rather rebuild for a school house.' (Mr Robin McDowall first drew my attention to this delightful building.)

72 *C.C.R.*, XXIV, 1830, 275. At this date there were eighteen boys and twelve girls on the foundation, with an unspecified number of paying pupils.

73 *C.C.R.*, XXXII, 1837, 731. See also R.C.H.M., *Monuments threatened or destroyed: a select list* (1963), 37. (There are also photographs in the N.M.R.) The building was still standing in 1968.

74 There is a good account of the Rotherham charity school in Guest, J., *Historic notices of Rotherham*, Worksop: White, 1879, 417–23, from which most of the details in this paragraph are taken. I am grateful to the Borough Librarian at Rotherham for further information and to Messrs Vere & Sons, Ltd, bakers, for permission to examine the building. The building was designed by John Platt (see Potts, *op. cit.*, 14).

75 *C.C.R.*, XXIV, 1830, 442. There were twenty-eight boys and twenty-eight girls on the roll at this date.

76 The details in this paragraph are from Webster, D. H., 'A study of Anglican charity education' (Leicester M.Ed. unpublished thesis, 1966), ch. 8.

77 Day, *op. cit.*, 108, 122.

78 Webster, *ibid.*

79 My quotations are from the second edition printed by Joseph Downing, London, 1711, and dedicated to the S.P.C.K. (Spelling modernized.)

80 *Ibid.*, 94, 99.

81 *Ibid.*, 84–5.

82 *Ibid.*, 87f. (and see p. 96f., 'Of rewards and punishments', where Talbott, though admitting the necessity for corporal punishment in some cases, argues for discretion in its use).

83 Simon, *op. cit.*, 64, calls Talbott's book 'the official handbook for teachers published by the S.P.C.K.', and maintains (p. 89) that it is wrong to assume 'that the average parish school can automatically be classified as a charity school' in the S.P.C.K. sense. On the other hand, Robson, *op. cit.*, 95–6, gives two Cheshire examples of 1716 and 1791 to show that the 'standards set by the S.P.C.K. continued to influence the founders of parish schools'.

84 *Proceedings for Sundays* [*sic*] *schools and a plan of that in St Stephen's, Norwich, established October 16th 1785* [by Lancaster Adkin] (printed by W. Chase, Norwich), 3–4.

85 In Wales, the provision of separate elementary schools for adults and children can be dated very exactly to 1811 (McLeish, J., *Evangelical religion and popular education*, Methuen, 1969, 6).

Eight

The building of elementary schools 1800-40

I

When we reach the nineteenth century, we naturally find that the surviving evidence, both architectural and documentary, becomes much more plentiful: in fact, the main difficulty is that of selecting significant examples from the large number of school buildings which survive. The great expansion of elementary education during the nineteenth century and the growing part played by the State in helping to provide schools has been dealt with extensively by educational historians, and we may therefore more suitably concentrate on the purely structural development of schools, using written evidence only where it is essential for interpreting the buildings and the educational ideas which affected their layout. Although the history of education in the nineteenth century has been well worked over in the past, a study of school architecture and organization does in fact throw fresh light on the general development of education during this period.

As is well known, many nineteenth-century elementary-school buildings are still in use, though their number is being reduced year by year. Many have been abandoned as schools and are now used as parish halls or for other secular purposes; many more – especially in large towns – have disappeared altogether. In 1962 the Department of Education and Science carried out a survey of maintained school buildings which was published three years later.[1] Table I overleaf summarizes the findings of this survey.

It will be seen that over 15,000 schools out of a total of just over 29,000 were built (at least in part) before 1903. Of these earlier schools, voluntary (mainly Church of England) schools naturally predominate because the great bulk of pre-1870 schools were built by the voluntary societies, among which the National Society, representing the Anglican interest, and the British and Foreign School Society, which tended to reflect Nonconformist opinion, are the best known. Again, it is to be expected that there are many more primary than secondary school buildings surviving from the nineteenth century, since secondary schools maintained by local education authorities, which are the only ones recorded in the table, were set up mainly in the present century, whereas the great expansion of primary education took place in Victorian times.

Table I Maintained school buildings in England and Wales (1962)

Age of oldest main building	*Primary*		*Secondary*		*All*
	County	*Voluntary*	*County*	*Voluntary*	
Pre-1875	1,809	5,345	194	181	7,529
1875–1902	4,390	2,349	733	187	7,659
1903–18	2,483	500	824	90	3,897
1919–44	2,221	438	1,566	136	4,361
1945–62	3,064	606	1,674	284	5,628
Totals	13,967	9,238	4,991	878	29,074

It is possible to obtain a more detailed conception of the main phases of elementary-school-building in the nineteenth century by seeing what happened in particular areas. Thus T. W. Bamford in his *Evolution of rural education, 1850–1964* (1965) has an interesting chapter on the elementary-school buildings of the East Riding of Yorkshire. Some of his findings are summarized in Table II.

Table II New elementary schools erected in the East Riding (excluding Hull), 1833–99

Date of erection	*Voluntary schools aided by grant*	*Voluntary schools not aided*	*Board schools*	*Total No. of new schools opened*	*Still in use in 1963*
1833–9	7	?	—	7 +	?
1840–9	25	?	—	25 +	?
1850–9	28	19	—	47	21
1860–9	9	9	—	18	13
1870–9	17	18	24	59	38
1880–9	1	2	5	8	5
1890–9	?	?	?	14	12
Totals	87 +	48 +	29 +	178 +	89 +

Dr Bamford shows from the East Riding evidence that the two principal decades of elementary-school-building were 1850–9 and 1870–9, and he suggests, from the evidence of school-building grants made to some voluntary schools by the central government, that the decade 1840–9 was also a time of rapid expansion. By contrast, the 1860s, the 1880s and the 1890s were relatively slack (though Dr Bamford shows that there was an increase in the number of extensions to existing schools during the last two decades of the century). He concludes that 'the real drive in rural education commenced with the 1840s' and that, although the passing of the 1870 Education Act led to a peak period of building activity, 'new schools were only being built (as short a time as ten years after the 1870 Act) to cope with problems of obsolescence'. He adds, however, that 'whether the same story holds for the large city school board of Hull must remain for future research'.[2]

A broadly similar pattern emerges from some related studies recently carried out in Lindsey (Lincs.) and Devon, the results of which are shown in Tables III and IV.

Table III Number of grants for school buildings in Lindsey, 1833–70

Dates	*No. of grants made to:*					
	National schools	*Other C. of E. schools*	*Wesleyan schools*	*British schools*	*Total No. of grants*	*Total value (£)*
1833–9	8	—	—	—	8	587
1840–9	32	—	1	1	34	3,136
1850–9	32	3	12	1	48	9,508
1860–70	19	9	6	—	34	6,121
Totals	91	12	19	2	124	19,352

Table III, which is based on Mr Russell's researches in Lindsey, lends support to the view that expansion really began after 1840 and carried on into the 1850s, but the decline in the 1860s is less sharp.[3] Mr Sellman's work on Devon village schools appears to confirm this, and also suggests that the real rise began in the 1830s, even though fewer grants were available (Table IV).[4]

It should be noted that Mr Russell's figures relate to grants for improvements to existing buildings as well as new schools, and that Mr Sellman's do not include over a third of the total number of village schools established in Devon during this period, because they could not be dated with certainty. The general picture which emerges is confirmed by a survey carried out by the Director of Education for Leicestershire in 1966. The head teachers of the 243 maintained primary schools in the county were asked to state the date of the oldest part of their present buildings. Fifty replied that

Table IV Village schools established in Devon, 1821–70

Date	*Church schools*	*British schools*	*Total*
1821–30	18	1	19
1831–40	42	1	43
1841–50	61	3	64
1851–60	44	5	49
1861–70	47	6	53
Totals	212	16	228

they were not sure (the majority of these buildings are of indeterminate nineteenth-century date). A further sixty-three were in wholly twentieth-century schools. A summary of the information received from the remaining 130 schools is given in Table V.

Table V Maintained primary schools in Leicestershire built before 1900 and still in use in 1966

Date of oldest part	*No. of schools (with location of the earliest)*
Pre-1800	2 (Appleby Magna, 1697*; Snarestone, 1717)
1800–9	1 (Congerstone, 1806†)
1810–19	3 (Claybrooke, 1813†; Barkestone, 1814; Sapcote, 1819)
1820–9	1 (Nailstone, 1828–36)
1830–9	6 (Ashby, 1836; Quorn, 1837; Thrussington, 1837; Market Harborough, 1838; Great Bowden, 1839; Sibson, 1839)
1840–9	22
1850–9	20
1860–9	18
1870–9	36
1880–9	11
1890–9	10
Total	130

*The Sir John Moore School, described in ch. 5.

†Much altered.

It has not been possible to check the accuracy of every return, and one would naturally expect the oldest buildings to be the least numerous. Even so, it appears that the 1840s, 1850s and 1870s were the three most active decades, as Dr Bamford found in the East Riding, and the reasons for this are not far to seek. The first Government grants for school buildings began in 1833 and were put on a new basis in 1839. The following twenty years were, as we shall see, a period when a specialized literature of school architecture began to appear and the Committee of Council on Education was particularly active. This period of rapid expansion (as in other branches of education) received a check when the Revised Code was introduced in 1862, but there was a marked advance in the decade following the 1870 Education Act and the setting up of school boards.

A proviso must be made, however, with regard to schools in the larger towns. In the county borough of Leicester, for example, where the existing school buildings were also surveyed in 1966, only one pre-1870 school building was still in use (the Belgrave C. of E. Infants' School, 1861). Furthermore, the Leicester school board had been consistently active during all three decades of its existence (1871–1903). This does not mean that the first wave of school-building came later in the towns than in the countryside. As we shall see, the problem of mass elementary education was first tackled in the new industrial areas of the early nineteenth century, and the reasons why in Leicester, and doubtless elsewhere, the school board was so active were because of the continued rise in population and the need to replace or supplement voluntary schools built earlier—and sometimes much earlier—in the century. There is also the point that the rate of general building development in the towns has been much more rapid than in rural areas, which has led to the virtual disappearance of early nineteenth-century school buildings in the towns, though some have survived, usually no longer used as schools and often in what are now slum clearance areas.

II

While it seems to be true that the main period of elementary-school-building began after 1840, the first forty years of the nineteenth century were in fact of crucial importance from the point of view of the development of ideas about how, in practical terms, the new problems associated with the mass provision of elementary education could be solved. We saw such provision beginning to be made with the coming of the Sunday schools towards the end of the eighteenth century, but it was not long before the limitations of schooling on only one day a week were perceived, particularly in the areas of rapid industrial expansion, where the Sunday schools chiefly operated. As David Stow wrote in 1836:

> The evil to be remedied is the exposed condition of the children of the poor

> and working classes, especially in large manufacturing towns. The only antidote which has yet been applied to meet that condition are Sabbath schools. . . . [Yet] every individual in the habit of visiting the poorer districts of cities, and who simply exercises his eyes and ears, must be fully satisfied that much open vice and profligacy prevail.[5]

It was this awareness of moral danger and the great increase in the number of children wandering about the streets which acted as the principal spur to the educational reformers of the time. Such conditions were not new (we noticed them, for example, in parts of London early in the eighteenth century), but they were now appearing on an unprecedented scale.

To meet this challenge a number of writers advocated radically new methods of organizing schools. All were preoccupied with the enormous size of the problem of popular education, as the sub-titles of their books testify—for example, Lancaster's 'account of the institution for the education of one thousand poor children', Wilderspin's 'how three hundred children . . . may be managed by one master and mistress', or Stow's 'system of moral training suited to the condition of large towns'.[6] The monitorial system, by which the older children taught the younger (a method of teaching already existing in embryo, as we saw, in many schools from the sixteenth century) was widely advocated. This system has been much discussed by historians of education,[7] so it will be sufficient here to concentrate on only one aspect of it, viz. the way in which it affected the layout of the schoolroom and the organization of classes.

Of these early writers—most of whom also sought to demonstrate their ideas in 'model' schools—Joseph Lancaster was perhaps the most conscious of the importance of the school building and its internal layout. In his *Improvements in education* (3rd ed., 1805), he refers to the 'bad accommodation common school-rooms afford to the poor children who attend them; many of whom suffer materially in health, by the confinement at their seats, winter and summer, without variation'. He adds that such schools rarely accommodated more than thirty children each, and that 'disorder, noise, etc., seem more the characteristic of these schools, than the improvement of the little ones who attend them'.[8] All the greater, therefore, was the need for larger and better-regulated schools. He has much to say about the detailed working of the monitorial system of teaching, but the elaboration of his ideas about the physical arrangements of the school did not come until a few years later: in *The British system of education* (1810) and *Hints and directions for building, fitting up and arranging school-rooms on the British system of education* (1811).[9] The first book advocated what was for that time a revolutionary layout, with the desks facing the master, instead of being arranged along the sides of the room. The desks were used for writing, but sufficient space was left at each side of the room for the children to assemble in small groups to practise reading, spelling and arithmetic under the supervision of the monitors. The second book goes into much more detail, and at the end of it is added 'a technical description of a plan for a school-room, intended for the guidance of a builder'.

The Lancasterian model plan of 1811 was for a schoolroom to accommodate 320 children. The room measured 70 by 32 feet and contained twenty rows of desks and forms arranged to face the master's platform and so spaced as to allow the monitors to move between the rows. (This gave each child a space of 7 square feet and provided for sixteen children to each 22-foot bench.) It is essential, says Lancaster, to leave aisles 5 feet wide on each side, so that the children, when not at their desks, can stand in semicircles facing the side walls, on which lesson-boards should be hung (for this reason also the windows should not be too low). The level of the floor should rise gradually towards the back of the room, so that the master could see every child clearly when all were assembled in their desks. The walls of the schoolroom need not be plastered—'let the bare brick be simply lime-whited' (a practice common in charity schools of the previous century and perhaps earlier). The provision of a ceiling is not recommended, since this would act as a sounding-board, so increasing the level of noise, which must in any case have been considerable when all the monitors were busy questioning the children in their groups. Similarly, he considers that floors of flagstones or wood are too noisy, and hard brick or rammed clay is suggested. His proposals for heating the room are also novel: there should be flues running at floor level along both sides, so providing warm air throughout the building, rather than open fireplaces, which only warm the children near them. He even suggests that heating by steam which 'has proved an important and successful experiment in manufactories' should be tried out in schools,[10] and he is also careful to plan sanitary accommodation (four closets and three urinal stalls in a small yard)—a provision sometimes overlooked in earlier schools, though we noticed a 'house of office' in Tudor plans (fig. 6, above).[11]

Lancaster's supporters formed the Royal Lancasterian Association in 1810, which developed into the British and Foreign School Society in 1814. Meanwhile, Lancaster had quarrelled with the Trustees, and in 1818 he departed for America, where he died in a street accident twenty years later. His ideas were further developed by the British and Foreign School Society, and had reached an astonishing degree of elaboration by 1831, when the Society issued their *Manual of the system of primary instruction.*[12] Illustrations are included in this manual of the plan and interior of the central or 'model' school of the Society at Borough Road, Southwark, which give an excellent impression of the fully-developed Lancasterian schoolroom (see pls. **120** and **121**).

The master stands on the extreme right of the picture, with a group of visitors on the extreme left. The 'general monitor of order' stands on a stool in the centre and is at this moment controlling the whole number of boys (some 365) who are sitting at long writing desks, with the 'monitors of class' standing at the left-hand ends of the desks. (The boys have their slates in front of them, except for those at the shorter desk in the front, who are beginners at the 'sand-desk'.)[13] Also at the left-hand ends of the desks are upright pieces of wood called 'standards', into which have been driven iron rods with the names of the classes from I to VIII attached to the tops. (The term 'standard', which was universally introduced in 1862 as the name of a class, no doubt owed something to earlier Lancasterian practice.) On the side and rear walls hang the 'lessons', or printed sheets pasted on boards. When particular lesson-boards were in use they were hung on nails at a lower level and the boys stood on semicircular lines called 'draft stations' facing the walls. The monitors used the pointers hanging on the walls to go through the lessons with the children. Baize curtains hang from the ceiling 'to check the reverberation of sound'. The floor slopes up from the front, rising 1 foot in 20 from the master's platform (which is not shown on this engraving).

While it is true that in the Preface to this *Manual* of 1831, it is stated that 'even in schools professing to be connected with the Society it is not expected that every regulation in this Manual will be strictly followed', the overwhelming impression left by a study of the Lancasterian model is one of rigidity. One further detail epitomizes this characteristic, viz. Lancaster's insistence that the wooden supports for the desks and benches should be driven into the ground to a depth of 12 inches, a recommendation elaborated in the 1831 *Manual*, which mentions cast iron legs 'fixed firmly in the ground'. And here it may be noted that Lancaster's recommendation about forming semicircles in the aisles has become by 1831 an instruction to mark them out with iron hoops sunk in the ground, or by incisions in the floor. How far the fully-developed Lancasterian specification was carried out in schools other than the much-publicized 'model schools' is open to question, but it is interesting to note that Andrew Bell, who first popularized the idea of monitorial schools (often called 'Madras schools' because he first experimented with them in India) was much less specific in his recommendations about the layout of the schoolroom, and as a result his system seems to have proved more flexible and to have been more widely adopted.[14]

Bell's *Experiment in education* was first published in 1797, but was reprinted with many additions in *The Madras school* (1808).[15] There is the same basic principle of the older children teaching the younger—the monitors are in fact called the 'teachers'. He also advocated a practice long known in the grammar schools (it was mentioned, as we saw, by Brinsley) of pairing the children as 'pupils' and 'tutors', so that the more proficient could help the less proficient to prepare the lesson for recitation to the teacher (in this case himself an older boy). This was the system which came to be known as 'mutual instruction', a term also applied to the somewhat different form used in the Lancasterian schools. Concerning the actual layout of the schoolroom, Bell, in marked contrast to Lancaster, appears to be indifferent. 'The chief and great expense', he says, 'consists in a roof to cover them. The rest, under the Madras system of tuition, is quite inconsiderable.'[16] He is also very willing to adapt to local circumstances: 'Every class in the school, or (where for the sake of room, the classes are arranged two and two, as at the Royal Military Asylum, and say their lessons alternately, the one occupying the ground which the other has quitted) every other class may be saying their lessons at the same time.'[17]

We therefore find that the detailed layout of Madras schools came in practice to be determined by Bell's followers, and particularly by the National Society for Promoting the Education of the Poor in the Principles of the Established Church, which was set up in 1811 to promote his ideas. The Society's fourth annual report of 1815 contains the following description of 'the present state of the Central School, Baldwin's Gardens', which was the model school established in London, near Gray's Inn Road:

> The Central School is divided into two rooms, well lighted and ventilated: one for 600 boys and the other for 400 girls, allowing six square feet for each child. The building is perfectly plain and fitted up in the simplest manner, the walls lime-whited and the floor level. Writing desks, having in front a single row of benches on which the children sit to write in successive portions, are placed round each school against the wall. . . . In one aisle are placed the sand trays, extending across the room, at which the alphabet and stops are taught. . . . The rest of the room contains only a desk, on which lies a book for the insertion of visitors' names, and a few moveable forms in the boys' school, and two large work tables and forms in the girls' school; the area being left as open as possible, to allow full space for the classes to form and the children to pass freely to and from their places.[18]

These details bring out the main points of difference between the Madras and Lancasterian schoolrooms. A somewhat later engraving and plan of the Central School (pls. **122** and **123**) show the children assembled in their places. Much of the teaching was done with the children standing up, and when they sat down for some of the lessons the benches were arranged in hollow squares reminiscent of a military formation. The right-hand portion of the plan shows the girls' school with the benches set out for sewing lessons: when the three Rs were being taught, the girls' benches were also arranged in hollow squares. As we have seen, the main body of the Lancasterian room was occupied by rows of writing desks fixed into the ground, and the children at other times said their lessons standing in the aisles. In the Madras room the arrangement is reversed, with the writing desks on the side walls and the main part of the room left for the children to stand in their classes. There is also an engraving of this period showing the interior of the Madras school at Clapham (pl. **124**), which was built in 1810 on an octagonal plan, as in the Wimbledon school noted earlier. It will be seen that most of the children are sitting at desks, though these are not fixed to the floor and are arranged more informally than would be possible in a strict Lancasterian school. (The smaller boys on the right are making letters with their fingers in the sand tray.)[19] In Frederic Iremonger's *Dr Bell's system of instruction* (1825) the importance of leaving the 'middle space of the room' clear is again stressed, and it is suggested that the children should stand on lines chalked on the floor.[20] John Wood, who adopted the Madras system in his school, gave a good description of the internal arrangements in his *Account of the Edinburgh Sessional School* (1830), where he pointed out that a major advantage of the system was that 'seats are required for only one half of the scholars, and convenient accommodation is afforded to a far greater number, than could be obtained under any other arrangement'.[21]

In the National Society's fifth annual report of 1816 there is a report of 'the sub-committee appointed to propose a plan for building schools, so as to unite the greatest possible convenience with the least possible expense'.[22] It begins with the statement (which was to be repeated right through to the 1830s) that 'a barn furnishes no bad model, and a good one may be easily converted into a school'. The report recommends that 7 square feet per child should be allowed in determining the floor area of a school, though it adds that it is often safe to allow only 6 square feet, since not all the children on the roll will attend every day. The structural details follow Lancaster fairly closely, but allow more variation in detail. The floor should preferably be of brick, but wood is not ruled out; the room should be heated if possible by flues or iron stoves, 'but common fireplaces will answer the purpose very well, if less expensive'. The same spirit of practical compromise is shown in the recommendations about the 'separation of sexes'. Like Lancaster, the sub-committee thought that if large numbers were involved, there should be separate rooms for boys and girls either next to each other or on two floors one above the other; but, if funds do not permit this, they suggest that the same room should be used, with the boys separated from the girls by a curtain or folding doors.

The sub-committee also included an interesting list of actual schools built in the period 1812–16, the salient details of which are given in Table VI.

Table VI National Schools built, 1812–16

Name of school	*Date*	*Cost £*	*No. of scholars*	*Length × breadth in feet*
Ightham	1815	122	120	41 × 19
North Creake	1816	599	83	28 × 13 (upper)
				25 × 24 (lower)
Wheathampstead	1815	183	100	36 × 15
Cowfold	1814	180	60	32 × 18
North Elmham	1812	239	150-200	? × 18
Huntingdon	1813	427	170	43 × 25
Keelby	1815	134	120	30 × 19
Louth	1812	291	300	45 × 28
Sittingbourne	1816	150	200	62 × 20

It will be seen that four of these schools were built for about £1 per place. The others were rather more expensive, and the high cost of the school at North Creake was clearly an embarrassment to the sub-committee. They explain that 'the whole of this work is most *substantially* done' (their italics), and, though the list is repeated unchanged in the annual report of 1820, North Creake is replaced in 1823 by the school at Buxted, built in 1819 and costing £153 for 140 scholars.[23]

The recommendations of 1816 were reprinted again in 1835 and entitled 'General observations on the construction and arrangement of school-rooms'.[24] A new recommendation is that if both sexes are accommodated in one schoolroom, then 'it may be well to increase the length of a room and diminish the breadth of it' with a partition or curtain to separate boys and girls (which probably accounts for some of the long, narrow rooms which may still be found in a few schools of this period). There is also a new section on dwelling-houses for schoolmasters and mistresses, which states that, although the National Society cannot make grants for building such houses, they were nevertheless very desirable and need cost no more than a local cottage (an interesting reflection on the social position of the elementary-school teacher). The point is made that a schoolhouse should preferably be built on to one end of the school and not between two schoolrooms for boys and girls, since this might make it difficult to extend the schoolrooms if numbers rose. (This advice was ignored, as we shall see, at the National School at Great Bowden, Leicestershire (1839), where the school house had later to be converted into a schoolroom.) The 1835 report also gives a new list of schools actually built, as shown in Table VII.[25]

Table VII National schools built, 1821–35

Name of School	*Date*	*Cost* £	*No. of scholars*	*Length* × *breadth in feet*
Bangor (N. Wales)	1821	675	300	86 × 32
Burnley (Lancs.)	1827	718	640	Two storeys, 58 × 33
Carrington (nr. Manchester)	1833	200	260	Two storeys, 35 × 23
Cheapside (nr. Burnley)	1832	230	200	51 × 24
Little Casterton (Rutland)	1832	72	25	20 × 12
St Julian's (Norwich)	1830	585	300	Two rooms, 44 × 22
Stevenage (Herts)	1833	406	266	Two rooms, 40 × 20
Tinwell (Rutland)	1834	65	40	20 × 15
Walsham le Willows (Suffolk)	1832	125	100	32 × 20
York	1835	325	250	50 × 30

It will be seen that there is still a good deal of regional variation in cost per place, and that several very large schools are included; the separation of boys and girls into different rooms or separate floors of the same building has also become more common. The only other development which may be noted is that it appears that all but the poorest schools followed the example of the Central School of the National Society in providing benches for the children to sit on when saying their lessons in the main body of the schoolroom. This was an advance on the previous practice of making the children stand in semicircles on chalked lines; it was now usual to form hollow squares, a shape dictated by the use of straight benches.[26]

III

The monitorial system held sway during the first forty years of the nineteenth century and continued to influence the elementary schools for many years thereafter. But even before 1840 it was being challenged, or at any rate modified, mainly, it would seem, as a result of the introduction of separate schools for infants. The monitorial system, mechanical as it was, required a minimum of teaching ability or at least disciplinary power on the part of the older children who acted as monitors. Inevitably it worked less well, or did not work at all, when it came to teaching children under seven years old. When, in the period after about 1820, the importance of infant schools came to be realized, new methods had to be devised. These resulted in important changes in the design of school buildings which eventually affected the schools for children above the infant level.

It is to Samuel Wilderspin that the chief credit is due for enunciating a distinctive theory of infant education in England.[27] He opened a model school at Spitalfields in London in 1820 and described his work there in *The importance of educating the infant children of the poor* (1823). We must leave aside his interesting and perceptive views on the education of very young children and concentrate on those practices which most influenced school design. He was a pioneer in urging the provision of a 'play ground' equipped with circular swings (similar in appearance to maypoles) on which the children could exercise. Inside the schoolroom, much use was made of pictures, which were fixed on poles for all the children to see. Even with the extensive use of pictures and a certain amount of use of older children as monitors, much direct teaching had to be done by the master and mistress themselves—certainly much more than was usual in the monitorial schools. Wilderspin also considered it to be essential to have a smaller room opening off the main room so that the master could teach each class in turn, the mistress in the meanwhile supervising the work in the main room. It is in this connection that we meet the phrase 'class room', one of the earliest uses of this term in educational literature and consciously distinct from the more usual 'school room', as the following quotation shows:

> The class that has done first is taken into a separate room, where the children have each another lesson, though in a different way from the first, for in what we call the class room, the children. . . being formed into a square. . . all say their lessons together.[28]

This was the germ of the system which later came to be called the 'simultaneous method', by which all the children in the room received instruction at the same time and from the master himself. This was clearly different from the monitorial system under which the children received instruction one at a time from older or abler pupils, and it was also a departure from the long-established system in the grammar and other schools, where the boys used to say their lessons in turn to the master. The monitorial system—particularly the Madras version of it—was merely the old system simplified and extended by multiplying the number of 'teachers' and pupils. But Wilderspin and Stow established the system later characterized by 'chalk and talk', which eventually became the orthodox method of teaching children in all types of schools. It is interesting to reflect that the post-1944 experiments in group teaching and individual 'programmed learning' are really reverting to much older forms of teaching.

It is not absolutely clear why Wilderspin insisted on a separate classroom for the direct teaching of the children by the master (instead of using some part of the schoolroom itself). He realized, however, the importance of a variety of activities for very young children, and says of the work in the classroom that 'as it is an entire change of scene to what it was in the large room, the children generally like it'; and again a few pages on: 'The reason why the children are not taught . . . in the same way [in the classroom] is because they are taught so by each other in the large room, and it is necessary to vary the scene because it pleases the children and they come to it with greater delight.'[29] (There were also, of course, fewer distractions in the smaller room.) Later, in his *Early discipline illustrated* (1832), he hit on the idea of the 'gallery lesson', so using a structural device to introduce the simultaneous method into the schoolroom itself. His practical experiments which resulted in the construction of a gallery are interesting, for he writes:

> Whatever children can *see* excites their interest, and this led to the idea of grouping them together, to receive what are called 'object lessons'. First, they were placed at the end of the room, but this was inconvenient; parallel lines were then drawn in chalk across the room, and they sat down in order on these; but, though the attention was arrested, the posture was unfavourable; some pieces of cord were afterwards placed across to keep them in rank and file, but as this led to a see-sawing motion it was discontinued; I then made various experiments with seats, but did not succeed, until, at length, the construction of a gallery, or succession of steps, the youngest occupying the lower and the eldest the higher, answered the desired end.[30]

David Stow further developed Wilderspin's ideas in his model school at Glasgow, which had opened in 1826. In his book on *Infant training*, published in 1833, he summarized the essentials of his system in terms of an enclosed playground, picture lessons of objects, and 'a gallery fitted to seat the whole children . . . where the eyes of all may more easily be fixed upon the master and upon the object or picture presented to their attention'.[31] It is worth remarking that, whereas Lancaster recommended a sloping floor so that the master could see the children clearly, Wilderspin and Stow altered the floor-level for an exactly opposite reason.

Stow's debt to Wilderspin (which he freely acknowledged) is obvious, and it may be noted that the use of the gallery did not make the classroom superfluous, for it was still used for teaching each class in rotation. Stow's ideas were further elaborated in his book, *The training system*, first published in 1836, but reissued and expanded many times subsequently, so that it must have become one of the most influential books on educational practice published in the nineteenth century. Already in the 1836 edition Stow was urging that the simultaneous method (including the use of a gallery) should be extended from the infant into the 'juvenile' schools, and it is not surprising that Stow was closely associated with new methods of teacher-training, since adult skills were needed to work his system properly.[32] This same edition contains a number of plans of infant and juvenile schools, all of which show a gallery in the main room, and a separate classroom. There are also engravings of the interiors of both types of school, one of which (the infants' school) is reproduced as pl. **125**.[33] The boys and girls are shown seated on a gallery (separated from each other by a wooden rail). The master's chair and a Bible-stand are immediately in front, from which position the gallery lessons are given. In the main body of the room stand lesson-posts with pictures of objects attached to them. When not in the gallery, the children stood in circles around these posts, at each of which a monitor was stationed. Benches for the children run along each side wall. In the juvenile school, writing desks stand along the side walls and the lesson-posts are dispensed with, but the children would still assemble in groups in the main part of what Stow now calls the 'school hall' when they were not being taught all together on the gallery or class by class in the classroom. The 1836 edition also has illustrations of school apparatus, such as the circular swing used in the playground, a lesson-post, a ball-frame, various pictures used for lessons, an 'orthographical desk' used for learning to spell (an early 'teaching machine'?), as well as descriptions, varying from the familiar blackboard to the less familiar 'gonigraph', which is described as 'a small instrument composed of twelve flat steel rods connected by pivots which, at pleasure, are formed into all possible geometrical figures'. Very few objects of this kind seem to have survived in museums or elsewhere—the emphasis has hitherto been on collecting toys and games.[34]

Leaving aside essential differences of methodology, it will be seen that Stow's schoolroom combines several features, not only of Wilderspin's school, but of Lancaster's and Bell's also. The inclined floor of the Lancasterian school may be said to some extent to have foreshadowed the gallery while the lesson-posts are clearly analogous to the boards hung up in Lancasterian schools, but the classes stand in the main body of the room and write at desks on the sides, as in the Madras school. It was Robert Owen, however, who, in his pioneer school at New Lanark, pointed forward most accurately to future developments—not only in his well-known provision for dancing and teaching from pictures,[35] which Wilderspin and others also practised, but in an interesting piece of self-criticism, as recorded by his son in 1824:

> We may here remark that it is probable the facility of teaching the older classes particularly would have been greatly increased had some part of the building been divided into smaller apartments, appropriating one to each class of from twenty to thirty children, provided such an arrangement had not encroached either on the lecture room, or principal schoolroom.[36]

Before, however, we follow up some of these further ideas, let us examine some surviving buildings of the period 1800 to 1840 to see what light they throw on the subject and how far the writers with whom we have dealt influenced the design of actual schools.

IV

So far in this chapter we have been concerned with the interior plans of elementary-school buildings, and the educational ideas which influenced them. It is fortunate that the writers whom we have been discussing gave so much attention to this aspect of the subject, since, although buildings of this date have certainly survived, their interiors have been remodelled, and in effect one is left with little more than the shells of the original buildings. The main points of interest are their overall dimensions relative to the numbers they were first designed to accommodate, the external architectural character of the buildings and their relationship to the surrounding area. A study of the subsequent alterations made to the buildings can throw light on later educational developments, but here we are attempting to reconstruct their original forms, their original architectural character and the social and physical environment as it was when these schools were built. This is no easy task, since the structural histories of these schools are often difficult to disentangle and the sources for the study of individual schools of this type are diverse and fragmentary.

Thus, we can usually no longer rely on the reports of the Charity Commissioners, since these monitorial schools were in general maintained by subscriptions and not endowed with land or other property. In only a minority of cases have school minute or account books survived, and the best initial sources are often local directories, though they give relatively little information for the early decades of the century. Local newspaper accounts of school openings and alterations can be very useful, but much research is needed to explore the history of even one such school from so voluminous a source. Records held by the National and other voluntary societies, and the official Education papers now in the Public Record Office can also be useful, but there are many gaps, especially for the early nineteenth century.[37] Thus very often the major piece of surviving evidence is the building itself, frequently much altered, given over to other uses, or simply standing empty and neglected.

As for the architectural character and social setting of such schools, these also are best examined on the ground. It is often possible to determine by physical inspection what parts of the building are original, and occasionally one can compare the building as it is now with engravings in early topographical works which show what it used to look like. If we also consider—as we should—the relationship of a particular school to the area as it was when the school was first built, one enters the field of urban history which has its own techniques of investigation.[38] This is a very large and rapidly-growing field, and the only reference which can be made to it here is to mention the value of early town maps for the study of the building of schools as an important aspect of nineteenth-century urban development. Further reference is made to the use of maps, and some of the other sources here described, later in this chapter.[39]

There are a few categories of elementary-school buildings of this period which can be largely ignored for the purposes of this present study. These are the schools which followed the traditional pattern of provision which we examined in the previous chapter: the individual benefactions and the schools founded in an earlier period, but extended to meet increased local demand or housed in new premises during the nineteenth century.[40] From among the fairly numerous examples of the first category, we may mention two which record their origin in carved inscriptions on the surviving buildings: Handsworth (near Sheffield) originally founded by the will of the Rev. F. Lockier in 1734, but housed in a new building in 1800 (pl. **126**) and Barkestone (Leics.) where an attractive oval plaque records that the school was built in 1814 by Daniel Smith for the education of twenty-six poor children (pl. **127**). Extensions to earlier buildings are also fairly common, as may be seen at Haughton (Notts.), where a small English school of 1692 was extended in the nineteenth century, and Laughton-en-le-Morthen (West Riding), built in 1605 and added to in 1805 in the same local stone and traditional style. Some of the larger charity schools of the eighteenth century were completely rebuilt during the nineteenth, and continuity was often emphasized by continuing to make a feature of the statues of charity school children—indeed, using the statues from the original building when possible. Thus in Northampton the Corporation charity school was rebuilt in Bridge Street in 1811, with two niches to contain the figures of a charity boy and girl.[41] Nearby, in Kingswell Street, the Beckett and Sargeant Charity School of 1735 was rebuilt in the Gothic style in 1862 and a figure of a charity girl was placed in the centre of the façade (pl. **189**; cf. pl. **101**). In London, the 'St Bride's and Bridewell Precinct Schools', originally established in 1711, were rebuilt in 1840 in eighteenth-century style and with the original figures of charity children. (This building survives as Nos. 16–17 Bride Lane, between Fleet Street and New Bridge Street, though the statues have been removed to St Bride's church.)[42] Similarly, in Leicester, St Mary's School, which until recently stood in Castle Street, was rebuilt in the Gothic style in 1869, but the design included the eighteenth-century figures of a charity boy and girl from the original school (pl. **190**).[43]

Our main concern, however, is with the new type of elementary school, built as a result of the social conditions created by the Industrial Revolution, financed by local subscriptions and often associated with the new voluntary societies. Inevitably there was a time-lag between the enunciation of the ideas of educational reformers and the actual building of schools. I do not know of a single surviving example of a subscription school of the new type built before 1810. Thereafter they become more numerous, though at first mainly in the towns. The difficulties of setting up monitorial schools in rural areas with a scattered population were described by the Vicar of Kildwick and Skipton in the Yorkshire dales, who informed the Archdeacon of York in 1815, in reply to the question, 'What causes operate to prevent the adoption of the method of instruction recommended by the National Society?' that:

> it is also requisite that Schoolrooms be fitted up in conformity with the new plan, which is some expense: and, what is no less curious than true, 50 scholars are not sufficient to obtain every benefit of the system; 100 are not quite enough, and 200 are better than 150; and the larger the number, of course it would be more expensive in accommodation of room and all requisite materials.[44]

In the towns, however, committees associated with the National and British Societies were formed in the second and third decades of the century to promote the building of new schools. Such committees seem to have been well informed about the latest developments in school design, though lack of funds often caused them to be modified in actual practice. For example, the Northampton branch of the National Society, meeting in 1829, reported that a new infants' school measuring 46 by 28 feet had been built in Northampton, but it was regretted that a house for the master and mistress adjoining the schoolroom could not be afforded, 'as such a house besides its obvious convenience, would be a means of protecting the property, and of rendering a large salary to the Master and Mistress less necessary, and would contain a classroom, which is considered of great importance in such schools'. Clearly, they were influenced by other than purely educational considerations, but at least they were aware of the Wilderspin model.[45]

Of the early monitorial school buildings which survive, those associated with the British and Foreign School Society are much less numerous than those of the National Society; what evidence there is suggests that, so far as external appearance was concerned, there was at first little or no difference between British and National schools of similar date. It may be useful to list the early British schools examined, with a brief note of the results, which will also indicate the general state of the architectural and documentary evidence of elementary-school buildings of the period 1800 to 1840:

1812. Wakefield (Yorks.). A school with a plaque bearing the words 'Lancasterian School 1812' survived in Margaret Street until 1959, when it was demolished to make way for extensions to the technical college. There is a photograph of it in the National Monuments Record, which is reproduced as pl. **130**. It will be seen that most of the windows have been altered, and it is probable that they all originally had semicircular heads, like the one below the pediment. The promoters' earliest surviving report (1823) mentions that there were 220 boys on the roll. The school was reorganized in 1856, and two years later there were 108 boys, fifty-eight girls and eighty-four infants. The school must have been extended later, presumably at the rear, for there were 658 children in attendance in 1880. Thereafter the numbers declined and the school was closed in 1901.[46]

1812. Leeds. A British school was built in Alfred Street, Boar Lane, in 1812 at a cost of £2,000. There was accommodation for 500 boys and the school was supported by voluntary subscriptions and the children's pence. The last reference to it in local directories is in 1872. The Ordnance Survey maps of Leeds printed in 1850 on the scale of 5 feet to the mile show the school, and also the arrangement of the desks, which occupy the main body of the room facing the master in Lancasterian manner. A building of four storeys still survives on this site, but it has been so much altered that it is impossible to guess at the appearance of the original school of 1812.[47]

1816. Shelf (near Halifax). A British school was built by public subscription in Carr House Lane in 1816. It consists of a long, single-storey schoolroom with a two-storey teacher's house attached. There is a carved stone dated 1816 and bearing the words 'School for the Children of Parents of all Religious persuasions upon the plan of the British and Foreign School Society (Late Lancasterian)', together with a list of the patrons of the Society and a quotation from Prov. iv., 13. There is no information as to the number of children who attended, but a new classroom was added in 1904. The building is now used by the Bethel Methodist Society as a Sunday school, and is illustrated on pl. **132**.[48]

1834. Kettering (Northants.). The minutes of the British School, which survive in Kettering Public Library, show that a school was built in what is now School Lane in 1834 and had accommodation for 100 boys and seventy girls. It was altered in 1864 in order to comply with the requirements of the Committee of Council and so become eligible for grant (there was much argument, as in other places, between those who desired State aid and the 'voluntaryists', who opposed it). The school was virtually rebuilt on the same site in 1874, and this is the school which survives as a youth centre. (Its long, low, shed-like appearance preserves something of its original character.)[49]

1834. Corby (Northants.). Although a British school was built in Meeting Lane (a significant Nonconformist name) in 1834, it has been so much altered that the original plan cannot now be reconstructed. The tablet formerly over the school door is now built into the wall of the school-house garden, which adjoins the school. It records that the school was erected by William Rowlett in 1834 and 'transferred by deed of gift to the British and Foreign School Society of London'. The school is still called the Rowlett School, but is under the control of the L.E.A.

1836. West Ham (now part of the London Borough of Newham). The Stratford British Boys' School was built in what is now Station Street in 1836 and was still standing in 1968, though derelict. Like the former school at Wakefield, it is a single-storey brick building with a pedimented central section. The schoolroom was an oblong with the long side facing the street, i.e. the pedimented portion does not indicate any internal division. The school cost £900 (part of which came from Government grant) and in 1846 there were 160 boys on the roll. In 1871 the report of the local school board (which, as elsewhere, carried out a survey of existing schools) gave the capacity of the school as 241 and the attendance 165. It was transferred to the board in 1873; five years later two classrooms were added, but lessons were hindered by the noise of the railway. The railway company used compulsory powers provided by Act of Parliament to acquire the freehold of the school, which closed in 1889.[50]

1836. Ross-on-Wye (Herefs.). This is a four-storeyed stone building of impressive appearance which still stands in Wye Street (see pl. **136**). An inscription below the pediment reads: 'The Royal Ross & Archenfield British Schools Established under the Patronage of Her Royal Highness the Princess Victoria Oct. 7th 1836', and below the top-storey windows are the words 'British & Foreign School'. Very little information is available about this school. The British Society's annual reports state that it cost £1,500 and was designed for 200 children, though by 1840 there were 184 boys and 104 girls on the roll. A directory of 1858 gives the name of the master and mistress, and another of 1867 states that the average attendance was 120 boys and seventy girls. The view of the building from Wye Street gives a somewhat false impression of its size, for it is built into the side of a hill, and the two lower storeys measure externally only 32 by 24 feet; these are lit entirely from the front and were probably used as living accommodation by the master and mistress. The boys' and girls' schoolrooms must have been in the third and fourth storeys, which measure externally about 32 by 48 feet. The room on the top floor was well lit from the side as well as the front and back, and can be entered from the top road (the main road to Monmouth); these windows have now been blocked up and the room is used as a Masonic hall.[51]

1838. Market Harborough (Leics.). The original British school, built of brick, survives as part of the Fairfield Road Infant School. Additions have been made to it, but the plan can be reconstructed (see fig. 26 (*a*) on p. 154). It consisted of a single-storey schoolroom measuring 70 by 28 feet, with a teacher's house at one end measuring 41 by 28 feet. The teacher was originally accommodated on two floors, but the roof line is a continuation of the schoolroom. This part of the building is the least altered, and retains the original round-headed doorway, windows with original panes, and external brick pilasters; the interior has, however, been remodelled and at one time contained an infants' gallery. (It is possible that this was an original feature, in which case the area occupied by the teacher would have measured only 21 by 28 feet.)

V

The National schools which survive from the period before 1840 are more numerous, and it is proposed to describe those examined in somewhat less detail. Many of these buildings were much larger in size than the elementary schools of the previous century, and in this respect the monitorial schoolrooms resembled the major grammar-school foundations, which, as we saw in earlier chapters, often included one very large teaching room (for example, Berkhamsted, 70 by 27 feet, and Shrewsbury, 78 by 21 feet). Lancaster in 1811 had recommended a schoolroom measuring 70 by 32 feet for 320 children, and the British and Foreign School Society's manual of 1831 one of 62 by 34 feet, designed for 304 children. We also noticed that the National Society included in its list of 1816 a school at Sittingbourne measuring 62 by 20 feet for 200 scholars, while in its list of 1835 was one of 86 by 32 feet for 300 scholars, at Bangor. The large schoolrooms of the new elementary schools were usually gaunt and barn-like in appearance. A good impression of the interior of such a school may be seen in the former National school at Daventry (Northants.), which was built in the period 1826 to 1874 and abandoned as a school in 1913 (see pl. **133**).[52]

The earliest monitorial school connected with the Church of England which I have examined is the school on Pound Hill, Cambridge, built in about 1810 (when tenders for its erection were invited in the local Press). The schoolroom measures 74 by 32 feet, which is almost exactly the size suggested by Lancaster. The original teacher's house also survives on the north-west end, and here it may be noted that, when funds permitted, it was usual to provide accommodation for the teacher alongside the school: this was traditional practice, as we have seen, and there was the further advantage mentioned by the Northampton committee in 1829, that a rent-free house meant that a lower salary could be paid to the teacher. The school at Pound Hill has been much altered and is no longer in use as a school, but it retains its original plaque with the words: 'Free School supported by voluntary contributions' (pl. **128**). A school of similar T-shaped plan, but with the teacher's house facing the road, still stands in King Street, Cambridge (built 1816); it is now used as a garage. Also in Cambridge, near to the Pound Hill school, between Albion Row and Mount Pleasant, is a former elementary school and teacher's house of *c.* 1825.[53]

These early nineteenth-century schools at Cambridge are virtually devoid of any architectural embellishment. Similarly, the first National school built at Cheltenham (Gloucestershire) in 1816 (which survives as St Luke's Hall in Bath Road) was originally an extremely plain, box-like building without decorative features of any kind.[54] At the same time there are some places where schools of an attractive, if simple, appearance were built, sometimes with the help of a wealthy patron. A good surviving example—

still in use as a school and therefore well-maintained—is on the borders of Shropshire and Flintshire (actually in the latter county). This is the building at Penley still called the Madras School, which has a pleasant hipped roof of thatch and its original plaque commemorating its foundation in 1811 by the second Lord Kenyon (pl. **129** and fig. 25 (a)). This plaque also has a carving of a Bible and Prayer Book, to indicate the Anglican allegiance of the school.[55]

Further research might show that other early nineteenth-century schools owed something to vernacular building styles, and certainly it would seem that there was

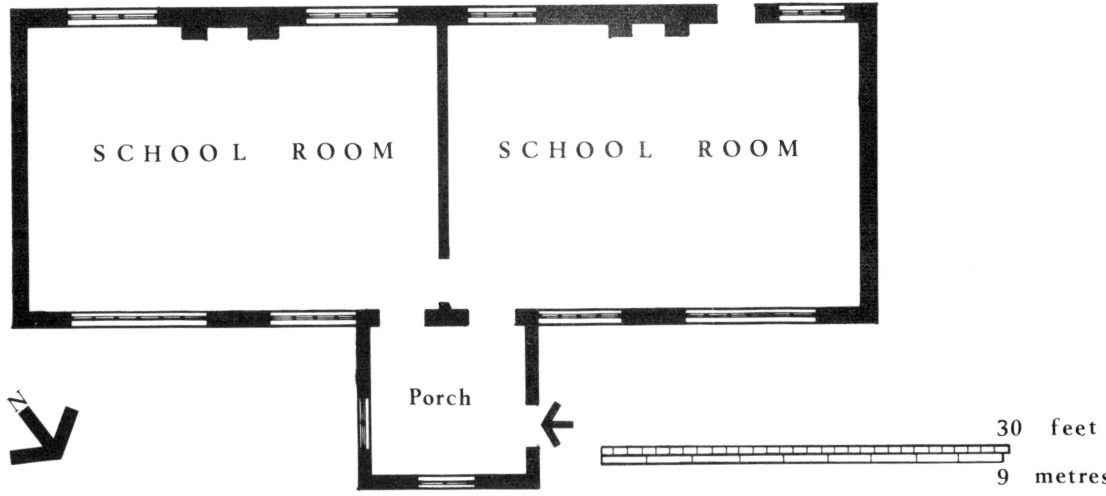

Figure 25 (*a*) Penley, Madras School, 1811, ground plan.

Figure 25 (*b*) Wisbech, Girls' School, 1814, ground plan.

some regional variation. In Devon, for example, Mr Sellman has shown the importance of the 'Church House' schools. The Church Houses were apparently used in the eighteenth century to accommodate pauper children and adults. When new workhouses were set up after the Poor Law Amendment Act of 1834 some of these buildings were remodelled entirely for school purposes (as at Chawleigh): and, since in the Church Houses it was usual for the adults to be on the ground floor with the children above, Mr Sellman tells us that in the 1820s a number of elementary schools followed this local tradition and were built with the teacher's rooms below and the school above (as at Lamerton, Sydenham Damerel, Lustleigh and Kentisbeare).[56] In parts of Leicestershire, too, there are country schools of the 1830s which have very similar external features—for example, the school at Sibson (1839) is an exact copy, though somewhat smaller, of the school at Nailstone (1828–36), four miles away. It was not until after 1840 that elementary-school plans began in a certain sense to be 'mass-produced', a point to which we return in ch. 10.

In the towns a common stylistic character seems to have emerged for the new elementary schools—usually they were lofty, single-storey buildings, built of brick and with strip-pilasters and pediments which serve to enhance the general effect of strict severity. A good early example is the former school in Hill Street, Wisbech (Cambridgeshire), where the inscription reads: 'The School for Girls Built by the Burgesses of Wisbech A.D. 1814: supported by the bequest of Mrs E. Wright and the benefactions of Abraham Jobson D.D., John Edes Esq. and others, aided by voluntary subscriptions' (pl. **131** and fig. 25 (*b*)). The schoolroom on the ground floor (now a furniture saleroom) measures 62 by 32 feet, and there is a row of iron columns down the centre, helping to support the upper floor. The character of the brick-work appears to be the same on the whole of the front of the building, but the different shape of the first-floor windows and an alteration in the bonding of the bricks on the gable end may indicate that this school was originally single-storey. Another good example is the former National school in Market Street, Kettering (Northants.), which was built in 1820, with a teacher's house facing the London Road. This building is now occupied by the Weights and Measures Department of the County Council, but the original schoolroom of 70 by 20 feet can still be made out, though now subdivided.

Most of the elementary schools of the 1820s and 1830s are classical in style, but it is interesting to trace the beginning of Gothic—or, more accurately, of the Tudor (Late Perpendicular)—style which had come into 'official' use after the passing of the Church Building Act of 1818 (the 'economical Gothic' of the 'Commissioners' churches').[57] The earliest elementary-school building in this style known to me is one which is still in use, the Clerkenwell Parochial School in Amwell Street, Finsbury (pl. **137**). This was an exceptionally large building erected in 1828 to cope with a rapid increase in the school population in that part of London. The building cost £3,000 and was designed by W. C. Mylne, architect to the New River Company, which adjoined the school. It consisted of a boys' school on the ground floor measuring 90 by 40 feet and a girls' school on the first floor which was 30 feet shorter, but the same width; in 1834 there were 253 boys and 164 girls on the roll. Because Clerkenwell was one of the 'most populous districts of the Metropolis', the National Society made an exceptionally large grant of £500 towards the cost of building.[58] The same amount was granted in 1828 to the new National school at St Martin-in-the-Fields (which opened two years later), since this was an 'important parish' and the school was 'to form a conspicuous object among the improvements contemplated in that part of the Metropolis'. As in the case of Clerkenwell, there were two large schoolrooms on separate floors, each room being designed to accommodate 250 children. The National Society was informed in 1828 that the cost would exceed £3,000, 'exclusive of the site, with which His Majesty has graciously been pleased to present the parish' (a fact recorded in large letters on the building itself). This school, which is illustrated on pl. **134**, is still standing in Adelaide Street behind the church, but it ceased to be used as a school in 1965.[59]

St Martin's School, the design of which is attributed to G. L. Taylor, has been much admired as a piece of architecture and certainly it is in a class by itself so far as elementary-school buildings of this period are concerned. It will be seen that the ground floor is rusticated and the upper storey ornamented with giant Ionic pilasters, since for a 'prestige building' of this kind a classical style was preferred to the parsimonious Gothic of Clerkenwell. During the 1820s and 1830s both styles were used, in simpler form, when building schools outside London. A handsome example of the classical style—complete with portico—is the school at Sandford in Devon, built in 1825,[60] while a more modest example of the same style persisting in elementary-school building may be seen in the former National school in Barker Gate, Nottingham (pl. **135**). This was opened as a girls' school in 1834, later became a boys' school, and seems to have ceased to be used as a school before the end of the century (it is now used as a store by a local firm). In 1833 an application was made to the National Society for a grant, and on the form of application it was stated that a school was needed to accommodate 600 girls on two floors, each room to measure 60 by 22 feet. In fact, the existing building measures externally exactly 60 by 30 feet, which would give the minimum 6 square feet per child which the National Society seems to have insisted upon (i.e. 300 girls on each floor of 1,800 square feet: the Nottingham promoters seem not to have taken account of wall-thicknesses).[61]

On the whole, however, it is the Tudor Gothic rather than the classical style which begins to predominate in the 1830s and continues into the 1840s and 1850s. An early provincial example is the school at Milton Abbot (Devon), where one of the last endowed elementary schools in the county was built in Tudor style by the Duke of Bedford in 1829.[62] Another example—this time dating from 1839 and incorporating the teacher's house in the design—is the National school at Great Bowden, near Market Harborough in Leicestershire (pl. **139**). The promoters applied to the National Society for a grant in 1838 and stated that they proposed to build a school with separate rooms for 60 boys and 60 girls, each measuring 25 by 15 feet, with a house for the master and

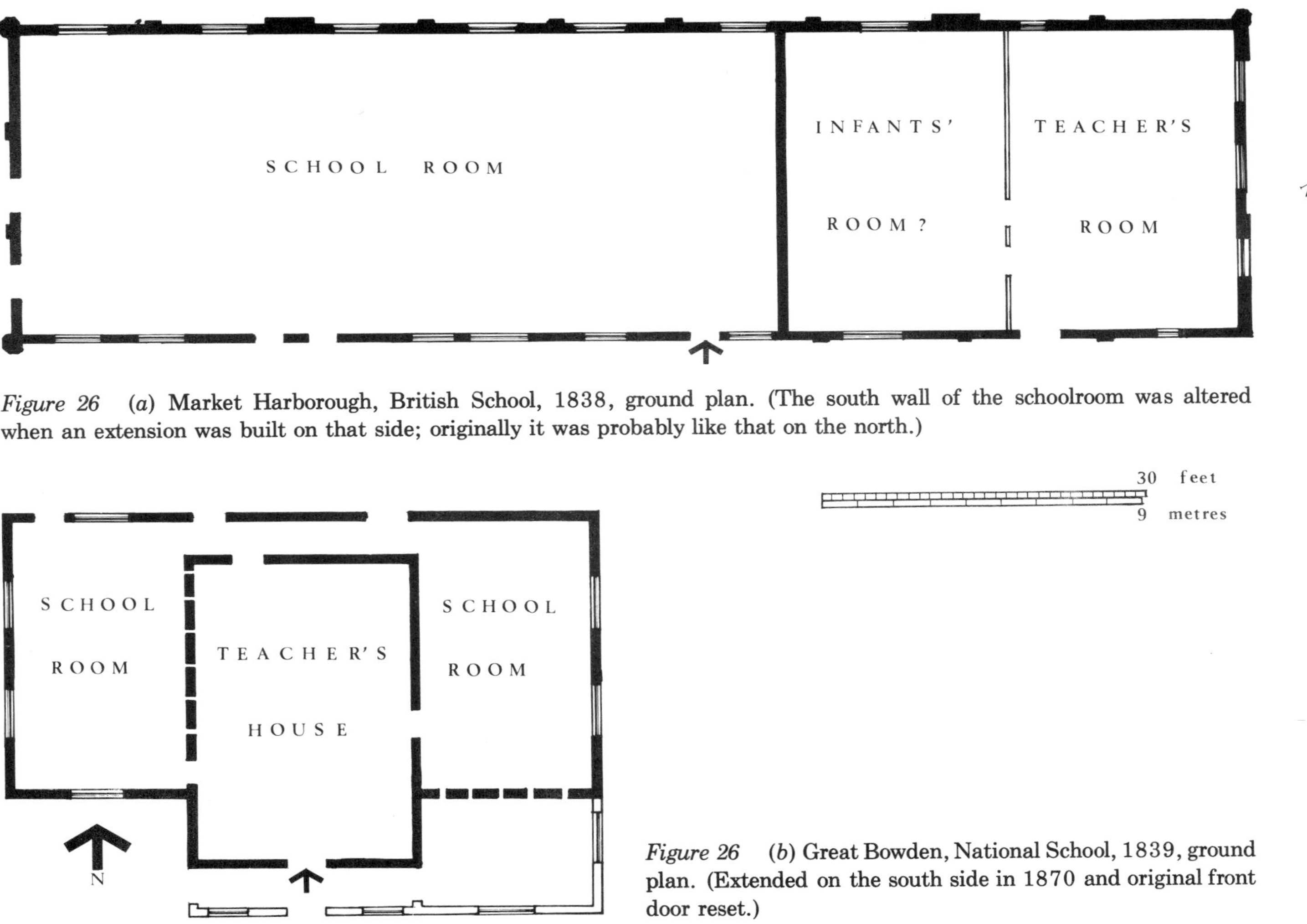

Figure 26 (*a*) Market Harborough, British School, 1838, ground plan. (The south wall of the schoolroom was altered when an extension was built on that side; originally it was probably like that on the north.)

Figure 26 (*b*) Great Bowden, National School, 1839, ground plan. (Extended on the south side in 1870 and original front door reset.)

mistress. They estimated the cost at £350, and stated that £290 had already been collected by subscriptions. The school as actually built (and still in use as a school) originally consisted of two schoolrooms 25 by 15 feet, separated from each other by the master's house, which was of two storeys. A further application was made to the National Society in 1870 for enlargements estimated to cost £480, and it was probably at this date that the internal walls in the master's house were removed to make a classroom, one of the original schoolrooms extended and a porch built at the front, with the original door re-set (see fig. 26 (*b*)).[63]

The Perpendicular style was coming to be considered particularly appropriate for schools because of its frequent use in scholastic buildings during the great educational expansion of Tudor and Stuart times. We may, for example, compare the windows and doors of the school at Clerkenwell with those of similar design on the school at Guildford built in 1557 (pl. **19**) noticing the similarity of form, but also perhaps the relative lack of vigour in the Clerkenwell design. Perpendicular forms had persisted even longer in vernacular buildings: a fairly late example is the village school built in the local style at Billesdon (Leics.) in *c*. 1650. Certainly on the Stone Belt there was nothing incongruous in reviving this style of building, so that, for example, the Catholic school built in Broadway (Worcs.) in 1851 fits in well with the other local buildings.[64] Two other charming examples—this time from further south—are the schools at Osmington (Dorset), built in 1835, and at Cruwys Morchard, near Tiverton in Devon, built in about 1840 (see pls. **138** and **140**).

VI

There is one final aspect of elementary-school building during the first forty years of the nineteenth century which requires further comment. As we saw earlier in this chapter, separate schools for infants began to be advocated in the 1820s. The first infant school at Cheltenham, for example, was built in 1827, that at Leicester in 1828 and that at Northampton in 1829. These buildings no longer exist, and indeed very few early infant schools seem to have survived. On the whole, it appears that the main changes came after 1840, when, as we shall see, it became usual to provide a separate room for infants in schools designed for the whole age-range; or one finds that an extra room for infants was built on to an existing school. I have, however, examined two schools which were originally designed for the use of infants only and date from 1830 and 1840 respectively.

The first of these was built in Cheltenham and survives, though altered and extended, in St James's Square (it is now a Post Office sorting depot). The design of the school was apparently approved by Wilderspin himself, who was living in Cheltenham at the time. It is known from documentary sources that the school accommodated 300 pupils aged from two to seven, and contained a 20-foot gallery where unison lessons were taken. An examination of the building (see pl. **141** and fig. 27 (a)) shows that it consisted of one large room measuring 60 by 30 feet (so giving the usual 6 square feet per child). The position of the gallery can still be made out at one end of the room, where there is a recess 20 feet wide; there was no separate classroom, but a contemporary painting shows that the playground was equipped with circular swings, as recommended by Wilderspin.[65]

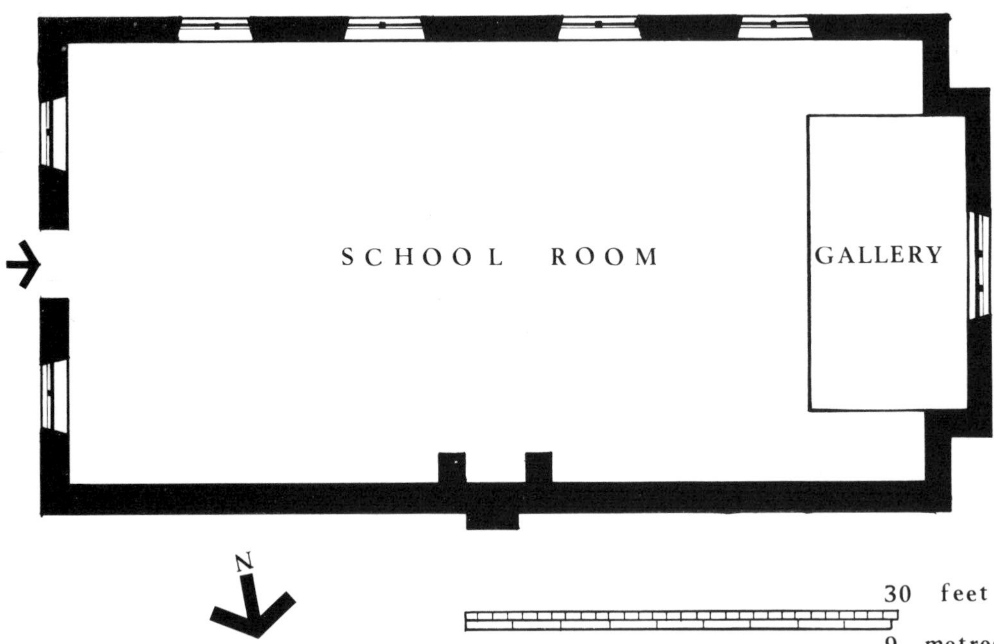

Figure 27 (*a*) Cheltenham, school for 300 infants, 1830, ground plan. (The south wall and gallery have now been removed and the original entrance blocked up.)

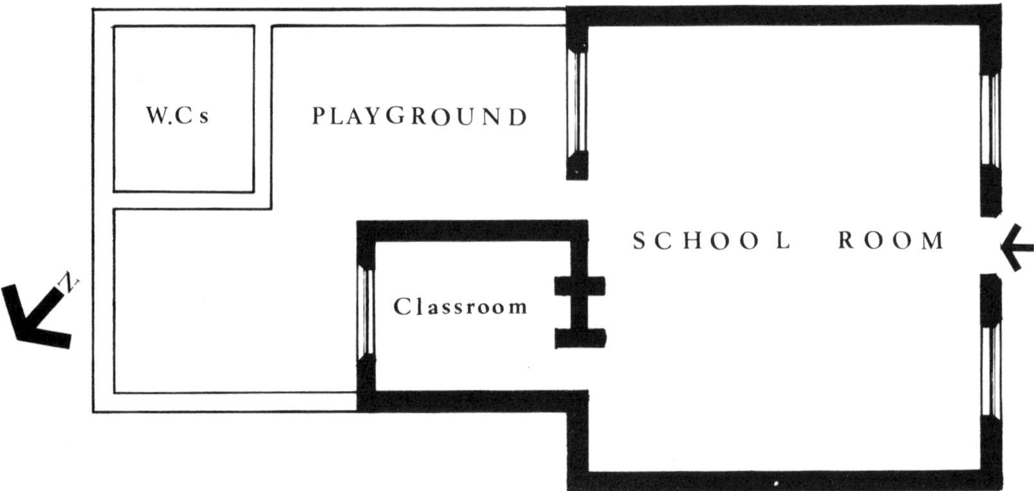

Figure 27 (*b*) Newark-on-Trent, school for 200 infants, 1840, ground plan. (The gallery must originally have been on the south side of the schoolroom.)

Our second example has been altered very little, though the gallery has been removed. This is the former infant school in King Street, Newark (Notts.), now used as an artist's studio (pl. **142**). It is situated in a working-class district first built up in the 1830s and 1840s, and the whole area is an interesting example of early industrial development (much of it is now being cleared away, but the original layout of the streets, with their narrow passages and courtyards can be reconstructed with the help of the 25-inch Ordnance Survey map). The school has the inscription 'Infants School 1840', and consists of a main room measuring 30 by 27½ feet, with a room 13 by 10 feet adjoining it, which must have been the classroom; the playground was relatively large for that date, and contains three water-closets (see fig. 27 (*b*)). According to local directories, the school was built by subscription to accommodate 200 infants. By modern standards, this would have made for severe overcrowding, and the classroom in particular appears to be very small indeed. One must remember, however, that only one class at a time used this room and that the playground was regarded by Wilderspin and Stow as an 'uncovered schoolroom'. In Stow's *Training system* (1836), his plan for 200 infants recommends the provision of a main room measuring 52 by 25 feet, a classroom 16½ by 12 feet and a playground 90 by 50 feet. If one includes both the main room and the classroom, this gives over 7 square feet per child; the Newark dimensions give less than 5, though it may be noted that in later directories the accommodation figure is reduced to 150.[66]

To conclude our examination of these early elementary-school buildings, we may perhaps say that, although their architectural appeal is often very limited, they justify detailed consideration because of their importance from the social and educational points of view. However barn-like in appearance and however inadequate by present-day standards they may have been, it is worth remembering that many thousands of children were taught inside their walls.

Notes

1 Department of Education and Science, *The school building survey, 1962,* H.M.S.O., 1965, especially Table 2.

2 Bamford, T. W., *The evolution of rural education 1850–1964*, Institute of Education, University of Hull, 1965, 44–53.

3 Russell, R. C., *The foundation and maintenance of schools for the poor*, Lindsey C. C., 1965, 76.

4 Sellman, R. R., *Devon village schools in the nineteenth century*, Newton Abbot: David & Charles, 1967, 25 and 35–7.

5 Stow, D., *The training system adopted in model schools of the Glasgow Educational Society*, Glasgow: McPhun, 1836, 53–4.

6 The sub-titles of Lancaster, J., *Improvements in education*, Darton & Harvey, 3rd ed., 1805, Wilderspin, S., *On the importance of educating the infant children of the poor*, Goyder, 1823, and Stow, D., *The training system, op. cit.*

7 Most recently in Sturt, M., *The education of the people*, Routledge & Kegan Paul, 1967, ch. 2. See also Salmon, D. (ed.), *The practical parts of Lancaster's 'Improvements' and Bell's 'Experiment'*, Cambridge U.P., 1932.

8 Lancaster, *op. cit.*, 188, 165.

9 *The British system of education: being a complete epitome of the improvements and inventions practised at the Royal Free Schools, Borough-road, Southwark*, London, 1810. This has a number of illustrations, including 'a representation of the boys at eight stations, generally called reading stations, but equally applicable to reading, spelling or arithmetic' (reproduced in Seaborne, M., *Education*, Studio Vista, 1966, pl. 109). *Hints and directions* . . . was printed by the author and sold at the Royal Free School, Borough Road.

10 The Friends' school at Ackworth was heated by steam from 1810 (*Reports on the state of Ackworth School, 1810–12*, in Leeds Institute of Education library).

11 Special provision was not always deemed necessary in earlier times, e.g. Harsnett's ordinances for Chigwell School stated 'that no scholar upon pain of whipping do make water within the walls of the courtyard, and that for their other needful occasions they resort to some such retired place as shall be appointed unto them by the governors and not elsewhere'. The school's historian writes that 'Harsnett, otherwise so thorough, made no permanent arrangement for privies', and says that 'the retiring place used to be the churchyard' (Stott, G., *Chigwell School*, Ipswich: Cowell, 1960, 160). Lancaster's plan shows 'conveniences for the boys where they may make water'; Stow's plan of 1836, referred to later in this chapter, shows girls' and boys' 'water-closets' and a 'retiring place' for the boys. On this whole subject, see Wright, L., *Clean and decent*, Routledge & Kegan Paul, 1960.

12 *Manual of the system of primary instruction pursued in the model schools of the British and Foreign School Society* (The Society, 1831). There are several other illustrations in this book, and three plans for schools to accommodate 304, seventy-two and forty children (inside measurements: 62 by 34, 30 by 18 and 16 by 16 feet).

13 Sand appears to have been first used by Bell for teaching the shape of letters and numbers: Lancaster used wet sand, but changed to dry sand on Bell's advice. The use of 'sand trays' in elementary school continued into the twentieth century.

14 Bell's style is as generalized as Lancaster's is specific. Cf. Meiklejohn, J. M. D., *Dr Andrew Bell*, Edinburgh: Blackwood, 1881, 173: 'The Educational works of Dr Bell amount to several thousand pages; but they cannot be recommended to the perusal of even the most enthusiastic student of education. There is much dust, chaff, and inorganic matter in them; and it is only here and there that one finds something worth picking up.'

15 *The Madras school, or elements of tuition: comprising the analysis of an experiment in education made at the male asylum, Madras, etc.*, Bensley, 1808.

16 *Ibid.*, 116 (sermon preached in support of Lambeth Charity School).

17 *Ibid.*, 45. This practice of alternating classes seems to have become a regular feature of the Madras schools—see also Wood's description of the Edinburgh Sessional School quoted below. We find an echo of it as late as 1912, when an H.M.I. visiting Foleshill School, Coventry, noted that the entire school of 100 children were being taught in one room, and in 1920 that the space was 'so limited that some of the children of one class must always stand so that others may have room to write' (Docking, J. W., *Victorian schools and scholars*, Coventry Branch of the Historical Assoc., 1967, 8).

18 National Society, *4th annual report*, 1815, 93–4. The later history of these schools may be traced through subsequent reports, but the basic form of organization remained the same. There is a (reversed) illustration of the interior of the school at Baldwin's Gardens facing p. 284 of Birchenough, C., *History of elementary education*, University Tutorial Press, 1932, but I have not been able to locate the original engraving. The engravings reproduced as pls. **122** and **123** are credited to Hamel, J., *L'enseignement mutuel*, Paris, 1818, in Lange, H., *Schulbau und Schulfassung der frühen Neuzeit*, Berlin: Belz, 1967, 534–5.

19 This undated illustration is in the archives of the Greater London Council, and bears the caption, 'An internal view of Clapham school. Conducted on the system of the Madras school invented by Andrew Bell, D. D., etc. This school was erected in 1810 for the education of 200 boys.' This may well have been the school referred to in critical terms by Lancaster in *Hints and directions . . . , op. cit.*, 16. An octagonal school-house of 1819 still survives in Birmingham, Pennsylvania (Building Bulletin No. 18, *Schools in the U.S.A.*, H.M.S.O., 1961, 300), and another of 1824 at Mildenhall (Wilts.).

20 Iremonger, F., *Dr Bell's system of instruction broken into short questions and answers for the use of masters and mistresses in the National schools*, Rivington, 1825. Included in *Religious tracts dispersed by the S.P.C.K.*, vol. ix, 1827. It uses, characteristically, the catechetical method of exposition.

21 Wood, J., *Account of the Edinburgh Sessional School*, 3rd ed., Edinburgh: Wardlaw, 1830, 75.

22 National Society, *5th annual report*, 1816, 185–90.

23 *Ibid.*, *12th annual report*, 1823, 36f. The present school at North Creake (Norfolk) dates from 1887: I have not been able to locate the original National school of 1816.

24 *Ibid.*, *24th annual report*, 1835, Appendix.

25 The school at Tinwell (Rutland) mentioned in the list still exists, as may some of the others. An inscription on the Tinwell school reads: 'School room built by subscription aided by the National and County Societies 1831.' (The last figure is faint and could be 4.)

26 This is inferred from the plans of National schools included in *Minutes of the Committee of Council on Education*, 1839–40, to which further reference is made in ch. 10. A few schools had horseshoe-shaped benches, e.g. at Scremerston, Northumb., 1839 (see document 16 in Hogg, G. W., and Tyson, J. C. (eds.), *Popular education 1700–1870*, University of Newcastle upon Tyne, Dept. of Education, 1969).

27 For a discussion of early pioneers of infant education and Wilderspin's contribution, see Stewart, W. A. C., and McCann, W. P., *The educational innovators, 1750–1880*, Macmillan, 1967, 241f. See also McCann, W. P., 'Samuel Wilderspin and the early infant schools' in *B.J.E.S.*, Vol. xiv, No. 2 (May 1966), 188f., and, more generally, Salmon, D., and Hindshaw, W., *Infant schools, their history and theory*, Longmans, 1904.

28 Wilderspin, *op. cit.*, 18–19.

29 *Ibid.*, 19 and 27.

30 Wilderspin, *Early discipline illustrated; or the infant system progressing and successful*, 1832, 5, quoted in Salmon and Hindshaw, *op. cit.*, 61–2.

31 *Infant training. A dialogue, explanatory of the system adopted in the model infant school, Glasgow*, by a Director [D. Stow], Glasgow: Collins, n.d., but Introduction dated 1833, 14, and cf. 95–6. The form of the dialogue (between 'Granny', who needs to be convinced of the value of the new system, and the children, master and mistress) was similar to that used, as we saw, by Brinsley.

32 See Cruickshank, M., 'David Stow, Scottish pioneer of teacher training in Britain', *B.J.E.S.*, *op. cit.*, 205f.

33 Stow's illustrations in *The training system, op. cit.*, face pp. 67 and 119, with plans on pp. 231–7. Similar (unprovenanced) illustrations showing a Wilderspin room and playground are included in Birchenough, *op. cit.*, between pp. 306 and 307.

34 There are a number of items of early educational equipment in the Kirk collection at the Castle Museum, York. Lancaster sold equipment at the Borough Road school, as did Wilderspin when he was staying in Alpha House, Cheltenham. Further search of early educational writers would no doubt bring details of other items of school equipment to light. Some items may also be seen at the Bridewell Museum, Norwich.

35 The illustration of the interior of Owen's school at New Lanark has often been reproduced from the unprovenanced copy in the *Radio Times* Hulton Picture Library, but I have not been able to trace the original. On Owen's school, see Stewart and McCann, *op. cit.*, 53f. and plate facing p. 49. The original school building at New Lanark is described by Owen, R. D., in *An outline of the system of education at New Lanark*, Glasgow: Wardlaw & Cunninghame, 1824, 9–10. For what remains of Owen's buildings at New Lanark, see article by Garnett, R. G., 'A housing association for New Lanark', in *The Amateur Historian*, Vol. 6, No. 4, (1964), 118f., including illustrations.

36 Owen, R. D., *op. cit.*, 10.

37 The most useful records of school buildings of this earlier period are the files on individual schools kept at the National Society, Great Peter Street, Westminster. When a school applied for a grant from the Society, the managers had to complete an application form giving details of existing provision and the proposed new building or addition. The comparable records for British schools were destroyed by bombing during the war, but the annual reports survive at the British and Foreign School Society, Stone Buildings, Lincoln's Inn, and also at Borough Road College, Islington. The sets of school plans formerly kept by the Education Dept. at Whitehall have been distributed to local record offices, and occasionally include plans of schools before they were altered in the period 1840–70 (see, further, in ch. 10). Also see, more generally, the article by Pugh, R. B., 'Sources for the history of English primary schools' in *B.J.E.S.*, vol. 1, no. 1 (1952).

38 See Dyos, H. J., (ed), *The study of urban history*, Arnold, 1968.

39 See *The historian's guide to Ordnance Survey maps* [by Harley, J. B., and Phillips, C. W.] reprinted from *The Amateur Historian* (The Standing Conference for Local History, 1964). Also, Dyos, *op. cit.*, 'The use of town plans in the study of urban history', by Conzen, M. R. G., 113f. and 'Maps and plans of towns', by Harley, J. B., in *The Amateur Historian*, Vol. 7, no. 6, (1967), 196f.

40 Details of these schools are usually included in the reports of the Charity Commissioners.

41 The two charity children in the room south of the tower in All Saints Church, Northampton, probably came from the now empty niches of the school in Bridge Street, now being restored (1969).

42 Pevsner, *London*, I, 2nd ed., 1962, 316.

43 This school was demolished in 1965, but is more fully described in ch. 10, below. For examples of the ways in which eighteenth-century charity schools adapted to the monitorial system, see *Durham Blue Coat Schools 1708–1958* [by Chadwick, R., 1958] and *The story of a charity school* [Blewbury, Berks., by Northeast, P., 1964]: both are stencilled booklets published by the schools.

44 Extract from a return in the Borthwick Institute of Historical Research. (I owe this reference to the Archivist there.)

45 Minute book of the National Society, General Committee (later the Northants. Church Education Board), preserved in the Northants. Record Office. (The book begins in 1827, though the Committee began earlier; this extract is from the minutes of July 1829.)

46 Details from Walker, J. W., *Wakefield: its history and people*, Wakefield: West Yorks. Printing Co., 1934, supplied by the City Librarian.
47 I am grateful to Professor M. W. Beresford for drawing my attention to this school, and to the large-scale O.S. maps of Leeds. The other information is from the Leeds Education Committee's *Education in Leeds; a backward glance and a present view*, 1936.
48 The school at Shelf is mentioned in Parker, J., *Illustrated history of Wibsey, Low Moor . . . and Shelf*, 1902. I owe this reference to the Archivist, Central Public Library, Halifax; I am also indebted to Mr H. C. Morris of the Halifax Photographic Society for supplying photographs of the building.
49 See also Lenton, A., *History of the British School, Kettering*, Kettering, 1908 (copy in Kettering Public Library).
50 Details from Sims, W., 'Essay on the voluntary schools of West Ham' (unpublished typescript in East Ham Public Library), which also contains photographs.
51 The high cost of the school of Ross was no doubt due to the difficulties of the site. (Details supplied by Librarian, Borough Road College.)
52 The National school at Daventry was merged with the local charity school. The surviving ironstone building opposite the church is now called the Abbey Buildings, since it is on the site of a former Abbey. The charity school accounts are in the Northants. Record Office (ref. DFA/5), and show that the school was built in 1826 and enlarged in 1874. The two main schoolrooms are side by side on the first floor and now stand empty; the rooms on the ground floor are used by a private nursery school.
53 These schools are fully described in R.C.H.M., *City of Cambridge*, II, 1959, 318. The subsequent history of the Pound Hill and Albion Row schools is confusing, because both served the parish of St Giles.
54 As shown on engraving in Griffith, S. Y., *History of Cheltenham*, Cheltenham, 1826. This shows two rooms for boys and girls in one single-storey building.
55 The Madras school at Penley was opened on 30 September 1811 for 150 pupils. The only early record which survives is a visitors' book now held by the Vicar. An early print in the Flints. Record Office, Hawarden, shows that the school was originally thatched. There is also a thatched school at Barrington (Cambs.), 1839. Another school which probably preserves in its street-name its association with Bell is the former National school in Bell Row, Haslingden (Lancs.), which was built above the Court House in 1829 (plan in Lancs. Record Office, ref. DDX/118/139/5); it survives as a decorator's workshop. A good example of the use of traditional building materials may be seen at the Belfry School, Cromer Road, Overstrand (Norfolk), where pebbles were used (1830).
56 Sellman, *op. cit.*, 19 and 26. The school at Lamerton is illustrated facing p. 48, and that at Chawleigh facing p. 65. On the origin of Church houses in Devon, see Barley, M. W., *The English farmhouse and cottage*, R.K.P., 1961, 7–8.
57 Cf. Betjeman, J., (ed.), *Collins guide to English parish churches*, Collins, 1958, 65, Jordan, R. F., *Victorian architecture*, Penguin, 1966, 72, and Inglis, K. S., *Churches and the working classes in Victorian England*, Routledge & Kegan Paul, 1963, 6–7. Of the 214 churches built under the 1818 Act, 174 were Gothic. The analogy between official grants to church buildings and those to schools after 1833 is clear.
58 National Society, *18th annual report*, 1829, 16, and *23rd annual report*, 1834, 40. Other information from Pinks, J., *History of Clerkenwell*, 1865, supplied by the Librarian, Finsbury.
59 National Society, *17th annual report*, 1828, 15. See also *Survey of London*, vol. **xx**, L.C.C., 1940, 55; Pevsner, *London*, I, 2nd ed., 1962, 311; and Nairn, Ian, *Nairn's London*,

Penguin, 1966, 71.

60 Illustrated in Sellman, *op. cit.*, facing p. 49.

61 A directory of 1844 states that the building cost £767 and that only 150 pupils attended. After 1853 it is described as a boys' school, and the last entry is in the 1894 directory (ex inf. City Librarian, Nottingham).

62 Sellman, *op. cit.*, facing p. 48.

63 Details from school files in National Society offices. Schools of similar plan and date are mentioned in R.C.H.M., *Monuments threatened or destroyed*, 1963, 60 (in Old Schools Lane, Ewell, Surrey), and R.C.H.M., *County of Cambridge*, vol. 1, West Cambs., 1968, 8, school and schoolhouse at Barrington, 1839, with plan.

64 This is the School of the Virgin Mother of God, in Willersley Road, Broadway. In the High Street is St Michael's C. of E. School, built in the Gothic style in 1869, which Pevsner considers a *gaffe* in a street otherwise Tudor and Stuart in character (*Worcestershire*, 1968, 106).

65 I am indebted to Mr Trevor Hearl for drawing my attention to this school, and to others in Cheltenham. The painting of 'Cheltenham Infants School' is by T. Westall, dated 1832, and recently acquired by Cheltenham Museum. The plan is based on this, as well as an examination of the existing building.

66 I am grateful to Professor A. Everitt for drawing my attention to this building; to Anne Cooper for further information; and to Mr R. Kiddey for allowing me to examine the building and providing a plan. (For a school of 150 infants, Stow recommended a schoolroom of 42 by 25 feet and a class room of 16½ by 10 feet.)

Nine

Tradition and innovation in school-building 1800-40

I

The monitorial-type elementary schools described in the previous chapter form a well-defined group; but there were several other kinds of school buildings of the early nineteenth century which cannot be so readily classified. The period from 1800 to 1840 was, in fact, essentially one of transition, in which new pressures were being felt, but had not yet found full expression in well-defined types of school. It is, for example, still premature to make any firm distinction between elementary and secondary schools,[1] or to attempt any clear differentiation at this period between public, grammar and private schools, or even between those which took boarders and those which did not. Certain broad tendencies may be discerned, however, which form the main themes of the following chapter, viz. the growing influence of the commercial middle classes, the greater importance attached to the teaching of modern subjects (which had significant effects on internal school organization), and—on the purely architectural side—the increasing adoption of the Gothic style of building.

The usual picture given of the grammar schools in the early nineteenth century is one of severe decline. This view has, as we shall see, to be modified to some extent, but it is certainly true that the widespread introduction of what would now be called secondary education came after 1840, when new foundations began to be made on a scale unprecedented since Tudor and Stuart times. We may obtain some indication of this by analysing the dates of foundation of the 200 schools which in 1968 belonged to the Headmasters' Conference, membership of which is often regarded as the present-day criterion of 'public school' status.[2] This analysis is given in the tables overleaf.

When one also recalls that the overwhelming majority of schools founded before 1800 were radically reorganized (often including a new set of buildings) following the Public Schools Act of 1868 and the Endowed Schools Act of 1869, it will be realized that the public-school system as we now know it is very much the creation of the Victorian era.

Table I Dates of foundation of H.M.C. schools (1968)

Period	*No. of schools*
Pre–1600	76
1600–99	19
1700–99	8
1800–99	85
1900–68	12
	200

Table II Classification of nineteenth-century foundations by decades

Decade	*No. of schools*
1800–9	2
1810–19	6
1820–9	4
1830–9	4
1840–9	18
1850–9	8
1860–9	19
1870–9	8
1880–9	11
1890–9	5
	85

However one defines the term 'public school' (and the difficulties of doing so for the early nineteenth century are virtually insuperable), there is no doubt that the first forty years of the nineteenth century was a time of few new foundations.[3] This relative paucity, taken with the often-cited evidence of the decline of many local grammar schools, may be thought to combine to make this period a particularly barren one from the point of view of the development of school architecture and organization. This, however, is far from being the case. While there is a great deal of evidence of mismanagement and lack of pupils in many schools which may have originated as grammar schools, modern writers have perhaps been too much influenced by the strictures on the earlier system made by the Schools Inquiry Commission, which thoroughly investigated school endowments in the 1860s. Also, in relation to the early nineteenth century, the criticisms made by Nicholas Carlisle in his well-known survey of the endowed grammar schools in 1818 have tended to lead educational historians to accept as evidence of decline any modification of the traditional type of classical teaching. We have already shown in earlier chapters that many schools founded to teach Latin grammar also taught English subjects, and, as the usefulness of Latin declined, so modern subjects began to find their way into the curricula of schools of many kinds. Then, in the late eighteenth and early nineteenth centuries, the new impetus towards providing elementary education for the poor (which we examined in some detail in the previous chapter) also came to have an important effect on the endowed schools, including those originally founded to teach Latin and Greek—and here we may note once more that many local schools either did not have detailed statutes confining their curricula to the teaching of the classics, or were from the beginning founded as Latin/English or wholly English schools. To imply, as Carlisle frequently does, that an old-established school was no longer truly functioning because it was teaching largely elementary subjects is not to say that it was not still fulfilling a very useful educational purpose and one wholly in conformity with local demand.

This point has been demonstrated in two recent studies of the grammar schools during this period. It has been shown that many schools, especially those controlled by local bodies in touch with the needs of the community, were very active in the elementary sphere and that it was only in the second half of the nineteenth century that the poorer classes were effectively excluded.[4] The teaching of elementary and to a lesser extent commercial subjects helps to explain the building of 'English schools' connected with local grammar schools which took place during this period. This bifurcation of the curriculum affected the design of schools, as we shall see, and gives added interest to the story of school-building during this period. If, in addition, we consider the schools which for various reasons were rebuilt, the continuing work of the private schools, and the relatively few but very important pioneer schools which appeared at this time, it will be seen that the first forty years of the nineteenth century were by no means sterile from the point of view of school design and construction.

II

Of the new foundations of the early nineteenth century, two were Roman Catholic (Ampleforth, 1802, and Downside, 1814) and, like the Jesuit college at Stonyhurst (1794), can be accounted for by the flight of Catholic schools from the Continent during the Revolutionary and Napoleonic wars. The most notable development was at Stonyhurst, which occupied a Tudor country house extended in 1808–10 to include not only schoolrooms, playrooms and dormitories, but also an 'academy room' where science was taught. The early nineteenth century also saw the foundation of a number of Nonconformist schools. The most important was the 'Protestant Dissenters' Grammar School' founded at Mill Hill, near London (1807). In addition, the Methodists founded a school at Woodhouse Grove, near Bradford (1812); the Congregationalists schools at Lewisham in Kent (1811, later at Caterham, Surrey) and Silcoates near Wakefield (1820); and the Quakers schools at Sidcot in Somerset (1808) and Bootham near York (1823). The Methodists and the Quakers had, as we have seen, been active in founding schools in the previous century, but these new foundations demonstrated the greater emphasis which was now being placed on the provision of middle-class schools. The Bootham school, for example, was the result of a desire to establish—in the words of its promoters—'a school under the control of the Quarterly Meeting of York which would afford a liberal, guarded and religious education, on moderate terms, to the sons of Friends who are not considered objects of Ackworth School'. The latter school had been established for the children of Friends 'not in affluence', whereas the school at Bootham was specifically for 'a class between those who are suitable to be educated at Ackworth and those who can afford to pay the usual terms of private schools'.[5] Both boarders and day-boys were taken and the fees were very moderate. The course of instruction comprised the English subjects (reading, writing, arithmetic, English grammar, geography and history), together with mathematics and the 'elements of natural philosophy' (or science, as we should now call it). Latin, Greek, French and German could be learnt for an extra fee.

These early Nonconformist schools were all notable for the importance they attached to the teaching of modern subjects, but in most cases there was little opportunity to experiment with the design of new school buildings. Bootham School occupied an ordinary house,[6] while at Woodhouse Grove a barn was converted for school use[7] (as was being advocated, as we saw, by the National Society). When the Dissenters first established their school at Mill Hill, they took Eton and Harrow as their models and adopted a predominantly classical curriculum; also, in true eighteenth-century style, they abandoned the idea of a day school in favour of a boarding school, since 'there would be dangers, both physical and moral, awaiting youth while passing through the streets of a large, crowded and corrupt city [i.e. London]'.[8] In actual practice, however, they began to take cognizance of new developments in education: mathematics and English were taught from the start, while French and natural philosophy were added in 1821. And when in 1825 they built a new school, though they looked to the previous century in adopting a strictly classical style complete with colonnades and pediments, they made an important break with tradition in abandoning the idea of building one large schoolroom and building instead separate rooms for each master (see pl. **146**, which shows four separate 'schools' and a 'writing school'). The architect was William Tite, and the cost £15,000.[9]

The provision of separate 'schools' in a building designed for 125 boys and five masters was of great significance for the future planning of schools, and formed a marked contrast to the other major schools of the period. If, for example, one looks at the illustrations included in Ackermann's *History of the colleges of Winchester, Eton, etc.* (1816), one finds that in every case all the formal teaching is shown taking place in one or two large schoolrooms. At Winchester the arrangement was unusual, in that the 'scobs' or desks were distributed in the main body of the room (cf. pl. **64**); at Eton, as we have already seen, there were two schoolrooms (upper and lower), with the boys sitting on benches at the sides and the masters on raised 'thrones'; at Westminster the masters sat in chairs, with the boys on benches at a higher level; at Charterhouse, St Paul's, Merchant Taylors', Harrow, Rugby and Christ's Hospital the boys sat on benches arranged along the side walls and raised in tiers, usually with desks for writing. (Even in the writing school at Christ's Hospital, illustrated on pl. **69**, it will be noted that the boys sat facing each other and not the master, in contrast, as we saw, to the Lancasterian schoolroom.)[10]

It is worth looking a little more closely at some of these schools at this particular period of their history, bearing in mind the earlier phases of their development, dealt with in previous chapters. Westminster School, starved of funds by the Dean and Chapter and rigidly adhering to its classical course, declined sharply from 324 boys attending in 1818 to only sixty-seven in 1841. Harrow, having successfully resisted an attempt by the townspeople to gain entry for their children, became a little-patronized aristocratic preserve, with its numbers dropping from 295 in 1816 to seventy in 1844.[11] Charterhouse had built a new schoolroom in 1803, but it was on entirely traditional lines.[12] A bold attempt to introduce the Madras system for classical, instead of the more usual elementary, teaching at Charterhouse was startlingly successful during the period 1818–25, but failed equally dramatically, with the numbers declining from 480 in 1825 to 104 in 1833.[13]

Equally conservative was St Paul's School, which was obliged to rebuild in 1824 because its old building was in such a poor state that it had to be shored up. The number of boys was restricted to the statutory 153 from 1806 to 1877, and this number was successfully maintained because the school was regularly supported by the clergy and professional classes. The new school of 1824 (pl. **145**) was built in classical style to the design of George Smith, with an internal layout exactly corresponding to the old school, which had been erected in 1670 after the Great Fire of London, i.e. with the schoolroom in the centre and wings at each end for the masters and boarders, a plan which went back, as we saw, at least as early as Berkhamsted (1545) and had continued at—among other places—Witney (1660) and Wolverhampton (rebuilt, 1713).[14]

The new schoolroom at St Paul's was raised on columns, somewhat in the manner of Upper School at Eton (1688) and the dormitory at Westminster (1722). This was to leave space for a playground below, which was described in 1858 as 'a gloomy cloister filled with pillars which support the upper part of the central edifice: it looks like the exercising ground of a prison rather than the playground of school-boys'.[15] At Merchant Taylors' School, which had been rebuilt in 1675 and continued in use until 1875, there was a similar space beneath the schoolroom, together with rooms for the assistant masters. It remained a well-patronized school throughout this period because Bellamy, the Headmaster from 1819 to 1845, saw the need for 'an extended system of education' and, by arranging for lessons to begin at 9 a.m. instead of 7 a.m. as laid down in the statutes, made it possible to increase the number of day-boys. In 1829 he was able to persuade the Governors to convert the masters' rooms beneath the schoolroom into two writing schools, and so, to a limited extent, was able to modify the building to meet the growing need for separate classrooms for more modern subjects.[16]

Of the other major schools, the two most successful were Eton and Rugby. Eton, which had 364 boys in 1800, had nearly doubled in size—to 627—by 1833, and continued around the 500 mark during most of this period, actually reaching 806 by 1861. It did this in spite of constant and often bitter criticism in the Radical Press arising from its rigid adherence to classical teaching and persistent reports of brutality and corruption.[17] It was, moreover, able to expand without diluting its aristocratic entry or undertaking any major building programme. Winchester during this period was in decline, partly at least because of the domination of the school by the Warden and Fellows of the college;[18] at Eton similar factors operated, but did not stop the school from growing. How are we to account for this? Eton, as we saw, had built up its reputation as the leading school in England during the previous century: its connection with royalty, its patronage by the ruling class and its association with leading members of the aristocracy made it an obvious target for Radical attack, but were also the source of considerable strength. Minor reforms were made—notably the dividing up Long Chamber (1846) and the abolition of the 'Montem' ceremony (1847), the expense and disorder of which had become altogether excessive.[19] While it is true that, apart from visiting masters who taught such accomplishments as dancing, the curriculum remained almost wholly classical, it can be argued that this was also, in the case of Eton, a source of strength. It was still true that for the leisured classes a purely literary education was thought to be the most appropriate, and indeed may have been valued all the more because its very lack of practical application bestowed an exclusive social *cachet*.[20] If we ask how the very large number of boys was accommodated and taught, we find the answer in the continued growth of the system of private boarding and tuition, which was already well-established at Eton and had the great advantage of flexibility.

Eton is perhaps the earliest example of a school which economically dominated its surrounding area: the provision of food and accommodation, as yet largely outside the official control of the college authorities, must have become an important local industry, and the same was soon to happen in several other places where major schools were revived or established for the first time. As for the actual teaching, most of this was done on a private basis in the 'pupil-rooms' of individual masters, as we saw beginning to develop in the previous century. Nicholas Carlisle, writing in 1818, when there were 471 boys at Eton, says that

> the Independent Scholars, or 'Oppidans', as they are universally denominated, are very numerous. Some, mostly of high Birth or the Children of opulent Parents, are boarded in the Houses of the Lower Master and the Assistants;—some few in private Houses under the care of Individuals, who are locally stiled [*sic*] 'Private Tutors';—and the rest in the respective Boarding-Houses, the presiding Masters and Mistresses of which enjoy the prescriptive Title of 'Domine' and 'Dame'.[21]

Later, he tells us that

> it seems not generally understood of Harrow and Eton, that the Education chiefly goes on in the Pupil-room of each Master with his own Pupils. They meet in the School in certain forms only to undergo Examinations in Lessons, which have been previously prepared in the Pupil-rooms.[22]

This system showed itself capable of adaptation both to the declining numbers at Harrow and the continued rise at Eton.

Rugby School had also established itself firmly in the previous century. James had, as we noticed, introduced some new subjects, as well as setting up separate 'schools' for several of the forms. In default of a tutorial system on the Eton model, the development of separate rooms for each form or class, i.e. stage of the classical curriculum, was probably inevitable once numbers increased beyond a certain point. Even in the sixteenth century it had been usual in the larger schools for the upper and lower forms to be taught in separate rooms, and, as the numbers at Rugby rose, it became necessary to engage extra staff and give them separate rooms in which to teach. The novelty of this arrangement was, however, stressed by Carlisle in 1818 when he wrote that at Rugby 'each Form has its peculiar Master who attends to no other'.[23] James had converted barns and outhouses for use as schoolrooms, but early in the nineteenth century a large surplus of funds—and no doubt a desire to erect an impressively large building which might compare with Winchester and Eton—led the Governors to rebuild the whole school.[24] As the historian of the school writes:

> It had long been felt that some change was necessary. James had found it as much as he could do to house his classes, and was reduced to using an old almshouse for one of them, sheds for others, and a barn for the chapel. He had erected some new rooms, together with a long line of sheds for shelter in rough weather. What with these and the barns and hedges, 'cow-lodges' and 'hog-lodges', the School must have looked somewhat like a small chapel gone astray in a large farm-yard.[25]

The Governors of Rugby School, with valuable land in London, had accumulated no less than £40,000, while the annual income of the school was more than double its expenditure. They also had the important advantage of a large site. Henry Hakewill was commissioned as architect, and rebuilding went on from 1809 to 1816, comprising what is now known as the 'Old Buildings'. Tradition was followed in forming the various rooms around a quadrangle, and it is interesting to note that the Tudor Gothic style was chosen, an obvious attempt to emulate the architecture of earlier academic buildings. The main schoolroom of 1750 was demolished after a relatively short existence and the various barns and sheds were cleared away. The very fine trees were, however, retained, and here we may note that the siting and surroundings of schools were again beginning to receive attention, as they had earlier in the time of Mulcaster and Hoole. Dignified and if possible 'countrified' surroundings were now considered important for the new middle-class schools. A setting similar to that of a country house helped to create an image suitable for a school designed to attract the sons of the gentry or would-be gentry, as some private schoolmasters of the previous century had also realized.[26]

Hakewill's block consisted of School House (i.e. accommodation for the Headmaster and his boarders, for which purpose it is still used) and what is now called the Old

Quadrangle. This is entered through a gateway in Lawrence Sheriff Street. Opposite the gateway, on the south side of the quadrangle, is Schoolhouse Hall, designed and still used as a dining-room for the Headmaster and the boys of his house (see pl. **147**—this was built on the site of the school of 1750 and, like the old school, had schoolrooms above it). Alongside the hall were four 'schools' or form-rooms, opening on to cloisters (pl. **148**), together with individual boys' studies, which are still in use today for their original purpose. On the west side of the quadrangle is Hakewill's Big School, which was used for general assemblies and for teaching two of the forms. On the north side were further 'schools' and on the east side two floors of studies over the cloister; there were dormitories over the 'schools' on the south and west sides (see fig. 28 for general layout).[27] Hakewill was also engaged to build a school chapel, again in Tudor style (1819–21). This was later rebuilt, though the west door, with the date 1820, was retained. In 1827 his plan for a school library was also accepted.[28]

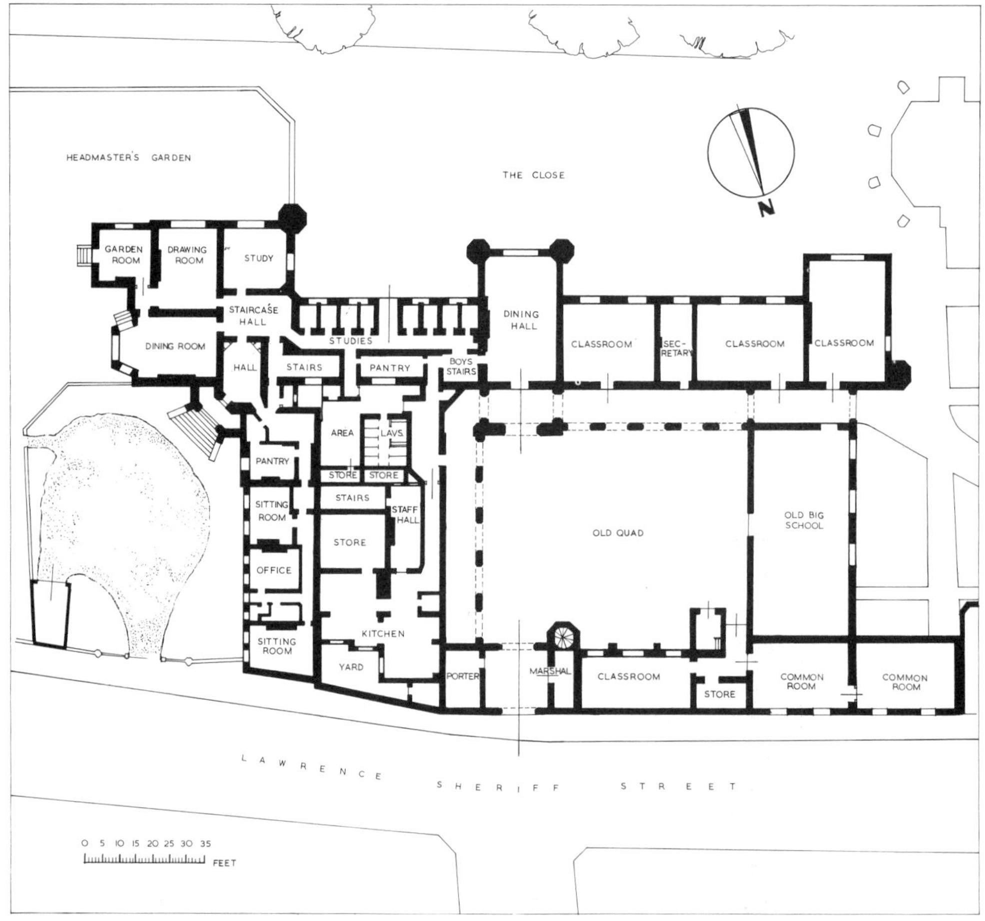

Figure 28 Rugby, School House and Old Quad, 1816, ground plan. (The common rooms in the north-west corner, and possibly the Secretary's room, were originally classrooms. School House has been remodelled since this plan was drawn.)

All this building work took place before Arnold became Headmaster in 1828, apart from the library, which was built in 1829 over the main gate and was the room used by Arnold when teaching the Sixth Form. Arnold's own additions to the building were of a minor character, though characteristic of him: he had steps erected leading to his study to enable boys to call on him with the least possible difficulty, and he arranged for a flag to be flown from the school house tower to show when he was available.[29] Arnold, of course, had no need to undertake further building, and in fact the number of boys rose very little during his headmastership. Nor was he an innovator in matters of the curriculum, being largely content to consolidate what James and Wooll (his immediate predecessor) had established. His achievement lay rather in improving the academic and, more particularly, the moral tone of the school, as to a lesser degree Samuel Butler was doing at Shrewsbury (1798–1836)—also, it may be noted, without altering the building.[30]

Arnold's major contribution to the development of school organization was not so much in making fuller use of the Sixth Form (which James had to some extent anticipated) as in bringing the boarding houses under the control of the school, and in this way providing an additional source of income for the assistant masters and the possibility of increased authority for the headmaster.[31] At Harrow the last of the dames' houses survived until 1841, but in most schools after about 1840 the boarding houses, though not as yet specially designed for the purpose, gradually came under the official control of the school authorities, with a corresponding improvement in the behaviour of the boys. There is no doubt that Rugby under Arnold led the way in this important new development.

III

The description given above of the changes taking place in the major schools helps to make clear some of the old as well as the new forces at work in education during the first forty years of the nineteenth century. When we turn to consider the small local grammar schools, we similarly find evidence that educational changes were taking place at different speeds in different parts of the country, and that the incidence of rebuilding is a good indication of the rate of development. During the first two decades of the century the classical style of architecture seems everywhere to have continued: we may cite as examples the schools at Ashby-de-la-Zouch (Leics.), built in 1807, and Colne (Lancs.), built in 1812. The school at Ashby was of two storeys and still stands near the parish church (pl. **143**). The ground floor was divided into two rooms, one of which was used by the headmaster for the classical school and the other by the trustees; the whole of the upper storey was used by the English school, the establishment of which had been authorized by the Court of Chancery in 1806.[32] This was the result of local demand for more than classical teaching, and it may be noted in passing that traditionally the Latin master occupied the 'upper school' in two-storey buildings: the reversal in this case, and the larger floor area given to the English school, is an indication of the importance attached to the teaching of non-classical subjects at this time, though still within the same foundation. The school which survives alongside the churchyard at Colne is also of two storeys (pl. **144**). The school which it replaced was described as 'an antique building, supported upon crooks', i.e. it was of traditional cruck construction, presumably with plaster walls. The new school of 1812 was built in stone by public subscription, and it is likely that one of the two floors was used for English teaching.[33]

The Perpendicular Gothic style seems to have been adopted for local grammar-school buildings in the 1820s, at about the same time as it was beginning to be used for elementary schools; it had already, as we have seen, been used for the new buildings at Rugby.[34] That it was not fully accepted even by 1829 is, however, indicated by the Charity Commissioners' report on the school at Wirksworth (Derbs.), which was rebuilt in that year and still stands near the parish church of St Mary. The Commissioners reported that the old school building of 1576 was in bad condition and that work had started on a new school in 1828. The trustees had, however, shown a 'considerable degree of negligence' in managing the school endowment, and the new building was criticized because

> no regular estimate was obtained previously to the commencement of the building, of the expense thereof, which has been considerably increased by the introduction of unnecessary and ill-placed decorations of the outward walls and roof [cf. pl. **151**]. We cannot but think that if due attention had been paid on the part of the trustees, a much smaller expenditure would have been sufficient for the erection of a substantial building, well calculated for the purpose for which it was intended.

In fact, this school is now regarded as one of the more attractive examples of neo-Gothic building of the period.[35]

A school of similar architectural style, but providing for the headmaster's house as part of the same design, is still in use as a school at Market Bosworth in Leicestershire (see pl. **150**, the headmaster's house being the three-storeyed section on the right). The plan of this school (fig. 29) shows that there was the traditional large schoolroom on the first floor, but that provision was also made for two smaller schoolrooms below, occupied by the under-master and the writing-master. A Chancery scheme of 1826 had decreed that the teaching of English, writing and arithmetic was consistent with the will of the Elizabethan benefactor of the school, and had authorized the appointment of a third master to teach these subjects. This again shows how an old (and at this point moribund) foundation was successfully adapted to meet local demands for non-classical teaching, and the building erected in 1828 is also a good example of the first stage of separating off the work of a school into different classrooms (still called 'schoolrooms', however).[36]

Figure 29 Market Bosworth, Dixie School, 1828, ground and first-floor plans.

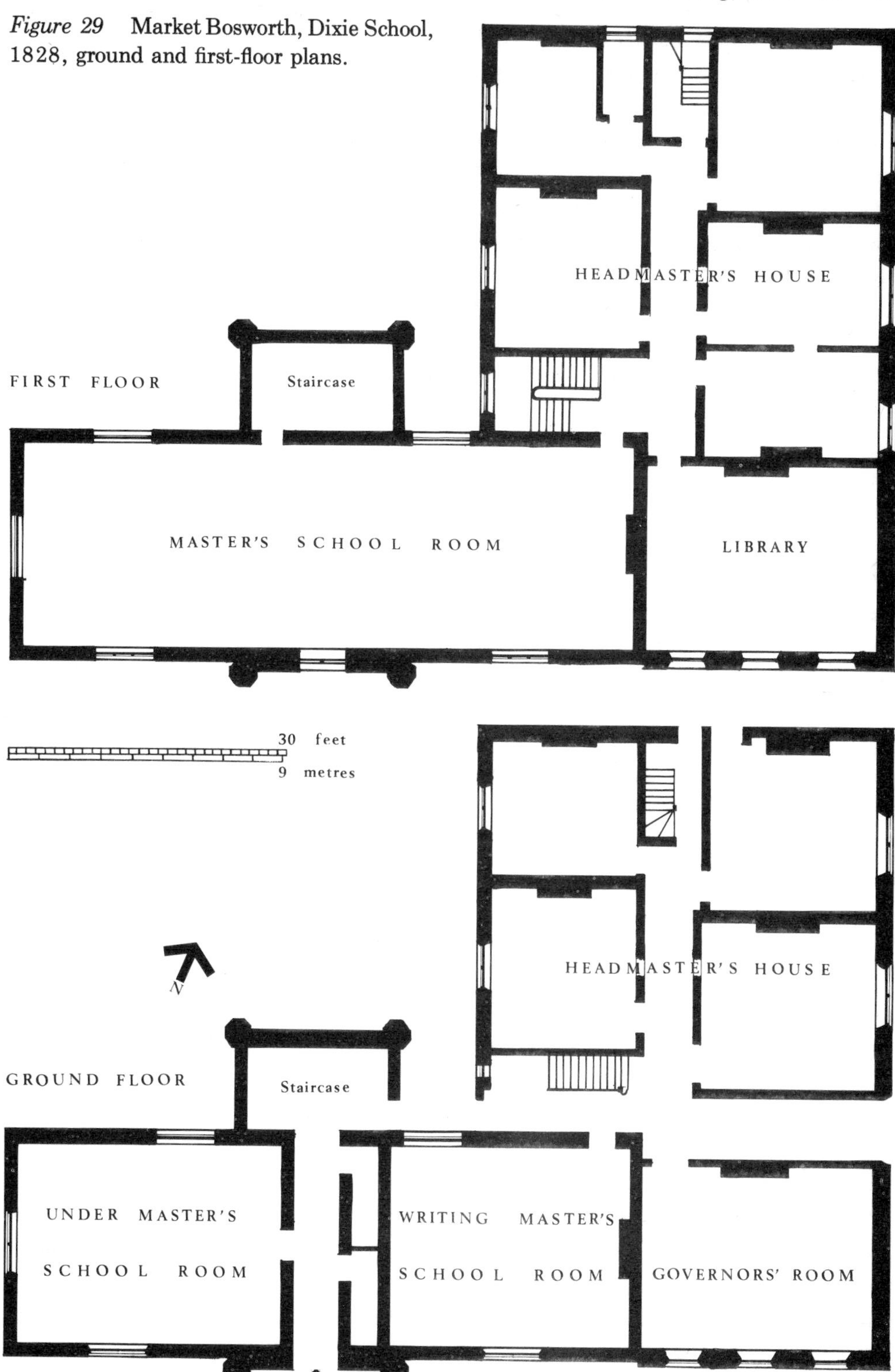

Two other schools, also of Gothic style, may be cited to illustrate more complex forms of organization resulting from the new educational pressures. At Loughborough (Leics.) there was a school financed by the Burton Charity which, even before 1800, seems to have taught reading and writing as well as Latin and Greek. Early in the nineteenth century the demand for elementary teaching had increased to such an extent that the Lancasterian system was introduced into the school, whose building was clearly showing itself to be inadequate to cope with the greater numbers. The new school built in 1825 was pulled down in the 1930s, but a photograph of it has survived (pl. **149**). The Charity Commissioners, who visited the school in 1837, reported that no less than four schools were accommodated in the same building: a grammar school with about eight boys learning Latin and Greek; a school for reading, writing and arithmetic with eighty boys; a Lancasterian school with 250 boys learning reading and writing; and a similar girls' school with eighty girls learning reading and needlework. It appears that the first two schools were on the first floor and the other two on the ground floor. One assumes that the eighty boys upstairs, who learnt arithmetic as well as reading and writing, were of a somewhat higher social class than the boys in the Lancasterian school below, and were being educated for commercial posts in what was an expanding town; the classical school, it will be noted, was almost defunct.[37]

The school at Loughborough shows very clearly the way in which old foundations were modified and different types of education provided out of the same endowment, before the various elements were separated off. From the upper schools at Loughborough developed a grammar and commercial school which moved to new premises in 1852, the 1825 building being taken over by the elementary schools and eventually transferred to the school board. Equally remarkable was the development of the Sebright foundation at Wolverley in Worcestershire, whose new building of 1829 also provides an early example of pointed neo-Gothic (see pl. **152**; the date on the front of the building (1620) refers to the original endowment of the school, and not to the building). As at Loughborough, the endowment was a wealthy one: in addition to building a new grammar school (which in 1852 had eighteen scholars), an elementary school for boys was erected and the old school building used as an elementary school for girls (in 1852 there were eighty boys and sixty girls in these schools). Two infants' schools were added in 1835 and 1851, so that by 1867 there was a total of 400 children in five schools. Later still, the endowments were reorganized in favour of the grammar school, which moved to new buildings in 1891 and has since become a member of the Headmasters' Conference (as has Loughborough Grammar School, which similarly received the lion's share of the Burton Charity).[38]

From 1825 the Tudor Gothic style was used for almost all schools which laid claim to any architectural pretensions, and when it was not used it was often in conscious reaction against it. It was the Gothic style which was chosen for rebuilding Christ's Hospital, Newgate Street, in the years 1820–32, to the designs of John Shaw and his son, who succeeded him as surveyor to the Hospital.[39] We have said a good deal about the earlier history of the buildings of this school, or complex of schools, in previous chapters, and yet again we find it setting the pace, for it provides an outstanding example of a school hemmed in on all sides, but succeeding in breaking its bonds. As the towns grew, so the problem of school sites became crucial: most of the big London schools were rebuilt outside it towards the end of the century, and in the other large towns the migration of schools from crowded city centres was to become an important feature of later school development.

At Christ's Hospital the problem was faced earlier than elsewhere and dramatically solved, though the solution lasted only until 1902, when the school moved to Horsham in Sussex. The Hospital had, as we saw, grown up around the former cloister garth of the Grey Friars. To the north was the Town Ditch, the main sewer which had been covered over in the sixteenth century, but still presented a major obstacle; to the south was the church and to the east and west a mass of small property. In spite of these difficulties, however, the school site was considerably extended (1825–32). New grammar and mathematical schools were built across the Town Ditch, over which a playground was laid out, while to the west a magnificent new hall and infirmary were erected. Other parts of the Hospital were rebuilt and it is fortunate that, although the buildings were demolished soon after the move to Horsham, photographs have survived which give a good impression of them (see pls. **153** and **154**). As in the late seventeenth century, the wealthy merchants of London rebuilt on the grand scale: the hall, in particular, with its embattled and pinnacled summit, octagonal towers at the ends and lofty windows with an arcade below, was greatly admired at the time. 'The interior', said a writer of 1842, 'forms, next to Westminster Hall, the noblest room in the metropolis.'[40]

Elsewhere the building of separate English departments, which we have already noticed beginning soon after 1800, continued as the demand for an elementary—or, where tradesmen had the principal voice in a school's affairs, a commercial—education grew. At Newark (Notts.) an English school was built in 1835, following a decree of the Court of Chancery in the previous year, which ordered that a new school for the teaching of English and arithmetic should be built out of the funds of the Magnus Charity. Indeed, the whole group of buildings which survives in Appletongate at Newark is symbolic of the development of many local educational charities. First, there is the original grammar school (now called Tudor Hall), built in 1532; alongside it, and effectively masking it from the road, is the much larger headmaster's house, built in 1818 at a time when the headmaster was trying, as in many other places, to build up a fee-paying boarding school concentrating on the classics, in defiance of the demands for the teaching of modern subjects; and, finally, at right angles to the master's house, is the English school of 1835, the building of which marked the temporary triumph of the non-classical party. None of these buildings is now used for school purposes, but Tudor Hall is open to the public at stated times, while the English school is now the municipal Museum.[41]

Similar changes took place in the major provincial towns, though the architectural evidence has largely disappeared, owing to the rapidity of urban development. Thus at Nottingham the new school built on the old site in Stoney Street in 1830 (and demolished in the 1950s) made provision for separate classical and writing departments,[42] while at Manchester, where the Grammar School had developed into a classical boarding school, a new scheme of 1833 made it possible to extend the curriculum beyond Latin and Greek, and to build a new English school in 1837.[43] At Birmingham, although the proposal to set up a separate English school was successfully resisted, the new grammar school designed by Charles Barry, soon to become the architect of the Houses of Parliament, contained two large rooms, one called the grammar school and the other the library, which was in fact used as the principal room of the English department. This school was completed in 1838 in Tudor Gothic style, and Pugin, who was working in Barry's office during this period, is credited with most of the interior work of the grammar schoolroom (pl. **159**). The plan (fig. 30) shows a compact design around two open courtyards, a revival of earlier layouts for large schools (cf. Guildford, fig. 4). The headmaster and second master were accommodated inside the building, as was traditional practice, but changing ideas of school-planning were shown in providing

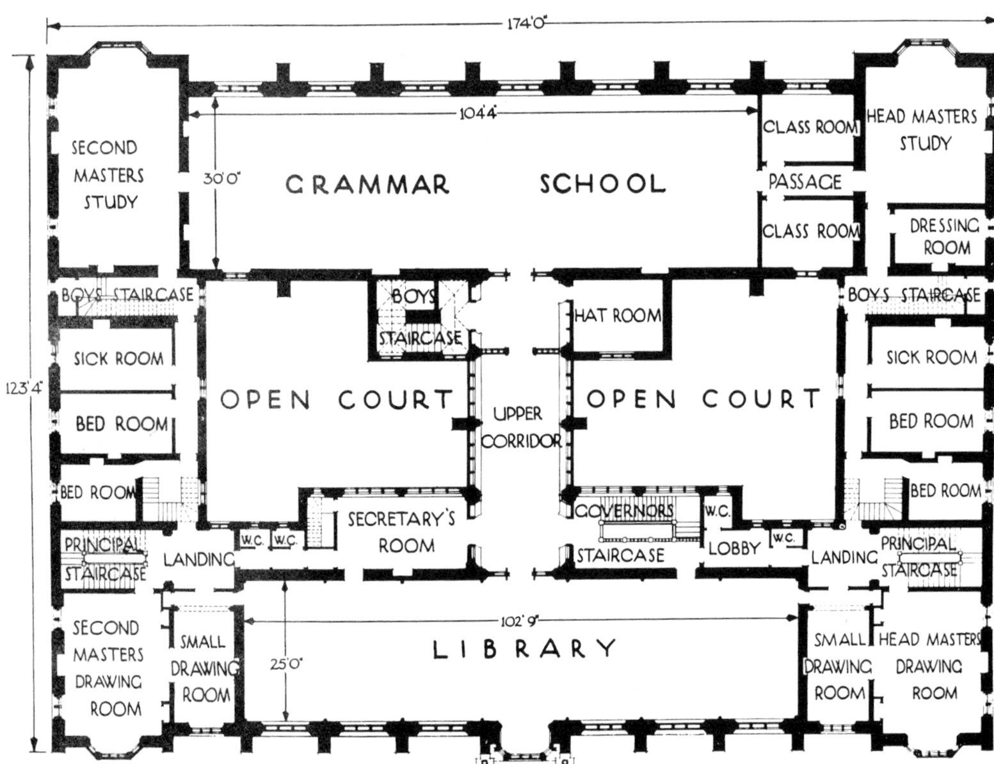

Figure 30 Birmingham, King Edward's School, 1838, plan of principal floor. (The English school occupied the room originally intended for the Library.)

a number of smaller classrooms in addition to the two big 'schools'. The school moved from New Street to Edgbaston in 1936 and the Barry buildings were later demolished, though the chapel was re-erected as part of the present school in 1952.[44]

Probably the most notable surviving building resulting from the development of English schools during this period is Bedford Modern School. The Harpur Endowment (like the Magnus Charity at Newark and the Burton Charity at Loughborough) existed for a number of different charitable purposes, and in Bedford a separation between the Latin and English departments has been detected as early as 1764. An Act of 1826 authorized the allocation of funds for the building of new schools, which were opened in 1834. The large neo-Gothic building was designed by Edward Blore, and incorporated not only an English or commercial school, but also boys' and girls' National schools and a hospital school, all of which were deemed to benefit under the terms of the Harpur Trust. The architectural result was impressive, the total effect being best appreciated from Blore's drawing reproduced as pl. **155**. The buildings may still be seen in Harpur Street, Bedford, where all the buildings designed by Blore are now occupied by the Modern School, which developed from the commercial school and is now a direct-grant grammar school for boys.[45]

The Trustees had held a competition for the best design, and their notification to architects competing (1828) included the following interesting passage:

> As the Trustees have resolved that the buildings shall be of stone and as they wish them to be in the style of what may be called the Collegiate, conventional and domestic English architecture of the period comprising the reigns of Edward VI, Mary and Elizabeth, they request that no plans may be sent in imitation of the Grecian, Roman, or Anglo Italian styles. The only deviation that could be allowed would be the admission of the perpendicular or Florid style of the purely English architecture of the reign of Henry VIII. The Trustees are anxious that the buildings should (if it be practicable) present such features as may recall the era of the dawn of the Reformation, the foundation of Endowed Public Schools, and the memory of Sir William Harpur.[46]

The prize was awarded in 1829 to a local architect, John Wing, but in the following year Edward Blore, a London architect who was becoming prominent because of his neo-Gothic (Tudor) designs, was asked to advise, and he redesigned Wing's scheme, particularly the front elevation.[47] A proposal to include an infants' school in the design was dropped, but there were still four basic elements in the plan as completed (shown in fig. 31).[48] There was a National school consisting of two large, single-storey schoolrooms for boys and girls; the Trustees' committee room and clerk's house; a hospital or boarding school for twenty-five boys and twenty-five girls, with two schoolrooms separated by an 'eating room', and sleeping accommodation on the floor above; and, finally, a commercial school in a room measuring 48 by 30 feet, with a classroom and a preparatory schoolroom adjoining. In 1821, before the new schools had been

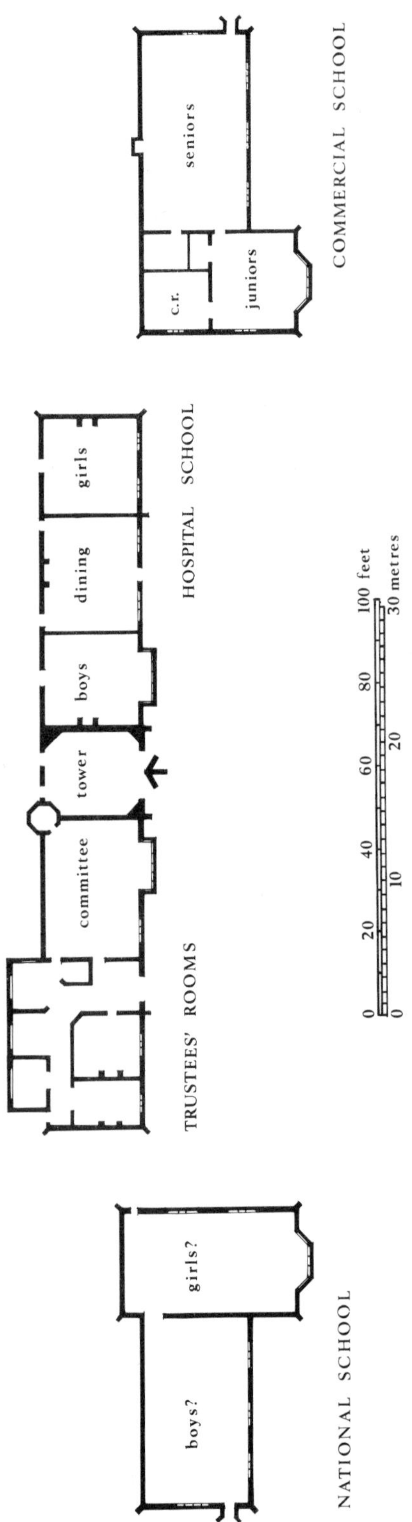

Figure 31 Bedford schools, 1834, ground plan. (The whole complex of buildings is now occupied by Bedford Modern School.)

built, there had been 100 boys in the writing (i.e. commercial) school and 250 boys and 170 girls in the National schools, including the hospital children. By 1868 the new buildings had been extended and accommodated no less than 1,400 children, while a separate school had also been erected for 250 infants.[49] All this was apart from the original grammar school (now Bedford School), which occupied a fine Georgian building, now the Town Hall in St Paul's Square, quite close to the Blore buildings.[50]

IV

Clearly, the provision made for English schools within or alongside the grammar-school buildings was an expression of changing ideas about the content of the curriculum, as it was being influenced by the new social and economic conditions of the early nineteenth century. In many parts of the country the classical curriculum traditionally offered by the grammar schools seems to have been little valued: again and again one finds that grammar schools which adhered to the letter of their original statutes and offered only classical instruction went into decline, and often out of existence altogether. Where the classics were successfully taught, it was usually by developing the boarding side, so making it possible to attract boys from well-to-do families outside the immediate locality of the school. Where elementary or commercial departments were set up, the relationships between the classical and English master were invariably strained; if one large room had to be shared, partition walls were often erected and rules made forbidding the boys in each department to mix socially.

This is the interesting and inconclusive picture which emerges from the detailed histories of many endowed schools during this period. The presence of poor children receiving an elementary education in some of these schools was to be a temporary phenomenon, for they were increasingly being provided for in the new-style elementary schools, and were eventually to be elbowed out of the major endowed schools by middle-class pressure. A more subtle conflict was that between the county and town interests and between the classical and commercial departments of the schools. On the whole, however, it was not until after 1840 that the urban middle classes began to gain control of the endowed grammar schools, introducing modern subjects and even finding a continuing role for classical teaching—a theme to which we return in ch. 11.

When one considers the legal and other complexities which governed the large number of educational charities accumulated over the centuries, it is not surprising that their remodelling took a considerable time to accomplish. Nor is it surprising that the most advanced educational thinkers of the early nineteenth century saw the best hope of reform in founding wholly new schools, where novel ideas could be tried out untrammelled by tradition. The early nineteenth century was also the hey-day of the private schools, which, as we have seen, were well-established long before 1800. In general, the private schools were still small and relatively short-lived, and for this and other reasons they have received comparatively little attention from educational historians. Evidence about them is very fragmentary, and serious research into their history involves much painstaking work on local newspapers and other very diverse sources. What can be achieved in spite of these difficulties has been shown by Mr Harrison in his recent study of private schools in Doncaster during the nineteenth century.[51] Even so, from the point of view of the development of school architecture and organization, the results are meagre, because few of these schools operated on a sufficiently large scale to stimulate new ideas on this aspect of education, though their influence on the development of the curriculum was considerable. Most of the buildings were merely private houses adapted for school use, and only rarely were they specially designed for educational purposes. Indeed, one finds that all kinds of buildings were pressed into service—as, for example, the race-stand at Doncaster, which came on to the market because it proved to be too far out of the line of the course; the building was then used by a number of private schools before being taken over by the Yorkshire School for the Deaf.[52] So, too, the doyen of nineteenth-century private-school masters, William Barnes, used a succession of buildings of various kinds in Dorset and Wiltshire, and only in his last school (1847–62) was there a purpose-built schoolroom.[53] Mr Harrison notes only two purpose-built private schools in Doncaster, erected in 1829 and 1832 respectively.[54] The second of these had a juvenile gallery, which indicates acquaintance with the latest teaching methods and also reminds us that there was little attempt to separate the elementary from the secondary stage of education given to middle-class children at this date.

Doncaster was during this period a centre for private schools, and is an interesting example of a prosperous market town with good road communications, but with its endowed schools at a very low ebb, so that almost every kind of education depended on private enterprise. Similarly, in Manchester it was found in 1834 that there were thirty-six boys' and seventy-eight girls' 'superior private and boarding schools'.[55] This was before the new English school for boys had been opened, while the complete lack of publicly-provided schools for middle-class girls in the town is clear from the large proportion of girls' private schools noted.

The same transitory character which we have noticed in what may be called the more orthodox private school sector was also apparent in the attempts made during this period to set up radically different kinds of school. The importance of the writings of such men as Jeremy Bentham and J. S. Mill, and of the experimental schools set up by reformers like Robert Owen at New Lanark and the Hill brothers at Hazelwood, lay mainly in the future. In that they contributed to the ferment of ideas about the best kind of education suited to the new industrial age, their influence was incalculable, but the wholesale remodelling of the school system took place long after their ideas were first enunciated.

If, for example, we consider Bentham's *Chrestomathia* (1816), which has been called a book which 'was to have a seminal influence on the educational thought and practice of the Radical bourgeoisie',[56] we find a highly abstract and complex set of ideas, and relatively little concern with the practicalities of putting them into operation. So far as school organization was concerned, Bentham upheld the Lancasterian system, already modified in actual practice and soon to be discredited even for elementary instruction.[57] His ideal school building was to be on the 'Panopticon principle of construction', since

> security, in this respect is maximized, and rendered entire: viz. partly, by minimizing the distance between the situation of the remotest Scholar and that of the Master's eye; partly, by giving to the floor or floors that inclination, which, to a certain degree, prevents remoter objects from being eclipsed by nearer ones; partly by enabling the Master to see without being seen; whereby, to those who, at the moment, are unseen by him, it cannot be known that they are in this case.[58]

What Bentham seems to have had in mind was a large circular room sloping towards the middle and with the master in the centre, like a spider in a web. He also stated as an 'architectural rule' that 'by height, or otherwise, so order the windows, that, so far as such exclusion can be made consistent with the admission of sufficiency of light, no object, exterior to the building, shall be visible in any part of it occupied by the Scholars'.[59] These ideas were only fully adopted in a number of new prison buildings erected at this period on the circular plan, though one finds echoes of the 'panopticon principle' in the lecture-rooms built at Edinburgh High School in 1825 and the City of London School in 1837, more of which is said later in this chapter. In his exclusion of classical teaching, religious tests and the boarding element, Bentham summed up three of the most important principles of Radical middle-class reform, but his views on school organization read like the *reductio ad absurdum* of Lancasterian practice.

Probably the fullest practical expression of Benthamite ideas was at the Hill Top School near Birmingham, which moved to Hazelwood at Edgbaston in 1819. Here T. W. Hill and his five sons successfully taught a wide range of subjects by novel methods, as well as introducing an elaborate system of self-government into the school, which was also open to all religious denominations. The school building at Hazelwood is said to have been designed by Rowland Hill (the later originator of the Penny Post) and to have contained 'numerous classrooms as well as a large schoolroom seating 250'. The building was reconstructed in 1820, with, according to some authorities, 'a built-in heating and ventilation system, an observation platform on the roof for astronomical observation and surveying operations, in addition to studies, a library, a reference library, a gymnasium, and a swimming-bath'.[60] Another brother, M. D. Hill, described the system in operation at the school in his *Public education of boys* (1st. ed., 1822).[61] His style is business-like and the incidental references to the building seem to be to a somewhat more modest structure than the above quotations would imply. He tells us that 'the school consists of about seventy boys, who are arranged into classes for each department of study, according to their proficiency in that department'.[62] The studies listed are orthography, geography, parsing, shorthand, mathematics, French, Latin and Greek; mention is also made of weekly lectures on natural experimental philosophy.

It is interesting to notice that, owing to the diversity of subjects taught, the basic teaching unit has become the class (and not the whole school, as in at least the smaller, classical, schools).[63] Later in the book, however, it is stated that 'the boys arrange themselves in a certain part of the school-room, in the classes in which they are about to receive instruction', and there is no mention of separate classrooms.[64] The gymnastic lessons took place in the playground, and in the summer the boys went 'to a bath which has been made for them in a retired spot, at a short distance from the play-ground'.[65] The new teaching methods used and the elaborate system of school government by committees of boys have recently been fully discussed, as has the system of merit-marks and the absence of corporal punishment, which was replaced by fines or, in the last resort, 'confining separately in the dark'.[66] Here, indeed, was a system by which merit alone conferred rank, while token-money, distributed by a boy-banker, served as reward.[67] What M. D. Hill called 'the noble art of money getting' was the basis of school organization and made an obvious appeal to some middle-class parents, though the school at Hazelwood had a relatively short life, closing in 1833. (A sister school, begun at Tottenham in north London in 1827, continued until 1891, though in less radical form.)

The complexity of the internal organization of Hazelwood school made it, as a recent writer has remarked, 'virtually inimitable'. But in its stress on teaching a wide range of subjects, including science, and its emphasis on organization in separate classes, it probably influenced the important new publicly-controlled 'High' schools which were set up in the 1830s.[68] Above all, Hazelwood was a distinctively middle-class school, to be clearly distinguished from the monitorial schools for the 'lower classes', the limitations of which M. D. Hill exposes in a penetrating analysis.[69] Hazelwood showed what could be achieved when—as Hill remarks—'cost is an object of minor importance'.

V

The problem of cost was overcome by opening 'proprietary' schools, where new subjects could be taught free from religious restrictions. Such schools appealed to middle-class parents of all religious persuasions, and they readily bought shares in what were in effect joint-stock companies. The first of these schools was probably the Liverpool Institute (1825) and, so far as developments in school-planning were concerned, Mill

Hill School, already described, and the new Edinburgh High School served as the models. (The latter school, on which building began in 1825, contained three principal classrooms and eight 'side classrooms', in addition to a writing classroom, a library and public hall.)[70] The whole reforming movement received a great impetus from the opening of the new University College in London in 1828, followed by King's College in 1831. Both of these colleges had junior departments, and the University College School in particular was based on the same Radical outlook which had inspired the founders of the main college: modern subjects, including science, were taught, corporal punishment was forbidden, and the abuses associated with the contemporary boarding schools were circumvented by taking day-boys only. King's College School also proved to be a very well-supported school and for many years the income from the school greatly exceeded the fees obtained from the senior departments of the college.

So far as buildings were concerned, both schools were restricted because of the subordinate position which they occupied in the constitutions of their colleges, a subordination which was shown in the physical arrangements made for both schools. At University College, the school used two rooms on the ground floor, and the great hall above, from 1833 to 1836, when this part of the building was burnt down; it then moved into the large room originally intended for the library, on the first floor of the south wing. As the numbers rose, a small adjoining room was brought into use (1849), and a new wing was finally built for the school between 1869 and 1876 (it was not until 1907 that the school became a separate corporation and moved to its present site at Hampstead).[71] At King's College the school occupied rooms in the basement, and further rooms were not brought into use until 1841, when the number of boys had reached nearly 500. The school moved to its present site on Wimbledon Common in 1897.[72]

Revolutionary as these two schools were in their curricula, they had little opportunity to experiment with new forms of building. But a school of what was for the time revolutionary design was built in London soon afterwards. This was the City of London School, which was erected in 1835–7 at the expense of the Corporation to the design of J. B. Bunning.[73] It was built on the site formerly occupied by Honey Lane Market in Cheapside, and it will be seen from pl. **156** that the Perpendicular Gothic style was chosen. This was not a proprietary school, though similar middle-class pressures brought it into being. It was financed by making use of a moribund but wealthy charity founded in the fifteenth century by a former Town Clerk of London. The story of the struggle to secure these funds for building a middle-class 'High School' is a very interesting one, since one body of opinion was more in favour of using the money to build a school of purely elementary type. Symbolic of the origin of the school is the fact that the foundation stone was laid by the famous reforming peer, Lord Brougham, in defiance of a threat of arrest made by the Lord Mayor.[74]

The curriculum adopted for the City of London School was modelled on that of the University and King's College Schools and included English, French and German as well as Latin and Greek. The school also taught theoretical science and claims to have been the first school in England to give practical science lessons (1838).[75] Boys of all denominations were allowed to attend, and it was a day school from the beginning. Its internal organization was similarly of a pioneer character, with separate classrooms as shown in fig. 32. On the ground floor was a 'grammar' room, and on the first floor a 'Latin classroom', which together were the equivalent of the large classical schoolroom traditional in most grammar schools. But, in addition, there were five senior and four junior classrooms, as well as a library and masters' room. The names of the classrooms indicate that the boys were arranged roughly according to age, but the real novelty of the school was its sub-division into classes taken by specialist-subject teachers. It is said that on the first day the Headmaster gave the order 'Sort those boys!' to the French master, who proceeded to arrange them in order of height.[76] Although this story may well be apocryphal, it serves to indicate a genuine feature of the new school—namely, the disregard for precedent, and the fluidity of the internal school structure which made possible a radically different kind of organization.

Since the old classical schoolroom had in effect been abolished, provision was made for general assemblies in a circular theatre, in some respects not unlike Bentham's 'panopticon' described above. On the basement floor was sanitary provision, together with a wash-room (later the French classroom); a science laboratory—certainly one of the earliest in an English school—was fitted up in a basement corridor. There was, however, one serious deficiency in the building, and that was the absence of a playground, or indeed any space for future expansion (the school occupied an island site, hemmed in on all sides). Perhaps we may remark that this may in part have been the result of the founders' Benthamite self-sufficiency, their feeling that perfection had been reached, so that provision for future change was not thought to be necessary. In the event, the boys played in the 'horseshoe' corridor below the theatre, and the Headmaster's living rooms were later converted into further classrooms. Even so, the school was forced to move out in 1882, when it occupied its present buildings on the Victoria Embankment, the old school being converted into warehouses.[77]

The example of these three important London schools was soon imitated in the provinces, but with considerably less success. Architecturally, the proprietary day schools outside London showed the same tendency to provide separate classrooms, while another interesting architectural development was that religious differences, which soon appeared among the middle-class supporters of these schools, were expressed in the choice of the Gothic style by the Anglicans and of the classical by the Nonconformists. There are also points of interest regarding the siting of these schools. Their middle-class character was usually emphasized by siting them in what were at the time the more exclusive suburbs. At Leicester, for example, the Anglican proprietary school (known as the 'Collegiate School') was built in 1836 in what is now Prebend Street, well away from the old centre of the town; it was only because of chance factors that

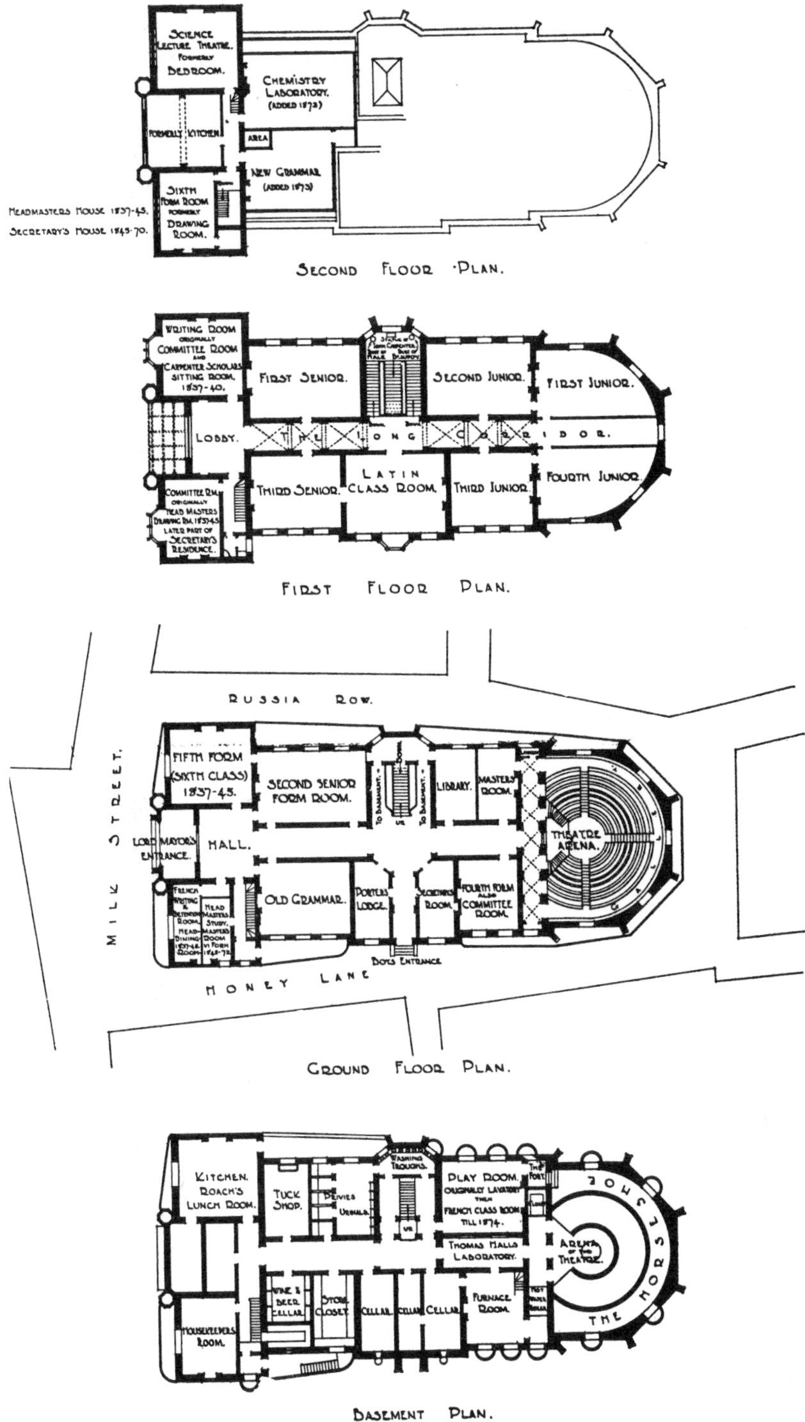

Figure 32 City of London School, 1837, plan of basement, ground, first and second floors, with alterations to 1882.

the housing which later came to this area proved to be of an inferior type.[78] The Nonconformist proprietary school, which opened a year later, was in the fashionable New Walk, and the promoters, who had originally bought a plot of land nearer to the centre of the town, decided to sell it only a few months later in order to obtain the more desirable position.[79]

The development of the two Leicester proprietary schools sums up an interesting episode in educational history and one which was shared by several other large towns. The driving force behind the foundation of the Collegiate School, which was the first to be built, was made clear by a speaker at the opening ceremony:

> The public Schools of our Country, with Eton at their head, I regard with unfeigned admiration. But unhappily, it is not in the power of every one to go there. . . . Those Schools are more particularly the happy resort of the young members of the noblest and wealthiest families in the land. But we, of the middle classes, must strive to *hold our own*; we will labour to maintain our proportionate rank—to support our middle station, and, if possible, to elevate that station.[80]

Here we find a new class-consciousness, but also a ready acceptance of the position of the established upper-class schools. The promoters of the Collegiate School also conformed to the now orthodox style of school-building in choosing the Perpendicular Gothic, to the design of J. G. Weightman, who had served in the office of Charles Barry and later, in association with M. E. Hadfield, designed a number of churches and other public buildings in the north of England.[81] It was in fact Weightman's design for the Anglican proprietary school in Sheffield (pl. **157**), which was adopted with very little alteration for the school at Leicester.

The Leicester Collegiate School seems to have consisted of a central hall flanked by two classrooms on each side—what one might call a moderately progressive plan for the period (fig. 33 (a)).[82] The Headmaster took a certain number of boarders in his house adjoining the school, but most of the pupils were day-boys. The school opened in 1836 with about 100 boys on the roll, and never rose much above this. Some modern subjects were taught and the school appears to have been reasonably well attended, but it was obliged to close in 1865, owing to financial difficulties. The premises were put up for sale and, somewhat ironically, the school-house came to be used as a girls' private school of Nonconformist origin, while the main schoolroom became a Congregational chapel. Later still, it was purchased by the City Education Committee and is now a girls' grammar school. The building has been altered and extended, and the main elevation has been spoiled by the recent erection of science laboratories immediately in front of it.[83] The twin school at Sheffield, which also opened in 1836, similarly suffered a series of financial crises, though it was kept going until 1885 when the revived Grammar School took over the building which still stands

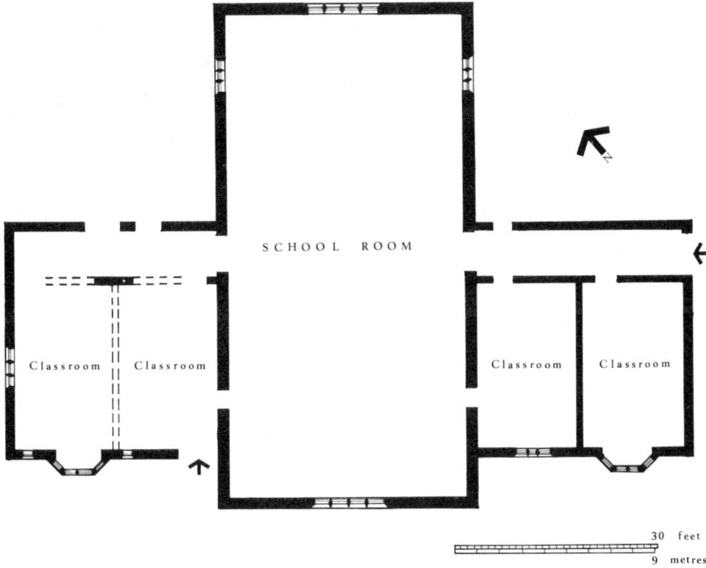

Figure 33 (a) Leicester Collegiate School, 1836, ground plan. (The building was extended to the east in 1883 and the bay window in the east classroom has been re-positioned. The door on the south side may have replaced an original window; if not, then it must have given access to one rather than two classrooms.)

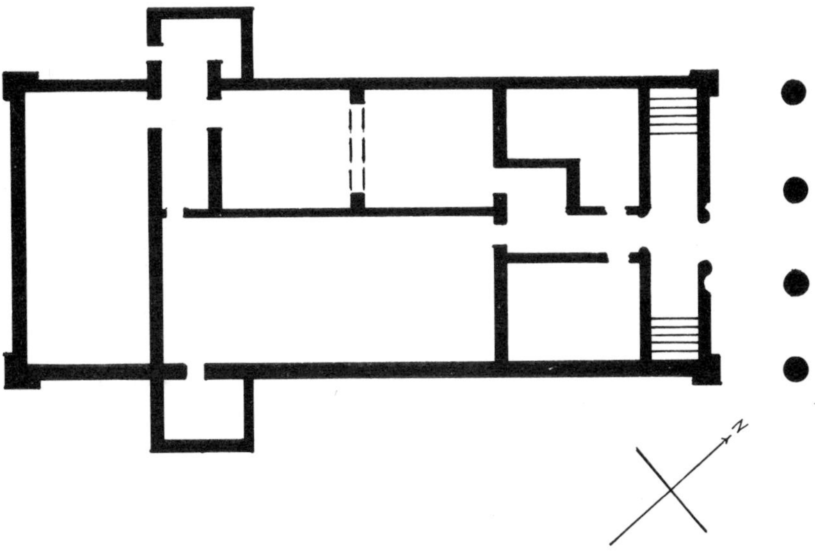

Figure 33 (b) Leicester Proprietary School, 1837, ground plan.

in Ecclesall Road. Then in 1905 the Grammar School combined with Wesley College—the Nonconformist proprietary school of 1837, which had met with more success than its rival—to form King Edward VII School and the Collegiate School became Sheffield Teachers' Training College.[84] It has since been considerably altered and extended, but something of its original architectural character has survived.

The Nonconformist Proprietary School in Leicester opened in 1837 and lasted only until 1847, though the original building has survived as a public museum (pl. **158**). It had been planned in direct opposition to the Anglican-orientated Collegiate School, and was in every way more Radical in its approach, though equally dominated by the middle classes (the fees were the same as at the Collegiate School, and a headmaster's house was similarly provided for boarders; the length of the school building, 100 feet, was exactly the same as its rival). It taught a wider range of modern subjects, however, including science, and the plan of the original building, which can be reconstructed (see fig. 33 (*b*)), shows that great emphasis was placed on classroom teaching.[85] There was a large room on the first floor, reached by stairs near the main entrance, but the ground floor was divided up into two large and four smaller classrooms. A somewhat pretentious classical style was chosen for the building, which was designed by J. A. Hansom. He had helped to design Birmingham Town Hall (1832–4), and later patented his 'safety cab', which has made his name well known. The speakers at the opening of the school, who included M. D. Hill, previously of Hazelwood School, all stressed their desire that the school should break away from the traditional type of classical teaching and prove itself according to the Benthamite maxim that 'to be successful, it must be useful'. References were made to London University 'and the excellent school attached to it', and also to the work of Lord Brougham, who had been invited to perform the opening ceremony but was unable to do so because of the illness of his daughter. The 'barbarous' discipline of the major public schools was denounced and the importance of freedom in religion stressed. The mayor also spoke with considerable passion about the choice of the classical style for the building:

> He rejoiced greatly that they had adopted the Grecian style of Architecture in preference to the Gothic;—the former, simple, chaste, and beautiful and suitable to every species of building—the latter deriving its beauty from its costly and profuse ornaments and stupendous magnitude and sinking into the burlesque in smaller edifices. To those whose associations fondly clung to the dark Monastic exploded institutions of our country, who love to dwell rather on the gloomy periods of our history, than to contemplate the blaze of light and knowledge which has since burst upon the world—to such persons he was aware the Gothic style of Architecture had great charms; but in an institution for the education of youth it was desirable that every association of the mind should be connected with a People who had carried literature to the highest point of perfection, whose love of liberty, of knowledge, of the fine arts, whose writings

> in History, in Poetry had never been excelled, rather than with the superstitions of our Gothic ancestors, who, with the exception of Architecture, were remarkable only for their ignorance and barbarism.[86]

The speaker did not seem to realize that by excluding architecture from among the shortcomings of 'our Gothic ancestors' he was to some extent weakening his case; even more remarkably, he went on to attack the teaching of Greek and Latin in schools.

As for the plan of the building, Hill had written, as we saw, of the classes at Hazelwood arranged around the various parts of the schoolroom; now we have the next stage of development in which physical form is given to the subdivision into classes, and it is interesting to note that the Headmaster of the Leicester school regarded the introduction of class-teaching as the greatest advance which he would be able to make in the new school, as he explained in the following extracts from his address at its opening:

> Perhaps the most serious of the many disadvantages attaching to those ordinary boarding schools to which alone the middle classes have been hitherto compelled to look for the instruction of their children, arises from the fact that far more than half the time of the pupil is spent, during the hours of school, in turning over the leaves of a lexicon, and either groping out for himself the substance of his lesson, or improperly and unprofitably assisted by his companions. Hence, a comparatively short time is occupied in what is called, 'saying the lesson'; and consequently, a very scanty opportunity is left to the master of making those connecting and explanatory remarks, and communicating that collateral and general knowledge which constitutes the most truly valuable part of scholastic instruction. . . . The plan intended to be pursued within these walls is entirely opposed to this. The preparatory studies of the pupils will be conducted within the intervals of their attendance, in order that, during the hours of school, they may reap all the advantage to be derived from the explanations, lectures and examinations of those to whose charge they are committed.[87]

Thus, just as Wilderspin and Stow had begun to introduce the simultaneous method into the elementary schools, so the importance of oral teaching also came to be realized in the new middle-class schools. Separate classrooms were necessary, not merely because of large numbers (as at Rugby), or even because of the introduction of new subjects (as at the City of London School), but because of an essential change in the whole method of teaching. Under the old system, the level of noise must have been considerable, but not unbearable, since the boys spent much of their time working by themselves or in pairs. Under the new system, however, separate classrooms were indispensable if the 'explanations, lectures and examinations' in a variety of subjects were to be clearly heard. Henceforth, the masters' voices were to reign supreme.

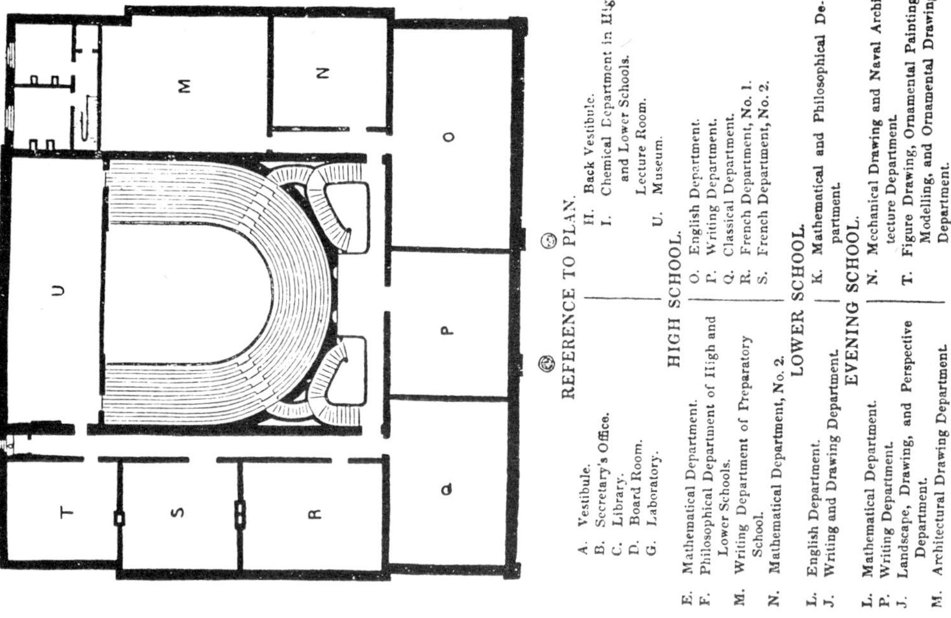

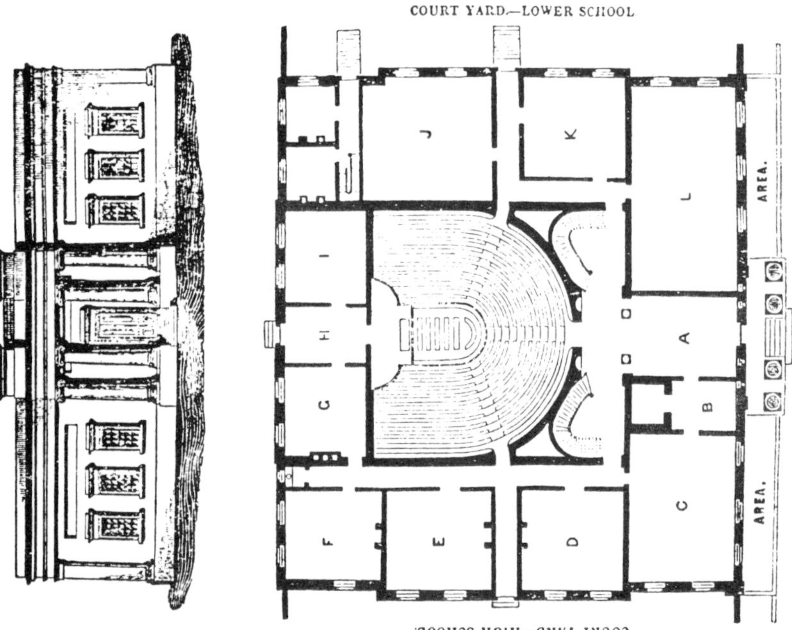

Figure 34 Liverpool Institute, 1837, ground and first-floor plans.

Similar considerations seem to have influenced the design of the Liverpool Institute School, which moved from temporary premises to a new building in Mount Street in 1837, the foundation-stone having been laid two years earlier by Lord Brougham. As with the Leicester Proprietary School, a classical façade was chosen, and the internal layout included the same basic elements, but with provision for a lower and an evening school (the latter connected with the mechanics' institute) as well as a high school. However, instead of placing all the classrooms on the ground floor with the hall above, as at Leicester, the classrooms in the Liverpool school (no less than sixteen in all) were arranged on two floors around a central hall, which was of horseshoe shape, as in the City of London School (see fig. 34).[88]

The Liverpool Institute School survives today as a boys' grammar school, but, in spite of its promising start, the Leicester Proprietary School lasted for only ten years, and similar schools in other towns were also relatively short-lived. The reasons for the failure of many of the proprietary day schools outside London are not entirely clear. Certainly, when one reads the detailed minutes of such schools as the Leicester Proprietary School, it is hard to see how so much effort and enthusiasm should have failed in its purpose. The day schools in London could, however, draw on a very large population, and in other places the supply was more limited. In this connection, it is worth noting that most of the proprietary schools founded after 1840 were boarding establishments, and were much more successful on that account. It also has to be remembered that the smaller private schools were still doing a flourishing business and continued to attract middle-class parents. In general, the proprietary day schools lacked both the tradition of the endowed schools on the one hand and the resilience of the private schools on the other. Although most of them failed to maintain this intermediate position, the proprietary day schools were of great importance because they showed the true direction of future reform. It is not without significance that several former proprietary school buildings were later taken over by local grammar schools which had been reformed and extended, as at Sheffield, Wakefield and York.[89]

After about 1840 there began a new phase in the development of what came to be called 'secondary education', and fresh attention was paid to the old educational endowments which existed in many parts of the country. It was now coming to be realized that local schools could be remodelled to the advantage of the middle classes and that charitable endowments could help to cover the cost. As the influence of the middle classes grew with the passing of the Reform Bill in 1832 and the repeal of the Corn Laws in 1846, so the educational system of the country came more and more to be shaped in accordance with their requirements.

Notes

1 The term 'secondary school' was taken from the French *école secondaire*, a phrase first used by Condorcet in 1792. R. L. Edgeworth, who was in touch with contemporary French educationalists, used the expression 'secondary school' in 1812. It was also used by Dr Arnold in 1831, but did not come into general use until after 1850, when it was used by Matthew Arnold and others (Board of Education, *Report of the Consultative Committee on the education of the adolescent*, H.M.S.O., 1926, 266–7).

2 The Headmasters' Conference was founded in 1869. In considering the election of a headmaster to the Conference, account is taken of 'the measure of independence enjoyed', 'the number of resident undergraduates . . . educated at the school' and 'the proportion of boys in the Sixth Form'. See Preface to *The Public and Preparatory Schools Year Book*, A. & C. Black, 1968.

3 Cf. Bamford, T. W., *Rise of the public schools*, Nelson, 1967, Introduction. Certain schools had come to be recognized by 1820 as major public schools, but it is very doubtful that these alone could claim to be 'public schools'. Bamford notes the foundation of only two 'public boarding schools' in each of the first four decades of the nineteenth century (*ibid.*, 18).

4 Simon, B. (ed.), *Education in Leicestershire 1540–1940* (Leicester U.P., 1968), ch. 5. See also Sanderson, J. M., 'The grammar school and the education of the poor, 1786–1840', in *B.J.E.S.*, XI, 1, November 1962, 42f: 'In the late eighteenth and early nineteenth centuries, elementary education for the vastly increasing lower orders aroused the most attention, and for insufficiency of other means the grammar schools concerned themselves with it. That they did so does not imply that they "declined" or "decayed," but rather that as always they adapted to the society in which they found themselves.'

5 Pollard, F. E. (ed.), *Bootham School 1823–1923*, Dent, 1926, 21–2.

6 *Ibid.*, drawing facing p. xviii, showing the school at Lawrence Street in 1840 (this included a workshop, library, dining-room, play-room, schoolroom and senior classroom).

7 Slugg, J. T., *Woodhouse Grove School* (Woolmer, 1885), drawing facing p. 21.

8 Brett-James, N. G., *The history of Mill Hill School 1807–1907*, Melrose, n.d., 17.

9 *Ibid.*, 60. Sir William Tite's buildings included the Scottish Presbyterian Church, Regent Square (1824–7), Nine Elms Railway Station, Battersea (1838), the Royal Exchange, Threadneedle Street (1841–4), and railway stations at Carlisle, Edinburgh and Perth (1847–8).

10 It may be noted that Ackermann illustrated all the schools later examined by the Clarendon Commission on Public Schools (1861–4), except Shrewsbury, which was just beginning to re-emerge under Butler.

11 The only major building at Harrow during this period was the construction of a new speech-room (1819) alongside the old school, which was re-faced in the Tudor style, pl. **55**.

12 Illustrated in Brown, W. G., *Charterhouse past and present*, Godalming: Stedman, 1879, facing pp. 149 and 155 (the internal arrangement shown in Ackermann is slightly different). The schoolroom of 1803 was on the site of the north cells of the great cloister and was demolished in 1872.

13 *Ibid.*, 151, 157. The chaotic conditions at Charterhouse, with seven masters in charge of 400 boys, are described in Davies, G. S., *Charterhouse in London*, Murray, 1921, 270f. Thackeray entered Charterhouse in 1828: he spent nearly all his time drawing, but used to bring a volume of Byron and a novel to fall back on.

14 McDonnell, M. F. J., *History of St. Paul's School*, Chapman & Hall, 1909. The 1670 school is illustrated facing pp. 234 and 384 (interior, p. 362). The new school of 1824 cost £23,000, and the architect, George Smith, also built at this period St Peter's Church, London Colney, Herts. (1825), Whittington's Almshouses, Archway Road, Highgate (1825), and the Town Hall, St Albans, Herts. (1829), also with a giant portico. The 1824 school is fully described in McDonnell, 390–1, and illustrated facing pp. 390, 402, 406. The similar plan at Witney is noted above in ch. 5; for the Wolverhampton school of 1713 see Mander, G. P., *History of Wolverhampton Grammar School*, Wolverhampton: Steens, 1913, 179 and illustration facing p. 208.

15 McDonnell, *op. cit.*, 414.

16 Draper, F. W. M., *Four centuries of Merchant Taylors' School*, Oxford U.P., 1962, 126–9, and *Merchant Taylors' School*, The Merchant Taylors' Company, 1861, 68.

17 Cf. Bamford, T. W., *op. cit.*, 5. He points out that at Rugby periods of publicity coincided with large entries, and 'it did not seem to matter whether or not the publicity was adverse'.

18 The only new building at Winchester during this period was the reconstruction of 'Old Commoners' to form 'New Commoners', 1839–42, described further in ch. 11, below.

19 On the 'disgrace of Long Chamber' see Lyte, H. C. Maxwell, *History of Eton College*, Macmillan, 1877, 420f. On the abuses of 'Montem' see Ogilvie, V., *The English public school*, Batsford, 1957, 133–5.

20 Bamford, T. W., *op. cit.*, 8, argues more generally that for 'schools in the top bracket . . . the actual pabulum of learning was of no practical importance', since 'only if the head of the household had a large family and limited funds was the possibility of a future occupation important'.

21 Carlisle, I, 81–2.

22 *Ibid.*, II, 148.

23 *Ibid.*, II, 677.

24 Arnold, who was a Wykehamist, made this point explicitly when he had five painted windows put in the chapel at Rugby: 'I envy Winchester its antiquity and am therefore anxious to do all that can be done to give us something of a venerable outside, if we have not the nobleness of old associations to help us' (Stanley, A. P., *Life of Thomas Arnold*, Murray, 1901, 137).

25 Rouse, W. H. D., *History of Rugby School*, Duckworth, 1898, 195–6.

26 Bamford, *op. cit.*, 12: 'Perhaps the vision of gentry-like surroundings for top-class schools was new.'

27 For the 'Old buildings' see Rouse, *op cit.*, 200–4. I am very grateful to Mr J. B. Hope Simpson for showing me around the buildings, and to Mr K. G. Kellett, F.R.I.B.A., for providing the plan here reproduced.

28 Hakewill's chapel is described in Rouse, *op. cit.*, 205–6 and illustration facing p. 230. For the library in the tower chamber over the front gate, *ibid.*, 233–4 and illustration facing p. 234.

29 Simpson, J. B. Hope, *Rugby since Arnold*, Macmillan, 1967, 7.

30 This follows Simpson, *op. cit.*, 5–8. The highest number of boys at Rugby during Arnold's time was 362 in 1841 (Simpson, 13), compared with 380 under his predecessor (*ibid.*, 5).

31 Cf. Rouse, *op. cit.*, 236: Arnold 'resolved that no more dames' houses should be allowed, and as each fell vacant . . . he transferred the house to one of his assistants. . . . The assistants were no longer allowed to take curacies along with the school work, and their services were claimed on Sundays as on week-days, if necessary'. The relationship of housemasters to headmasters has not yet received adequate treatment; the former could claim considerable independence in certain circumstances.

32 Fox, Levi, *A country grammar school*, Oxford U.P., 1967, 66–7. The classical schoolroom measured 29 by 20 feet and the English schoolroom 60 by 20 feet. (Plan in possession of County Architect, Leics.; another classroom was later added at the rear. This building, known as the Hood extension, is now used by Ashby Grammar School.)

33 The school at Colne does not appear in *C.C.R.* or Carlisle. The details given are from Baines, E., *History of the County Palatine and Duchy of Lancaster*, Heywood: Croston, 1890, III, 362. There is a brief mention in *V.C.H.*, *Lancs.*, VI, 1911, 536.

34 The earliest provincial grammar school built in the Tudor revival style which I have come across is at Midhurst (Sussex), 1821.

35 *C.C.R.*, XXI, 1829, 22. The date-stone of the earlier school (1576) is built into an external door lintel. Cf. Pevsner, *Derbyshire*, 1953, 248.

36 The building was designed by Thomas Cook (d. 1842) of Leicester. He also designed several workhouses in Leicestershire and Derbyshire. His library and instruments were sold by auction and are listed in the *Leicester Advertiser* of 4 February 1843 (see Bennett, J. D., *Leicestershire architects 1700–1850*, Leicester Museums, 1968, under 'Cook'). The events leading to the rebuilding are given in Hopewell, S. *The book of Bosworth School*, Leicester: Thornley, 1950, 67f. For the layout of the building see *C.C.R.*, XXXII, 1838, 190. There is also a plan of the site and the original indenture made with the builder (1827) in the Dixie papers in Leicestershire County Record Office.

37 *C.C.R.*, XXXII, 1837, Part 5, 386f. A plan of the school dated 1858 in the Leicestershire County Record Office (Ma/E/BG/207/8), shows a ground-floor room measuring 53 by 30 feet, and states that there were two rooms on the first floor. An inscribed stone from the 1825 building survives in the grounds of Limehurst Secondary School, Loughborough. It records the erection of the school in 1825 and its enlargement 'by voluntary contributions and by a grant from the Privy Council' in 1858, i.e. following the removal of the Grammar School six years previously.

38 The history of the school is summarized in *V.C.H.*, *Worcs.*, IV, 67–8 and is given more fully in Murray, A. L., *Sebright School, Wolverley, a history*, Cambridge: Heffer, 1953. The earlier grammar school, rebuilt 1787, still exists, and is illustrated facing p. 30. The building of 1829, as shown on pl. **152**, has arches which do not reach to the ground, since the school was built over an old right-of-way, which remained as a covered passage. Behind the façade was the schoolroom, at first-floor level (Murray, 39–40). For the siting of the various schools on the foundation, see map facing p. 58 of Murray. See also Pevsner, *Worcs.*, 1968, 289–90.

39 See Pearce, E. H., *Annals of Christ's Hospital*, Methuen, 1901, 63–4. This also has a ground plan of the buildings (between pp. 300 and 301).

40 Knight, C. K., (ed.), *London*, Knight, 1842, II, 341–2. The hall was 187 feet long, 51 wide and 46 high. There are interior views in the N.M.R.

41 The 1818 building is described in Jackson, N. G., *Newark Magnus*, Nottingham: Bell, 1964, 121 and illustration facing. The English school is described on 137f. and illustration facing p. 224. A plan of the whole complex faces p. 241.

42 Thomas, A. W., *History of Nottingham High School 1513–1953*, Nottingham: Bell, 1957, 131f.

43 Graham, J. A., and Phythian, B.A., (ed.), *The Manchester Grammar School 1515–1965*, Manchester U.P., 1965, 34f.

44 Hutton, T. W., *King Edward's School, Birmingham 1552–1952*, Oxford: Blackwell,

1952, ch. 17, on 'Barry's building'. An Act of 1831 empowered the Governors to borrow £ 30,000 for two new schools, a grammar school and an English school, but the advertisement invited architects to submit designs for a new grammar school only. Later, however, the design was amended to accommodate 'that large class of persons who are desirous of educating their children for mercantile life'. Barry's school cost £55,000 and was designed for 400 boys. The site in New Street was eventually sold for £400,000.

45 Conisbee, L. R., *Bedford Modern School*, the School, 1964, 18–19.

46 From the Trustees' minutes (copy kindly supplied by the Clerk of the Trust, R. N. Hutchins, to whom I am grateful for further information and permission to examine the original plans in his custody).

47 Blore's other designs include the Pitt Building, occupied by the University Press in Trumpington Street, Cambridge (1831), the front elevation of which closely resembles the Bedford Modern School.

48 The diagram here reproduced is based on a first-floor plan signed by Blore and Wing, with other details from ground-floor layouts signed by Blore alone, which are on a larger scale and show minor changes. (Plans kept in what is still the original committee room at the school.)

49 *C.C.R.*, VI, 1821, 19, and *S.I.C.* report, 1868 (copy at School). The 1868 figures were: commercial school, 320; preparatory commercial school, 237; National schools, 370 boys and 490 girls; and infants' school, 250. The grammar school, in its separate building, contained only 194 boys. Total number of children being educated by the Harpur Trust was therefore 1,861.

50 This small area of Bedford contains an interesting complex of school buildings. The Grammar School, endowed by Sir William Harpur in 1566, was rebuilt in 1767 (the present Town Hall) and extended in 1861 (the present Civic Theatre). Pevsner calls it 'the only Georgian public building of interest in the county'. Next to the 1767 building is the former Girls' Modern School (now county offices) which was designed by Champneys in 1886 (see Pevsner, *Bedfordshire*, 1968, 50-1, on the school buildings of Bedford generally).

51 Harrison, J. A., *Private schools in Doncaster in the nineteenth century*, Parts 1 to 5, Doncaster Museum and Art Gallery Publications, nos. 20 (1958), 23 (1960), 27 (1961), 28(1962), and 36(1965), but paginated continuously. In general, these schools were quite small, tending to vary between twelve and forty pupils, and were mainly for boarders, sometimes supplemented by day-boys from the town (Harrison, 89f.).

52 *Ibid.*, 33 and illustration, p. 52. Built, 1809; demolished, 1959.

53 Barnes used the Old Clock Room, Mere, Wilts. (1823–7), Chantry House, Mere (1827–35), two houses in Dorchester (1835–7 and 1838–47) and 40 South Street, Dorchester (1847–62). In the garden of the last, Barnes built a two-storey schoolroom, with a playroom on the ground floor and the schoolroom above; demolished, 1965. See Hearl, T. W., *William Barnes the schoolmaster*, Dorchester: Longmans, 1966.

54 Harrison, *op. cit.* These were both on Thorne Road, at the fashionable end of the town, viz. Prospect House Academy, with large playground and spacious gardens (pp. 25–6), and Edenfield House Academy (pp. 46, 106–7 and illustration facing p. 48). A prospectus of 1871 mentioned a schoolroom, lecture-room and reading-room as well as a swimming-bath, gymnasium, etc. (p. 68). See also sale plan of J. H. Crouch, auctioneers, October 1892, in Sheffield City Library.

55 Quoted in Simon, B., *Studies in the history of education 1780–1870*, Lawrence & Wishart, 1960, 113: eighty-nine of these schools had been established since 1820 and a high proportion of the teachers were Dissenters.

56 *Ibid.*, 79f.
57 The Lancasterian system had a limited vogue in a few secondary schools. Charterhouse has already been mentioned. It was also used at Edinburgh High School; see Bentham, J., *Chrestomathia*, Payne & Foss, 1816, 86f.; also at Newark Grammar School (Jackson, N. G., *op. cit.*, 120f.).
58 Bentham, *op. cit.*, 'Chrestomathic tables' at end of book, 12–13 (an ugly sentence for an ugly idea). On Bentham's obsession with the 'Panopticon principle', see Himmelfarb, G., *Victorian minds*, Weidenfeld & Nicolson, 1968, ch. 2, on his projected model prisons. For prisons on this plan, see Mayhew, H., and Binny, J., *The criminal prisons of London*, Griffin, Bohn & Co., 1862, and Hobhouse, S., and Fenner Brockway, A., (ed.) *English prisons today*, Longmans, Green, 1921, 87, which describes the two systems of construction, the radial system, with the cells radiating from a central tower, exemplified in Pentonville Prison, and the block system exemplified in Wormwood Scrubs.
59 *Ibid.*, 20.
60 Stewart, W. A. C., and McCann, W. P., *The educational innovators 1750–1880*, Macmillan, 1967, 100. This book contains a good general account of Hazelwood School, pp. 98–123.
61 This is the title on the spine of the book; on the title-page it is *Plans for the government and liberal instruction of boys in large numbers*, Whittaker, 1822, no author given. Stewart and McCann, *op. cit.*, use the 2nd ed. of 1825, which may account for some of the discrepancies concerning the building and the organization of classes.
62 *Ibid.*, 14.
63 *Ibid.*, 2: 'The boys learn almost every branch of study in classes, that the Master may have time for copious explanations; it being an object of great anxiety with us, that the pupil should be led to reason upon his operations.'
64 *Ibid.*, 33. The whole section on 'Miscellaneous Arrangements' (31–7) speaks of the 'school-room' and the classes at their 'respective stations'; cf. Lancasterian terminology.
65 *Ibid.*, 63.
66 *Ibid.*, 25. Solitary confinement was used as a punishment in a number of Nonconformist schools at this period. At Sidcot School, Somerset, founded by the Quakers in 1808, the offender was locked in a 'coffin', a wooden upright box measuring internally 5 feet 6 inches by 1 foot 8 inches by 1 foot 9 inches. See illustration facing p. 81 in Knight, F. A., *History of Sidcot School*, Dent, 1908. This book also has a plan of the school as rebuilt in 1838 (facing p. 102), showing residential accommodation in the centre, with the boys' and girls' schoolrooms in opposite wings. Cf. the plan of Great Bowden School (Leics.), described in ch. 8.
67 The use of token money was common in contemporary commercial life, and much of it was produced in the Birmingham area (Rowland Hill was himself for some years a part-time official in the Birmingham Assay Office). On this subject generally, see Mathias, P., *English trade tokens*, Abelard-Schuman, 1962.
68 The phrase 'high school' was coming into use for progressive secondary schools modelled on the high schools of Scotland; cf. Douglas-Smith, A. E., *The City of London School*, Oxford: Blackwell, 1937, 48.
69 Hill, *op. cit.*, 123–5: 'We are not only called upon to put the key of knowledge into the hands of our pupils; we must open the cabinet and display its treasures.'
70 There is a plan of this school in Steven, W., *The history of the High School at Edinburgh*, Edinburgh: Maclachlan & Stewart, 1849, facing p. 224. The principal classrooms measured 37 by 27 feet, the side classrooms mostly 30 by 16 feet, and the public hall, with seats arranged in oval plan, 75 by 42 feet.

71 Bellot, H. H., *University College, London, 1826-1926*, University of London Press, 1929, 169–74, and an excellent plan between pp. 172 and 173.

72 Hearnshaw, F. J. C., *The centenary history of King's College, London, 1828–1928*, Harrap, 1929, 63–7, 101–4, and 153–9.

73 J. B. Bunning was afterwards City Architect. His work includes the Coal Exchange, Lower Thames Street (1847; now demolished), Holloway Prison (1849–51) and the Caledonian Market, Islington (1855).

74 Douglas-Smith, *op. cit.*, 66. A key part was played by W. S. Hale (ch. IX).

75 *Ibid.*, 83–4.

76 *Ibid.*, 72.

77 *Ibid.*, 241.

78 Freebody, N. K., *The history of the Collegiate Girls' School, Leicester, 1867–1967*, the School, 1967, 21, referring to the absence of an adequate road system in this area.

79 A writer of 1847 called New Walk 'the only respectable street in Leicester' (quoted in Patterson, A. T., *Radical Leicester*, Leicester U.P., 1954, 367).

80 *Leicester Journal*, 12 August 1836.

81 Weightman joined Hadfield's firm in Sheffield in 1837. Their buildings include the Town Hall, Glossop (1838), the Roman Catholic Cathedral, Salford (1845), St Mary's Church, Burnley (1846) and St John's Church, Chapeltown (1859).

82 The Leicester Collegiate School has in fact a shorter west wing than the school at Sheffield. It is possible that originally there was one classroom on each side of the main schoolroom, and a third further east, on the site of the 1883 alterations.

83 The history of the school is given in Freebody, *op. cit.*, and in Simon, B., (ed.), *Education in Leicestershire, 1540–1940*, Leicester U.P., 1968, 122–4, 128–9.

84 Millington, R., *A history of the City of Sheffield Training College*, the College, 1955, ch. 2. The Wesleyan School, which still forms part of King Edward VII School, was in the Palladian style favoured by the Nonconformists.

85 The Proprietary School building in Leicester was purchased by the Corporation in 1849 for £3,000 to house the museum collection of the Leicester Literary and Philosophical Society. The first report of the Museum Committee of the Town Council (1873) gives the layout of the building, which seems to have been little altered until after this date. The original school is now mainly one storey and a new staircase has been inserted. The history of the school is outlined in Simon, *op. cit.*, 124–8.

86 *The Leicestershire Mercury*, 5 August 1837.

87 *Ibid.* The germ of this idea may be detected in Hill, *op. cit.*, (see note 63, above).

88 Tiffen, H. J., *A history of the Liverpool Institute Schools 1825 to 1935*, Liverpool Institute Old Boys' Assoc., 1935, ch. 4, from which fig. 34 is taken. The sixteen teaching rooms included a laboratory and rooms for chemistry, mathematics and French, as well as for classical and English subjects. See also the engravings in the *Illustrated London News*, 2 March 1844.

89 The Sheffield schools have been mentioned above. At Wakefield, the West Riding Proprietary School was erected in 1834 and purchased by Queen Elizabeth's Grammar School in 1854. The Collegiate School at York was opened in 1838 and was combined with St Peter's School in 1844. Both buildings were in the Perpendicular style preferred by the Anglicans.

Ten

Church schools and State intervention 1840-70

I

It was the pressing need for elementary-school buildings which led to the first Government grant for education in 1833, and the desire to exercise control over its disbursement which lay behind the decision to appoint a Committee of the Privy Council on Education six years later. A Treasury minute of August 1833 had stated that local subscribers must raise at least half the estimated cost of a new school before a grant could be made, and that applications for a grant must be supported by either the National or British School Societies. More elaborate conditions were laid down in 1839: the Committee of Council reserved the right to inspect all schools aided by grant, the building plans had to allow at least 6 square feet per child (the standard which already applied in National and British schools), and applications for a grant, instead of being forwarded through the two societies, had to be made by the school promoters direct to the Committee. The National and British School Societies could, of course, continue to make their own building grants, but they were now relieved of all responsibility for Government assistance to schools.[1]

The controversies which arose between the various Church bodies and the Government over such matters as the inspection of schools have been extensively dealt with by historians of education, and the increasing amount of money paid by the Exchequer in support of elementary education in the period following the first grant of 1833 has also been frequently noted. Our concern here is with only one aspect of State intervention, though an important one. For at a time when denominational differences were at their height and when any Government attempt to influence the curriculum of the schools would have caused an uproar, the less controversial issue of school design and construction provided a principal sphere for detailed supervision and control by the central Government. School-building grants continued to form a major part of Government expenditure on education. In the period from 1839 to 1859 more than £1 million was granted for 'building, enlarging, repairing and furnishing elementary schools' out of a total grant expenditure of £4·4 millions.[2]

In fact, although a very keen interest was taken by the Committee of Council in the design of schools, it was some years before a standard layout for new grant-aided schools was established. Already the Lancasterian and National school promoters had well-developed views on this subject, as we saw in a previous chapter, while the architectural ideas of Stow were also receiving much attention. How, if at all, could these rival systems be reconciled?

Only a year after the setting up of the Committee of Council on Education, the Committee issued a lengthy 'minute explanatory of the plans of school-houses', to which was attached a series of plans 'to enable the promoters of schools to avoid considerable expenses in the erection of school-houses, and to diffuse an acquaintance with the arrangements which have been sanctioned by extensive experience, as best adapted to the different systems of instruction'.[3] The minute attempted to steer a careful course between what was traditional and novel in the theories of school-planning at the time. It gave a full account of the layouts recommended by the National and British School Societies (quoting at length from the *General observations* of the former and the *Manual* of the latter, which we described in ch. 8); it also discussed in some detail the system of 'mutual instruction' advocated by Lancaster and Bell and the 'simultaneous method' associated particularly with the name of David Stow. The essential difference between these two methods, the development of which we discussed in an earlier chapter, was succinctly stated by the Committee as follows:

> the simultaneous method is distinguished from the method of mutual instruction by arrangements which enable the children to receive instruction immediately from the master or one of his assistants, instead of from the most advanced of their fellow-pupils, from which [latter] practice the method of mutual instruction derives its name.

In the Lancasterian schools classes of eight to twelve children, and in the National schools classes of twelve to thirty children, were taught by monitors 'individually and in succession', with the master acting mainly as a supervisor; but in schools where the simultaneous method was in use the master could himself teach classes of from sixty to 100 or more children all together, so that 'the mind of each child [is] at all times under the influence of the master'.

The Committee—anxious no doubt not to seem too radical in their proposals—advocated the adoption of a 'mixed method of instruction', which would combine both mutual and simultaneous teaching. In this way the drilling of the children in the three Rs would continue to be conducted in small classes taken by monitors, but 'general instruction' of up to 120 children would be undertaken by the master himself, making use either of the whole schoolroom or of a gallery 'like that used in infant schools'. We noticed in a previous chapter that Wilderspin had introduced the gallery into the infants' schoolroom and Stow later brought it into the schools for older children as well. This idea was now taken up by the Committee of Council, who pointed out that in small schools the monitorial system had rarely been adopted in its entirety, since the master could personally teach each class in turn, or instruct the whole school by the simultaneous method. But in large schools the Committee realized that the simultaneous method could only be fully adopted by introducing additional adult teachers. On the Continent adult teachers were more widely employed than in England, though they were often wretchedly paid and were put in charge of very large classes.[4] The Committee hoped that further progress could be made in English schools by using pupil-teachers on the Dutch model. The pupil-teacher would be apprenticed to a master from fourteen to seventeen years of age before going to a 'normal school' to qualify as an assistant teacher. In the meantime, the Committee thought that schools should be designed in such a way as to make it possible to increase the amount of simultaneous teaching. The pupils' desks should be placed on steps, not as high as the galleries used in infants' schools, but so arranged that relatively large groups of children could see the master clearly when from time to time he gave a simultaneous lesson instead of merely supervising the monitors with their smaller groups. If, as the Committee hoped, the bigger schools were able to provide a separate infants' room with a gallery, the older children could also receive some simultaneous instruction in the gallery when the infants were at play. Finally, the Committee thought it desirable for living accommodation for the master and his family to be provided as part of the total design for the school. This had become the established practice in many places, as we have seen, though expenditure on such accommodation was not recognized for grant until 1843.

These general principles were worked out in detail in the sixteen plans attached to the minute of 1840. The plans attempted to show what the adoption of the 'mixed method' of instruction would mean in terms of the layout of schools of various sizes, though the equivalent Lancasterian and National school layouts were also inserted on each plan for purposes of comparison. Two of the Committee's plans are reproduced as pls. **160** and **161**. The first is for a small school of fifty-six children, and shows the master's seat facing the children, who are arranged in four rows of tiered desks. This block of desks is divided centrally by a movable wooden partition, so that the boys and girls could be separated if desired, but in general the Committee supported the principle of co-educational teaching on the Scottish model, with the boys and girls sitting on alternate benches in four separate classes, according to their proficiency in the three Rs. Thus the master could either teach the whole school simultaneously, or he could call out each class in turn to stand in a semicircle round his desk, the other classes meanwhile being taken by monitors. In this way it was thought that simultaneous and monitorial teaching could be effectively combined.

The second plan shows the same principles adapted to a larger school (150 infants and 144 older children). The older children are divided into four classes of thirty-six, taught by the master, an assistant teacher, and two pupil-teachers. As pl. **161** shows, each pair of 'class rooms' is divided by a partition, which does not, however, extend the whole width of the room. This would make it possible for the master or the assistant teacher in one classroom to keep an eye on the less experienced pupil-teacher in the adjoining room. In effect, each pair of classrooms was a separate school, but the attempt to subdivide the schoolroom even in this tentative way proved to be premature, as we shall see. There were to be four monitors—one for each class—to help with books

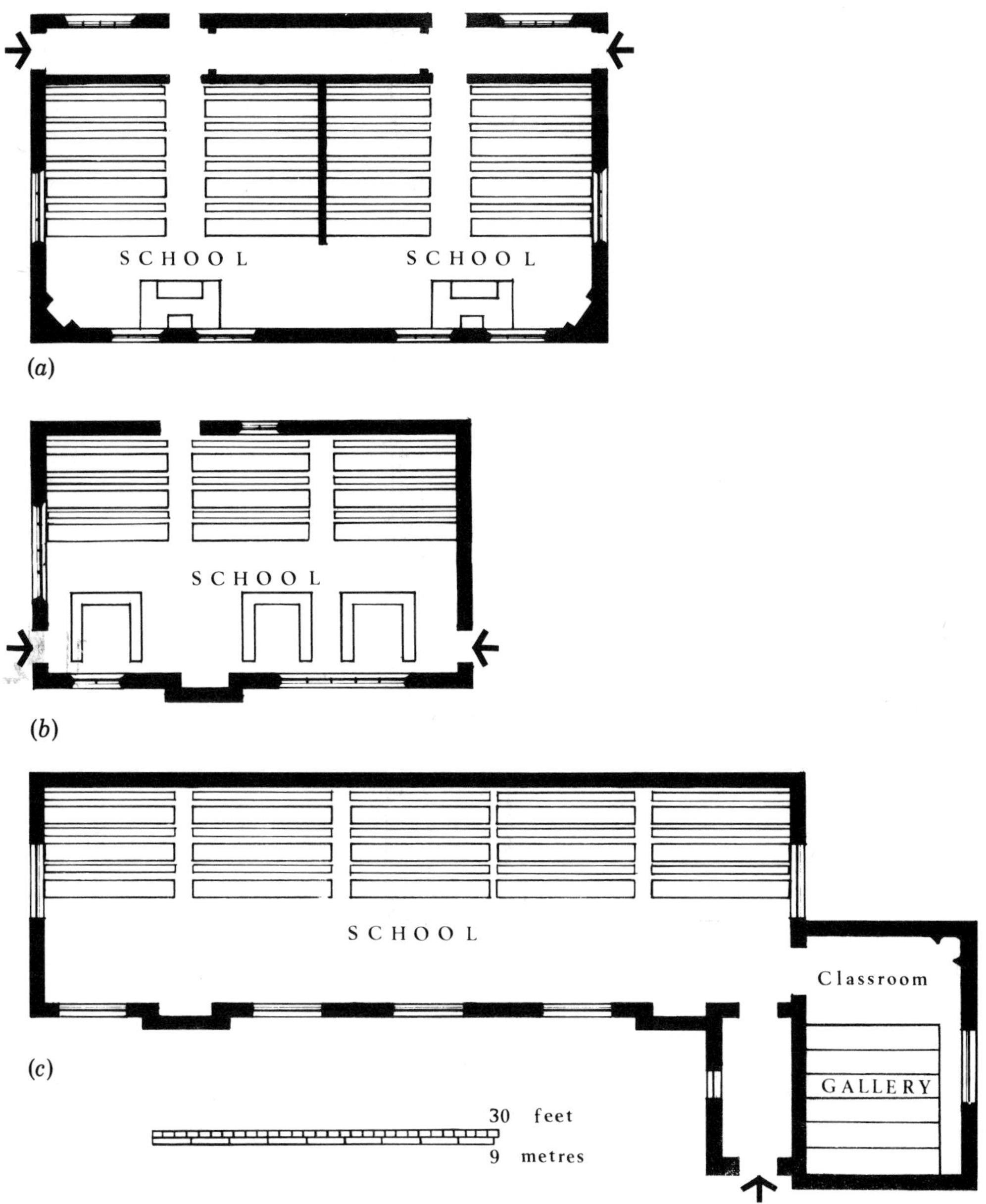

Figure 35 Plans issued by the Committee of Council on Education, all to the same scale: (*a*) Plan for 112 children, 1840 (Series B, No. 3). (*b*) Plan for 116 children, 1845 (No. 1). (*c*) Plan for 120 children, 1851 (No. 5).

and apparatus, but most of the teaching was to be given collectively to the whole class, with a limited amount of individual instruction given round the teacher's desk, group by group. The infants had their own master or mistress with a separate schoolroom: they were to be taught in groups in the 'hall' or open part of the schoolroom, but simultaneous instruction would be given in the gallery—all of which was by now well-established practice for infants. The section drawing in the top left-hand corner of pl. **161** shows that in the classrooms for the older children the desks and benches were placed on wide, shallow steps, whereas the steps of the infants' gallery were steeper and had seats (but not desks) fixed to them, since writing was not required for a 'gallery lesson'.

Looking at these plans more generally, it will be seen that although the Committee of Council were advocating a mixed method of teaching, their plans were in reality much more suitable for simultaneous than monitorial instruction. Their plans were also more generous in floor-area than the commonly accepted standard of 6 square feet per child, and were therefore more expensive to build. Thus, in the school for fifty-six children already referred to, the children were to occupy a room measuring 31 by 18 feet, or 10 square feet per child; in the school for 150 infants and 144 juveniles, while the infants were allocated the usual 6 square feet each, the older children occupied over 8. Since most of the floor-space was taken up with desks and benches, the internal layout recommended for the rooms used by the older children more closely resembled the Lancasterian than the National school plan. It could also be argued that the stepped floor was in some respects a development of the sloping floor already in use in the Lancasterian schools, though it is probably more correct to see it as a modification of the infants' gallery of Wilderspin and Stow. Yet the Lancasterian plan had never been as popular as that adopted by the National Society, which, as we have seen, had always made a feature of having a large open space in the middle of the room for monitorial teaching. It was, in fact, a fundamental weakness of the Committee's plans that they depended for their successful working on the employment of pupil-teachers, who were not yet, however, readily available.

It is therefore significant that the Committee of Council on Education issued a new set of plans in 1845—this time without any explanatory remarks—and that these plans show a reduction of floor-areas to 6 square feet per child, and also the allocation of half of the floor-space to monitorial teaching, with benches arranged in hollow squares in the National school manner, as shown in fig. 35 (*b*) (this is for a school of 116 children in a room measuring 35 by 20 feet; compare fig. 35 (*a*), which is the 1840 plan for a school of 112 children in a room measuring 48 by 19 feet).[5] The layout of 1845 was adopted in, among other places, St Mary Newington School, Southwark, and an interesting photograph of 1893 shows the schoolroom still arranged on these lines (pl. **162**).[6] This basic plan was reprinted by the Committee in their *Instructions to the architect or builder employed by the promoters of the school* (1848) which gave detailed guidance about the submission of plans and specifications, and drew attention to the importance of the proper siting, ventilation and sanitation of schools.[7]

It is clear that the Committee were obliged to approve National and British school plans based on the minimum requirement of 6 square feet per child. Almost certainly, therefore, a truer reflection of the layout of elementary schools as actually built in the 1840s—and probably later—are the plans given in *The school-room: its arrangements and organization*, which was written in 1848 by J. J. A. Harris, organizing master of the National Society.[8] This book, the author tells us, was written 'in compliance with the reiterated request of many clergymen and school-managers, who are anxious to be up and doing in the great work of National Education, and who have in vain sought in existing works upon the subject for the information it is intended to offer here'. It contains fourteen plans, showing schools of three shapes, viz. oblong, square and L-shaped, all of which, according to Harris, were commonly in use. In almost every case, the 'school' is a single room, and the 'classes' are arranged in hollow squares, each made up of three long benches, with the monitor sitting on a box (which contained slates and books) to complete the square. Indeed, it is clear that all these plans were based on the continued employment of monitors as class-teachers, and the time-tables which the author also gives show that the master's job was to teach at least one half-hour lesson each day to every class in turn, in the meantime supervising the whole school. The children were arranged in their 'classes' in the main body of the room, standing up to read and sitting down when writing on slates. Only the older children wrote on paper and, when doing this, they sat at desks facing the walls. The usual 6 square feet per child were allowed in calculating floor-areas.

All this was in the tradition of the Madras school, as we saw earlier. Harris believed that the monitorial system had been unfairly criticized: it was not the system, but its inefficient implementation, which was at fault. At only one point in his book does he admit to a limiting factor. This is when he says that the youngest and oldest children presented the main problems. The youngest were not accustomed to school discipline (even though the National schools were normally for children above infant age), while, as regards the older children, 'their size will make it more dangerous for a monitor to enforce discipline . . . and their age will often cause them to be unwilling to be governed by a schoolfellow, no older, or perhaps even younger, than themselves'. Harris therefore suggests that the oldest and youngest classes should be placed nearest to the master's desk, so that he could keep a close eye on them both. Later in the book, however, he proposes an alternative solution to the problem of inattentive older children, viz. the introduction of a certain amount of oral teaching, using the 'simultaneous method'. For this reason, he tentatively suggests that the writing desks should be turned round to face the master and placed on steps (as, in fact, the Committee of Council had proposed in their plans of 1840 and 1845).

Harris also reproduces the plan of the boys' schoolroom at the National Society's model school at the Sanctuary, Westminster (it had moved there from Baldwin's Gardens in 1832).[9] This, which is shown in fig. 36 (*a*), was for a main schoolroom with three rows of tiered desks at the back, facing into the room; in addition, there were two small classrooms, the larger of which was used by the top class. This class would in any event have needed a separate adult teacher, since their syllabus included drawing, ciphering, some history and geography and the 'elements of astronomy'—subjects well beyond the reach of the ordinary monitorial schools of the day. The model school at Westminster was, of course, a teacher-training establishment as well as a school, and where the help of students was available it was beginning to be possible to plan a room

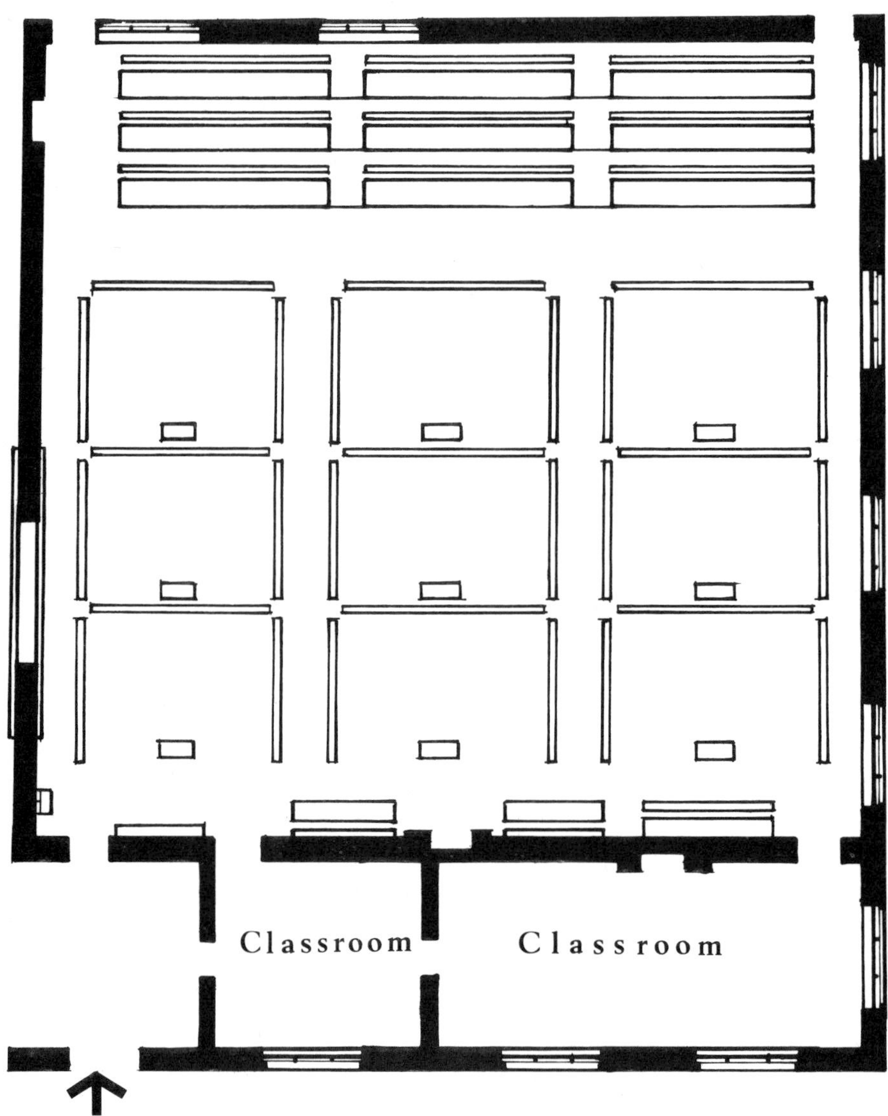

Figure 36 (*a*) National Society's Central Boys' School plan, *c*. 1843.

with the classes physically more distinct than had hitherto been usual. A layout of this transitional character, which anticipated the arrangement later encouraged by the Committee of Council, was adopted in 1844 in the practising school of St Mark's College, King's Road, Chelsea (now the College library), where an octagonal building was used for classes taken by students under the control of an experienced master, who sat in a central position supervising the whole school.[10] Fig. 36 (*b*) shows four main teaching areas: three of them were divided by curtains to form six classes, and the fourth

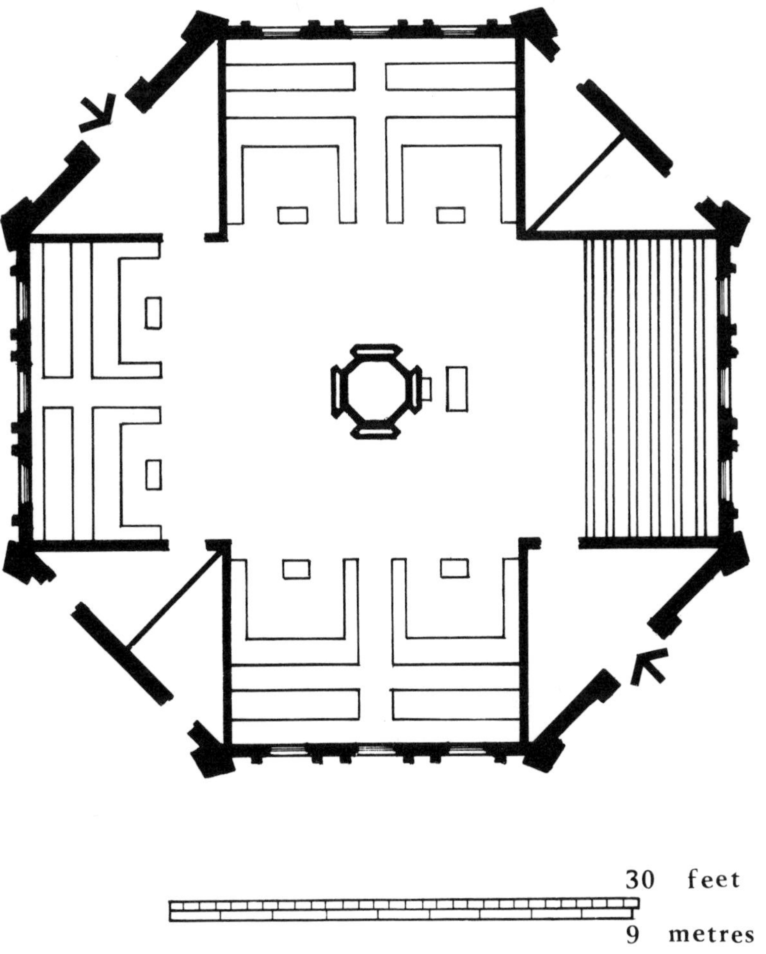

Figure 36 (*b*) St. Mark's College, Practising School plan, *c.* 1844.

was occupied by a gallery (the school contained 150 pupils taught by batches of eight students). The shape of the building was said to be in imitation of an Italian baptistry, but we noted earlier octagonal schools at Wimbledon and Clapham, and a somewhat similar octagonal plan was also adopted at this period in the United States, where it was commended as a 'model of fitness and close economy'.[11]

The internal planning of the British, like the National, schools was also developing very slowly. A report made in 1847 by Joseph Fletcher, one of Her Majesty's inspectors of schools, remarked on the varying quality of the British school buildings which he had inspected. Among the 'handsomest of those last visited' he includes the schools at Market Harborough and Ross-on-Wye referred to in ch. 8, and he states that although some British schools were 'altogether ill-contrived and mean', such schools were the exception rather than the rule: 'the school-rooms are generally lofty, well-lighted and airy', the chief defect being inadequate heating arrangements. He also remarks that 'some of the school-houses are connected with places of worship and the chief use of several of those classed as village schools appears always to have been as Sunday-schools'.[12]

Mr Fletcher's lengthy report also makes it clear that the internal layout of the British schools had changed very little since Lancaster's time. Plans reproduced from the British Society's manuals show the usual layout of long desks facing the master, with a passage on each side, except in the case of the smaller schools, where the passage was on one side only (see, for example, the photograph of the boys' school in the Old Meeting Schools in Birmingham, taken as late as 1882, and reproduced as pl. **163**). Fletcher notes that in only a very few schools were there separate classrooms with galleries on the Stow model. Even in the 'normal' schools (i.e. for teacher-training) which were rebuilt on the Borough Road site by the British Society in 1842, the boys' and girls' schoolrooms were little altered, the main change being the addition of two classrooms for boys and one for girls, into which smaller groups of children could be taken.[13]

In general, however, the development of physically-separate classrooms in the elementary schools had to wait until the supply of adult teachers increased. The 1850s and 1860s constitute a transitional period, characterized by the growing use of pupil- and assistant-teachers, a development which owed much to the policy pursued by the central Government. The Committee of Council offered financial inducements to the employment of pupil-teachers in a minute of 1846, and further minutes of 1851 and 1852 provided that ex-pupil-teachers might be appointed as assistants to certificated teachers at a salary of £25 p.a. The historian of teacher-training in the nineteenth century remarks that:

> This provision for adult assistant teachers was a significant thing. Previously the elementary school had been looked upon as essentially a one-man place, but as the monitorial system came more and more into disrepute, and the

> 'simultaneous' method more and more popular, the need for class teachers as distinct from head teachers was felt. As the assistant teachers became an established institution in the schools, it became increasingly common for students from training colleges to become assistant teachers before taking on the responsibility of a head teacher. This change of policy in the schools had an obvious bearing on the work of the training colleges, for an assistant teacher did not need the same knowledge of actual school organisation as the sole teacher of a school.[14]

Equally important were the effects on the planning of schools. Classes could if necessary be larger than under the monitorial system, and each class could be regarded as a self-contained unit; but since the assistant teachers, and especially the pupil-teachers, were relatively inexperienced, the classrooms, as in the practising schools attached to training colleges, had to be arranged so that the headmaster could readily supervise the whole school. The introduction of pupil-teachers therefore led to a very important change in building policy, which was announced in 1851 by the Committee of Council in a *Memorandum respecting the organization of schools in parallel groups of benches and desks*—a somewhat uninspiring title for a new type of internal organization which in fact influenced the layout of elementary schools for the next twenty years, and indeed later.[15] It therefore merits close attention.

The essential rationale of this document is given in the 'preliminary remarks', which show the importance attached to pupil-teachers in the future planning of schools; for 'where such assistants are maintained at the public expense, it becomes of increased importance to furnish them with all the mechanical appliances that have been found by experience to be the best calculated to give effect to their services'. The *Memorandum* then continues:

> The main end to be attained is the concentration of the attention of the teacher upon his own separate class, and of the class upon its teacher, to the exclusion of distracting sounds and objects, and without obstruction to the head master's power of superintending the whole of the classes and their teachers. This concentration would be effected the most completely if each teacher held his class in a separate room; but such an arrangement would be inconsistent with a proper superintendence, and would be open to other objections.[16] The common school-room should, therefore, be fitted to realize, as nearly as may be, the combined advantages of isolation and of superintendence, without destroying its use for such purposes as may require a large apartment. The best shape . . . is an oblong about eighteen feet in width. Groups of desks are arranged along one of the walls. Each group is divided from the adjacent group or groups by an alley, in which a light curtain can be drawn forward or back. Each class, when seated in a group of desks, is thus isolated on its sides from the rest of the school. The head master, seated at his desk placed against the opposite

> wall, or standing in front of any one of the classes, can easily superintend the school; while the separate teacher of each class stands in front of it, where the vacant floor allows him to place his easel for the suspension of diagrams and the use of the black board, or to draw out the children from their desks, and to instruct them standing, for the sake of relief by a change of position. The seats at the desks *and* the vacant floor in front of each group are *both needed*, and should therefore *be allowed for* in calculating the space requisite for *each class* [their italics].

The introduction of pupil-teachers and the new arrangement of classes marked the real beginning of the change-over from monitorial to collective teaching, and it will be noted that, in the extract quoted above, while the children might still be called out to stand in the empty space in front of the desks, this was 'for the sake of relief by a change of position' rather than to be taught in monitorial groups, as envisaged in the Committee of Council's plans of 1845. The plans attached to the 1851 *Memorandum* show very precisely how the new elementary schools should be organized. The basic form is shown in fig. 35 (*c*) on p. 201, which is the plan of a school for 120 children in five classes of twenty-four in a room measuring 65 by 18 feet. It will also be seen that a separate classroom (20 by 14 feet) is provided, with a gallery 'capable of containing two of the classes'. The five classes of children would sit at desks arranged in three parallel rows in the main schoolroom and separated from each other by curtains. These classes would be taken by pupil-teachers, supervised by the master. In addition, the master could himself withdraw any two of the classes into the classroom for a 'gallery lesson', which was regarded as the purest form of simultaneous instruction. Or, in a smaller all-age school, the classroom could be used mainly by the infants, for whom the gallery had, of course, originally been devised.

The furnishing of the schoolroom also appears to have shown some development. The *Memorandum* of 1851 includes drawings of desks arranged both on the level floor and on shallow steps, unlike the 1840 plans, which show stepped floors only. Probably a stepped floor was now considered less necessary, since a separate gallery was to be provided in all schools. Also, it seems that more attention was now being paid to the varying sizes of children and to the need to vary the heights of the desks. If the tallest desks were placed in the back row, the need for a stepped floor largely disappeared. Benches and desks were 12 feet long and were supported on cast-iron legs; the benches were without backs, since it was thought that the children received sufficient support by leaning forward on the desks. It may also be noted that the desks and benches were quite separate pieces of furniture: the idea of combining them seems to have been a later development. The *Memorandum* further suggested that the furniture should not be fastened to the floor—a compromise, perhaps, between the rigidity of the Lancasterian arrangement of desks and the fluidity of the National school system of benches.[17]

Bearing in mind the usual allocation of 6 square feet of floor space for each child, it is particularly worth noting that the plans of 1851 allowed 9 square feet per child—and this was exclusive of the classroom, which was now regarded as an essential adjunct to the schoolroom. Wilderspin, as we saw earlier, had made use of a classroom in his model infant school, and Stow had also insisted on a classroom in his model infant and juvenile schools. Now, after a considerable time-lag, such provision became part of the official policy for all schools.

The 1851 schoolroom had an optimum width of 18 feet. The length could be varied to suit the number of children to be accommodated, but the Committee felt that a schoolroom longer than about 65 feet was undesirable. Clearly, a greater length would have resulted in a corridor-like room, occupying a long, narrow site of a kind difficult to obtain in many areas; in addition, there was a limit to the number of classes arranged along one of the walls which a single master could adequately supervise, even when the pupil-teachers were doing much of the actual teaching. The Committee therefore suggested that, where the number of children was too large to be accommodated in a room 18 by 65 feet, an additional schoolroom should be built, either on the same site or elsewhere. If this proved to be impossible, the schoolroom should be L-shaped, with an experienced master or mistress supervising the teaching in each arm of the L. A second possibility would be in effect to place two of the narrow oblongs together to make a schoolroom over 30 feet wide, with the desks arranged along both side walls. This last plan was not, however, generally favoured by the Committee, since the children would have to face each other across the room and the teachers might also get in each other's way when teaching from the open space in the centre of the room. Nevertheless, we shall see that such plans were by no means uncommon in urban areas, where the number of children was great and sites expensive or hard to come by.

We can recapture something of the internal appearance of schools built on these lines from nineteenth-century photographs showing such schools in operation. The first (pl. **164**) is of a school at Dowlais, near Merthyr (Glam.), and shows an assistant or pupil-teacher facing a class, with two other teachers sitting in the front row and the master sitting at his desk behind her. On the left of the photograph may be seen a curtain, with the rod along which it was drawn running across the top of the picture.[18] The second (pl. **165**) is of a large London school which is arranged with the children facing each other in the manner not favoured by the Committee of Council. A gallery (with seats only, and extending considerably higher above the level of the floor) is at one end of the room. The young women assistants and pupil-teachers may be seen, and also the master, who stands in the centre of the schoolroom taking a dumb-bell lesson with some of the girls. The curtain-rods, which made it possible to separate the classes, may also be seen.[19]

The recommendations contained in the *Memorandum* of 1851 dominated school-planning during the 1850s and 1860s. Charles Richson's *The school builder's guide* (1850) was a compendium of official rulings made for the benefit of school-promoters, and was published before the new policy had been announced.[20] In the United States a comprehensive guide to *School architecture* had been written by Henry Barnard in 1848, and his *Practical illustrations of the principles of school architecture* appeared three years later.[21] While, however, there was certainly an equally marked interest in the subject of school architecture in contemporary America, it appears that there were not the rival systems of organization which had complicated the development of school-planning in England and delayed the adoption of a uniform layout for schools. Most of the plans advocated by Barnard merely show single or dual desks arranged in rows facing the teacher. An attempt to popularize Barnard's work in this country was made in R. S. Burn's *On the arrangement, construction and fittings of school-houses* (1856),[22] but, as a reviewer of Burn's book commented, 'it would be a waste of time in any case where assistance from the Committee of the Privy Council on Education is desired, to found plans on those given by Mr Barnard, as no pecuniary aid is granted unless the plans are in accordance with the arrangement laid down as the best by the Committee of Council' (i.e. those of 1851).

Educational opinion was now becoming convinced of the value of the Committee's plans of 1851. A very interesting contribution to this question was made in 1860 by Harry Chester in a pamphlet entitled *Hints on the building and management of schools*.[23] This was the text of a lecture given at South Kensington in December 1859 by the recently-retired assistant secretary of the Committee of Council on Education.[24] He admitted that the Committee's efforts to improve the planning of schools had at first been resented and that difficulties had arisen because of the variety of methods of organization then in vogue, but he felt sure that a real solution had been found in 1851:

> Given the case that we have to deal with in educating the poor, i.e. given one principal teacher, assisted only by pupil-teachers, to instruct the greatest possible number of children, I am satisfied that the organization recommended by the Committee of Council on Education, and commonly used in the best National and many other schools, is on the whole by far the best.

Chester also spoke firmly, and with much good sense, on the subject of the layout of schools:

> In the first place, no school can be so organized that six square feet per child will afford a sufficient area; and, in the second place, you can no more determine how many square feet per scholar will suffice in a particular school, without reference to the peculiar organization of that school, than you can determine how many guests can sit down to dinner in a dining-room without knowing the shape of the room, and whether the table is round or oblong. The capacity of a school-room depends on the organization of the school, and on the positions of the doors and fire-places.

He added the remarkably perceptive comment, that in planning a school building the first essential is to discover its system of organization; when that has been determined 'you may surround the scholars (as it were) with the proper walls'.

Throughout the 1850s and 1860s official pressure was exerted to ensure the adoption—at any rate in schools which applied for grant—of the system of 'parallel groups'. In 1856 the various official agencies offering grants for educational purposes united to form an Education Department, and in 1863 the Department issued a set of *Rules to be observed in planning and fitting-up schools*, which was largely a reprint of the 1851 *Memorandum*.[25] This was the era of the Revised Code, and the issue of these Rules is equally a reflection of an increase in central Government control. They may be regarded as the precursors of the present-day School Building Regulations, and certainly they marked the decisive intervention of the central Government in the detailed planning of schools.

II

So far in this chapter we have been mainly concerned with the development of the internal planning of elementary schools in the period 1840 to 1870. When we turn to consider the external architectural character of these buildings, we find that equally important changes were taking place. We have seen that the Tudor style had been growing in popularity from about 1830. This was also the style chosen for the elevations given in the Committee of Council's plans of 1840, including doors with four-centred arches, and mullioned windows with square hood-moulds. In the official plans of 1845 the stylistic features of Tudor buildings were further emphasized, with detailed drawings of roofs, doorways and windows.[26]

The architectural style chosen for these official plans, although certainly a reflection of the Gothic revival, was on the whole secular in character. The 1840s, however, marked the beginning of a more distinctively ecclesiastical style for schools, especially those erected with the help of the National Society. Pugin's *Contrasts; or a parallel between the noble edifices of the fourteenth and fifteenth centuries and similar buildings of the present day; shewing the present decay of taste* had been published in 1836 and his *True principles of Pointed or Christian architecture* appeared in 1841. This was also the year of Newman's *Tract XC*, and the height of the controversy aroused by the Oxford Movement. The building of schools came to rank second in importance only to church-building as a means of spreading distinctive religious views among the rapidly-growing population in both town and country. It was now felt to be desirable that the school buildings should themselves reflect the religious aspirations of their founders, and in particular it is interesting to trace the introduction of thirteenth- and fourteenth-century Gothic styles into elementary school architecture after 1840. A relatively early example is the school at Lound in Chapeltown, near Sheffield, which opened in 1845. It was designed by J. G. Weightman, who (as we saw earlier) had designed the collegiate schools at Sheffield and Leicester. Parliament had recently authorized the division of large parishes into ecclesiastical districts and given bishops power to license any suitable building for divine service—a belated attempt to provide for newly-industrialized areas. Thus the school at Lound was designed to accommodate 276 children and to be used on Sundays for Anglican services. The *Sheffield Times* printed an engraving of the school, which is reproduced as pl. **166**. (The building survives in Chapeltown opposite St John's Church, which was built by Weightman and Hadfield in 1859–60.) This newspaper also included the following description of the school building, which is indicative of the emphasis now beginning to be placed on an ecclesiastical (though still humble) architectural style for schools:

> Although substantial in construction, a pure and refined taste marks every portion of the edifice; and, although ecclesiastical in character, it does not pretend to rank in elevation of style with what they, who are interested in church-building, ought to feel it their duty to see carried out in every temple dedicated to the service of Almighty God. The school-house comprises two apartments for the children, and a residence for the master. The large school has an open roof and mullioned windows, with a quaint porch and bell-cot. The style of architecture is of the fourteenth century, faithfully carried out in all its details; and the general effect of the pile is particularly school-like, distinct from the mere secular or every-day architecture of modern times, and having sufficient character to inform the passer-by that it has been reared for the service of the God of Charity.[27]

Very similar ideas were expressed by Henry Kendall, junior, in his *Designs for schools and school houses*, published in 1847 as a folio volume, with Gothic print and elaborately decorated lithographs.[28] In his preface he refers to the need for 'a return to a better and purer style' for school buildings and pays tribute to the work of 'Pugin and others' for 'kindling amongst us a love of ancient art'. He goes on to express the opinion that 'the styles of the Middle Ages . . . are best suited for school houses . . . because the buildings themselves (like the pious and charitable institutions of olden times) partake, or ought to partake, of a semi-religious and semi-ecclesiastical character'. His twelve designs range in style from Early English, through Decorated and Perpendicular, to Elizabethan and the 'fantastic medley manner of building in the time of James I'. Purity of style was not considered essential: two of the designs are in what Kendall calls the 'mixed Tudor' style, 'the general aim being rather to produce a picturesque combination, than one strictly correct with reference to style, or consistent in detail'.

Seven of Kendall's designs are of schools which were actually built under his supervision, and some of the salient details of these schools are summarized in Table I opposite. It will be noted that five of the seven schools were provided with accommodation for the teacher as part of the design: in such cases, the cost per place varied between

Table I. Schools designed by Kendall, 1840–47

Date	*Place*	*No. of children*	*No. of schoolrooms*	*Cost,* £*	*Cost per place, £*
1840	Willesden (Middx.)	80 B & 80 G	2	500	3·1
1842	Bury St Edmunds Poor Boys' School, Bridewell Lane	300 B	1	760	2·5
1844	Childerditch (Essex)	60 M	1	120	2·0†
1845	Stanmore (Middx.)	100 I	1	430	4·3
1846	Bury St Edmunds Commercial School, College Street	170 B	1	300	1·7†
1847	Battle (Sussex)	100 B & 100 G	2	800	4·0
‡	Bury St Edmunds Poor Girls' School	150 G	1	575	3·8

* Exclusive of site and internal fittings.

† No teacher's house provided.

‡ To be erected.

B = Boys. G = Girls. I = Infants. M = Mixed.

£2 10*s*. and £4 6*s*. The internal plans, which were based on the usual 6 square feet per child, were conservative in spirit: two of them have the National school layout recommended in the book by Harris referred to earlier, and the rest show most of the floor-area taken up by long benches, with writing desks provided for the older children—the main aim apparently being to provide seating for the maximum possible number of children. In most cases all the teaching was to take place in one schoolroom, though boys and girls were accommodated separately in the larger schools. In no case was a physically distinct classroom provided, and it is clear that these schools were designed for places where the undiluted monitorial system was still the order of the day.

The real novelty of Kendall's book lay in his popularization of a wide variety of medieval and Tudor styles for school-building, and in his plea for the employment of professional architects in what had hitherto been regarded as an unimportant sphere. We have noticed in previous chapters that architects had usually been engaged by the major public-school foundations, but their use for elementary-school buildings was altogether exceptional before the 1840s. Kendall's father had been one of the founders of the Institute of British Architects (1834), and his son's plea for the regular employment of qualified architects should be seen in relation to the expansion of the architectural profession which was taking place during this period. Kendall junior was careful to point out that elaborate styles need not mean greater expense, so long as the school was professionally designed—indeed, his designs reached such a degree of elaboration that only a specialist could supervise their construction. He saw it as 'the duty as well as the policy of the profession to stimulate the growing taste of the community for the study of architecture', and he considered that the expansion of elementary education presented a 'noble opportunity for the exhibition of national architecture and for contributing to its general diffusion'. In this way Kendall could claim that religion, patriotism and the need for popular education all united to make the architect indispensable.

In this connection, it may be noted that many of the plans submitted by promoters of schools to the Committee of Council on Education were signed by local architects, and that both the Committee of Council and the National Society were prepared to advise on school design, the latter employing Edward Blore (whose work at Bedford we noticed in the previous chapter) to draw sets of model plans which were sent to school-promoters in the provinces.[29] The appearance of Kendall's book was welcomed by *The Builder*, which particularly commended—and in fact reproduced—his design for a 'picturesque adaptation of some distinguishing features and the character of Early English Collegiate Edifices' (see pl. **167**, which shows the boys' schoolroom on the left, the girls' in the centre at right angles to it, and the master's house on the right). *The Builder* added that 'we look upon this book as a well-timed volume, and trust it will have the effect of leading other architects to publish designs, to counteract the effects of the melancholy exemplars put forth by a former Committee of Privy Council on Education'—for *The Builder* never seems to have had a good word to say for any plans sponsored by Government bodies.

This hope was shortly realized by the appearance of Joseph Clarke's *Schools and school houses* (1852), which illustrates eleven schools and a school-house on twenty-five plates.[30] Further details are given in Table II. It will be seen that the cost of many of these schools was higher than that of those designed by Kendall. It should be noted, however, that the village school at Clifton Hampden was the result of 'private munificence'; Foxearth School was paid for by the Rector, and that at Leigh by the Bishop of Moray and Ross. The building at Leigh included provision for a curate's house, three schoolrooms and a house for the schoolmistresses, and as Clarke remarks, 'this building can hardly be looked on as belonging to the ordinary class of village schools; it forms in fact a parochial establishment based on a collegiate system' (see pl. **168**).

Clarke had a large practice in church restorations and ecclesiastical and school buildings. He was a founder of the Architectural Museum (from which the Architectural Association developed) and became President of the Ecclesiastical Surveyors' Association. In 1851 he had designed the Oxford Diocesan Training School at Culham, on a quadrangular plan in late Decorated style.[31] His designs for parish schools are, however, disappointingly conventional. They were mainly of a simple, Tudor style, with some use of half-timbering for decorative effect. They show the traditional National

Table II. Schools designed by Clarke, c. 1852

Place	*No. of children*	*No. of school-rooms*	*Cost, £*	*Cost per place, £*
Monk's Horton (Kent)	50 M	1	120‡	2·4§
Lydd, Romney Marsh (Kent)	200 B & G	2	750‡	3·8
Little Bentley (Essex)	80 B & G	1†	350‡	4·4§
Clifton Hampden (Oxon.)	100 B & G*	1†	800	8·0
Coopersale (Essex)	110 B & G	2	900	8·2
Willesborough (Kent)	70 M	1	500‡	7·1
Brabourne (Kent)	100 B & G	1†	800‡	8·0
Boreham (Essex)	120 B & G*	1†	600‡	5·0
Foxearth (Essex)	120 M	1	900	7·5
Hatfield-Bishops (Herts.)	200 G & I*	2	600‡	3·0
Leigh (Essex)	260 B, G & I*	3	2000	7·7

* Estimated from floor-area given.
† Divided by curtain or folding partition.
‡ Includes grant from Privy Council.
§ Teacher's house not provided.
B = Boys. G = Girls. I = Infants. M = Mixed.

school layouts, with the usual allowance of 6 square feet per child. Clarke comments of one of his schools that it was planned 'on the scale originally laid down by the Committee of Council, but this number [of children] is far too many to be taught efficiently'. In fact, as we saw, the Committee had suggested more generous floor-areas in 1840, but had not succeeded in making them obligatory until 1851. Clarke reproduced the Committee's plans of 1851 in an addendum to his book, noting the 'marked improvement' which had lately taken place and the fact that 'school buildings are now looked on with far more interest . . . coupled with an evident desire to make them, to a certain extent, ornamental as well as useful'. *The Builder*, in its review of Clarke's book, commented characteristically that the plans given in the addendum showed

> the arrangement of schools as now directed by committee of council. We say *now* directed because the committee appear to have thrown overboard all the designs and regulations which up to that time they had issued for guidance, and without attention to which there was very little chance of obtaining a grant. The number of bad churches, bad schools, bad workhouses, and unhealthy

> dwellings, which we owe to Government commissioners, the Privy Council and Acts of Parliament, is distressingly large.

This was in fact far from the truth: the Committee of Council had been obliged to reconcile, as far as they were able, the rival plans of Lancaster, Bell and Stow; they had also faced opposition from the Churches; and they had drawn systematic attention for the first time to the importance of the proper siting, ventilation and sanitation of schools. That it took ten years to achieve an acceptable series of plans was hardly surprising.

In spite of its prejudice against the Committee of Council on Education, *The Builder*, which began as a weekly publication in 1843, is itself a valuable source of information about school buildings in many parts of the country, as we shall shortly see. Here we may make the general point that it provides further evidence of the increasing interest in school architecture and of the growing popularity of Gothic designs for schools. This was clearly a period of elementary-school building on a mass scale: in 1843, for example, *The Builder* announced that the Wesleyans were planning to spend nearly £200,000 on schools over the next seven years,[32] and three years later it reported that thirty infants' schools were to be built in Birmingham by an association of clergymen and others, financed by local funds and grants from the National Society and the Privy Council.[33] All this was apart from the individual benefactors who featured prominently in the building of schools for the poor during this period.

Virtually all the designs given in *The Builder* were for schools in Gothic style. In 1849 it noted a Wesleyan school built in the 'Grecian style', but this seems to have been exceptional.[34] Even the Nonconformists were now losing their distrust of medieval styles. When in 1850 the Society of Friends restored a Gothic building for use as a school, *The Builder* remarked on the contrast it made with the plain appearance of the meeting-house nearby, adding that 'it is worthy of notice, as indicating the progress of architecture in the nineteenth century, that the Quakers, of all men the most indifferent to the claims of art, have caused to be restored an ecclesiastical structure of the Middle Ages'.[35]

A well-informed observer of 1860[36] stated that he had seen 'many excellent Gothic designs, some good Elizabethan designs, and some few very bad Italian designs for schools'. He, too, was impressed by the progress made during the previous twenty years. 'When the Committee of Council on Education was first created in 1839', he wrote, 'so little attention had been given to the planning of schools, that they were very commonly erected by the village brick-layer and carpenter, by rule of thumb, without any plans at all.' Such schools were usually 'low, thin, dingy and ill-drained' and contained 'no furniture but a teacher's desk, a few rickety forms, a cane and a fool's cap' (cf. pl. **118**). But now all this had changed: 'educational societies vie with each other in architectural exploits, and the land is adorned with schools. The most celebrated architects undertake to design these buildings, and give their minds to the design. No one now thinks that a school can be built anyhow, without any reference to the uses to which the building is to be applied.' Thus it was that elementary-school building became a recognized branch of architecture and was swept forward as part of the Gothic revival.

III

These general remarks serve to introduce a more detailed examination of individual school buildings of the period. Certainly there is no lack of evidence, though it has so far been largely neglected by educational and architectural historians. Apart from the many buildings which survive, there are the very numerous plans of schools which are now kept in local record offices and ecclesiastical record repositories.[37] The first circular issued by the Committee of Council in 1839 stated that every application for grant must be accompanied by a plan of the school. 'This plan should be neatly drawn according to scale, and should display the dimensions of every room, and the arrangement of the benches, desks, gallery, and other school apparatus.' The name of the school and of the architect should also be given on every drawing.[38] The same instructions were repeated in the Committee's minutes of 1847–8.[39] The plans received

Table III. Analysis of elementary schools in Leicestershire for which Committee of Council plans survive

Period	*No. of schools with at least one plan dated in period shown*	*No. of schools built in period shown*
Pre–1840	—	8
1840–9	5	14
1850–9	17	13
1860–9	10	10
1870–9	5 (to 1872)	11 (to 1875)
Undated	19	—
Totals	56	56

Note: Many of the dated plans refer to alterations to earlier buildings. In the case of new schools, there was naturally a time-lag between the submission of plans and the completion of the buildings. The Elementary Education Act of 1870 withdrew all building grants from the voluntary societies, but this took a year or two to take effect.

by the Committee of Council were retained among the records of the central department until a few years ago, when they were distributed to local record offices. They form an invaluable source of information about elementary-school buildings in all parts of the country.

We may take as a sample those now kept at the County Record Office in Leicester, where there are about 250 plans relating to fifty-six schools. Most of these plans are undated and it is not always easy to date them from internal evidence. Our analysis of the development of school layouts dealt with earlier in this chapter, however, enables us to proceed with a certain measure of confidence. It is also not clear whether the schools for which plans survive were the only ones in the area which qualified for building grants, but, assuming that the surviving plans are a representative selection, it may be noted that the great majority of them relate to National or Church of England schools (in fact, all but the British school at Ibstock, the Lancasterian school at Loughborough and the Wesleyan school at Worthington).[40] More detailed notes on the Leicestershire collection of plans are given in Appendix 1; the accompanying Table III provides a comparison between the dates given on some of the plans and the dates of the original buildings as stated in local directories and sometimes on the buildings themselves.

In an attempt to compensate for the possibly distorted picture resulting from an examination of plans in only one area—and that a predominantly rural one—the volumes of *The Builder* from 1843, when it began publication, to 1870, when a fresh wave of school-building started, have been examined for references to schools. A few of these references are to elementary schools in Wales, Scotland and Ireland and a few more to residential elementary schools, such as orphan and industrial schools.[41] No account has been taken of these, but a list of the illustrations relating to elementary day schools in England included in *The Builder* up to 1870 is given in Appendix 2 (many more are referred to without any plan or elevation being given). Table IV is an analysis of the schools illustrated, divided by decades.

We are now in a position to review the evidence available from some of the

Table IV. Elementary day schools in England illustrated in *The Builder*, 1843–69

Period	*No. of schools with elevation only*	*No. of schools with plan and elevation*	*Totals*
1843–9	4	1	5
1850–9	11	12	23
1860–9	4	7	11
Totals	19	20	39

plans submitted to the Committee of Council, the volumes of *The Builder* and a selection of surviving elementary school buildings, and to draw some tentative conclusions.

First, it appears that, although the taste for Tudor Gothic continued strongly into the 1840s, the plainer, classical style persisted in some places. Thus we may note that the 1841 plan of the school at Wigston Magna (Leics.), now demolished, was of classical design, while the Boys' National School at Berwick-on-Tweed (Northumberland), shown on pl. **169**, was built a year later with strict classical proportions. Similarly, a classical pediment and round-headed recesses were used on the National School in Russell Street, Cambridge, in 1845 (see pl. **170**). This school had separate entrances for boys and girls, still marked by massive brick piers. The boys' schoolroom, measuring 50 by 29 feet, was on the ground floor and was entered from the east side; the girls entered from the west and mounted a staircase to their schoolroom on the first floor. (The staircase was positioned immediately behind the classical façade, with the blocked recesses masking it from the road.)[42] Other classical examples still to be seen are the Jubilee School, dated 1850, at Barnby-in-the-Willows (Notts.), where the idea of blank round-headed recesses appears once more, and the school alongside the parish church at Staveley (Derbs.), built in 1844, with an octagonal teacher's house occupying the corner of an L-shaped site and the schoolrooms radiating from it. Simple classical detail is also used on the school facing the village green at Gretton (Northants.), built in 1853 (pl. **171**). The interior of this building was divided into two by a partition to make separate schoolrooms for boys and girls, for it may be assumed that there was no shortage of land and therefore no need (as at Berwick-on-Tweed and Cambridge) to build in two storeys. Later, as in many other places, an infants' schoolroom was added.

It was, however, the Tudor style which firmly established itself as the characteristic style for elementary schools during the 1840s. The Nonconformists seem to have preferred the so-called 'Elizabethan' style, as, for example, in the British School at Ibstock (Leics. 1846), and the Crescent Chapel Schools at Liverpool (1846) illustrated in *The Builder*, but the majority of schools were Anglican and were built in the earlier Tudor style. The authors of the recent *Inventory of historical monuments in West Cambridgeshire* (1968) remark of the elementary schools in that area dating mainly from the 1840s that 'the prevailing style is Tudoresque, generally following that considered appropriate at the same time for parsonages, but with rustic or cottage overtones suited to the accommodation of the rural labouring classes'.[43] The same may be said of Leicestershire, where three of the five schools of the 1840s of which Committee of Council plans survive are in this style, as are many other schools built in Leicestershire during this decade.[44] We noticed 'Tudoresque' schools beginning to appear, not only in London, but in rural counties, such as Dorset and Devon, in the 1830s, and from Lancashire we may note the school founded by Janet Shuttleworth at Habergham, near Burnley, in 1848. This building, which is illustrated on pl. **175**, consists of the main schoolroom with its gable end facing the road, a further schoolroom (with unusual, possibly later, clerestory windows) at right angles to it, and the teacher's house at the end. A small school in the same style, with the teacher's house forming a cross-wing to the schoolroom is illustrated from the school built in 1846 at Heydon, Cambridgeshire (pl. **173**)—again a common arrangement.

Two of the plans of the 1840s in the Leicester County Record Office shed further light on the internal arrangement of schools of this type. That at Kibworth Beauchamp (1842) is illustrated on pl. **172** and fig. 37 (*a*), and shows how it was possible to include accommodation for the teacher in the same building as the school. It will also be noted that two small classrooms were provided—an indication, as we saw earlier, of the beginning of simultaneous as distinct from monitorial teaching. The school at Queniborough built in 1847 (pl. **174** and fig. 37 (*b*)) also included a classroom, but the arrangement of the schoolroom shows that it was still possible for a school to be given a Government building grant even though it retained the traditional National school layout (as, equally, did the British school at Ibstock, built in the previous year, with the typical Lancasterian arrangement of desks). Other schools of this date show the modified plan mentioned by Harris, i.e. with the desks facing the master, but still allowing plenty of room for monitorial groups, as at Sheepy Magna, 1847. It may also be noted that the Tudor style was often used for two-storey buildings, as at Thurmaston, Leicestershire (1844) and—a more elaborate example—the Cavendish Street Schools, Manchester, illustrated in *The Builder* (1849).

Another variation of the 1840s which may be noted—though it was not a new one—was to place the teacher's house between the boys' and girls' schoolrooms. This was not an arrangement recommended by the National Society, as we saw earlier, but it was nevertheless commonly used up to at least the 1850s (as at the Trinity Schools, Margate (1850) and St Mildred's Schools, Canterbury (1855), both illustrated in *The Builder*). Our two illustrations of this type of school are strongly contrasted in origin. The first is the school in Windsor Great Park established by Queen Victoria in 1845 'for the education of the children belonging to those families in her Majesty's immediate service, such as game-keepers, gate-keepers, gardeners, etc.'. The *Illustrated London News*, whose engraving of the school is reproduced as pl. **176**, hoped that the seventy-five children attending would be 'brought under the influence of sound religious training, and education in its true meaning', so that they may 'go out into the world with knowledge befitting their station'. It also expressed the hope that 'the example set by the first lady of the land will be emulated by the patrons of kindred institutions';[45] in fact, it was Prince Albert who was probably instrumental in building this school, his philanthropic energies also making themselves felt at Windsor in his model housing scheme of fifty-eight cottages in what is now Alexandra Road, the preservation of which has recently been the subject of concern.[46]

Of similar plan are the two schools founded by the Chartist colonists in 1848 at Snig's End and Lowbands (Glos.), two of the large estates bought by the ill-fated Co-operative Land Society sponsored by Feargus O'Connor. The school at Snig's End, now

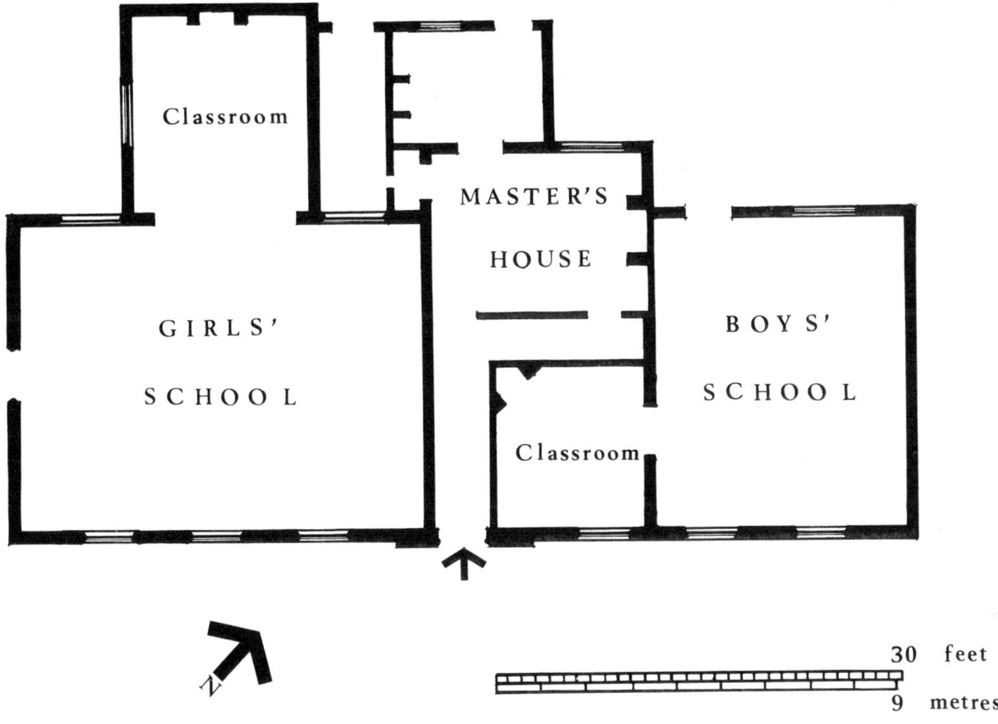

Figure 37 (*a*) Kibworth Beauchamp Parochial School plan, 1842.

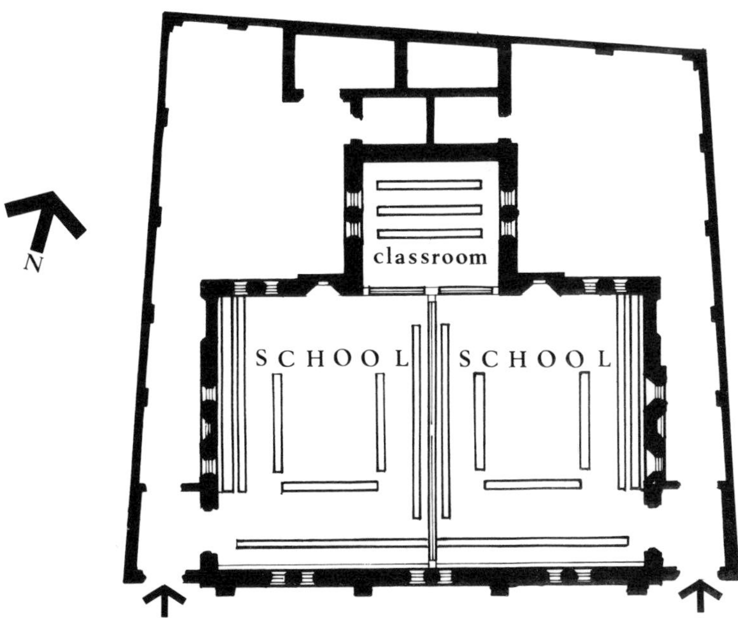

Figure 37 (*b*) Queniborough National School plan, 1847.

the 'Prince of Wales' public house, has been somewhat altered, but that at Lowbands (illustrated on pl. **177**) is in virtually its original state, though it has long ceased to be used as a school. It consists of two schoolrooms each measuring 28 by 15 feet, with the teacher's house in the centre. As at Windsor, the contemporary cottages which also formed part of this model scheme may still be seen, but separated from each other in their own plots of land.[47]

When we come to consider the evidence about individual elementary schools of the 1850s and 1860s, we find that the Committee of Council's *Memorandum* of 1851, discussed earlier in this chapter, had a very marked influence on interior layouts, while the ecclesiastical Gothic styles of the kind advocated by Kendall and others were coming to be adopted on a nation-wide scale. The rate of building was also accelerating: in the towns larger individual schools were being built, sometimes of more than two storeys, a feature which had earlier been quite exceptional.[48] The number of village schools also increased because even the smaller villages now began to have their own school buildings—usually rudimentary, single-cell structures, it is true, but nevertheless marking the furthest limit of the penetration of formal education into the countryside, and a limit from which, in terms of buildings, we have in the present century been steadily retreating.[49]

The change from Tudor to earlier Gothic forms may be seen in *The Builder* from 1849: the Free Schools at Yarmouth were in the Early English style similar to that which we saw had been adopted at Lound, near Chapeltown, four years earlier, while the style of the Northern Schools of St Martin-in-the-Fields was described as 'approximating to the Gothic of the north of Italy'. The elementary schools illustrated in *The Builder* after 1850 are invariably in ecclesiastical Gothic style, and tend to become increasingly ornate and elaborate. Similarly, the external architectural features of a number of surviving Leicestershire schools illustrate what appears to have been a national trend. The small school building at Knipton (1854), for example, is still in Tudoresque style, with square-headed windows and hood-moulds (pl. **178**). That at Burton Overy (1857), however, incorporates Gothic tracery in the windows (pl. **179**), as does the school at Husband's Bosworth, where E. F. Law, a well-known Northampton architect, designed a main schoolroom and master's house in 1858 and two years later an infants' schoolroom at right angles to the main room (pl. **180**). Much more elaborate window tracery was employed in the school at Enderby, which opened in 1860 with separate schoolrooms for boys, girls and infants (pl. **181**). This school was designed by the Leicester firm of architects, Millican and Smith, and was later extended in similar style on the north side.

As for the plans of schools built during this period, the impact of the 1851 *Memorandum* is clearly visible in the volumes of *The Builder*. Before that date, the interior layouts of schools were not given at all, possibly indicating a lack of interest among architects in the 1840s in this aspect of school-planning. The plan of the Trinity School, Reading (1852), was that recommended by the Committee of Council in 1845 and did not include a classroom, but its allowance of 9 square feet per child was more generous than had earlier been usual. That of the Hythe National School, also dated 1852, shows the desks arranged in groups, though not quite as the 1851 *Memorandum* suggested. The layout of the rooms in the National School at Mansel Lacy, Herefordshire, however, which dates from 1853, corresponds with those given in the *Memorandum*, as do all the school plans included in *The Builder* for the rest of the 1850s and 1860s. Typical of these plans was the one given in 1855 for the National School at Ludlow (Salop.), which is illustrated on pl. **182**. It consisted of an L-shaped schoolroom and associated classroom on each side of an infants' schoolroom. The provision of playgrounds, w.c.s and accommodation for the teachers was also normal by this date.

The plans relating to Leicestershire schools similarly illustrate the alteration of internal layouts. The plan of Frisby National School dated 1852 gives the 1845 arrangement which left most of the floor area free of desks to permit monitorial teaching. That of the National School at Rothley, however, also dated 1852, shows the arrangement recommended in the 1851 *Memorandum*, with three rows of parallel desks 2 feet 6 inches, 2 feet 3 inches and 2 feet 0 inches high. There is also a draft plan of the schoolroom with the note 'Council offices 18 Sept. 1852', which suggests that the layout was sketched in by an official of the Committee of Council on Education for the guidance of the school promoters. The plan of Thurlaston National School, dated 1853, and all subsequent plans in the Leicestershire collection, conform in virtually every respect to the *Memorandum*. Many record the alteration of existing schools in order to comply with the *Memorandum*, including the addition of classrooms.

Almost all of the Leicestershire plans are of single-storey buildings. In rural areas large sites were usually available, but in the towns this was far from being the case, and the increasing number of multi-storey schools is clear from the illustrations given in *The Builder*. The Northern Schools at St Martin-in-the-Fields (1849), mentioned above, were designed for the considerable number of 720 children. The ground floor was occupied by a schoolroom for 320 infants, and on the first floor were separate schoolrooms for 200 boys and 200 girls. A novel feature here was the construction of a playground on the roof, an idea later adopted in some of the London Board schools. A number of schools in Liverpool illustrated in *The Builder* show that three-storey buildings were erected to accommodate infants on the ground floor, with boys on the first and girls on the second floor. These were the St John's Schools (1850) in Great Croshall Street (now used as offices by a firm of engineers), St Augustine's National Schools (1853) in Salisbury Street (which were still standing, though derelict, in 1967) and St Mark's Schools (1854) on the corner of Roscoe Street and Back Knight Street (now demolished), where the need for access to the upper floors made it necessary to group the desks, somewhat unusually, in the centre of each schoolroom.[50]

In other major towns, schools of several storeys were also being built. Thus, St Giles's National School, built in Endell Street, Bloomsbury, London, in 1860, was of five storeys and was designed for no less than 1,500 children (pl. **184**). In the basement was a soup kitchen and an industrial school; on the ground floor an infants' school, with the residence of the master and mistress on a mezzanine floor above; on the next floor was the girls' school, and on the top floor the boys' schoolroom. This school—or, more strictly, complex of schools—was built in a neighbourhood which was considered to be 'one of the worst in London', and the notice of it in *The Builder* felt sure that it would be 'a powerful means for good'. The building, corresponding exactly to the illustration in *The Builder*, was still standing in 1969.[51]

The incorporation of infants' schools in buildings designed also for older children was a noteworthy feature of elementary schools of the 1850s and 1860s. The point seems to be that infants' schools had fully established their place by 1850 and entirely separate buildings for them appear more rarely than in the 1830s and 1840s. Of the fifty-six schools in Leicestershire of which Committee of Council plans survive, only two (at Loughborough, 1852, and Melton Mowbray, 1853) were for infants only. One such school, illustrated in *The Builder* in 1853, was built in Pile Street, Redcliffe, in Bristol, and shows that the planning of infants' schools had developed hardly at all, though the architectural style had become much more elaborate.[52] The plan was a simple one, and, apart from the addition of a teacher's house at the side, showed no real advance on, for example, the infants' school at Cheltenham, built in 1830, which we examined in ch. 8: there was still the one large schoolroom with a gallery at one end and benches along the sides of the room. But the main elevation (reproduced as pl. **183** from the engraving in *The Builder*), with its Gothic windows, ornate chimneys and tall pinnacles, forms a very marked contrast with the relatively plain style of the Cheltenham school built only twenty years before (pl. **141**).

Some development in the planning of infants' schools did, however, take place in the 1860s, probably because of the growing influence of Froebelian ideas. One of the few books on the subject of school buildings which seem to have been written in the 1860s related specifically to buildings for infants. This was *Hints on school building* (1863), by J. S. Reynolds, the Secretary of the Home and Colonial School Society, which had been founded in 1836 to popularize the methods of the Swiss educational reformer, Pestalozzi, especially in infant schools.[53] Reynolds mentions the value of the kindergarten occupations which derived from the work of Froebel, and it is clear that teaching methods were changing, but, so far as infant-school buildings were concerned, we find that the usual large room, with one or more galleries and a small classroom adjoining, was still being recommended. He does, however, also recommend that a 'babies' room' for children of two to four years of age should be provided in every school, either as a separate classroom or in part of the schoolroom partitioned off for the purpose. The layout of Reynolds' model infant school is shown in fig. 38. It will be seen that wash-basins were provided at one end of the schoolroom and that one of the two classrooms had writing desks for the older infants. Separate w.c.s were provided for boys and girls and more than half of the total site area was occupied by the playground, which was equipped with swings, parallel bars, etc., and partly covered over for use in wet weather.

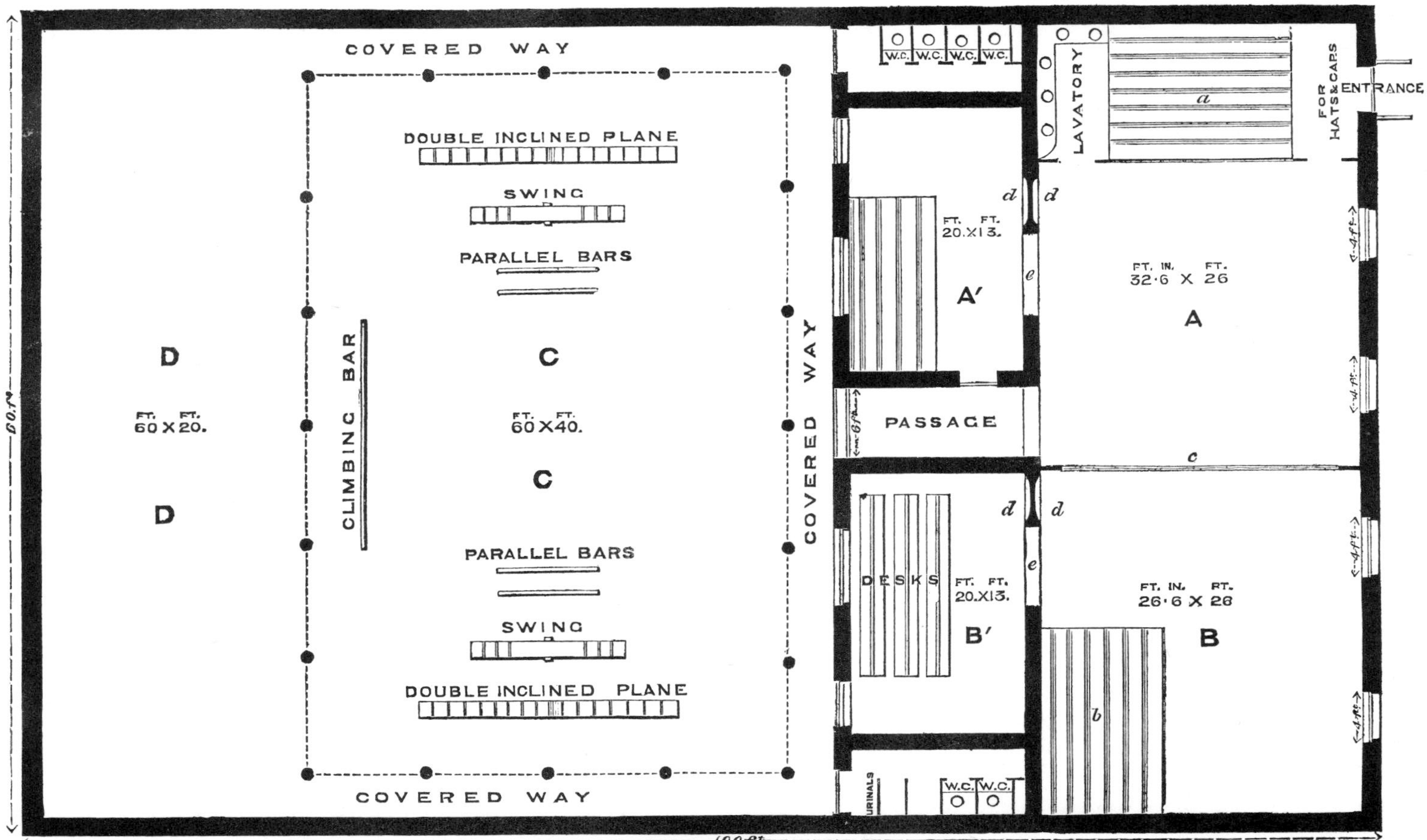

Figure 38 Plan of Model Infants' School, 1863 (with number of children, where given): (A) principal schoolroom, 155; (A′) babies' room, 45; (a) gallery, upper section, 80; (B) Middle section; (B′) upper section, classroom; (b) gallery, middle section, 75; (C) open playground; (c) curtain dividing the sections; (D) covered playground; (d) fireplaces; (e) large windows.

The relative lack of books on school architecture in the 1860s, taken with the decreasing number of illustrations of elementary schools included in *The Builder*, seems to have been symptomatic of a declining interest in the subject or at any rate of a slackening in the rate of building. This may have been an indirect result of the introduction of the Revised Code in 1862, though probably more significant was the Government's decision in 1860 to withhold building grants for new schools which failed to permit non-Anglican parents to withdraw their children from religious instruction, which appears to have led to a decline in the building of National schools.[54]

Table V Cost of the school at Harby (Leics.), 1861

	£	s.	d.
Expenditure:			
Original contract	560	2	6
Extras	141	8	3
Stone-getting	31	19	0
Sundries	71	15	9
Architect	55	17	10
	861	3	4
Receipts:			
Subscriptions raised in parish	253	13	0
Extras paid by Rev. M. O. Norman	141	8	3
Sale of old school	12	13	6
Collections	29	2	1
Sundries	45	1	1
National Society	30	0	0
Government grant	290	0	0
Balance	59	5	5
	861	3	4

There is also some evidence that the cost of building schools was rising, though this could also be a reflection of better-quality building. We noticed earlier in this chapter that the schools designed by Kendall in the 1840s were built at between £2 10*s*. and £4 6*s*. per place, while those designed by Clarke in *c*. 1852 varied considerably from £2 8*s*. to as much as £8 4*s*. A recent survey of thirty schools built in the Durham area in the period 1830–50 shows an average cost per place of as little as £2.[55] Unfortunately, the figures given in *The Builder* (see Appendix 2) are not easy to interpret, since it is rarely clear whether site works, accommodation for the teachers and interior fittings were included in the contract price, while the number of children to be accommodated sometimes varies in the descriptions given of the same school. Trinity School, Reading

(1852) cost £9 per place, but this included the teacher's house, fences and fittings 'complete for occupation'. Most of the other schools for which costs per place can be calculated from figures given in *The Builder* seem to have varied between £3 and £4. At St Saviour's School, Paddington (1867), the cost was four times as high, but this included extensive site works, and the architect also made the exceptionally lavish allowance of over 12 square feet per child. A full account survives of the cost of the school at Harby, Leicestershire (1861), which was designed for 100 children and cost £861.[56] The building is still in use (pl. **185**) and the details of its cost are set out in Table V.

A tightening of central government control over building standards is also apparent in the *Rules* of 1863, which we mentioned earlier. These were based on the *Memorandum* of 1851, but with some significant changes of emphasis. Thus, the 1851 *Memorandum* had considered that a classroom with a gallery should be attached to each schoolroom for use by the classes in turn; the Education Department's *Rules* of 1863, however, permitted the total number of children on the roll to be increased if a classroom was provided. Most of the plans given in the *Rules* allowed 10 square feet per child, but for schools with over 200 children on the roll they permitted 9 square feet, and the official figure used for assessing accommodation in the 1860s was 8 square feet. The plans given in *The Builder* show considerable variation in the number of square feet allowed (details in Appendix 2), but it has to be remembered that during a period when absenteeism was rife the figure for actual attendance was often well below the official accommodation figure.[57]

One paradoxical development of the 1860s was that, although the total amount spent on school buildings seems to have declined, those schools which were built were often more elaborate—and therefore more expensive—than before. In particular, it is interesting to notice that the architectural style of Anglican schools built without grant tended to reflect their ecclesiastical connections more strongly than ever. Thus we find that many schools of the 1860s were notable for their profusion of external ornament, especially of the Gothic variety. The remarkable fenestration of the school built in 1861 in Eastern Road, Brighton, to the design of George Somers Clarke was an extreme example of this stylistic development (pl. **186**),[58] while the Decorated Gothic of Paulerspury School, Northants., was an accurate reflection of the High Church views of the Rector, the Rev. W. H. Newbolt, who built the school in 1861 at his own expense. It was designed for 110 children and consisted of a schoolroom measuring 44 by 20 feet, giving 8 square feet per child; further classrooms were added later at right angles to the schoolroom. Newbolt placed his own coat of arms on the building, and surmounted the design with a carved pinnacle (pl. **187**). He refused to admit the children of Nonconformists into what he regarded as his own private school, and chapel-goers were obliged to build their own school two years later.[59]

Another school of simple plan but ornate exterior was St Mary's Parish School, built in Castle Street, Leicester, in 1869 and demolished in 1964. Incorporated in the façade were the figures of a boy and girl taken from the charity school of 1786, which it replaced (pl. **190**). The building was H-shaped, with the infants' schoolroom in the centre and the boys' and girls' schoolrooms on either side. The architect was Joseph Goddard, who in the previous year had designed the clock tower which still stands in the centre of Leicester. One further example—which represents perhaps the height of Gothic lavishness in an elementary school of this period—is the village school built in 1860 at Ford, Northumberland (now Lady Waterford Hall) where the main schoolroom was decorated with elaborate coloured scenes taken from the Bible.[60]

Taking these and other similar buildings into account, we may say that rarely before had the architecture of schools expressed so clearly the social and religious outlook of the time in which they were built.

IV

There is one other aspect of elementary-school-building in the period 1840–70 which is well worth commenting on, albeit in summary form. This is the siting of schools and their relationship to other buildings in the areas in which they were placed. The Committee of Council drew attention to the importance of the school site in its first circular (1839), which instructed the architects of proposed new schools to state whether there were 'any vitriol-works, tanneries, size manufactories, slaughter-houses, or other noxious trades' situated near the site and also whether it was 'in the neighbourhood of any undrained marsh or swampy ground, any large uncovered drain, or large stagnant pool'.[61]

It may be that schools which received a grant did in fact take such considerations into account. Nevertheless, the sites chosen for schools were not always of the most salubrious kind. The Abbey Girls' School built in 1841 in the country town of Worksop (Notts.), for example, which is still in use as a girls' secondary modern school, is situated between the church burial ground on the one side and a stream which actually touches the school walls on the other.[62] Many other examples of unsuitable siting could be given both for this and later periods, though often the unsuitability arises from development subsequent to the building of the school—as in the case of Cliffe (E. Yorks.) where a railway level-crossing was later built alongside the school.

The commonest arrangement, especially for National schools, was to place the school near to the church. This practice, as we have seen, dated back to at least the sixteenth century, and it is not surprising that the same feature occurred in the nineteenth century when a fresh wave of elementary-school building took place, with a renewed emphasis on the religious and moral role which such schools were intended to perform. When a curate's or teacher's house was built at the same time as the school—as frequently happened—these buildings often formed a group with the church. From numerous examples we may illustrate the church, parsonage and school at Coalville (Leics.), *c.* 1840 (pl. **191**) and the church, school and teacher's house at Theddingworth

(Leics.), 1844 (pl. **192**). Nonconformist schools were also sometimes built in close architectural association with chapel and manse: two surviving examples quoted in a recent survey of west Cambridgeshire are at Elsworth (*c.* 1830) and Gamlingay (1848), the latter in a strong Dissenting area.[63]

Catholic schools, too, were frequently built close to the church; sometimes, indeed, the school was built first and used for services until there were sufficient funds to complete the church. An outstanding Catholic grouping of this kind was illustrated in *The Builder* in 1853, viz. St Augustine's Church, school and residence built by A.W. Pugin at the extremity of West Cliff, Ramsgate, Kent (pl. **193**). It will be noted that, architecturally, the church dominates the school, as with St Vincent's Catholic school, Howard Hill, Sheffield (1863), shown on pl. **194**, where the subordinate position of the school is exaggerated owing to a change of ground level.[64] Sometimes it is the teacher's house which is dominated by the school, as at the Anglican school of St Peter (1848) in Waterloo Street, Cheltenham, which is still in use (illustrated on pl. **195**). In ways like these, contemporary social attitudes were accurately expressed in architectural terms.

The school at Coalville, referred to above, illustrates not only the grouping of schools with churches, but also the importance of looking at individual schools in their wider economic and social context. A local directory of 1846 stated that

> This large colliery village has sprung up in consequence of the great extension of the neighbouring collieries of Snibston and Whitwick. Schools and chapels have been built by the proprietors of these coal works, for the use of their numerous workmen, and they also contributed liberally towards the erection of Coalville church.[65]

Thus the school was built as a direct result of new economic development and shows the value of studying elementary schools of this type as an important aspect of what is now called 'industrial archaeology'.

The subject of new industrial settlements has only recently been opened up, and much work remains to be done on the educational arrangements frequently made by enterprising industrialists during this period.[66] The factory and colliery schools of Wales have found their historian, but their numerous counterparts erected in the new industrial areas of England have received very little attention.[67] We cannot attempt to do more here than note a few examples of these important categories of school. Probably the best known are the schools at Saltaire, four miles north of Bradford. This new town was founded in 1851 by Sir Titus Salt, who had become one of the largest manufacturers in the Bradford textile trade. It was designed as a model town, with 820 cottages supplied with gas and water, but no public house, and was carefully sited near the River Aire and the Leeds-Liverpool Canal.

The educational buildings financed by Sir Titus Salt were given a central position when he laid out the town (see pl. **196**).[68] The school, which is illustrated on pl. **197**, cost £7,000 and was opened in 1868. It provided accommodation for 750 children, with the boys' and girls' schoolrooms placed at opposite ends of the building and the infants in the centre. The two principal schoolrooms measured 80 by 20 feet and were divided into classes by curtains, as recommended in the *Rules* of 1863. The building was in the Italian style and was designed by Thomas Milnes of London; it will be noted that Salt's Nonconformist outlook led him to avoid the Gothic style, though his architect indulged in a good deal of external ornamentation, including a central pediment with coat of arms, a bell turret decorated with figures of children holding instruments of instruction, and sculptured lions at the corners of the building which are said to have been originally prepared for Trafalgar Square. The initials 'T.S.' (Titus Salt) also appear on various parts of the building (pl. **198**). Opposite the school in Victoria Road is the Club and Institute, which opened in 1872 and conducted classes under the Science and Art Department. The former factory school became a high school in 1877, when new Board schools were opened for elementary education, and this developed into the Salt Grammar School, which moved to new premises only in 1963. Since then the former factory school has been used as an annexe of the Bingley College of Education. The Club and Institute now house the public library and Victoria Hall.

Saltaire is perhaps the best known of a very large number of new industrial settlements: many other industrialists provided model houses and schools, though usually on a smaller scale. Dr J. D. Marshall has drawn my attention to schools connected with newly-colonized industrial areas at Galgate, Caton and Low Mill, near Lancaster, and at Eagley, Barrow Bridge and Belmont, near Bolton.[69] At Belmont, the 'Sabbath School' built in 1832 by local factory-owners may still be seen, and an interesting group of buildings also survives in Halliwell Road, Bolton, erected in 1847–57 by J. H. Ainsworth, the owner of a local bleach works: in the centre of this group is St Paul's Church, with a cottage block and a school dated 1847 (now the parish hall) on one side of it, and another cottage block and a school of identical design dated 1856 on the other. Another noteworthy example is the school in Scotswood Road, Newcastle upon Tyne, which was built in 1866 by Sir W. G. Armstrong and partners of the Elswick Ordnance Works (pl. **199**). It was divided (like the building at Saltaire) into schools for boys, girls and infants, and was open to the children of workers, who made 1*d*. or 2*d*. a week payment out of their wages, in return for which they elected the majority of the managing body and also had free use of the adjacent mechanics' institute.[70] This school still stands opposite the Armstrong-Vickers factory and is now used as a works canteen; it is, however, due for demolition in the near future (1969). Among numerous other examples of former factory schools which could no doubt be discovered is the school at Cuckney (Notts.), where there is an eighteenth-century worsted mill which between 1786 and 1805 was largely worked by pauper apprentices and was converted into a National school by the Duke of Portland in 1846 (this is still in use as a primary school).[71]

Also awaiting their historian are the schools built or partly financed by railway companies during the 'railway mania' of the period after 1840. The directors of these companies were keenly alive to the importance of providing for the spiritual and educational welfare of their workers in the new railway settlements which were springing up. The London and North Western Railway Company, for example, set up a special 'Church and Schools Committee', whose minutes date from 1849 and show that the committee considered numerous requests for financial assistance for the promotion of schools.[72] The company were prepared to make grants to bodies of any Christian denomination, but in practice most of the money went to Anglican schools. Many requests of marginal importance to the company—such as an application to help finance the cost of a new organ at St Albans Abbey—were turned down, but in certain major railway centres the company were very ready to assist. At Wolverton (Bucks.) they paid part of the incumbent's stipend, helped to repair the church and school, and paid the salaries of the teachers. At Church Coppenhall, on the outskirts of Crewe, a barn was converted into a National school in 1842 and was replaced by a new building in Broad Street (1861) which is still in use. In Crewe itself, the company supported National schools in Moss Square (1847) and New Street (1866), both now demolished. Following the rapid increase in the size of the town between 1861 and 1871, they built new schools in Adelaide Street and Edleston Road (1875), Wistaston Road (1879; later rebuilt) and West Street (1887–90)—all of which are still in use. These schools were conducted as National schools, so as to comply with the provisions of the Elementary Education Act of 1870 without the need for setting up a school board with the power to levy a school rate on property (including the extensive railway property) in the town. Meanwhile the Wesleyans built their own schools (1862, 1869, 1887), as did the Roman Catholics (1854; replaced 1879) and the Scottish Presbyterians (1869).[73]

Similarly, the Great Northern Railway Company built schools for its employees at Peterborough and Doncaster. The original railway settlement known as 'New England' may still be seen at Peterborough, with its terraced rows of model cottages (due for demolition, but still standing in 1969). A temporary (? corrugated) iron school was erected here in 1856, and soon afterwards the shareholders provided £700 for a permanent building, which was later extended and used also by the mechanics' institute. It was replaced in 1891 by the school which still stands in Walpole Street. A new church (St Paul's), almost wholly financed by the directors, was built in Walpole Street in 1869 to the design of James Teale and E. B. Denison (later Sir Edmund Beckett, Lord Grimthorpe), son of the Chairman of the company.[74] Lord Grimthorpe also had a hand in Scott's design for St James's Church, built near the railway works at Doncaster in 1858. The adjoining schools were designed by the company architect, Mr Godard, and were opened in 1854. They were subsequently burnt down, but were rebuilt on the same site in 1897, and these buildings are still in use as a primary school (pl. **200**).[75]

There are many points in this chapter which could be further developed, nor has any account been taken of the very numerous dame-school type of buildings (rarely if ever purpose-built), which, as the Newcastle Commission of 1861 showed, were usually deplorable. But enough has perhaps been said to indicate that great advances were made in elementary-school-building after 1840 and before the Elementary Education Act of 1870 brought in the new principle of universal compulsory education. The intervention of the State, especially after 1851, was of great importance, but the amount achieved by voluntary effort should not be underestimated. The mid-Victorians, with their boundless energy, have left behind them a remarkable legacy of school buildings, and it is less than fair to blame them for having built so substantially that in many cases their buildings have outlived their usefulness.

Notes

1 The legal aspects are summarized in Gosden, P. H. J. H., *The development of educational administration in England and Wales*, Oxford: Blackwell, 1966, 1–3, and Bartley, G. C. T., *The schools for the people*, Bell & Daldy, 1871, 31–4.

2 *Report of the commission appointed to inquire into the state of popular education in England*, H.M.S.O., 1861, I, 23, 579.

3 *Minutes of Committee of Council on Education* (hereafter referred to as *Minutes*), 1839–40, 46–92. The sixteen plans are bound in at the end of this volume as follows: Series A, Nos. 1–5; Series B, Nos. 1–5; Series C, Nos. 1–3 and Series D, No. 1; with two plans of a combined orphan house, normal school and model school.

4 The best description of contemporary Continental methods is in Robson, E. R., *School architecture*, Murray, 1874, chs. 5 (France), 6 (Germany), and 7 (Austria). See also Lange, H., *Schulbau und Schulverfassung der frühen Neuzeit*, Berlin: Beltz, 1967.

5 The plans of 1845 (nineteen in all) are bound in at the end of *Minutes*, 1844.

6 This school was built in 1820 and demolished in 1966 (ex inf. Borough Librarian, Southwark). Cf. 1845 plan No. 7.

7 *Minutes*, 1847–8, I, cxlviii-clv.

8 Harris, J. J. A., *The school-room: Part I, Its arrangements and organization*, The National Society, 1848. Copy in the Society's offices in Great Peter Street, Westminster. (Only *Part II, Its discipline and supervision* is in the B.M.)

9 Harris, *op. cit.*, Plan V on p. 59, which is the same as the plan reproduced in the National Society's *Annual Report*, 1843.

10 Plan reproduced as frontispiece of National Society's *Annual Report*, 1844. Also described in Rich, R. W., *The training of teachers in England and Wales during the nineteenth century*, Cambridge U.P., 1933, 91–2. This arrangement may have owed something to the 'Panopticon principle' advocated by Bentham (as discussed in ch. 9, above).

11 Barnard, H., *School architecture; or contributions to the improvement of school-houses in the United States*, New York: Barnes, 1848, description and plan of octagonal school on pp. 73–5. The octagonal plan is well suited for group work, and for that reason has been revived for some English primary schools of the 1960s.

12 *Minutes*, 1846, II, 3f. The first British school at Cheltenham, Glos., *c.* 1820, met in the basement of the Countess of Huntingdon's chapel (ex inf. T. Hearl). The way in which Nonconformist day schools grew out of Sunday schools attached to chapels is remarked on in Chaloner, W. H., *The social and economic development of Crewe, 1780–1923*, Manchester U.P., 1950, 223.

13 See ground plan of the normal and model school of the British and Foreign School Society facing p. 334 of *Minutes*, 1846, II.
14 Rich, *op. cit.*, 129–30.
15 *Minutes*, 1851–2, 78–91. The arrangements officially adopted in 1851 were anticipated in the plan of Norwich model school for boys shown in *Minutes*, 1850–1, 411–16.
16 Because funds were limited, it was a question of building either one large schoolroom or several classrooms. One of the objections to the latter was the impossibility of addressing the whole school at the same time; the large schoolroom could also be used in the evenings for social activities.
17 There is a useful (illustrated) description of the development of elementary school furniture in *The Building News*, XVII (1869), 243f., 254f., and 429f. This makes clear that stepped floors in the main schoolroom were not used by this date, i.e. as distinct from the galleries proper. Other details may be obtained from the plans of the Committee of Council and in Robson, *op. cit.*, chs. 9 and 18.
18 This was the school of 1855 described by Evans, L. Wynne, in 'Sir John and Lady Charlotte Guest's educational scheme at Dowlais in the mid-nineteenth century', *National Library of Wales Journal*, IX, 3, 1956.
19 The name of this school is not known (photo in G.L.C. Record Office).
20 Published by Darton & Co. (Only copy located is in D.E.S. library.) Reviewed in *The Builder*, VIII (1850), 453.
21 Barnard was Secretary of the Board of Commissioners of Common Schools in Connecticut. *Practical illustrations* ('extracted with modifications from the author's *School architecture*') was published by Case, Tiffany & Co., Hartford, 1851. See also Johonnot, J., *Country school houses*, New York, 1859; not in B.M.; copy in D.E.S. library.
22 Published by Blackwood, Edinburgh. Reviewed in *The Builder*, XIV (1856), 167.
23 Published by Chapman & Hall, 1860. Missing in B.M., but copy in D.E.S. library. Extracts quoted in *The Builder*, XVIII (1860), 461–2.
24 Harry Chester (1806–68) was the third son of Sir Robert Chester of Bush Hall, Hatfield; educated at Westminster and Trinity College, Cambridge; became a clerk in the Privy Council office in 1826 and Assistant Secretary to the Committee of Council on Education, 1840–58 (Venn, J. A., *Alumni Cantabrigienses 1752–1900*, Cambridge U.P., 1944). For his work in connection with the Royal Society of Arts, see article, on 'Harry Chester' by J. S. Hurt in *The Journal of the R.S.A.* vol. CXVI, nos. 5138–40 (January, February, March 1968).
25 There are in the D.E.S. library (ref. D. 11. Of.) copies of these *Rules* dated 1863, 1871 and at intervals to 1900. The (1872?) version is printed in Robson, *op. cit.*, Appendix B. On the legal status of Departmental rules see Gosden, *op. cit.*, 16–17. See also p. 227, below.
26 The 1840 plans were drawn by Sampson Kempthorne, Architect, Piccadilly, and those of 1845 by W. Westmacott. Kempthorne's works are listed in Ware, D., *A short dictionary of British architects*, Allen & Unwin, 1967, 141–2. Some school plans were included in Loudon, J. C., *Encyclopaedia of cottage, farm, and villa architecture and furniture*, 1833 and later editions.
27 *The Sheffield Times*, 12 December 1846, p. 5.
28 Kendall, H. E. *Designs for schools and school houses, parochial and National*, Williams, 1847. Copy in R.I.B.A. library; reviewed in *The Builder*, VI (1848), 78–9.
29 I owe this information to Miss Iris Blake of the Records Dept. of the National Society, but none of Blore's model plans appear to have survived.

30 Clarke, J., *Schools and school houses: a series of views, plans, and details, for rural parishes*, Masters & Bell, 1852. Copy in R.I.B.A. library; reviewed in *The Builder*, X (1852), 380.

31 Illustrated in *The Builder*, IX (1851), 754–5.

32 *Ibid.*, I (1843), 517.

33 *Ibid.*, IV (1846), 596. The following C. of E. elementary schools of the period 1840–70 were still standing in Birmingham in 1968 (ex inf. D. Leinster-Mackay): 1840, Quinton, Hagley Road West, B'ham 32; 1842, St. James', Sandwell Road, Handsworth, 21; 1843, All Saints, All Saints Street, 18; 1856, St John's, Gilby Road, Ladywood; 1857, St Clement's, High Park Street, Netchells, 7; 1860, Bishop Ryder's, Gem Street, 4; 1860, St Peter's, Old Church Road, Harborne, 17; 1861, St Jude's, New Street; 1862, St Michael's, Piers Road, Handsworth, 21; 1868, St Mary's, Avenue Road, Aston Brook, 6.

34 *Ibid.*, VII (1849), 383, viz. South Myton Wesleyan schools, near Great Thornton Street chapel (not illustrated).

35 *Ibid.*, VIII (1850), 91 (Friends' School, Bristol).

36 Chester, *Hints . . .*, *op. cit.*

37 In addition to the plans referred to below, others survive in diocesan record offices, e.g. plans relating to schools in the diocese of London are kept in the Guildhall Library. Also, school buildings are included in the plans deposited with local authorities subsequent to the 1848 Sanitary Act, e.g. in Leicester Museum Archives Dept. are about 30,000 plans dating from 1848 to 1900 and relating to buildings of all kinds.

38 *Minutes*, 1839–40, 6f.

39 *Minutes*, 1847–8, I, cxlviiif.

40 Few Wesleyan school buildings seem to have survived. The plan of the Wesleyan school at Griffydam, Worthington (1852), shows the usual infants' room with gallery on the ground floor. On the first floor the schoolroom was divided by a curtain—on one side were benches of different heights running parallel to the end wall, and on the other desks and benches faced each other across the room; adjoining was a small room divided by a curtain to form two very small teaching areas, with desks. On Wesleyan school plans see Robson, *op. cit.*, 13–15, and, more generally, Bartley, *op. cit.*, 69f.

41 On the neglected subject of industrial, reformatory and workhouse schools, see Bartley, *op. cit.*, 243f., 254f., and 272f. Also article by Pallister, R., 'Workhouse education in County Durham: 1834–1870', in *B.J.E.S.*, XVI, 3 (October 1968) 279f. Ragged schools (Bartley, 382f.), when they came to have purpose-designed buildings, represent an interesting intermediate type, with dining-rooms and workshops, but no dormitories (e.g. see plans of Newcastle Ragged Schools by John Dobson, dated 1854, in Northumberland C.R.O.—a reference I owe to D. Webster).

42 This school is fully described (with plan) in R.C.H.M., *City of Cambridge*, II, 1959, 318.

43 R.C.H.M., *W. Cambs.*, I, 1968, lvi.

44 Further details in Appendix 1. The schools at Kibworth, Twyford and Queniborough still exist (all Tudor style), but the 'Elizabethan' school at Ibstock and the classical style school at Wigston have been demolished. The Tudor style continued in Leicestershire into the 1850s and 1860s, one of the last being at Thurnby (1865).

45 *Illustrated London News*, 26 December 1846, 403–4.

46 *Guardian*, 26 August 1968 (report on activities of the Windsor and Eton Society).

47 See also the article by Kirby, E. E., 'Three acres and a spade', in *Country Life*, 22 December 1955, 1473; Joy MacAskill on 'The Chartist Land Plan' in Briggs, Asa (ed.), *Chartist studies*, Macmillan, 1959, 304f.; and Armytage, W. H. G., *Heavens below*, R.K.P.,

1961, 224f.

48 The main exceptions were a few of the larger charity schools in London mentioned in ch. 7.

49 Even of one of the remotest rural areas, it has been written that 'By 1860 voluntary effort had provided schools in nearly all the major parishes' (Pigott, D. A., 'Education in Wildmore and West Fens of Lindsey, Lincs., during the 19th century', unpublished M.Ed. thesis, Leicester, 1969, 242).

50 See the plan reproduced in *The Builder*, XII (1854), 534. I am grateful to the Archivist, Liverpool Record Office, for information about these schools. (A photograph of St Augustine's School is kept in that office.) The only Liverpool school illustrated in *The Builder* which is still in use as a school is St Anne's, Overbury Street, Liverpool 7 (see *The Builder*, XI (1853), 504–5).

51 There are photographs of this building in the G.L.C. Record Office. The architect was E. M. Barry, who also designed the new grammar school at Leeds (see ch. 11, below).

52 This school no longer exists. Reece Winstone in *Bristol as it was 1874–1866* (The author, 1966) reproduces a photograph of 1872 (No. 43) showing the building as 'an unfamiliar chapel' (ex inf. City Librarian, Bristol).

53 The full title is *Hints on school building, and on the management and superintendence of infant schools* (Home and Colonial Society, 1863); on the spine the title is *Hints on infant schools*. Cf. Marenholz-Bülow, B. von, *Fröbel's system of infant gardens*, Darton, 1855, including drawings of kindergarten activities, and Bartley, *op. cit.*, 112–15 and illustration facing p. 40.

54 I owe this point to Norman Morris of Manchester University. See also Bartley, *op. cit.*, 57, and Burgess, H. J., and Welsby, P. A., *A short history of the National Society*, National Society, 1961, 27. And compare Tables II and III in ch. 8, above.

55 'An economic study of elementary education in County Durham in the early part of the 19th century', (Pallister, R., unpublished M.Ed. thesis, Durham, 1966, 187).

56 Original poster survives at the school. It is not clear how the architect's fee was calculated. The usual fee was 5 per cent of the contract price, plus travelling expenses (see Beckett, E., *A book on building*, Lockwood, 1876, 22f.). Beckett is also interesting on the subject of rising costs, pp. 227–8, though the index of building costs 1845–1938 given in Mitchell, B. R., *Abstract of British historical statistics*, Cambridge U.P., 1962, 240, shows that costs during the 1860s remained stable.

57 Pallister, thesis, *op. cit.*, 186, finds that in 1849 only three out of fifty-two schools in the Durham area had less than 6 square feet per child in average attendance; thirty had between 10 and 20 feet and may well have been the less efficient and therefore less well patronized schools.

58 This was built as the Brighton School for Blind Boys at 179 Eastern Road; demolished, 1959 (ex inf. Public Librarian, Brighton).

59 I owe this information to the Headmaster, quoting from a pamphlet on the school published in 1907 by J. C. Harrison. The classroom was added in 1892.

60 I owe this reference to Professor B. Simon. This was an estate school in a model village financed by the Countess of Waterford.

61 *Minutes*, 1839–40, 6.

62 This school in Priorswell Road, Worksop, is a good example of Victorian Early English, with lancet windows. It was originally one large room in the north-west corner of the churchyard; an extension by one classroom towards the road and in the same style was made in 1875 (plan in Notts. C.R.O., which also has a plan of the nearby Rectory Infants' School, Cheapside, erected 1859). I owe the details about the school at Cliffe to Dr T. W. Bamford.

63 R.C.H.M., *W. Cambs., op. cit.*, 86 and 108.
64 The earliest Roman Catholic elementary-school building known to me is at Leyburn (N. Yorks.)—a small limestone building, with the inscription 'Catholic school 1836'. It was built over a stable and has a niche in the wall inside which housed a statue (ex inf. M. Rumford). On early R.C. schools, see Bartley, 78f.
65 White, W., *History, gazeteer and directory of Leicestershire*, Sheffield, 1846, 565. See also Hawthorn, E., *A short history of Christ Church, Coalville*, Coalville, 1953, 2–3.
66 See chapter by Marshall, J. D., 'Colonization as a factor in the planting of towns in north-west England', in Dyos H. J. (ed.), *The study of urban history*, Arnold, 1968, 215f. Also Sanderson, M., 'Education and the factory in industrial Lancashire 1780–1840', in *Economic History Review*, 2nd series, xx, August 1967.
67 See the articles by Evans, L. Wynne, in *The National Library of Wales Journal*, IX, 3 (1956) X, 2 (1957) XIV, 4 (1966) and XV, 1 (1967). Also, for the Durham area, see Pallister thesis, *op. cit.*, ch. 9.
68 There are good contemporary descriptions of the schools at Saltaire in Bartley, *op. cit.*, 516–22, and in Waddington-Feather, J., *The Salt Grammar School*, Bingley: Harrison, 1968, 23–4. There are also useful illustrations in the *Calendar of the Salt Schools, Shipley*, Bradford, 1906, and a book of plans (ref. 19685. H39) kept in the Institute (now the Public Library). I am grateful to Miss M. Tattersall for further information about the Salt Schools.
69 The Sabbath school of 1832 at Belmont is one of the earliest buildings designed as a Sunday school which I have come across. But see the Sunday schools in Preston Old Road, Blackburn (1825), Newtown Linford, Leics. (1822) and Old Bridge Street, Truro, Cornwall (1836). Dr Marshall has also referred me to schools built by industrialists at Warthfold, near Bury, (*c.* 1860) and Farington near Leyland (1843); also a very good group with a school and Athenaeum at Compstall, Cheshire, built by Messrs Andrew & Son (cotton and print works) in the 1860s.
70 *Newcastle Daily Chronicle*, 10 April 1866 (ex inf. City Librarian). As at Saltaire, the Gothic style was avoided. See also the plan of Elswick Works in Cockrane, *History of Elswick* (1909). John Dobson designed the Institute, but apparently not the school.
71 I owe this information to the Headmaster of the school, who refers to a register of apprentices kept from 1786 to 1805.
72 British Transport Historical Records (66 Portland Road, Paddington), LNW 1/574 (1849–55) and 575 (1855–65).
73 These details are from W. H. Chaloner's book on Crewe, *op. cit.*, 61–4 and 222–48—one of the few economic histories which includes the educational aspect. Plans for schools at Edleston Road and Hightown, Crewe (1874) are in B.T.H.R., LNW 3/255.
74 The New England school of 1857 (now demolished) is illustrated in Perrin, R., *The history of the old railway church schools* (privately printed in connection with Lincoln Road Schools Jubilee, Peterborough, 1961), 14.
75 Ex inf. Public Librarian, Doncaster. (The girls' school is now a primary school and the boys' school a craft centre for the disabled.) See also Grinling, C. H., *The history of the G.N.R.*, Methuen, 1903, 148–9.

Eleven

Middle-class schools 1840-70

I

The great resurgence of interest in elementary-school-building during the first thirty years of Victoria's reign had an important, though indirect, influence on the provision for what was now coming to be called 'secondary' education. Social-class divisions were apparent from the outset, since the new elementary schools were invariably seen as providing only for the poor, and were certainly not of the kind to which their usually middle-class promoters would have considered sending their own children: the distinction commonly made was, in fact, between middle- and lower-class rather than elementary and secondary education in the modern sense. Nevertheless, the widespread provision of elementary schools for the poor stimulated interest in middle-class education, and it was now becoming usual for writers on education to chide middle-class parents for giving an education to their own children only marginally better than that available to the working classes in the National and other voluntary schools.[1]

It is sometimes suggested that the reform of secondary education was a direct consequence of the remodelling of university and professional education which took place in the 1850s and 1860s, and thus to date the expansion of middle-class schools to the period following the Public Schools Act of 1868 and the Endowed Schools Act of 1869.[2] From another point of view, however, one may see these two important statutes as the culmination of a period of reform which had its origin in schools like Hazelwood in the 1820s and in the proprietary schools which, as we saw, began to emerge in the 1830s. More broadly, we may say that the power of the new commercial and industrial middle classes was growing from the beginning of the nineteenth century, so that the reform of secondary education, though gradual and piecemeal, was a continuous process in which the intervention of Parliament marked only one stage of development.

The commissions of inquiry into the major public schools (the Clarendon Commission, 1864) and into the other endowed schools (the Schools Inquiry or Taunton Commission, 1868) provide the *terminus ad quem* of the present chapter.[3] The former examined the nine schools (viz. Eton, Winchester, Westminster, Charterhouse, St Paul's, Merchant Taylors', Harrow, Rugby and Shrewsbury), which, though they had had a chequered career, appeared in the 1860s to have established themselves as the leading schools, sharing the characteristics of providing a largely classical curriculum for mainly middle- and upper-class children in a predominantly residential environment. The Taunton Commission for its part included in its survey 2,175 endowed elementary and 782 endowed grammar schools, and found them to be, as we shall see, in a very unsatisfactory state.

The ample evidence of the need for reform in the nine major public schools and in the endowed grammar schools which these Commissions provided is, however, far from giving a complete picture of the situation regarding secondary education in the period 1840–70. Some of the nine leading schools—notably Eton and Rugby—continued to expand during the period, and Harrow underwent a marked revival under the headship of Vaughan (1844–59). Some of the smaller endowed grammar schools also took on a fresh lease of life and acquired new buildings in the process. Furthermore, the period after 1840 was notable for the founding of a number of middle-class schools which pioneered new forms of secondary education, not least because they were untrammelled by outdated curricula, antiquated endowments and decrepit buildings. As only one index of this, we may note that of the 200 schools which in 1968 belonged to the Headmasters' Conference, forty-five date their foundation to the period 1840–70, compared with twenty-four which originated in the subsequent thirty years (see Table II in ch. 9). Thus we shall find that the building activity which we described in the last chapter in relation to elementary education had its counterpart in the secondary sphere also.

Let us, however, first consider the nine schools examined by the Clarendon Commission, and the architectural changes which had taken place since we last looked at their development. The Commissioners required questionnaires to be completed which gave very full information about the state of these schools towards the end of 1861. Some of the details are summarized in Table I, which gives an impression of the relative sizes of the schools, the preponderance of non-foundationers (mainly boarders) and the number of masters employed.[4]

Eton and Winchester were both under the control of unreformed ecclesiastical bodies, but in the case of Eton this did not, as we saw earlier, stop the school from expanding. The number of boys at Eton had risen by 1861 to over 800, and this had been possible without much new building because of the highly flexible tutorial system which we described in ch. 9. The Commissioners found, for example, that a Fifth-Form boy at Eton spent only fourteen or fifteen hours a week in the schoolroom, but an equal or greater amount of time in private study or 'in pupil-room' under the supervision of a tutor, who was one of the assistant masters working in a different capacity.[5] The pupil-rooms were not in the main college buildings, but in houses nearby; similarly the number of boarding houses had risen to thirty by 1861, only four of which were now kept by dames, the majority being in the charge of classical assistant masters.[6] A certain amount of new building had, however, taken place. Long Chamber was divided up and the so-called 'New Buildings' erected at right angles to it in 1844–6 for the better accommodation of the Collegers. They were designed by John Shaw (whose work at Christ's Hospital we noted earlier) in Tudor Gothic style (pl. **201**). A small amount of mathematical teaching had been introduced in the 1840s and 1850s and a mathematical school was built, though it no longer survives. In 1861–76 the block still known as 'New Schools' was built, designed by Woodyer and containing thirteen rooms: it stands on the west side of the Slough road, opposite the main college buildings.[7]

Table I Analysis of the number of boys and masters at the nine schools examined by the Clarendon Commission (1861)

School	*On foundation*	*Not on foundation*	*Actual total**	*No. of masters*			*No. of classical divisions‡*	*Average size of division§*
				C	*M*	*ML†*		
Eton	61	722	806	23	8	1	22	36·6
Winchester	69	128	200	7	2	3	8	25·0
Westminster	40	96	136	5	2	2	6	22·7
Charterhouse	45	71	116	5	1	3	8	14·5
St Paul's	146	—	146	4	1	2	6	24·3
Merchant Taylors'	262	—	262	6	4	2	10	26·2
Harrow	33	431	481	16	4	2	14	34·4
Rugby	68	397	463	14	3	2	14	33·0
Shrewsbury	26	106	131	4	1	1	4	32·8
Totals	750	1,951	2,741	84	26	18	92	29·8

* The actual totals are sometimes different from the totals for foundationers and non-foundationers added together, owing to a slightly later return.

† The letters C, M and ML stand for classical, mathematical and modern languages masters.

‡ A 'division' means 'the group of boys ordinarily taught together in school by one master'.

§ Calculated by dividing the actual total number of boys by the number of classical divisions.

At Winchester there was an attempt, as at Eton, to improve the living accommodation of some of the boys, but in general the lack of building activity at Winchester accurately reflected the stagnation of the school. New Commoners was built during the period 1839–42, to replace 'Old Commoners', which had been erected in 1742. A friend remarked to Dr Moberly, the Headmaster, 'You have built a workhouse'; to which Moberly replied, 'My dear sir, that is the very thing I meant to do.'[8] One of the first actions of Ridding, the reforming Headmaster, was to close New Commoners (1869), and it was later 'adapted and adorned' by Butterfield. On the whole, the summary given by one of the recent historians of the college seems to be amply justified: 'In the classroom of the seventeenth century [i.e. the schoolroom of 1687] and amid the arrangements of the eighteenth, the boys of 1866 were being taught on the principles of the vanished Oxford of the thirties.'[9]

The four London schools—Westminster, Charterhouse, St Paul's and Merchant Taylors'—were in little better state. The Commissioners' main recommendation was that the first two, where boarders outnumbered the day-boys, should develop their boarding sides and rebuild outside London; the other two, which were already predominantly day schools, should remain in London, but on better sites. At Westminster, it had long been felt that the dilapidated state of the school buildings was a chief factor in the decline of the school since its great days in the seventeenth and early eighteenth centuries. 'Life in college', says the latest historian of the period before the Clarendon Commission, 'was unbelievably rough'—the school was starved of funds by the Dean and Chapter and only minor structural changes took place. In the 1840s the Queen's Scholars were provided with studies underneath their dormitory, which, it will be recalled, had been built in 1722. A classroom was not provided until 1861, and most of the teaching continued to take place in the one large schoolroom until 1884.[10] Even then there were those who regretted the change: one former pupil wrote that, though it might have been true that when all the boys were taught in the same room they were easily distracted, 'one thing is certainly lost when different forms do their work in separate school-rooms, and that is the common unity of feeling and the tie of interest which bound us all together, and, to me at least, was so impressive'.[11] The Commissioners themselves, as we shall see, were far from convinced of the value of separate form-rooms in any school, and produced some interesting arguments in favour of the traditional arrangement.

As events turned out, Westminster did not move to a new site, for in the 1880s it gained the use of Ashburnham House, a large seventeenth-century building adjoining the main schoolroom, which gave it the space so badly needed for new form-rooms, a school library and a natural science laboratory.[12] Charterhouse did, however, move from London—to Godalming in Surrey in 1872. Its old site was a spacious one, and a new schoolroom had, as we noted earlier, been built in 1803, but it had done little since then to improve the facilities available, and the Commissioners felt sure that 'as a boarding school it would thrive much better if removed to some eligible site in the country'.[13]

The two London schools which were predominantly day schools were also badly provided with buildings and were obliged to move, though still within the London area. St Paul's School, as we noticed previously, had been rebuilt in 1824, but along wholly traditional lines. There were no playing fields—a matter coming to be considered of great importance by the 1860s—and, says the school's historian,

> the din of the large schoolroom, added to the ever-increasing noise of traffic in St Paul's Churchyard, which necessitated laying down straw every year at the Apposition [a traditional ceremony], so as to enable the speeches to be heard, must have made teaching almost impossible in such difficult surroundings.[14]

Some of the rooms in the headmaster's house were used as classrooms after 1853, but the need to move to a new site was under discussion well before the Clarendon Commissioners recommended that a move should be made. The Trustees had accumulated a surplus of £33,000 by 1860, but it was not until 1884 that the school moved to new buildings in West Kensington. (When St Paul's moved to Barnes in 1968 it was to its fifth set of buildings since 1509, for it had been twice rebuilt on its original site.)

The buildings of Merchant Taylors' School were perhaps the worst of any of the nine schools investigated by the Clarendon Commission. They dated from 1675 and were situated in what was by now a heavily built-up part of London—Suffolk Lane, one of the narrow streets which still run up from Thames Street near London Bridge. It was described in the 1840s as a 'long dingy brick building . . . adorned by six or seven gaunt chapel-looking windows with semicircular tops'; it was surrounded by tall warehouses and when in the 1850s a five-storeyed printing works was erected opposite the school, 'the poisoned air from the windows of a reeking printer's office' was added to the nuisances of the district. In spite of the provision of writing schools on the ground floor in 1829 (which we noted in ch. 9) the building was wholly inadequate for the new type of secondary education now in demand—indeed, until the 1850s the boys still had to work by the light of candles and kneel at their benches when they needed to write.[15] A number of boys boarded with the headmaster, but there was general agreement with the Commissioners' recommendation that Merchant Taylors' should become primarily a day school on a new site in London. The school moved in 1875 to the Charterhouse site now left vacant, though most of the former school buildings there were demolished. (Merchant Taylors' moved to its present site in Northwood, Middlesex, in 1933.)

Of the three remaining schools examined by the Clarendon Commission, Harrow and Rugby were well-established boarding schools, while Shrewsbury, though once a famous school, had only recently begun to revive under Butler (1798–1836) and Kennedy (1836–66). Shrewsbury, as we saw in ch. 4, had extensive buildings dating from the late sixteenth and early seventeenth centuries, but it lacked adequate accommodation for boarders, who had earlier tabled in the town, but now lived in the houses of the headmaster and second master, near the main school buildings. Kennedy, though a lover of classical learning and tradition, called the school buildings 'old, unattractive and in some respects inconvenient and inadequate', but it was his successor, Moss, who realized that in the new public schools up-to-date boarding accommodation and extensive playing fields were essential. After proposals to extend the existing site failed to materialize, the school acquired the buildings and grounds of the former foundling hospital at Kingsland, and moved to its new site in 1882.[16]

Harrow, on the other hand, continued to expand in piecemeal fashion. Numbers had been very low in the early 1840s, with only three boarding houses in use. Then, during the headship of Vaughan, the number of boys rose from sixty-eight to 438, and this was accompanied by a notable phase of new building. A small chapel had been built by Vaughan's predecessor, Dr Wordsworth, in 1839, but this was replaced (1855–7) by a 'larger and more elegant structure', designed by Gilbert Scott, the chancel of which was given by Vaughan himself. Several of the major schools already had chapels and, like Arnold, Vaughan saw the importance of the chapel for promoting a new spirit: the boys no longer used the parish church, and so the school could lay claim to their total allegiance. An additional block of schoolrooms, known as 'New Schools', was built by subscription in 1855, and the foundation-stone of the library erected in honour of Vaughan was laid in 1861. This was also by Scott (pl. **203**).[17] In the meantime, existing houses in the town were taken over for use as boarding houses and pupil-rooms, for, as at Eton, Harrow operated an elaborate tutorial system. By 1861 there were seven large and ten small houses belonging to the school.[18]

At Rugby also there was a new phase of building during the headships of Tait (1842–50), Goulburn (1850–8) and Temple (1858–69). Tait provided additional studies in School House and the masters raised the money required to add a north transept to the chapel built in Wooll's time. A room was also built adjoining the old Sixth-Form room to make a library in memory of Arnold. During Goulburn's period as Headmaster, subscriptions were raised for a south transept in the chapel, and a physical science lecture-room and laboratory (among the earliest in any public school) were erected by the trustees; Goulburn himself built a new boarding house and presented a new playing field.[19] Although Rugby had a tutorial system, it did not involve the use of pupil-rooms outside the main school buildings. It was still true that every form, or 'school', as it was called at Rugby, had its own master, and thus as the numbers increased so did the need for additional teaching accommodation. Dr Temple urged this need on the Clarendon Commissioners, but they were aware that, whereas there had been a very large accumulation of capital available when the school had been rebuilt earlier in the century, the trustees had very little left by the 1860s. The crucial decision whether to abandon the age-old system of teaching all the forms in one room, which had already been taken at Rugby, but which many other schools were now having to face, was not one which the Commissioners felt easily able to support. In an interesting passage of their report on Rugby, they wrote:

> Dr Temple seems to lay it down as a principle that two classes should, under no

circumstances, occupy the same apartment. . . . We are ourselves aware that there are great advantages for teaching, and some advantages for learning, in the system of allotting single rooms to single classes. . . . It is further not to be forgotten that to enable those branches of instruction of which we recommend the introduction to be well taught [i.e. science, mathematics and other non-classical subjects], some additional separate accommodation will be required. At the same time the following facts and considerations have also some bearing on the question. All the teaching of all the classes at Winchester School has for centuries been conducted in one room; the same has been the case with other Schools for long periods of time. . . . In all these Schools there has been a considerable amount of efficient teaching. There is no doubt that the tendency of recent years has been to provide a greater degree of seclusion for boys and masters. Boys were accustomed to learn surrounded by their companions, and classes were wont to be taught surrounded by classes. . . . They have been gradually secluded within private studies for the purpose of learning. While it was the main object of this arrangement, we believe, to secure them from positive molestation, it has been the effect of it, probably, to make them sensitive to slight disturbances, of which boys in past times would have been even unaware while studiously employed. The same tendency, too, which has secluded the boys while they learn is now acting to separate them while they say what they have learnt. But it may admit of doubt whether in both these respects Schools are not moving faster than the world, for which they are a preparation, has followed or will be able to follow them. It is necessary at the Bar, and in other careers of life, and in the Houses of Parliament, that much mental work should be done of all kinds, amidst many outward causes of distraction. It would be a matter of regret if Public School life should in any way disqualify boys for the conditions under which they must do their work as men.[20]

In spite of the lukewarm support given by the Clarendon Commission, Temple stuck to his principle of one form, one master, one room. The continued rise in numbers obliged him to convert a hay-loft into a schoolroom and to rent another in the Town Hall. In 1864 the Trustees agreed to convert a house for extra 'schools', but they were unable to support Temple's plan for a large new quadrangle with teaching rooms on two sides of it (the chapel making up the third side and the old 'Big School' the fourth). The masters raised £5,000 and Temple approached Butterfield to prepare plans, which the Trustees considered in May 1868, though they had already decided that the state of the school funds would not permit them to make any contribution themselves.

After the Masters' generosity [they minuted], the Trustees feel some delicacy in expressing any opinion or criticism of the plans now submitted to them. They

> however venture to state that they are unanimous in wishing greater congruity at least in colour with the old buildings, and they beg to know whether the Masters generally would acquiesce in their unanimous feeling on the subject so far as to allow the walls and roofs to be built of the same description of brick and slating as their present buildings, and the copings to be of the same kind of stone.[21]

In spite of this, Butterfield went ahead with 'New Quad' in red, yellow and black brick (pl. **202**), though it was not completed until after Temple had left Rugby to become Bishop of Exeter (1869). This was only the beginning of Butterfield's major work at Rugby: 'his influence is everywhere', says the school's latest historian, 'and Rugby is as it is'.[22]

There is one other aspect of the buildings of the nine major schools which is worthy of comment, since the findings of the Clarendon Commission cast light on the hitherto obscure subject of the boarding arrangements made for the boys.[23] At Eton the number of boys who slept in Long Chamber was reduced from seventy to twenty-one following the erection of New Buildings (which provided individual rooms) and was further reduced to fifteen, the present number, in 1863, when Long Chamber was divided into cubicles. In the houses it was usual for each boy to have a room to himself, in which he slept at night and sat during the day, his small bedstead being folded up during the daytime. At Winchester New Commoners was damp and ill-ventilated, but three boarding houses were opened in 1859–63 under the supervision of assistant masters.[24] The boys at Winchester slept five or six to a room, but did not use their bedrooms during the day; the twenty senior boys in the headmaster's house had small private studies, while the rest, when not in school, sat in hall, each at his own 'toy' or cupboard. At Westminster the large dormitory of 1722 was divided up in 1860 into forty cubicles, one for each of the scholars. The bedrooms at Harrow contained between one and five beds and, as at Eton, the boys used these rooms during the day as studies. At Rugby, from two to sixteen boys slept in each bedroom, but every boy had a small study for his own use, or shared it with one or two other boys. At Shrewsbury, where the system of large bedrooms persisted, it was by now usual for the senior boys to have individual or shared studies. In general, it may be said that the Commissioners' comment about the 'greater degree of seclusion' which had become apparent in the schools is borne out in the altered sleeping arrangements of the period 1840–70. Another important change, initiated, as we saw, by Arnold at Rugby, was to bring the boarding houses fully under the control of the masters.

As for the internal organization of the schools, considerable changes had taken place, especially at Eton, Harrow and Rugby, owing to the great increase in numbers. We saw in ch. 6 that at Eton in the eighteenth century there had been six forms (three upper and three lower), with a 'remove' inserted between the fourth and fifth forms. By 1861 there were no less than eleven forms or subdivisions of forms in the upper school alone—the Fourth Form was divided into three, the remove into two and the Fifth into five, with only the Sixth Form still undivided.[25] Even so, the number of boys in each form or division of a form was too large, and a separate system of 'classical divisions' had to be devised, wholly independent of the nominal form organization. Matters were further complicated at Eton by the tutorial system, by which tutors (who, when in the schoolroom, were each in charge of a division) took boys from various divisions in their own 'pupil-rooms'. The tutor went through the pupils' work, which was then gone over again by the masters in charge of the classical divisions to which they belonged.[26] The result was that the work in the schoolroom, which was still based on the time-honoured method of calling on individual boys to 'say' part of the lesson, had become largely a formality, and the Commissioners recommended that less time should be spent in the pupil-room and more in school, where the teaching should be made more exacting. It is significant that the building of 'New Schools' began at the time of the Commissioners' inquiry, for additional form-rooms were clearly needed if the classical divisions were to become the main centres of instruction (though the tutorial system has remained a distinctive feature of education at Eton).

It appears that there was still a wide age-range in any one form or division at Eton. In 1861 the Commissioners noted that nineteen of the twenty-eight boys in the highest division of the lower school were over fourteen years of age,[27] and in the upper school, although the average size of division was thirty-six, some masters had groups of well over forty, and again the age-range was wide. Entry into the Sixth Form was limited by examination, and the Commissioners suggested that there should be a systematic testing of attainments in the other forms also, so that no boy should be allowed to remain at Eton if he failed to reach the Fourth Form by the age of fourteen, the Remove by fifteen and the Fifth by sixteen.[28] It seems, however, that the traditional practice of mixing several age-groups in a given form or attainment-range continued to only a slightly less extent than before.

We may conclude this section by remarking that the Clarendon Commissioners, though in many respects conservative in outlook, drew attention to a large number of important problems, the solution of which was to affect the internal organization and curricula of these and other schools. The Public Schools Act of 1868 led to the reconstitution of governing bodies, which gave the schools the financial and legal independence they needed for further development: in particular, it freed Eton, Winchester and Westminster from the control of ecclesiastical corporations whose interests had frequently diverged from those of the schools. The main effect of the Act was, however, to confirm the position of seven of these nine schools (i.e. all except St Paul's and Merchant Taylors') as boarding establishments charging high fees. The Clarendon Commissioners considered that local qualifications should 'cease to confer any advantages', and in two cases this found architectural expression in the setting up of separate day schools for local boys: the Lower School of John Lyon at Harrow in 1876 and the Lawrence Sheriff 'Subordinate' School at Rugby in 1878. In short, social-class divisions were reinforced, with a corresponding differentiation of curriculum, organization and buildings.

II

David Newsome, in a perceptive book on Victorian education, has suggested that many features of nineteenth-century life and thought may be explained in terms of 'the re-awakening of the religious spirit, the appreciation of educational needs and the high regard for learning, the acceptance of the principle of competition as the doorway to honours and responsible public service', and he adds that 'one of the most important manifestations of this rising influence of the middle class was the emergence of the public schools as important national institutions'.[29] It may indeed be said that it was only in the period after 1840 that the phrase 'public school' came normally to mean a boarding school and the place to which well-to-do parents almost automatically sent their sons.

We described in ch. 9 the pioneering schools of the 1820s and 1830s and the reasons why many of them failed. Now, in the period after 1840, we find that schools were founded which incorporated many of the new ideas tried out earlier, but this time with a greater degree of success. So far as architectural features were concerned, there was a transition from Tudor to earlier Gothic forms, similar to that which we noticed in elementary-school-building of the time. Since, however, in the new middle-class schools special provision was usually made for boarders and for teaching a wider range of subjects, the architecture was on a more impressive scale, while the internal planning showed a greater amount of elaboration. The growing interest in these developments is shown in the details given in *The Builder* and *The Building News* (see Appendix 3), to which further reference will be made.

The relative lack of success of many of the day proprietary schools in the 1830s did not lead to the abandonment of the proprietary principle, but to a shift of emphasis from the day school to the boarding side. The colleges established after 1840 at Liverpool, Cheltenham, Marlborough, Rossall, and many other places, were all founded on the proprietary principle, by which the funds were raised through a system of shareholding. The Taunton Commission classified as proprietary schools all those which were neither endowed on the one hand nor run for purely private profit on the other. As their report pointed out, the proprietary method of financing schools marked an important transitional stage in the development of secondary education: the successful schools eventually became either endowed or private schools, but, because they broke the monopoly of the classics and introduced improved methods of school organization and building, the Taunton Commission's verdict of 1868 remains true: 'commercially the majority have not succeeded; educationally they have very largely succeeded'.[30] These developments, it may be noted, were taking place well before the Clarendon and Taunton Commissions issued their reports.

The use of the word 'college' rather than 'school' was indicative of the essentially middle-class outlook of the promoters of the new foundations which we propose to deal with in this section. Nowhere was this more apparent than in Liverpool, where, as we saw in ch. 9, a school of radical plan had opened in 1837, associated with the Mechanics' Institute. As in Leicester and other towns, this produced a strong Anglican reaction. The school of 1837 had included a 'high school' and a 'lower school', together with evening classes for adults; the promoters of the new 'Collegiate Institution', which opened in 1843, carried class distinctions a stage further by implementing a tripartite system, with upper, middle and lower schools, and with particular emphasis on the upper school, since, as they themselves wrote at the time, 'the wealthier classes of the town, by whom the bulk of the donations has been subscribed, became anxious that suitable accommodation should be made for the education of their children to enable them to receive equal benefits with those of the middle and working classes'.[31] Accordingly, the new school in Shaw Street was organized according to the social class of the boys and each of the long corridors in the school was divided by iron gateways into three parts. 'It has been conjectured', wrote Michael Sadler in 1904, 'that the Endowed Schools Commission of 1863–7 derived the idea of three grades of secondary education, subsequently adopted by the Charity Commissioners, from the tripartite arrangement of the institution in Shaw Street.'[32] As one would expect, the new college was built in Gothic style (pl. **204**) and was architecturally much influenced by the new grammar school which had been built in Birmingham in 1838. The architect was H. L. Elmes, who also built—though in the classical style still considered more appropriate for public buildings—St George's Hall and the Assize Courts in Liverpool. The upper school moved in 1883 to Lodge Lane in the suburbs and a new school building was erected there in 1886. The Shaw Street building was sold to Liverpool Corporation in 1907 to become the Liverpool Collegiate (Municipal Secondary) School, the upper school being known from that date as Liverpool College. Plans of the building made in about 1907 (see fig. 39 for the first-floor layout) show the original gates *in situ* and an octagonal assembly hall at the rear (compare the shape of the halls at the Liverpool Institute and City of London schools). The original plans do not appear to have survived and it is not possible to determine how the building was subdivided in 1843.

Liverpool College, though never a wealthy school, received sufficient support to succeed, even though it remained almost wholly a day school: in this respect it was unusual, but it may be noted that there was a large population to draw on, especially since Liverpool was served by a network of railways—indeed, the catchment area of Liverpool College (which is now an independent school) has always been exceptionally wide.[33] Other considerations enabled Cheltenham College to succeed with a considerable number of day-boys, though it later became mainly a boarding school (it was founded in 1840, and by 1863 there were 405 boarders and 222 day-boys).[34]

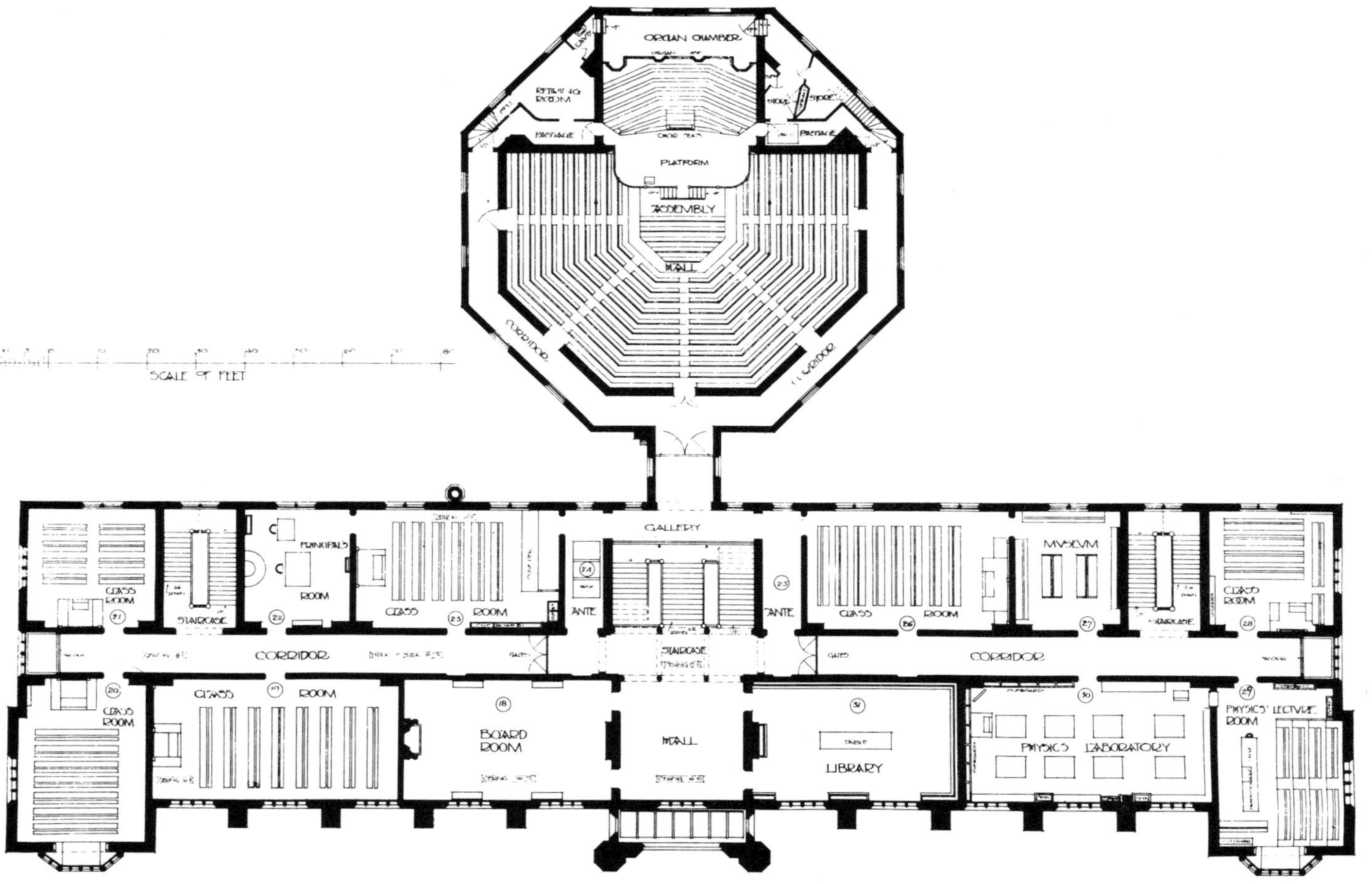

Figure 39 Liverpool College, 1843, first-floor plan, showing the layout in *c.* 1907. (The use to which the various rooms were originally put cannot now be determined with accuracy.)

Cheltenham itself, though not a large town and of relatively recent growth, had become a fashionable watering-place and had an abnormally high proportion of middle- and upper-class parents—parents, moreover, as sensitive about their social position as the promoters of Liverpool College, for the Committee which founded the new college at Cheltenham decided that only 'gentlemen' should be allowed to take out shares, 'no retail trader being under any circumstances to be considered'.[35] The popularity of 'taking the waters' was declining, but many parents settled in the town in order to take advantage of the schools, so that it has been said that the schools replaced the waters as the town's principal source of income.[36] (Cheltenham Ladies' College opened in 1854, but did not move into specially-designed buildings until after 1870.) Cheltenham in the 1840s was also an Evangelical stronghold, and the speech made at the opening ceremony by the Rev. Francis Close, the Vicar of Cheltenham, with its condemnation of 'the abominable mythology of the ancients', showed the distrust with which Evangelicals regarded some forms of classical learning.[37] Equally significant was the connection with the Army and Navy, which was an important factor in the decision to have a 'modern side' (also called the 'military and civil department') as large as the 'classical side'. A wide range of modern subjects was taught, and boys were specifically trained for the Army and Civil Service, both of which were now being thrown open to competition.

All these cross-currents of opinion were reflected in the original buildings of Cheltenham College.[38] The main block was in Perpendicular Gothic style (pl. **205**); this was by now usual for middle-class schools, but constituted an important breach in the Regency style, which until that date had been dominant in the architecture of the town. The architect was James Wilson of Bath, whom we shall meet again later in this chapter. The classical and modern departments formed the principal front and were divided by a central tower—a favourite plan in the 1840s and externally not unlike Blore's design for Bedford Modern School (1834), mentioned earlier. 'Big Classical' (the name given to the large room to the south of the tower) was opened first, in 1843; 'Big Modern' was not roofed over until 1850. The internal planning of the college developed rapidly during the 1850s as a result of increasing numbers and the introduction of the Rugby system of separate rooms for each form. In 1853 north and south wings, consisting of classrooms for the classical and modern departments respectively, were built. Five years later the open side of the quadrangle thus formed was closed by the first chapel, designed by a Cheltenham architect, D. J. Humphris. Humphris's chapel was replaced in 1896 by a new chapel to the north of the original quadrangle, which has itself been largely filled in by later building.

Most of the other middle-class schools which were founded at this time and developed into major public schools were built well away from centres of population. They therefore owed their success to their development as boarding schools and to the triumph of a new conception of middle-class education. Strong religious feelings usually provided the main ingredient, though the availability of funds from the new industrial and commercial classes enabled them to find full expression in architectural form. The moral aspect seems to have been more important even than the demand for the teaching of modern subjects, for without a real sense of the value of a religious education, how could so many middle-class parents have sent their sons to remote country sites, where masters, invariably brought up in the older public schools, dispensed—at least at first—a largely classical education? It has been suggested that the study of the classical languages still gave an exclusive social *cachet*, and was desired chiefly on that account.[39] Yet the masters themselves were genuinely convinced of the educational value of the classics and were even more conscious of the importance of religious and moral training in the communal life which these schools provided: many of the parents must have shared their views. At the same time, the desire to imitate some of the older foundations is also clear, not least in the choice of architectural styles.

Relatively few of the new foundations began in wholly new buildings, however. Since funds were usually very limited at first, rented premises were often used. It is interesting to notice that, just as in the sixteenth century surplus ecclesiastical buildings were taken over by schools, so in the mid-nineteenth century the equally momentous transformation of society brought about by the Industrial Revolution resulted in the occupation of many buildings associated with landed wealth by schools which directly or indirectly derived their resources from industry and trade. Marlborough occupied the coaching inn which had become redundant with the coming of the railways, but had been built as a mansion in the early eighteenth century by the Seymour family; Rossall took over the Hall given up by Sir Hesketh Fleetwood; Radley, the family seat of the Bowyers.

The early history of Marlborough College is a particularly interesting one, since it epitomizes the development of many new middle-class schools of the period 1840–70 and telescoped into thirty years what took over 300 years for some schools to achieve.[40] For it began in 1843 with a motley collection of boys, without either social or academic organization, and ended as a public school of Arnoldian type. The eighteenth-century mansion, which is now called C House (pl. **206**), was used as living accommodation. The architect, Blore, built the master's lodge and what are now A and B Houses in William and Mary style—the avoidance of Gothic was unusual, and perhaps Blore was influenced by the classical design of the original house. A large schoolroom (now demolished) was also provided, with classrooms for German and dancing. Thus there was some advance on the usual classical curriculum, but so far as the organization of the school was concerned, we are still in the sixteenth century. All the classes were taught in the one large room, there were virtually no studies for the boys and, although a Gothic chapel was built by Blore in 1848 (replaced, 1883–6), the religious life of the school during the first few years was at an extremely low ebb. Conditions both in the schoolroom and in the dormitories were primitive and the growing state of disorder culminated in the rebellion of 1851, which led to the resignation of the Headmaster. Then came the transformation, with the appointment of Cotton, formerly a master at Rugby. He introduced a prefectorial system on Arnoldian lines, grouped the boys into houses and introduced organized games. New form-rooms were built so that the Rugby system of one form to a room could be adopted. There was little change in the content of the curriculum, but the classical languages were now taught (as they had been by Arnold) in a more enlightened way: there was an approach to the method of discussion between masters and boys which Hill at Hazelwood School had earlier stressed.[41]

At Rossall, too, what had formerly been a large private house became the nucleus of the school buildings. (This was Rossall Hall, erected in *c.* 1750 and demolished in 1927.)[42] Commercial interests were very pronounced, for Fleetwood (Lancs.), owing to its situation near the sea and its good rail communications, made a particular appeal as a school site to the industrialists of the north-west of England, where major school foundations had always been few. The idea of the school was a product of the fertile brain of Signor Vantini, the manager of the large new railway hotel in Fleetwood. He had already managed the Euston and Victoria Hotels in London and was the first to establish a refreshment-room on a railway station, at Wolverton, on the London and North Western line. He persuaded the Vicar of Fleetwood that a large college could be financed on the basis of insurance and that Fleetwood was ideally placed to attract pupils. The Vicar modified the scheme considerably, but succeeded in obtaining the financial support of leading members of the aristocracy and of a number of industrialists and railway chairmen: life governorships could be obtained for £100 in shares and the right to nominate pupils for £50. The school opened in 1844 under the name of 'The Northern Church of England School' and at first faced similar disciplinary problems to those at Marlborough, but, since the numbers were smaller, they did not reach such serious proportions. And just as Cotton reorganized Marlborough, so the Rev. W. A. Osborne (Headmaster, 1849–70) built up Rossall so successfully—chiefly through his control over the prefects and by introducing science and games—that the school was able to buy the lease of Rossall Hall, the shares having been converted into donations shortly before Osborne took office. It was much the same story as at Cheltenham and Marlborough: the provision of better facilities was paid for by increasing the fees, and the schools were then able to support themselves without external financial help—in the process, of course, they became socially more exclusive.

Other schools started in new premises, or were able to afford them very early in their history. Thus, Brighton College (Sussex) was founded in 1845 by a group of prominent residents in the town in order to provide 'a thoroughly liberal and practical education in conformity with the principles of the Established Church'. The main block of buildings, designed by Gilbert Scott, was occupied in 1849, at which date only the principal front containing the classrooms was ready. The headmaster's house was finished in 1854, the chapel in 1859 and the dining-hall and dormitories (pl. **207**) in the 1860s—all by Scott. The buildings were considerably extended in the 1880s, and it was not until then that the big schoolroom was built.[43] It is significant that the classrooms were built first: we have seen that at Rugby and elsewhere the boys were taught in separate form-rooms, and at Brighton also the schoolroom was used only at times when the whole school needed to be gathered together.

The religious motives of the founders were most marked at Radley, Bradfield and in the remarkable group of schools inspired by Nathaniel Woodard. St Peter's College, Radley, near Abingdon (Berks.), was founded by the Rev. William Sewell, Fellow of Exeter College, Oxford, and opened in 1847 in Radley Hall, the family seat of the Bowyers. St Andrew's College, Bradfield (also in Berks.), opened in 1850 in the manor house of the Rev. Thomas Stevens, the Lord of the Manor and Rector of the parish.[44] Both colleges extended their buildings from these centres: at Radley a chapel (rebuilt, 1895) and a schoolroom (now used for dining) were opened in 1848 and dormitories in 1849 and 1859, while at Bradfield classrooms and dormitories were added between 1853 and 1862, with a dining-hall in 1856 (as at Brighton, 'Big School' was not opened until later—in 1872).

The High Church associations of Radley were particularly pronounced. Sewell realized that the buildings already on the site could not themselves provide the religious associations he desired, but interior fittings could. Turkey carpets were purchased second-hand, as were 'sixteen old panels exquisitely carved with Scripture subjects', ancient locks for the chapel doors, and copies of old paintings. A Flemish reredos of the fifteenth century was purchased in 1847 and, although it was at first sent back because it had 'a very Popish air', it was later installed in the chapel. The schoolroom was an Elizabethan barn converted for the purpose, but painted windows were placed in it and the walls lined with old panelling. A prefabricated corrugated-iron cathedral meant for a colonial town was purchased for use as a gymnasium (1859) and is now used as the school theatre. Sewell regarded the dormitory as next in importance to the chapel for encouraging the pursuit of a religious life. The long room used for this purpose was divided into separate cubicles measuring 9 by 6 feet (pl. **208**). Each was furnished with a bed, a washstand with a cupboard underneath for clothes, a chair and an oilcloth on which was placed a bath (kept under the bed when not in use). Radley was unique in providing separate bathing facilities for each boy and in its rigid insistence on the rule of silence in the dormitory, where the use of night-lights resembled not only the conditions thought to characterize religious life in the Middle Ages, but also the arrangements made, as we saw, by the Moravians at Fulneck and the Wesleyans at Kingswood in the previous century. These cubicles are still in use (pl. **209**).

It was in the Woodard schools, however, that a coherent philosophy of education found its most compelling architectural expression.[45] Woodard realized that the growing middle class included not only members of the lesser gentry and the ancient professions, but also men working at various levels in industry and commerce. In 1848, when Curate of New Shoreham in Sussex, he published a pamphlet entitled *A plea for the middle classes*, in which he outlined a scheme for providing a nation-wide system of schools, divided into 'three distinct grades', corresponding with the upper, middle and lower divisions of that section of society which lay between the rich and the poor: the rich were already catered for by the major public schools and the poor by the National schools. Woodard's proposal for three types of middle-class school was a development of the idea of separate educational provision which the founders of Liverpool College had tried to combine in a single building, but which Woodard succeeded in achieving with three distinct colleges in Sussex. Subsequently, other colleges on the 'Woodard Foundation' were established in other parts of the country.

Woodard founded the first college (St Nicolas) at Shoreham in 1848 and it moved to new buildings at Lancing in 1857. This was an upper school for the sons of 'clergymen and other gentlemen', and was followed by a middle school (St John's) for the sons of 'substantial tradesmen, farmers, clerks and others of similar station', which opened at Hurstpierpoint in 1850 and moved into permanent buildings there in 1853. The lower school (St Saviour's) for the sons of 'petty shopkeepers, skilled mechanics and other persons of very small means' occupied the building at Shoreham left vacant by the upper school and moved to permanent buildings at Ardingly in 1870. By 1868 Woodard had raised and spent nearly £250,000 on these three colleges, yet their buildings were still far from complete.

Woodard believed that Education should be the handmaid of Religion and that 'no system of education would be perfect which did not provide for the cultivation of the taste of the pupils through the agency of the highest examples of architecture'.[46] He sought to achieve these objects with the help of a number of architects, notably R. C. and R. H. Carpenter (the latter succeeding the former in 1855) and his own son, Billy. Woodard took a keen personal interest in all the details of the buildings and himself chose the school sites, all of which are magnificent. Each college was built on the same basic plan: there were two quadrangles, into which were fitted a chapel, large schoolroom, dining-hall and classrooms, with dormitories above. At Lancing—the principal foundation—both R. C. and R. H. Carpenter worked on the buildings, and the original chapel was replaced by a superb new chapel, begun in 1868 under the supervision of R. H. Carpenter and Billy Woodard. Hurstpierpoint was begun by R. C. Carpenter and completed by his son, who also designed (with W. Slater) the building at Ardingly. The layout of Ardingly, which was given in *The Builder* in 1867 (pls. **212** and **213**), illustrates the quadrangular design adopted in all three colleges. To the right of the central tower was the schoolroom (A) with the chapel over it, and to the left the dining-hall (D). The rest of the ground floor was occupied mainly by classrooms (B), no less than fifteen in all (some of which were not built, however). To the side of the main building was a yard with kitchen and other domestic offices. But the architectural climax of the Woodard colleges was—and is—the chapel at Lancing, built in French Gothic style and higher from floor to vaulting than any nave or choir in the country except Westminster Abbey, York Minster and Liverpool Cathedral (pl. **214**).

Non-Anglican bodies were equally active after 1840 in setting up new middle-class schools. The Roman Catholics were traditionally strongest in the north of England and the Nonconformists in the west, and the growth of schools in these areas helped to counteract the earlier concentration of schools in the south—indeed, the balance of population was shifting throughout this period, which also helps to explain the geographical spread of middle-class schools.

The Jesuit college at Stonyhurst (Lancs.), which had begun in 1794, continued to expand, and its interest in the teaching of science was particularly notable: an observatory was built in the school grounds in 1838 and another in 1866, though the rebuilding of the school of 1810 did not begin until 1876.[47] Mount St Mary's College was also founded by the Society of Jesus (1842) in the manor house of Spinkhill in north-east Derbyshire, while the Benedictines expanded their educational work at Ampleforth in the North Riding of Yorkshire, where Joseph Hansom was employed to design a church (1857; replaced, 1922–61) and a new school building (1861; illustrated in *The Builder*). The resurrected Douai seminary had established itself as St Cuthbert's College at Ushaw (Durham) in 1808; A. W. Pugin made a number of additions in Gothic style after 1840, and his son, Edward, designed a Junior College (illustrated in *The Builder*, 1860).[48] Catholic schools were also founded further south. The Benedictines had settled at Downside House in Somerset in 1814 and this was extended in 1823. A. W. Pugin made plans here too, but the new range of 1853–4 was by Charles Hansom. The Rosminian Order established a college at Ratcliffe, near Leicester, the original building being designed by A. W. Pugin in 1843–7 and enlarged by Joseph Hansom in 1854–8.[49] Pugin's front is illustrated on pl. **210**.

The Nonconformists, whose efforts to found day proprietary schools in the 1830s had largely failed, met with considerably more success with boarding schools after 1840. Like the Catholics, they had their favourite architects: in particular, James Wilson, who had designed the original college buildings at Cheltenham, was called in to design a number of important schools in the West of England. Queen's College in Trull Road, Taunton (Somerset), was founded in 1843 as 'The Wesleyan Collegiate Institution', and the building, designed by Wilson, was based on his Cheltenham plan of a central tower with wings on each side, in Early Tudor style. Wilson developed this plan at the new Kingswood School, which moved from Bristol to Landsdown, near Bath, in 1851, and was built in the shape of a letter H, with the large schoolroom and dining-room forming the side wings.[50] There was some stylistic development in Wilson's design for the Landsdown Proprietary College (now the Royal School, Bath, and illustrated in *The Builder*, 1858), which was in Geometrical Gothic (not Tudor) style, and included two large schoolrooms and five smaller 'halls of study'. A similar plan was adopted at the 'West of England Dissenters' College' (now Taunton School, in Staplegrove Road, Taunton), which was housed in a new building designed in Geometrical Gothic style by Joseph James of London and illustrated in *The Builder* in 1869 (see also pl. **211** and fig. 40 (*c*)).[51] This building, too, was H-shaped in plan: on the ground floor the dining-hall and the schoolroom occupied the side wings, the rest of the space being taken up with masters' and servants' rooms and five classrooms, each about 450 feet square: on the first floor were eleven dormitories, the largest measuring 30 by 15 feet. Other important Nonconformist schools were established during the 1860s at Tettenhall (Staffs.) and Bishop's Stortford (Herts.), the latter housed in the buildings of an unsuccessful proprietary school of 1852.[52]

It was at Wellington College (Berks.), however, that a number of new architectural and organizational features first appeared.[53] The college originated as a national monument to the Duke of Wellington, who died in 1852, and it was endowed by public subscription. It was intended as a college for the orphans of Army officers, and the architect chosen was John Shaw (the younger), whose design for the Royal Naval School at Deptford (now Goldsmiths' College) was much admired by the promoters of the new college: in addition he had, as we noted earlier, designed 'New Buildings' at Eton and worked with his father on the rebuilding of Christ's Hospital, the purpose and scale of which provided the nearest contemporary analogy with those originally adopted for Wellington College. The College, which opened in 1859 (pl. **215**), was, as Dr Pevsner has pointed out, highly important for the history of Victorian architecture.[54] The style chosen was not the usual Gothic, but in the manner of Christopher Wren's Chelsea Hospital and Hampton Court—that is (in the words of *The Builder*) 'of French-Italian design . . . with traces of the Jacobean manner', which later emerged on an extensive scale as the so-called Queen Anne style. *The Builder* also commended the 'chromatic character of the building' resulting from the use of Bath stone and two types of brick, purple-red made locally and orange-red from Reading. Shaw's plan, which is shown on pl. **216**, was strictly symmetrical, with the buildings arranged around two principal courtyards. The 'Hall Quadrangle' had the dining-hall on the south side and the main schoolroom on the north; the 'School Quadrangle' had two classrooms and a playroom on the west and the library with two further classrooms on the east. The two upper floors of the east and west buildings in the School Quadrangle contained dormitories for 250 pupils, each with separate cubicles measuring 10 by 7 feet. The infirmary and chapel, which were to occupy separate buildings on each side, were not, however, built to Shaw's design, owing to lack of funds. When they were built later, they were in a different style, and subsequent additions to the college have destroyed much of the symmetry which Shaw had aimed at achieving.

The idea of the college, and the choice of the site, architect and first Headmaster, were largely due to the Prince Consort, who, like the founders of some Nonconformist schools in the 1830s, disliked the Gothic style because of its 'monastic' associations. He also hoped that the college would develop 'those branches of scientific knowledge which have a special application to the arts, commerce and industry of the country' and, although it was soon decided not to limit entry to orphans, it remained the original intention to provide wholly for the sons of Army officers. But the first Headmaster, E. W. Benson, who had taught at Rugby under Goulburn and Temple, wanted a school modelled on Arnoldian lines. It was Benson who was largely responsible for the choice of Gilbert Scott to build a Gothic chapel in 1863 (shown on the right of pl. **215**); moreover, shortage of funds obliged the Governors, urged on by Benson, to increase the number of fee-paying children of civilian parents. As in the case of many older schools—though at Wellington the whole process was speeded up—the number of foundationers remained fixed, and they were soon greatly outnumbered by the non-foundationers. Hence Wellington developed into a public school very different in character from that which the Prince Consort had intended and comparable with the other major new foundations which were springing up during this period.

Wellington was significant in the development of school architecture, not only because it broke away from the Gothic style, but also because it was one of the first of the new middle-class schools to be planned *ab initio* on the grand scale. Although alterations and additions were made later, there was—at least in intention—no question of the kind of piecemeal development which characterized most of the other new foundations of the 1840s and 1850s; even the Woodard schools took many decades to be completed. The architectural conception of a major school building, complete with its many interrelated parts and extensive site, was itself proof of the strength of the middle-class demand for secondary education.

The new foundations of the 1860s were usually on an equally impressive scale. In 1858 the East India Company closed its college at Haileybury (Herts.), a large and splendid building designed by William Wilkins in 1809 (pl. **217**), and in 1862 it was occupied by a school 'intended for the Education of the Sons of the Clergy and Laity of the Home and Eastern Counties . . . conducted on the same principles as the Public Schools of Marlborough and Rossall'.[55] The other major foundations of the 1860s were, however, built in Gothic style: Clifton College (Glos.), illustrated in *The Building News* in 1861; St Mary's College, Harlow (Essex), illustrated in *The Builder* in 1862; Framlingham College (Suffolk), illustrated in both these journals in 1864; Malvern College (Worcs.), illustrated in *The Builder* in 1865; Trent College (Derbs.), 1866; Eastbourne College (Sussex), 1867; and the Bedfordshire Middle Class College, illustrated in both journals in 1868–9. All these colleges still exist, except for the one at Bedford, later called Elstow College, which closed in 1916 and was demolished in 1964. The college at Bedford is shown on pl. **218**: it was designed by Frederick Peck, who had also designed Framlingham College, and was built on an E-shaped plan, with classrooms occupying the main front, and two large schoolrooms and a dining-room forming the arms of the E (see fig. 40 (*d*)).[56]

A study of the original plans of these buildings shows how accurately they reflected the educational developments which we have been tracing. We saw that at Cheltenham provision had been made for the teaching of modern subjects in the original layout, and that further classrooms and a chapel had been added in the 1850s so as to form a quadrangle. We have also seen that Wilson in his later designs for schools had developed a layout around an open-ended quadrangle, while at Wellington and in the Woodard schools the quadrangular plan had been taken even further. It was therefore to be expected that the new middle-class schools of the 1860s would be built on variations of the quadrangular plan (see the diagrams in fig. 40 for a visual summary). Particularly

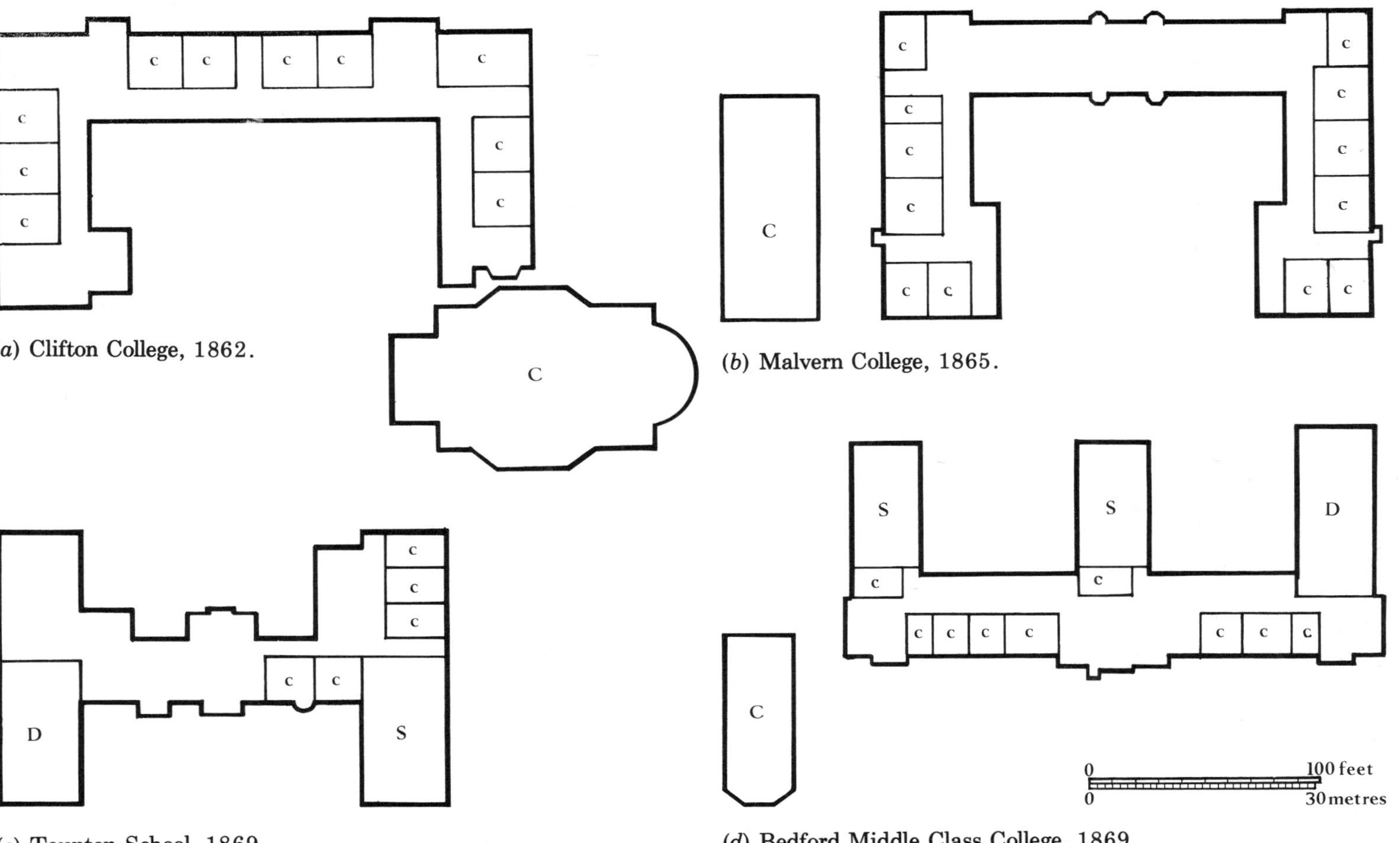

(*a*) Clifton College, 1862.

(*b*) Malvern College, 1865.

(*c*) Taunton School, 1869.

(*d*) Bedford Middle Class College, 1869.

Figure 40 Quadrangular plans of the 1860s (C = Chapel, c = classrooms, D = Dining-hall and S = Schoolroom).

outstanding in this group were Clifton and Malvern, which were both designed by Charles Hansom and contained a number of important features which are worthy of comment.[57] In the first place, a chapel, though regarded by the promoters of both Clifton and Malvern as essential, could not be provided immediately owing to limited funds, and we find that, as at Bedford, the design in each case placed the chapel adjoining to, but distinct from, the main school buildings. It is also important to note that the principal block contained only the teaching rooms (and not, as in earlier foundations, the dormitories and dining-room as well). The boarders were accommodated in separate houses nearby, partly at least to secure the physical conditions under which a 'house' system (such as had grown up spontaneously in many of the older public schools) could be developed; in addition, the space in the main building was needed for extra classrooms and specialist teaching rooms, e.g. at Malvern the design provided for twelve classrooms on the ground floor and, on the first floor, a 'classical school', a 'modern school', a drawing and modelling room and a laboratory. The teaching of classics still held an important place in the curriculum, but provision for it had now become only one element in the design.

The setting of a school was also considered to be of great importance, both for reasons of public prestige and because of the need for large playing fields in the new era of 'muscular Christianity'. The sites for the colleges at Clifton and Malvern were chosen with care—the former on the edge of a well-to-do suburb and the latter at the foot of the Malvern Hills. The total effect (now somewhat marred by later development) is perhaps best seen in aerial photographs, as reproduced on pls. **219** and **220**. The layout of these colleges may be said to have summed up thirty years of school planning and equally to have set the pattern for many other school buildings for the rest of the nineteenth century and later.

III

The new middle-class schools which we have been considering show, in general terms, two main types of plan. The first, exemplified at Marlborough and Rossall, may be called the 'nuclear' plan, in which a school grew from a nucleus or centre, usually an older building that had originally been rented for school purposes. The second, which may be called the 'quadrangular' plan, as exemplified at Wellington and in the Woodard schools, was the result of large-scale planning from the initial stages. We now turn to consider the changes which were taking place in the endowed grammar schools between 1840 and 1870 to see what impact was being made on the traditional system of secondary education by the new developments which were taking place independently of it. As we have already seen, those new developments had been made possible by privately-raised finance, or (in the case of Wellington) by public subscription. Now the need was increasingly being felt to reorganize the vast number of educational endowments which existed all over the country, and to turn this accumulated capital into new channels.

The need for reorganization on a national scale led to the appointment of the Schools Inquiry Commission in 1864, which reported four years later. The Commissioners' task was to report on the very large number of schools left unexamined by the Newcastle Commission of 1861 and the Clarendon Commission of 1864. Of particular importance was their review of the endowed grammar schools of the time. These varied from large and famous schools, such as Christ's Hospital, to small and obscure country grammar schools. Apart from Christ's Hospital, the Commissioners paid special attention to seven other schools where the educational endowments exceeded £2,000 a year, viz. at Southwark, Dulwich, Birmingham, Manchester, Tonbridge, Bedford and Monmouth. But few if any educational endowments escaped their net, and their voluminous report is a vast quarry of information about the endowed schools.[58] The first volume of their report included a chronological list of endowed grammar schools, with tables grouping them according to the subjects taught and the age of the pupils. Their final summary for the whole of England and Wales divided the 782 foundations into 820 'schools or departments', as shown in Table II.[59]

Table II Analysis of endowed grammar schools in England and Wales examined by the Schools Inquiry Commission (1868)

Type	*No. of schools*	*Net annual value of endowment, £*	*No. of boarders*	*No. of day-boys*	*Total*
Classical	209	113,597	6,762	9,498	16,260
Semi-classical	191	45,503	2,208	8,689	10,897
Non-classical	172	23,966	309	9,366	9,675
Elementary	198	8,762	Full details not given		
In abeyance	50	3,356	Full details not given		
Totals	820	195,184	9,279	27,553	36,832

This table illustrates two of the main points made by the Commissioners, viz. the considerable number of schools (over half) no longer teaching classical subjects and the large proportion (about three-quarters) of day-pupils. So far as the first point is concerned, we have already noted that many of the endowed schools had ceased to teach classical subjects, if indeed they had ever taught them, many years before, though they may still have provided for the real needs of the communities they served. As for the preponderance of day-boys, it is clear that we are here mainly concerned with purely local schools which had never recruited on more than a regional basis: they could all claim to be 'public schools' in the traditional sense, but very few had built up a national reputation by taking boarders from all parts of the country. The Commissioners were well aware of the significance of the boarding question and also of the importance of the buildings in which the schools were housed. The latter they discussed in a separate section of their report devoted to 'sites and buildings'.[60]

In general, the Commissioners considered that 'at least half of the grammar schools are without doubt insufficiently, and probably only one quarter can be considered fairly, provided'. They pointed out that a few of the leading schools had recently acquired new buildings, but that the majority were still in their original buildings, often several centuries old and invariably suffering from overcrowding, poor ventilation and unsuitable siting. In Suffolk the local grammar school typically consisted of one block containing the master's house and schoolroom and was 'old-fashioned, low, and often in bad repair'; in Westmorland there was often no master's house and 'only one schoolroom of the rudest description'; in Lancashire, one of the Assistant Commissioners reported that the grammar schools were 'almost uniformly mean, confined [and] unsuited to their purpose': the town schools were mainly 'old, ugly, ill-ventilated [and] in every way offensive', while in the country districts the grammar schools were described as externally 'plain, oblong structures, with low, almost square, sometimes heavily mullioned windows, occasionally a small porch in the middle, and a bit of bare ground in front enclosed by the stone palisade so common in the northern counties'. As for the inside, 'the interior is even more repulsive; the roof is low, and the small windows admit a feeble light. The walls are mostly whitewashed, or covered with a wash which once was white, but is now a grimy brown.' Another Assistant Commissioner reported in similar terms on some of the endowed-school buildings in London, which he compared unfavourably with the new National schools, a typical endowed school being 'as unprepossessing and repulsive in its exterior as the other [i.e. the National school] is cheerful and inviting'.

What these Assistant Commissioners were describing was the educational legacy of centuries of development, particularly of the Tudor and Stuart periods—that is, the vernacular buildings of the kind described in the earlier chapters of this book. The revival of interest in vernacular building since the Second World War enables us to view what remain of these 'repulsive' school buildings with a more sympathetic eye. Even so, one would be guilty of merely sentimental antiquarianism if one were to attempt to deny that many local schools had by the 1860s outlived their usefulness. Many, as the Commissioners pointed out, were in a poor state of repair; others, particularly in places where the population had grown rapidly as a result of the Industrial Revolution, were now much too small and very badly sited. At Maidstone (Kent) the school site was 'close to the river and surrounded by factories'; at Portsmouth (Hants.) 'the school is next door to a public-house'; while at Oldham (Lancs.) the school 'is placed in a filthy lane inhabited by the lowest of the Irish settlers, and is enclosed on two sides by a slaughter-yard'. Most of these buildings, especially in built-up areas, have disappeared, but one may occasionally recapture from Victorian photographs something of the air of squalor and neglect which overcame particularly the less well-endowed schools.[61] What a contrast they must have made, not only to the new elementary schools, but even more to the new colleges with which the Commissioners would have been familiar.

The Commissioners also remarked on the lack of classrooms in most of the older buildings. It is indeed clear that the changes in school organization and teaching methods which we have noticed in the new middle-class colleges had made little or no impact on the majority of the older endowed schools. The teaching continued to take place in one schoolroom: at Rotherham (Yorks.), for example, which was a comparatively large grammar school rebuilt in 1857, the forms were still being taught by the ushers in the same room, as an engraving of the 1860s shows (pl. **222**).[62] Similarly, traditional ceremonies continued, sometimes in medieval surroundings, as may be seen, for example, in the lithograph of the King's School, Canterbury, showing the delivery of speeches (derived from rhetorical exercises) in the Chapter House (pl. **221**).

This general picture needs to be modified, however, for some of the endowed schools, especially in the large towns, where the problem of providing adequate secondary education was felt most acutely. While the work of the Commissioners appointed under the Endowed Schools Act of 1869, and later under the Charity Commission, heralded a new era for many of the endowed schools, it is interesting to trace the earlier efforts of local trustees to adapt their educational funds to the new demands being made. In Liverpool and in many other provincial towns, as we have seen, new schools had been financed on the proprietary principle. In such places the endowed grammar schools were usually at a very low ebb, or had closed completely. In other towns, however, real efforts were made to reform and extend the local endowed schools. Birmingham, with the second largest endowment next to Christ's Hospital (£9,500 p.a.), is a case in point. There, as we noted in a previous chapter, Acts of Parliament obtained in 1831 and 1837 enabled the Trustees to build a new school, with an English as well as a classical department. Between 1837 and 1852 they also set up four branch schools 'for the free education of boys and girls of the humbler classes', each in separate buildings situated in Gem Street, Edward Street, Meriden Street and Bath Row. Later the classical and English departments in the New Street building came to be called the High School and the Middle School respectively, the branch schools being known as Lower Schools.[63] In 1828 the King Edward's School Foundation had been educating only 115 boys, but forty years later 1,600 children of both sexes were being taught in six schools in five separate buildings.[64] This situation was closely comparable with the development of the Harpur Trust in Bedford, where, as we saw in ch. 9, the number of children being educated by the Trust rose from about 600 in 1821 to 1,800 in 1868.

Manchester also had a well-endowed school, with an annual net income in 1868 of £2,480.[65] The Grammar School had been rebuilt, as we noted earlier, in 1776. It was situated in Long Millgate, which the Taunton Commissioners described as 'a disagreeable lane, away from the respectable parts of the town', though they later conceded that its central position near the railway stations enabled it to serve a very wide area. A new schoolroom for the teaching of English, arithmetic, mathematics and French had been built on the same site as the Grammar School in 1837. Twelve years later the High Master was forbidden to take boarders, which was a further blow to the classical side of the school. In the meantime the 'lower' department of the school had developed into an ordinary elementary school. Clearly the intention was to provide a system of day schools giving a mainly elementary and commercial education to local boys. In 1856 there were seventy boys in the Lower School, 150 in the English School and only 100 in the Upper (Classical) School. Then in 1859 a new High Master, F. W. Walker, was appointed. He transformed the school in a way not unlike Cotton at Marlborough or Benson at Wellington, except that, instead of boarders, Walker introduced fee-paying day-boys and, in place of the cultivation of moral character (which a day school could not hope to emulate), he emphasized intellectual distinction as the main criterion of success. Walker introduced an entrance examination and made Latin compulsory in the Lower and English as well as the Upper School, which now began to build up its reputation for winning open scholarships at Oxford and Cambridge. A scheme of 1867 confirmed that the school would offer 250 free places by open competition, but fee-payers were also admitted. Modern as well as classical subjects were to be taught to a high academic level, and further classrooms were opened on the Millgate site in 1871 to accommodate the extra pupils. The latest historians of the school suggest that, while Walker's great achievement was to convince the middle classes in Manchester that academic excellence (including the rigorous study of the classics) should be the aim of secondary education, the school had been essentially a middle-class school since the beginning of the nineteenth century, when the landed gentry had deserted it for the better-known boarding schools.[66] It also seems to be true, however, that the poorer classes—who, as in Birmingham, had previously attended the Lower School in large numbers—were now effectively excluded. The main justification put forward for this change was that elementary schools were increasingly being provided from public funds, and an elementary education was all that the overwhelming majority of the poorer classes were thought to need.

These developments at Manchester remind us that important changes could still take place without national legislation, or a major rebuilding programme. The same may be said of Bristol, where the population was also growing rapidly: from 40,000 in 1801 to 125,000 in 1841 (following a boundary extension) and to 154,000 in 1861. In this case, the school's historian makes the point that in the 1840s the public boarding schools were not sufficiently numerous or wholly acceptable to many middle-class parents, to which we may add that the day proprietary schools had not in general been financially successful; but 'the grammar schools lay ready to hand, if their endowments and properties could be rescued and set in order after the muddle of the previous era'.[67]

At Bristol the Grammar School had since 1767 occupied a hospital building of 1703, but it had closed through lack of support in 1829. A new scheme of 1847 reorganized the endowments and provided for the introduction of modern subjects. The school reopened in 1848, with pupils drawn almost entirely from the professional and middle classes. Fees were introduced and efforts made to revive the boarding element, but in 1860 the Master of the Rolls ruled that the Grammar School should be exclusively for day-boys, arguing that boarding schools were only 'for the sons of the higher classes of the community'.[68] Wealthier parents now sent their sons to Clifton College, the Grammar School later moving to another site, not too near Clifton, but in a newer middle-class area (1879).

Outside the large towns, reorganization took place very slowly, or not at all. In general, we may say that during the first thirty years of Victoria's reign new social and educational forces were clearly at work, but were finding expression in the piecemeal adaptation of existing foundations. A minority of schools, mainly in the towns, were able to obtain permission from the Court of Chancery or by private Act of Parliament to reorganize their resources, a reorganization which was sometimes symbolized by the erection of new buildings; elsewhere, however, reorganization and rebuilding did not take place until after 1870, and in such places—or where the local endowments were in any case inadequate—it appears that middle-class parents sent their children either to the new colleges or to local private schools. So far as the development of grammar-school buildings is concerned, we will have to concentrate on those places where rebuilding did take place and especially on those schools which were considered to be of sufficient interest to be noticed in the volumes of *The Builder* and *The Building News* (see also Appendix 3).

No grammar-school plans appeared in *The Builder* in the 1840s, and *The Building News* did not begin publication until 1855. What evidence there is suggests that the new grammar schools of the 1840s were planned on a modest scale in Tudor Gothic style and were very similar to those already considered for the 1820s and 1830s. Two surviving examples, no longer used as schools, may be seen at Dulwich (south London) and Doncaster (Yorks.). Dulwich College had been founded by Edward Alleyn in 1619 to provide for a master, warden, four fellows, twelve poor men and women and twelve poor scholars. They were housed in an early seventeenth-century building which survives as the 'Old College' in Dulwich Village. The east wing of this building was rebuilt in 1740 and, following the gift of a collection of pictures, a Picture Gallery designed by Sir John Soane was built alongside the college in 1814. Dulwich was a rapidly-developing area, and the demand arose that more of the funds should be spent on local education. Accordingly, Charles Barry, the surveyor to the College and architect of the new Houses of Parliament, was engaged to build a grammar school, which opened in 1842 on the corner of Burbage Road and Gallery Road (where it still stands). It consisted of the usual large room, which was divided by a wooden partition into an upper and lower school, the twelve poor scholars continuing to receive their education in the college.[69]

The Grammar School at Doncaster was also by this date totally inadequate for local needs and, as we saw in a previous chapter, the deficiency was made up by private schools. The Doncaster school had since 1560 occupied the chancel of the redundant church of St Mary Magdalen. In 1846 this building was demolished to make way for a new market hall, and a new grammar school was then built in St George's Gate. It opened in 1850, but three years later was taken over as a temporary church when the adjoining parish church was burnt down, reopening as a school in 1862. (This building was until recently used as part of the public library, but was due for demolition in 1969.)[70] Other grammar schools of the 1840s may be seen at Southwell, Notts. (1840–50, north of the Minster and now vacated by the school), St Bees, Cumberland (1842–4), Durham (1844, in Margary Lane), Chesterfield, Derbs. (1846, in Sheffield Road and now considerably extended) and Richmond, Yorks. (1849, in Station Road).

In the 1850s illustrations and plans begin to appear in *The Builder* and *The Building News*, and the number of surviving grammar-school buildings also seems to be greater. In 1851, for example, *The Builder* reported on the rebuilding of a school at Tamworth (Staffs.), which had been founded in 1820 by the father of Sir Robert Peel, the Prime Minister, whose constituency this was. The new building of 1850 was designed by Sydney Smirke in Tudor style and consisted of a schoolroom measuring 49 by 25 feet and two classrooms, one 'fitted up for chemical lectures' and the other with 'mechanical models and mathematical instruments'. There was already an established grammar school in the town, and although Peel's school was also described in *The Builder* as a grammar school, its declared aim was to offer 'a good commercial education at a very moderate cost', so that it was obviously seeking to respond to the new demand for a more modern type of secondary education. The Smirke building still stands in Lichfield Street, Tamworth, and is now used by a printing firm.[71]

Two older grammar schools which were rebuilt in the early 1850s may be seen at Wimborne (Dorset) and Loughborough (Leics.). The former (pl. **223**), which opened in 1851, consisted originally of one large and one smaller schoolroom in the centre, with accommodation for the headmaster and the undermaster (with their boarders) on each side.[72] The new school at Loughborough (pl. **224**), which opened in 1852, had a plan somewhat in advance of this, and one which reflected the curricular changes to be expected in a developing town, especially one with a large educational endowment. There was a central tower, with a grammar schoolroom and classroom on one side of it, and a commercial schoolroom and classroom on the other, so forming an H-shaped plan of the type discussed in our last section. A house for the headmaster and his boarders was also built by the side of the school, and is still used for this purpose, though the two schoolrooms have now had an additional floor inserted. The architects were John Morris and Charles Hebson of Lambeth, London, and, as at Wimborne, the Perpendicular Gothic style was chosen, with different-coloured bricks used for decorative effect (a feature which was imitated in the subsequent extensions at Loughborough). The Loughborough school was set in six acres of grounds on the outskirts of the town, in contrast to the cramped site of its former building (pl. **149**). The Taunton Commissioners particularly commended this school for the 'excellence of [its] buildings, situation and playground', which they felt encouraged the formation of '*esprit de corps* and moral tone among the boys'.[73]

The Taunton Commissioners also commended the new grammar school building at Ipswich (Suffolk). This school had from 1614 to 1842 used the former building of the Blackfriars, which was said to date from 1351. In 1842 the Blackfriars building was deemed to be unsafe and the Trustees decided to demolish it and erect a new school on a less-crowded site on the edge of the town. The architect chosen—after the usual competition and accusations of unfairness[74]—was an Ipswich architect named Fleury, who designed it in Tudor style, a conventional choice which was reinforced by the Trustees' desire to imitate Wolsey's Gate at Ipswich (pl. **17**). The Big School was 62 feet long, 31 feet wide and 20 feet high, with an open timbered roof. During the course of erecting this roof, the walls became unsafe and had to be buttressed, an episode which called forth the satirical cartoon reproduced as pl. **225**. The original building, which opened in 1852, also contained a senior classroom, a junior classroom and a library; a chapel was added soon afterwards. Most of the teaching, however, continued to take place in Big School.[75]

The school at Loughborough provided 'grammar' and 'commercial' courses and that at Ipswich 'classical' and 'general' courses, which seem to have meant much the same thing. We noticed earlier the appearance of 'English' departments in many schools after about 1800. In so far as working-class children were receiving elementary instruction in such departments, they now came increasingly to be excluded; but the attendance of lower middle-class children taking commercial subjects continued to be allowed for in the new buildings of the 1850s and 1860s. It has, however, to be borne in mind that the division into 'upper' and 'lower' schools was not that of the earlier period, when the division was by age, but indicated the organization of separate courses, depending on whether a mainly classical or modern curriculum was to be followed, and also—since the fees were usually different—on the social class of the pupils.

This point is well illustrated in architectural terms in the rebuilding of the principal endowed schools at Southwark in 1855 and at Leeds in 1859. St Olave's School, Southwark, had taught ciphering and accounts since Elizabethan times, no doubt because of its situation near the port of London. It was one of the wealthier schools, with an endowment income in 1868 of over £2,000 p.a. It had moved in 1839 from its original site near London Bridge to Bermondsey Street, and was obliged to move again in 1855 because of railway extensions—this time to Tooley Street in the parish of St John's Horselydown. The new building there (illustrated in *The Builder* in 1856) cost £24,000 and was designed in the usual collegiate Gothic style by the firm of Allen, Snooke and Stock. It included a classical schoolroom with cloisters below, giving access to a classical classroom, a mathematical classroom and a writing school, together with a separate English schoolroom, occupying two storeys. This building no longer exists, the school having been rebuilt on the same site in 1892–6. (The school moved to Orpington in Kent in 1967 and the Tooley Street building now forms part of Guy's Hospital.)[76]

At Leeds the Grammar School building dated from 1624, and a famous legal judgment in 1805 had restricted the teaching of modern subjects in the school. Mathematics and English were, however, being taught in 1820, and by 1844 there were over 200 boys, some of whom were accommodated in a nearby warehouse. In 1854 the Rev. Alfred Barry was appointed Headmaster and introduced commercial subjects; he also pressed for a new building on the outskirts of the town. The new building of 1859 (pl. **226**), which still forms part of the school, was designed by his brother, the architect E. M. Barry, and was notable for its use of the Decorated Gothic style. The design was strongly ecclesiastical, both in its external detail and internal plan, which was in the shape of a Latin cross and was considered to be of sufficient interest to be included in *The Building News* (pl. **227**). The long arm of the cross contained the lower schoolroom on the ground floor, with the upper schoolroom above (each 95 by 28 feet). The right-hand arm of the cross contained cloakrooms on the ground floor, with a classroom and library above (each 24 by 22 feet); the left-hand arm was occupied by a study and dormitories for the headmaster's boarders; and the upper part of the cross was taken up with the headmaster's residence.[77] It will be seen that, while the cruciform shape was consciously contrived—and in that sense novel—the main elements in the design were fairly traditional, since the teaching still took place in the large schoolrooms and only one classroom was provided. It will also be noted that the provision of accommodation for boarders in the headmaster's house—an arrangement which added to the headmaster's income and to the prestige of the school—was also usual in grammar schools of this as of earlier periods: most of the schools hoped to attract boarders, though in practice boarders rarely constituted more than a minority of the pupils, especially in the larger towns, where day-boys were readily available. If parents were really concerned to give their children a boarding education, it seems that they preferred to send them to schools which had already made their names as boarding schools or were situated in attractive country areas. Thus the grammar schools in the big towns like Leeds, Manchester and Birmingham tended to develop as day schools, stressing academic prowess rather than the more intangible moral qualities associated with boarding education.

During the 1860s the same influences were at work that we have noticed at Leeds and elsewhere. It was basically a matter of public pressure and the availability of funds, either from a reorganized endowment or by public appeal, the latter being mainly effective in the prosperous industrial towns. In general, the grammar schools aimed at reviving what was (often mistakenly) thought to be their ancient pre-eminence as leading local institutions. The reformers, in their invariable choice of the Gothic style, and in their continued emphasis on teaching in the big schoolroom, claimed to be traditional; but their buildings were, in fact, revolutionary in scale and style, and usually replaced quite modest structures which had been built at a variety of dates and in a variety of architectural styles. The rapidity of the change could be impressive. Thus, as we have already seen, the school at Loughborough, having acquired a new building in 1825, was rebuilt on another site in 1852; similarly at Doncaster, the school which had opened in 1850 was replaced by a much larger building on the edge of the town in 1869—a transformation which it owed in large measure to the efforts of the Vicar of Doncaster, C. J. Vaughan, who had previously done so much to revive the school at Harrow. At Nottingham the grammar school had been rebuilt on its original site in Stoney Street in 1830, but moved to a large new building in Arboretum Street in 1868. At Newcastle the Grammar School was from 1607 to 1844 housed in a former hospital building; in 1848 it migrated to a private house in Charlotte Square and in 1870 moved to a new school at Rye Hill, which was used until 1906.[78]

The new grammar-school buildings of the 1860s were usually ambitious in scale and incorporated classrooms as well as Big Schools. Thus the school at Nottingham, which opened in 1868 and still forms part of the premises of Nottingham High School, was T-shaped in plan and was designed by a local architect, Thomas Simpson. The main frontage (pl. **228**) originally consisted of a Classical or Upper School and an English or Lower School, each measuring 60 by 30 feet. These schoolrooms were of identical design and were separated by a central tower (a well-established layout, as we have seen), but inside the tower were sliding doors, which, when opened, gave an unbroken vista 160 feet long. To the north was a wing originally occupied by five classrooms, above which a Drawing and Writing School was built in 1880 (this wing has now been largely rebuilt). The English School, to the west of the tower (left in the photograph), has remained virtually unaltered and is now used as a library; the Classical School to the east has, however, had an extra storey inserted, and has been divided up into classrooms. More remarkable was the insertion during the 1870s and 1880s of a basement storey beneath the whole of the original front, a development made possible because the school was built on a ridge of soft sandstone. (The brick damp-course of the original building can still be seen, some 10 feet above the present ground-level.) The basement storey was at first used for science teaching, but now consists of ordinary classrooms.[79]

The 1869 building at Doncaster is also still in use as part of Doncaster Grammar School in Thorne Road. Like Nottingham, it was T-shaped in plan, but on a smaller scale, and originally consisted of a schoolroom measuring 82 by 35 feet on the first floor (pl. **229**), with open cloisters below and three classrooms at the rear. The school was designed by Scott, who had also been employed by Vaughan at Harrow and for the rebuilding of Doncaster Parish Church (1854–9).[80]

The most striking rebuilding of the 1860s was, however, at Dulwich, where, as we have seen, a new grammar school had been opened in 1842. The endowment was a wealthy one, ripe for reform, but the new Dulwich College of 1866–70 was very much a product of the new industrial age, since most of the money used to build it (nearly £100,000) came as compensation from two railway companies whose lines crossed the school estates. The architect, Charles Barry (the younger), broke almost fiercely from the conventional Gothic. The building was in a style called 'North Italian Renaissance' but has recently been described as showing 'fragments of all styles and scales' and as 'a fair candidate for the wildest nineteenth-century building in the whole of London' (pl. **230**).[81] The plan (reproduced as pl. **231**) shows that the college was designed in three blocks: the South Block was to house the upper school and the undermaster; the North Block the lower school and its master; and the Centre Block a lecture theatre and laboratory on the ground floor, with a library and Great Hall above. (The master was to be accommodated in a separate house, though this did not materialize.) The upper and lower schools were quite distinct, with different curricula and scales of fees.[82] In fact, however, the demand for places in the upper school was so great that both the South and North Blocks were used by the upper school. The lower school remained in the 1842 building and had to wait until the 1880s for a new building, when it was given the name of 'Alleyn's School', the upper school henceforth being called 'Dulwich College'.[83]

The internal organization of the buildings of 1866–70 is of particular interest. They were designed for 600 boys, who were to be taught, according to a leading article in *The Builder* in July 1868, on 'the classroom system', allowing $12\frac{1}{2}$ square feet per pupil.[84] A description of the buildings in 1877[85] states that there was a splendid hall, but it was only used 'as a place of muster for the whole school every morning, and there prayers are read before the boys proceed to their several class-rooms'. (The hall, which has recently been refurbished in its original style, is illustrated on pl. **232**.) Here we have the final transformation of the traditional schoolroom into the modern assembly hall, the actual teaching being done in separate classrooms. The provision for the teaching of science was also far in advance of most contemporary schools. The lecture theatre in the Central Block was used for class instruction in chemistry and physics; there were also two chemistry laboratories and classrooms fitted up for instruction in physics, anatomy and physical geography. If the colleges at Clifton and Malvern represent the highest points of development in the planning of the privately-financed secondary schools of the period before 1870, we may certainly say that the new college at Dulwich was the climax of the movement to reorganize the older endowed schools.

IV

There is one final aspect of the rebuilding of grammar schools in the period 1840–70 which needs to be mentioned. This is the way in which a certain number of local grammar schools—usually through the work of outstanding headmasters—managed to convert themselves into public schools of the Marlborough and Rossall type, following (from the architectural point of view) the same kind of nuclear development which we noted earlier, but with the original school building instead of a mansion as the nucleus. Such a development had occurred much earlier in a few places, notably at Rugby and Harrow, but now it took place on a much wider scale. While the revived grammar schools in the towns, in spite of their attempts to attract boarders, tended to develop as middle-class day schools under the control of local trustees, some of the country schools were able to take on a fresh lease of life by concentrating on the boarding side, which, when successful, enabled them to become increasingly independent of local (and indeed national) control. As we saw at Bristol, the day schools were by about 1860 regarded as most suitable for the lower middle or first-generation middle classes, while the upper middle or second-generation middle classes preferred to send their children to the more expensive boarding schools. And once the proprietary colleges had shown the way, some of the endowed schools were able to turn to advantage their rural situation—with its opportunities for character-training and organized games—and to supplement their often meagre endowments by charging boarding fees.

So we may trace the re-emergence of such schools as Sherborne, Repton, Sedbergh and others which had been founded much earlier, but only became prominent nationally after about 1850. Sherborne, for example, did not begin its revival until after the appointment of Harper as Headmaster in 1850, and Repton until after the appointment of Dr Pears in 1854; of Sedbergh, the school's historian says that the school was by 1870 in danger of extinction, yet it too revived under the Rev. Frederick Heppenstall after 1875.[86] The archetype of this category of school was, however, at Uppingham in Rutland under the Headmastership of Edward Thring, and it is proposed to conclude this chapter with a brief consideration of his work, particularly in relation to the school buildings and organization.

When Thring took up the Headmastership of Uppingham School in 1853, he found only twenty-three boys on the roll.[87] They were still taught in the schoolroom built near the parish church in 1584 (pl. **25**), and later extended to provide a room for the usher. It will be recalled that the founder of the school had also provided for an hospital or almshouse. The hospital building and adjoining master's house (also built in 1584) were some distance away from the schoolroom, off the High Street, and since the eighteenth century they had been used to accommodate boarders at the school, the fourteen old men provided for in the founder's will being paid annual pensions in lieu of residence. Under Thring the hospital buildings continued as School House, i.e. as living accommodation for the headmaster and his boarders, though they are now occupied by the library and the bursar's offices.[88] Thring was determined to expand the school, in spite of its relatively small endowment, and he did this by engaging assistant masters with sufficient private means to build their own boarding houses, the profits from which recouped them for their initial capital outlay. Eight new houses were opened in the first ten years of Thring's period as Headmaster, and by 1865 the number of boys (almost entirely boarders) had risen to 300. Thring wanted to avoid the 'barrack system' of the kind which he had endured as a boy in Long Chamber at Eton, and every boy at Uppingham was given a cubicle to sleep in and a study to work in during the day. Thring also insisted that no house should contain more than thirty boys, which was, in his view, the maximum number that one man could supervise properly.

Another of Thring's principles, and one which was to have enormous influence on the development of secondary education generally, was that 'every boy is good for something', the corollary of which was that a wide variety of subjects should be offered by the school. Music was introduced in 1855, drawing, chemistry and German in 1856, physical training in 1859 and carpentry in 1862. These subjects were taught in old buildings taken over by the school on ground now occupied by the Memorial Hall and classrooms of 1923, though the gymnasium which Thring built in 1859 survives as the buttery to the south-east of the hospital building (see fig. 41). This was the first purpose-built gymnasium in any public school,[89] and an interesting photograph of *c.* 1880 shows what it looked like in Thring's time, with its earth floor covered with 1 foot of sand, its parallel bars and other equipment (pl. **233**). Another photograph of the same date shows the chemistry laboratory (pl. **234**).

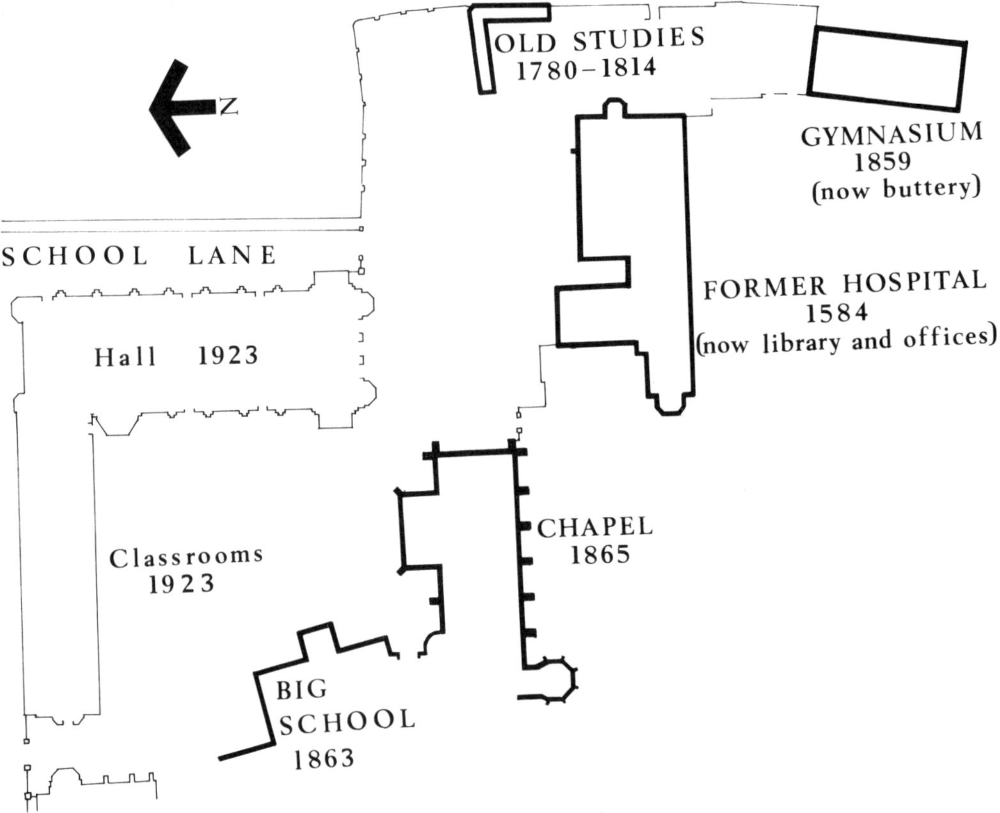

Figure 41 Uppingham School, sketch-plan showing position of buildings in Thring's time.

The difficulty of providing classrooms for the rapidly increasing number of boys at Uppingham was ingeniously solved by arranging for classes to be taken in the houses (an idea perhaps derived from the pupil-rooms at Eton), though some classes were also held in cottages and even cellars. Relief was provided by Thring's first major building, the Big School, which consisted of a large room at first-floor level used for general assemblies and for teaching two of the classes; on the ground floor was Thring's own classroom, a library and an open arcade. This building, which is still in use, was designed by G. E. Street and completed in 1863. Thring's other major building—again designed by Street—was the chapel, which opened in 1865. As with Temple and the New Quadrangle at Rugby, the Governors declined to contribute towards the cost, and the money was raised by Thring and the masters. A gallery was added in 1868, a transept to house the organ in 1880 and a Memorial side-chapel in 1921. In 1965 the main chapel was enlarged and renovated by the architectural firm of Seely and Paget, an enlargement which skilfully blends old and new materials and styles. (pl. **235**).

More than any of his contemporaries, Thring recognized the importance of the school organization and buildings—what he called 'the machinery' and 'the almighty wall'. Hence his emphasis on individual studies and cubicles, his limitation of each house to thirty boys, his building of the large schoolroom to promote a community spirit, and his provision of facilities for practical and other subjects. No-one believed more fervently than Thring in the need for an ideal physical environment for learning and teaching:

> Whatever men may say or think, the almighty wall is, after all, the supreme and final arbiter of schools. I mean, no living power in the world can overcome the dead, unfeeling, everlasting pressure of the permanent structure, of the permanent conditions under which work has to be done. . . . Never rest till you have got the almighty wall on your side, and not against you. Never rest till you have got all the fixed machinery for work, the best possible. The waste in a teacher's workshop is the lives of men.[90]

Thus it was that by introducing smaller classes and exercising close supervision through the boarding houses, the school was maintained in a state of civilized order almost unknown in earlier schools.

Notes

1 E.g. *The Builder,* XX (1862), 28, was voicing a common opinion when it wrote in connection with the founding of St Mary's College, Harlow, that, like Hurstpierpoint, Shoreham, Bloxham and Radley, these schools were 'all aiming at the same grand object, viz. the education of the middle classes, for which so little had hitherto been done'.

2 Cf. Archer, R. L., *Secondary education in the nineteenth century*, Cambridge U.P., 1928, 235: 'The progress in secondary education has been found in this country to follow the progress of university education. The revival of the old universities preceded the reawakening of the public schools; the founding of the provincial colleges preceded the institution of county and municipal schools.'

3 *Report of Her Majesty's Commissioners appointed to inquire into the revenues and management of certain colleges and schools and the studies pursued and instruction given therein*, H.M.S.O., 1864, hereinafter referred to as *C.C.* (Clarendon Commission); and Schools Inquiry Commission, *Report of the Commissioners (to inquire into the education given in schools not comprised within Her Majesty's two former commissions . . .)*, H.M.S.O., 1868, hereinafter referred to as *S.I.C.* (Schools Inquiry Commission), or the Taunton Report.

4 Table I is based on figures given in *C.C.*, I, 9 and 19.

5 *C.C.*, I, 20.

6 *Ibid.*, 98–100.

7 There is a useful description of the buildings at Eton (and a map showing their location) in Austen-Leigh, R. A., *An illustrated guide to Eton College*, Eton: Alden and Blackwell, rev. 1964. The 'New Buildings' are described on pp. 130f. and the 'New Schools' on pp. 124f.

8 Cook, A. K., *About Winchester College*, Macmillan, 1917, 493f.

9 Firth, J. D'E., *Winchester College*, Winchester Publications Ltd., 1949, 145.

10 Carleton, J. D., *Westminster School*, Rupert Hart-Davies, 1965, chs. 5 and 9, *passim.*

11 *Ibid.*, 128.

12 *Ibid.*, 127. (Ashburnham House is open to the public during holiday periods.)

13 *C.C.*, I, 184.

14 McDonnell, M. F. J., *A history of St Paul's School*, Chapman & Hall, 1909, 406. An 'Apposition' at St Paul's is illustrated in the *London Illustrated News*, 27 May 1843.

15 Details from Draper, F. W. M., *Four centuries of Merchant Taylors' School*, Oxford U.P., 1962, ch. 13. The school of 1675 is illustrated facing pp. 96 and 97.

16 Oldham, J. B., *A history of Shrewsbury School 1552–1952*, Oxford: Blackwell, 1952, *passim.* A plan showing an abortive scheme to enlarge the old school is reproduced facing p. 129. On the controversy concerning the move to Kingsland, see pp. 130–4.

17 Full details in Howson, E. W., and Warner, G. T. (eds.), *Harrow School*, Arnold, 1898, chs. 4, 5, 14. See also Laborde, E. D., *Harrow School*, Winchester Publications, 1948: Dr Vaughan's chapel, 95f., New Schools, 121f., Vaughan Library, 123f.

18 *C.C.*, I, 224.

19 Simpson, J. B. Hope, *Rugby since Arnold*, Macmillan, 1967, 14–15, 26–7.

20 *C.C.*, I, 287.

21 Quoted in Simpson, *op. cit.*, 48.

22 *Ibid.* For an architectural description of New Quad see Pevsner, *Warwicks.*, 1966, 388. The New Quad contained a music school, a drawing school, two science lecture-rooms, an electricity and chemistry room, and six classical schools (Sandford, E. G. (ed.), *Memoirs of Frederick Temple*, Macmillan, 1906, I, 206).

23 The details in the following paragraph are from *C.C.*, I, 49 and *passim,* and from the sections on boarding arrangements in the various schools contained in Staunton, H., *The great schools of England*, Low & Marston, 1865, which also has a number of illustrations of the schools at this date.

24 Firth, *op. cit.*, 135. Cf. Dilke, C., *Dr Moberly's mint-mark*, Heinemann, 1965, 101: 'The three Houses, which were to serve as the model for others, introduced a new phenomenon into the school life: one different from the medieval order of College and the disorder of Commoners.'

25 *C.C.*, I, 70.

26 The tutorial system at Eton is fully described in *C.C.*, I, 76f., and III (Minutes of Evidence, Eton), *passim.* One master at Eton summed up the teaching arrangements as follows: 'It seems to me to be the result of our system at Eton that an immense deal of work is got out of the masters, with comparatively little out of the boys' (III, 267).

27 *C.C.*, I, 93. The problem of the 'big lower boy', who tended to become a 'swell', is further discussed in III, 262.

28 *C.C.*, I, 109.

29 Newsome, D., *Godliness and good learning*, Murray, 1961, 35.

30 *S.I.C.*, I, 314. The whole section on proprietary schools (pp. 310–22) is a useful summary of this type of school.

31 Quoted in Wainwright, D., *Liverpool gentlemen. A history of Liverpool College*, Faber & Faber, 1960, 40. Other details in this para. are from this book. See also Mr Wainwright's article on the college in the *Architectural Review*, May 1959, pp. 349–50.

32 Sadler, M. E., *Report on secondary education in Liverpool*, Eyre & Spottiswood, 1904, 40. I am very grateful to Mr H. Hollinghurst, who tracked down a set of plans in the City Surveyor's office made, one imagines, when the building was taken over by the Corporation in 1907. The three-decker hall is illustrated in *London Illustrated News*, 21 December 1844.

33 Wainwright, *op. cit.*, 304.

34 *C.C.*, II, Appendix, 546f., which contains much information about the internal organization of Cheltenham College in 1863.

35 Quoted in Morgan, M. C., *Cheltenham College*, Cheltonian Society, 1968, 3.

36 Hart, Gwen, *A history of Cheltenham*, Leicester U.P., 1965, 225.

37 Quoted in Morgan, *op. cit.*, 5.

38 Described in Morgan, *op. cit.*, 15 and 27–9, and Little, B., *Cheltenham*, Batsford, 1952, ch. 6. (The old chapel is now the dining hall.)

39 Cf. Stone, Lawrence, 'Literacy and education in England 1640–1900', in *Past and Present*, no. 42, February 1969, 71: 'the latent functions of the classics . . . namely the reservation of higher culture as the distinctive monopoly of a social élite', etc.

40 Details in this para. from Bradley, A. G., *et al.*, *A history of Marlborough College*, Murray, 3rd ed., 1927. The buildings are described in Pevsner, *Wilts.*, 1963, 302f.

41 For Arnold's curriculum at Rugby, see Newsome, *op. cit.*, 64–6 ('The main aim of the teacher was to stimulate his pupils to acquire knowledge for themselves').

42 Details in this para. from Rowbotham, J. F., *The history of Rossall School*, Manchester: Heywood, n.d. I am grateful to the Bursar for further information.

43 See *V.C.H., Sussex*, II, 1907, 430–1.

44 Details in Leach, A. F., *A history of Bradfield College*, Frowde, 1900. For Radley, see Bryans, E., *A history of St Peter's College, Radley 1847–1924*, Oxford: Blackwell, 2nd ed. 1925, and Boyd, A. K., *The history of Radley College, 1847–1947*, Oxford: Blackwell, 1948. The cubicle system is described in Bryans, 66f., and Boyd, 42f. I am very grateful to Mr Paul Crowson for further information, and for showing me round the buildings at Radley.

45 Details from Kirk, K. E., *The story of the Woodard Schools*, Abingdon: Abbey Press, rev. ed., 1952, especially ch. 8 on 'Sites and buildings'. Also see *V.C.H., Sussex*, II, 1907, 431–4, and Nairn and Pevsner, *Sussex*, 1965, 256f., 398f., 542.
46 Quoted in Kirk, *op. cit.*, 144.
47 The early buildings are well described in Gerard, J., *Stonyhurst College*, Belfast: Ward, 1894, 128f. (including provision for science well in advance of most contemporary schools). Gerard also has a plan of the buildings in 1871 on p. 139.
48 For details of the Junior College (completed 1859), see Milburn, D., *A history of Ushaw College*, Durham: Ushaw College, 1964, 221f.
49 Details in Leetham, C. R., *Ratcliffe College 1847–1947*, Ratcliffian Assoc., 1950, 11f., 19f., 32f., 44f. The Rosminian Convent School in Park Road, Loughborough (1848), is said to have been the first Catholic day school supervised by nuns, but for an earlier convent school at Chelsea see the *Illustrated London News*, 19 April 1845.
50 *The history of Kingswood School*, by Three Old Boys, Kelly, 1898, gives a contemporary description of the 1851 building, pp. 199–200, with plan facing p. 200.
51 A few details of the 1869 building are in Record, S. P., *Proud century. The first hundred years of Taunton School*, Taunton: Goodman, 1948, 56f.
52 See Morley, J., and Monk-Jones, N., *Bishop's Stortford College 1868–1968*, Dent, 1969. It opened as the 'Dissenters' Proprietary School for the Eastern Counties'.
53 Details about Wellington are from Newsome, D., *A history of Wellington College, 1859–1959*, Murray, 1959, Bevir, J. L., *The making of Wellington College*, Arnold, 1920, and from *The Builder*, XIV (1856), 85–7, and XVII (1859), 55–7.
54 Pevsner, *Berks.*, 1966, 260.
55 Milford, L. S., *Haileybury College*, Unwin, 1909, 19. The dome was added by Sir Arthur Blomfield in 1876.
56 Ex inf. Borough Librarian, Bedford, who refers to an article in the *Bedfordshire Times*, 18 October 1963. The college stood in Ampthill Road, Kempston, on a site now occupied by Granada TV Rentals offices.
57 The original buildings at Clifton are described in Borwick, F. (ed.), *Clifton College annals and register 1862–1925*, Bristol: Arrowsmith, 1925, 1xvf., with plan facing p. lxviii. See also the essay on 'Clifton College buildings' by Betjeman, John, in Hammond, N. G. L. (ed.), *Centenary essays on Clifton College*, Bristol: Arrowsmith, 1962, 21f. For Malvern, see Blumenau, R., *A history of Malvern College 1865–1965*, Macmillan, 1965, ch. I, and Sayer, G. (ed.), *Age Frater. A portrait of a school*, Malvern College, 1965.
58 The twenty-one volumes of the Schools Inquiry Commission are listed in Higson, C.J.W. (ed.), *Sources for the history of education*, The Library Assoc., 1967, 164 (ref. E. 207).
59 *S.I.C.*, I, Appendix, 150.
60 *Ibid.*, 276–83 ('Next to a good master, there is nothing more important for a school than a good site and buildings').
61 E.g. the photograph of Nixon's School, Oxford (built 1659) in Seaborne, M., *Education*, Studio Vista, 1966, pl. 120.
62 The 1857 building at Rotherham is now a private house (no. 11 Moorgate Road), the school having moved to its present building (a former theological college of 1876) in 1890. See *Rotherham Grammar School 1483–1933*, Bradford: Lund, 1934.
63 Hutton, T. W., *King Edward's School, Birmingham, 1552–1952*, Oxford: Blackwell, 1952, 40–1, 187–8.
64 *S.I.C.*, I, 502.
65 *Ibid.*, 473. Other details in this para. from Graham, J. A., and Phythian, B. A., *The*

Manchester Grammar School 1515–1965, Manchester U.P., 1965, chs. 3–5.

66 Graham and Phythian, *op. cit.*, 67.

67 Hill, C. P., *The history of Bristol Grammar School*, Pitman, 1951, 79.

68 *Ibid.*, 84.

69 Details from Gayford, A. W. P., *History of Dulwich College*, the College, 1950, including plan of the Old College, p. 11, and a sketch map of the area, pp. 20–1. See also *Alleyn's College of God's Gift*, an illustrated brochure published by the College for the 350th anniversary (1969).

70 From *A short history of Doncaster Grammar School 1350–1950*, the School, n.d., *passim*. Since this chapter was written the 1850 school building has been demolished.

71 *The Builder*, IX (1851), 546–7. See also Palmer, C. F., *The history of the town and castle of Tamworth*, Tamworth: Thompson, 1845, 436–9. The school began in 1820 in Church Street, was rebuilt on the south side of Lichfield Street in 1837 and again in 1850 on the north side of Lichfield Street. The 1850 school survives as the printing works of Johnson & Allsopp Ltd., and still has two inscribed stones in one end wall (I am grateful to the Borough Librarian, Tamworth, for helping me to locate this building). What was almost certainly the 1837 building (of neo-Gothic design) also survives as Nos. 17 and 18 Lichfield Street, next to the Boot Inn.

72 Clegg, A. D. Lindsay, *A history of Wimborne Minster and district*, Bournemouth: The Outspoken Press, 1960, ch. 6; also contract and original plans in Dorset C.R.O. (ex inf. County Archivist).

73 *S.I.C.*, I, 277; other details from White, A., *A history of Loughborough Endowed Schools*, Loughborough Grammar School, 1969. I am grateful to the Headmaster, Mr N. S. Walter, for showing me around the buildings.

74 *The Builder*, IX (1851), 10, 26, 40, 63. For a similar dispute, see Thomas, A. W., *A history of Nottingham High School*, Nottingham: Bell, 1957, 170–1. On architectural competitions at this period, see Beckett, E., *A book on building*, Lockwood, 1876, 3–8.

75 Further details in Gray, I. E., and Potter, W. E., *Ipswich School, 1400–1950*, Ipswich: Harrison, 1950, ch. 8.

76 Details from *The Builder*, XIX (1856), 117–19, and Carrington, R. C., *Two schools. A short history of the St Olave's and St Saviour's Grammar School Foundation*, the Governors, 1962, which includes illustrations of the building of 1839 (frontis.) and 1855 (p. 49)—both neo-Tudor, the former by James Field and the latter by Henry Stock.

77 Details from *The Building News*, V (1859), 625, 1,014–15, Kelsey, P. H., *Four hundred years, 1552–1952. The story of Leeds Grammar School*, the School, n.d., and Price, A. C., *A history of Leeds Grammar School*, Leeds: Jackson, 1919, ch. 9. Other grammar schools rebuilt in the 1850s, according to Pevsner, may be seen at Lewes, Sussex (1851), and Morpeth, Northumberland (1859).

78 The Rye Hill school has been demolished to make way for part of the College of Commerce. (It is illustrated facing p. 43 of *The story of our school. The Royal Grammar School, Newcastle-upon-Tyne*, the School, 1924.) Surviving grammar-school buildings which, according to Pevsner, date from the 1860s, apart from those mentioned in this chapter, are: Felsted, Essex (1860–8); Norwich, former Middle School attached to Technical Institute (1861); West Buckland, Devon (1861); Highgate School, London (1865–8); Wormley, nr. Witley, Surrey (1867); Abingdon, Berks. (1869–70); Croydon, Trinity School of John Whitgift (1869–71).

79 Details from Thomas, *Nottingham High School, op. cit.*, including illustration of the unaltered school of 1868, facing p. 160; and an excellent article by Reynolds, C. L., on 'The buildings of Nottingham High School' in the *Transactions of the Thoroton Society*, LVII (1953), 33–42. (The original plan included nine classrooms, each 17 by 15 feet.) I am very grateful to Dr Thomas for conducting me around the building.

80 I am much indebted to Mr A. J. Lefley for information about the school at Doncaster, for showing me the building and for providing photographs. Scott's plans do not appear to have survived, but a later plan shows the original layout, including two classrooms measuring 14 by 12 feet and another above of 14 by 25 feet, all now extended. The cloisters beneath the schoolroom are now occupied by cloakrooms; the schoolroom is now the library, and retains its fine hammer-beam roof. The school before the cloisters were blocked up is shown on p. 18 of *A short history, op. cit.*

81 Nairn, I., *Nairn's London*, Penguin, 1966, 196 (where the architect is given as E. M., instead of Charles, Barry).

82 Details in Staunton, H., *The great schools, op. cit.*, 501–6. He says of the Lower School: 'This is not a Junior Department but a separate School, and is entirely distinct in its conduct and arrangements from the Upper School' (505).

83 Gayford, *op. cit.*, 25–6.

84 *The Builder*, XXVI (1868), 521–2. In the elementary schools of the 1860s, the usual allowance, as we noted in ch. 10, was 8 square feet per pupil.

85 Blanch, W. H., *Dulwich College and Edward Alleyn*, Allen, 1877, 23–5.

86 Further details in Gourlay, A. B., *A history of Sherborne School*, Winchester: Warren, 1951, Macdonald, A., *A short history of Repton*, Benn, 1929, and Clarke, H. L., and Weech, W. N., *History of Sedbergh School 1525–1925*, Sedbergh: Jackson, 1925.

87 The information about Uppingham is mainly drawn from Parkin, G. R., *Edward Thring*, Macmillan, 1910, *passim*, V.C.H., *Rutland*, I, 1908, 281f., and Bothamley, H. W., 'Some notes on the history of Uppingham School' (typescript in School library, 1949). I am very grateful to Mr Brian Belk for showing me the buildings and providing other information; and to Mr Anthony New of the Seely and Paget Partnership for details of the chapel.

88 There is an excellent study of the *Early buildings of Uppingham School*, by Heath, P., the School Press, 1967.

89 We noted earlier the building used as a gymnasium at Radley, which opened in January 1860, two months after that at Uppingham. A gymnasium had been opened at Addiscombe College in 1851 and open-air equipment was used at Cheltenham College in the 1850s (see Hearl, T., 'Military academies and English education', in *History of Education Society Bulletin*, no. 2, 1968, p. 15).

90 Parkin, *op. cit.*, 217–18.

Twelve

Conclusion

One of the curiosities of the literature on the history of English education is that on the one hand there are the general historical accounts dealing with legislative and other changes taking place mainly in London, and on the other hand a very large number of school histories dealing principally with the local aspects of school development and only rarely relating the story of a particular school to general educational history. Comparatively little attempt has so far been made to relate these two main categories of historical scholarship. Yet the importance of making such a link is surely vital. Certainly for the period before 1870 and the large-scale intervention of the central Government in education, it is almost impossible to consider general educational developments without basing one's conclusions on local examples; equally, it is highly undesirable to consider the history of one particular school without being aware of what was happening in other schools of similar type. All too often one finds that entirely commonplace changes are stressed in school histories, while new ideas go almost unnoticed. The time has surely come, however, when fresh attempts should be made to correlate the painstaking work of the numerous writers of school histories, and other local historians who mention education *en passant*, for this could lead eventually to a reinterpretation of many aspects of general educational history.

The picture that emerges from a study of individual school histories is inevitably fragmentary, and sometimes confusing. An attempt has been made in this book to adopt a consistent policy of referring the many changes which took place to the development of the school structure, both architectural and administrative. Here, it might appear, is a valid touchstone by which to assess the significance of particular events. For, it may be argued, if the changes made were of sufficient importance, then they are likely to have been reflected in alterations to the buildings and internal organization of the schools. Clearly, an increase in the number of children in a school will tend to affect its pattern of administration and lead to changes in its physical structure. Similarly, the ideas of educational reformers, if they are really to take effect, must sooner or later be expressed in organizational and architectural terms. Changes in the curriculum and methods of teaching are also likely to be reflected in the layout of the buildings and the arrangement of the classes.

It is true that these principles do not always apply, as we have had occasion to remark from time to time in the course of this study. For example, Eton expanded rapidly during the eighteenth and early nineteenth centuries, not by undertaking major rebuilding, but by expanding the tutorial system under which boys were boarded and taught in private houses. So, too, some of the headmasters who most influenced their schools, and in the process contributed to the general development of educational theory and practice, did so without altering the buildings, the most notable example being Thomas Arnold at Rugby. Occasionally one finds that important educational developments—as at Manchester and Bristol in the period 1840 to 1860—have not attracted the attention they deserve, partly at least because no major new buildings were provided during that period.

These, however, are the exceptions rather than the rule. In general, school buildings and internal organization are a true index, not only of the development of particular schools, but also of the educational and social outlook of the time. We may instance the emergence of distinct forms in the early grammar schools, the appearance of 'English' departments after about 1800, and the increasingly precise social-class differentiation which found expression in school buildings after 1840—as in the upper, middle and lower departments of Liverpool College and the various grades of middle-class school built by Nathaniel Woodard. There were also the schools built under the direct influence of new educational ideas, such as the so-called charity schools of the early eighteenth century, or the monitorial schools of the early nineteenth. Some of these ideas were particularly fruitful in terms of practical change, in which connection reference may be made to Wilderspin and Stow and their influence on elementary-school building, and to the founders of proprietary schools in the 1830s and 1840s who did so much to expand the contemporary conception of secondary education. It is often possible, not only to relate individual schools to general educational history, but also to relate theory to practice by examining changes in educational ideas and searching out actual examples of schools built in conformity with them.

This study has concentrated upon buildings which may still be examined on the ground, but it has also been found necessary to refer from time to time to schools now demolished or radically altered, in order to illustrate particular points. We have tried to give the famous schools their due, but have also broadened the inquiry to include even the humblest buildings. It may nevertheless be said that one can overemphasize the importance of the architectural evidence. Much as one may admire the spirit of Edward Thring at Uppingham, and his untiring efforts to improve the physical conditions of his school, it is not easy to agree wholly with his view that the 'almighty wall' is the 'supreme and final arbiter of schools'. On the other hand, when the Secretary of State for Education and Science gave his opinion in 1969 that the quality of education depends 70 per cent. on the teacher, 20 per cent. on the books and equipment, and only 10 per cent. on the premises in which it takes place, it may be wise to recall that he was speaking at a time of a possible surplus of newly-qualified teachers and a severe shortage of money for new buildings.[1] No doubt the truth of the matter lies somewhere between these two extremes.

One is obliged to admit, however, that the subject of school architecture and organization has been generally neglected by educational writers, in spite of notable exceptions from Mulcaster and Hoole to Lancaster and Thring.[2] A number of individual school buildings have been admired by some modern architectural authorities, but the architectural aspect has, in general, been similarly neglected, again with notable exceptions from Wren's concern with the layout of the school at Appleby Magna to the very definite views of the Gothic revivalists. A recent writer on the endowed schools at the beginning of Victoria's reign has suggested that with only a few exceptions, 'most were small and insignificant, mere adaptations of the country-cottage tradition'.[3] Such a statement does not take account of major buildings which were educationally unsuccessful and consequently no longer attract attention, such as those at Guilsborough (1668) and Kirkleatham (1709), or which have been replaced or destroyed, often because of their continued success, as with Ashbourne (1585) or the early buildings at Stonyhurst (1810). Even some of the relatively small and lesser-known schools rose well above the cottage type, such as those at Witney (1660) and Lucton (1708), and many others illustrated in this book.

From the purely architectural point of view, the most fruitful line of further inquiry may be to compare the development of school plans with changes in domestic architecture. The similarity of the school at Guildford (1557–86) to a Tudor town house has been noted, and clearly the main constituents of a school building, viz. the schoolroom (which corresponded to the hall or principal room of a house), the master's accommodation, and sometimes rooms for boarders, may be compared with the increasing complexity of house plans.[4] Similarly, the quadrangular plan of, for example, the Liverpool Blue Coat School and Ackworth School in the eighteenth century, and of some of the proprietary boarding schools in the nineteenth, bears comparison with the development of private mansions. Of equal interest is the value of school buildings in showing changes in architectural taste—as when the Commissioners at Wirksworth (1829) condemned 'the introduction of unnecessary and ill-placed decorations' on the new school there, at about the same time that the Trustees of the Bedford schools were specifically asking for a new building in a similar neo-Gothic style (1828); or when the Trustees of Rugby School expressed their distaste for the more flamboyant Gothic style of Butterfield's New Quad (1868). The transition from vernacular to classical styles, and then to the various forms of Gothic, has been dealt with in the course of this study and provides interesting side-lights on changing architectural fashions.

From the purely educational point of view, we have seen that the alteration or rebuilding of a school is invariably a sign of its success, or at any rate of important internal change. We have also seen how at certain turning-points in the history of

English education, new educational ideas were expressed, not only in theoretical treatises, but also in bricks and mortar. It is true that the internal planning of schools remained at a fairly rudimentary level for most of the period covered by this book. Even in the sixteenth and seventeenth centuries, however, we noted the building of upper and lower schools and of rooms for the teaching of classical and English subjects, as well as the appearance of school libraries; in addition, where boarding arrangements were made, as occurred particularly in the eighteenth century, the layout was further elaborated. The next major stage in the development of internal school-planning came in the elementary sphere with the monitorial schools after about 1810, and in the secondary sphere with the early proprietary schools of the 1820s and 1830s. A new era may finally be said to have opened in about 1850. The Committee of Council's model plans of 1851 had a major effect on the design of elementary schools, while the 1850s also saw the large-scale planning of a number of middle-class secondary schools. The complex factors at work have been discussed in the later chapters of this book, but we may perhaps say that the crucial change was, on the elementary side, from the system of mutual instruction to the simultaneous method, which resulted in the partial emergence of separate classrooms, and, on the secondary side, the comparable change to expository methods of teaching, which led to the introduction of classrooms and other rooms for specialist teaching, together with the transformation of the large schoolroom into an assembly hall. At the same time, the changes introduced by men like Sewell, Temple and Thring helped to bring the pupils—as, in a cruder way, was already the case in the elementary schools—under the closer control of the staff.

Thus the concept of education became fully institutionalized and a long period of uneven development ended with the triumph of the school as a distinctive social and architectural form.

Notes

1 Reported in *Education*, 27 June 1969, p. 840.

2 A revival of interest is, however, indicated by the special issue of the *Harvard Educational Review* devoted to the subject of 'Architecture and Education' (vol. 39, no. 4, 1969).

3 Bamford, T. W., *Rise of the public schools*, Nelson, 1967, 10.

4 For interesting work on the classification of house plans, see Eden, P., 'Smaller post-medieval houses in Eastern England', in Munby, L. M. (ed.), *East Anglian studies*, Cambridge: Heffer, 1968, further elaborated in Dr Eden's *Small houses in England 1520–1820* (Historical Assoc. pamphlet, 1969).

Appendices

Appendix 1

Sample survey: Leicestershire elementary schools with plans in County Record Office, c. 1840–70 (ex-Committee of Council, ref. Ma/E/BG)

Name of school	*Date of plan(s) (see note at end)*[1]	*Date of original building*	*Comments* (S.R. = Schoolroom. C.R. = Classroom B. = Boys. G. = Girls. I. = Infants.)
Arnesby National	1864	1860	Sch. built 1860 (White).[2] 1864 plan is for extra C.R.
Ashby National	n.d.	1836	Nat. Sch. 1836, 120 G. and 110 I. in 1877 (White). Sch. in North St. has plaque dated 1836. Plan shows infts. sch. with gallery and C.R., and Nat. Sch. adjoining (? *c.* 1850).
Barrow C. of E.	1857	1858	Nat. Sch. 1858, Inf. sch. 1868 (White). Plan shows usual 1851 layout[3] of S.R. and C.R.
Barwell National	n.d.	1871	Nat. Sch. 1871 (White). Plan shows separate S.R.s for B., G., and I. Typical 1851 layouts.
Birstall National	1860	1860	Nat. Sch. 1860 with 90 pupils (White). Plan shows S.R. with I. sch. or C.R. adjoining.
Buckminster National	n.d.	1841	Nat. Sch. 1841 (White). Includes early rudimentary plan with rooms for B. and G.
Burbage Parochial	1870	1870	Nat. Sch. 1870 (White). S.R.s for B., G. and I. Standard 1851-type layout.
Castle Donington National	1854	1854	Nat. Sch. 1854 (White). Plan shows S.R.s for B. and G. divided by movable partition. Similar to 1851 plan 7.
Coalville National	n.d.	*c.* 1840	Shows alterations of *c.* 1851 to sch. of *c.* 1840, demolished 1967.
Cosby Parochial	n.d.	1872	Nat. Sch. 1872, average attendance 85 (White).
Diseworth C. of E.	1861	1862	New sch. 1862 with C.R. and master's house attached (White).

Name of school	*Date of plan(s) (see note at end)*[1]	*Date of original building*	*Comments* (S.R. = Schoolroom. C.R. = Classroom B. = Boys. G. = Girls. I. = Infants.)
Earl Shilton National	1857	1859	Sch. built 1859 (White).
Enderby National	1858	1860	Nat. Sch. 1860, large room for 200, inft. sch. for 100 and 2 C.R.s. (White). Plan shows S.R.s for B., G., and I. standard 1851 layout.
Fleckney National	1872	1873	Nat. Sch. 1873 for 148 pupils (White).
Frisby National	1852	1854	Church Sch. built 1854 (White).
Gilmorton National	n.d.	1858	Nat. Sch. 1858 with 120 pupils (White).
Harby National	n.d.	1861	Nat. Sch. 1860 (White). Headmaster has poster showing sch. opened in 1861, designed for 100 pupils, average attendance 80.
Higham on the Hill National	1868	1869	Nat. Sch. 1869, 80 pupils (White).
Hinckley Trinity National	n.d.	1853	Nat. Sch. 1853 (White). Two-storey, B. on ground floor, G. above.
Hugglescote National	n.d.	1862	Nat. Sch. 1862, 150 pupils (White).
Husbands Bosworth National	1857/60	1858	Nat. Sch. 1858, Inft. Sch. added 1860 (White). Standard 1851 layout.
Ibstock British	1846	1847	Shows typical Lancasterian layout. Built 1847, closed pre-1877 (White).
Kegworth National	1856	1839	Nat. Sch. 1839 (White). Standard 1851 layout.
Kibworth National	1842?	1842	Original bdg. has plaque of 1842—plan includes two S.R.s and two C.R.s. Extended 1855 and 1872 (White).
Kilby National	1871	1872	Nat. Sch. 1872 (White).
Loughborough Emmanuel National Infants	1852/6	1852	Inft. Sch. in Victoria Road 1852, enlarged 1857 (White). Usual large room with gallery at end.
Loughborough Lancasterian	1858	1825	This is the old grammar sch. of 1825, altered 1858, now demolished.
Lubenham National	1857	1858	Nat. Sch. 1858 (White). S.R. for B. and G., standard layout of 1851.
Market Harborough National	1858	1836	Nat. Sch. 1836, upper storey added 1842 (White)—now the Adult School in Coventry Road.

Name of school	*Date of plan(s) (see note at end)*[1]	*Date of original building*	*Comments* (S.R. = Schoolroom. C.R. = Classroom B. = Boys. G. = Girls. I. = Infants.)
Markfield C. of E.	1861	1861	Nat. Sch. 1861—new Inft. Sch. added 1868 (White).
Melton Infant C. of E.	n.d.	1853	Usual room with gallery. Part of present St Mary's Inft. sch. has date-stone 1853. (Norman st.). Inft. sch. erected 1853 (White).
Narborough National	n.d.	1872	Nat. Sch. 1872 (White).
Netherseal National	1869	1871	Nat. Sch. 1871 (White).
Newbold Verdon Parochial	n.d.	1875	Parochial sch. 1875 (White).
Queniborough National	1847	1847	Shows typical early Nat. Sch. layout as given in 1840 *Minutes* of Committee of Council. Building has 1847 on it. 70 scholars in 1877 (White).
Quorndon National	1861	1835	Nat. Sch. 1835 and Inft. sch. 1836 (White). Present St Bartholomew's sch. has part said to date from 1837. Plan shows standard 1851 layout.
Rearsby Parochial	n.d.	1872	Nat. Sch. 1872 (White).
Rothley National	1852	1838	Sch. rebuilt 1838 and 1872 (White).
Sharnford National	n.d.	1845	Nat. Sch. 1845, enlarged 1871 (White). Plan shows S.R. for B. and G. separated by partition, with teacher's house adjoining. Later extension to make a mixed sch. and infts. room, with 1851 layouts.
Sheepy National	n.d.	1847	Nat. Sch. 1847 (White). Plan shows a Nat. Sch. layout consistent with this date.
Shepshed National	1870	1836	Nat. Sch. 1836, enlarged 1856 (White). One of the plans shows pre-1851 layout. The 1870 plan is of an infts. sch. with usual gallery. Another plan shows 1851 layout.
Sileby National	1858	1860	Nat. Sch. 1860 (White). Plan shows S.R. for B., G., and I. with usual 1851 layouts.
Stapleton C. of E.	n.d.	1847	Nat. Sch. 1847 (White).
Stoney Stanton Nat.	n.d.	1874?	Nat. Sch. presented to rector in 1874—C.R. added in that year (White).
Swannington National	1855	1862	Sch. built 1862 (White).
Thringstone National	n.d.	1844	Nat. Sch. 1844, C.R. added 1872 (White).

Name of school	*Date of plan(s) (see note at end)*[1]	*Date of original building*	*Comments* (S.R. = Schoolroom. C.R. = Classroom B. = Boys. G. = Girls. I. = Infants.)
Thurlaston National	1853	1855	Nat. Sch. rebuilt 1855, Inft. sch. 1859 (White). Usual 1851 layout.
Thurmaston National	1867	1844	Nat. Sch. 1844—200 pupils; teacher's house added 1856 (White). One plan shows sch. of two storeys (G. and B. over), 1867 plan shows addition of a C.R. on each floor. Building has date 1844 on gable (now Leics. Teachers' Centre).
Twyford National	1845?	1845	Nat. Sch. 1845, enlarged 1874 (White). Sch. dated 1845 stands opp. church
Waltham National	n.d.	1844	Nat. Sch. 1844/5, with C.R. and teacher's house—135 pupils (White).
Whitwick National	1857/67	1858	Nat. Sch. 1858 (White). Still stands in Market Place. Plan shows S.R.s. for B., G., and I., usual layout of 1851. 1867 plan shows proposed larger I. room.
Wigston Magna National	1841/69	1839	Nat. Sch. 1839 (White). 1841 plan is of sch. now demolished—also a plan of 1842 shows proposed addition of C.R. and teacher's house. 1869 plan is of a new sch. with usual layout for B., G., and I.—still in use as annexe of junior sch. in Long St.
Woodhouse Eaves Nat.	1860	1843	Nat. Sch. 1843—100 pupils—teacher's residence added 1860 (White).
Worthington, Griffydam Wesleyan	1852	1852	Plan shows Tudor Gothic elev. with datestone 1852. Other plans show a two-storey bdg., with I. on ground floor with usual gallery and C.R. Above is a S.R., divided by curtain, with C.R. adjoining.
Worthington National	1871	1872	Nat. Sch. 1872 (White).
Wymeswold National	1857	1845	Nat. Sch. 1845 (White).

Notes

1 Each school usually has several plans relating to it: where a plan is dated it does not necessarily relate to the earliest building on the site, or to a complete school. Many of these plans relate to alterations to an existing building and some are of proposals never carried out.
2 'White' is reference to Wm. White's *Directory of Leicestershire* (1877).
3 '1851 layouts' are those contained in the *Memorandum respecting the organization of schools in parallel groups of benches and desks*, in *Committee of Council Minutes, 1851–2*, pp. 78–91. These were the standard official layouts until at least 1870.

Appendix 2

Elementary day schools illustrated in *The Builder*, 1843–70

The numbers given in the columns headed 'Plan' and 'Elevation' are the pages of the annual volumes of *The Builder* on which the plan and/or elevation of the school appears. The number of square feet per child has been calculated on the combined area of schoolroom(s) and classroom(s), where given.

Volume	*Year*	*Name of school*	*Cost, £*	*No. of places*	*Cost per place, £*	*Architect*	*Plan*	*Elevation*	*Square feet per child*
IV	1846	Crescent Chapel Sch., Liverpool	3,500	1,160	3·0	J. A. Picton		546	
VI	1848	St Paul's Sch., Oxford	650			Not stated	223	223	
VII	1849	Cavendish St. Sch., Manchester	4,700			Edw. Walters		102	
		Free sch., Yarmouth		560		Messrs. Brown & Kerr		294	
		Northern Sch., St Martin-in-the-Fields, London	2,433	720	3·4	James Wild		451	
VIII	1850	Trinity Sch., Margate	1,033	300	3·4	Mr Caveler		259	
		St John's Sch., Liverpool	1,355			Mr Hay		462	
		Sch. at Croft, Hereford				W. B. Mountfort		571	
IX	1851	Free Sch., St Helen's (R.C.), Paddington, London	1,200			Mr Meyer	595	595	

Volume	*Year*	*Name of school*	*Cost, £*	*No. of places*	*Cost per place, £*	*Architect*	*Plan*	*Elevation*	*Square feet per child*
X	1852	Hythe National Sch.	1,270	480	2·6	Jos. Messenger	40	41	B. & G. 8·0; Infts. 5·3
		Trinity Sch., Reading	900	100	9·0	John Billing	409	409	9·2
XI	1853	West Meon Sch., Hants.	800	200	4·0	John Colson		117	
		Infant Sch., Redcliffe, Bristol	789			G. Godwin	248	249	
		St John's Sch., Angell-town, North Brixton	1,100	400	2·8	B. Ferrey		360	
		St Augustine's Sch., Ramsgate				A. Welby Pugin		377	
		Mansel Lacy National Sch., Herefordshire	600	140	4·3	Mr Nicholson	405	405	10·7
		St Anne's Sch., Edgehill, Liverpool	1,150			W. W. Lloyd	504	505	
		St. John's National Sch., Margate		350		G. Mair	547	547	8·7
		St Augustine's National Sch., Liverpool	2,800	900	3·1	H. P. Horner		655	
XII	1854	St Mark's Sch., Liverpool	2,200	600	3·7	T. D. Barry	534	535	8·0
		New houses & Sch., Fulham				F. & H. Francis	582	583	
XIII	1855	St Mildred's, Canterbury	1,700			Jos. Messenger	147	147	
		Ludlow National Sch.	2,400	600	4·0	T. Nicholson	438	439	B. & G. 7·7; Infts. 4·5
XIV	1856	Angmering, National Sch., Sussex				S. S. Teulon		583	
		St Peter's Parish Sch., Leeds	937			Dobson & Chorley	662	663	9·0 (stated)

Volume	*Year*	*Name of school*	*Cost, £*	*No. of places*	*Cost per place, £*	*Architect*	*Plan*	*Elevation*	*Square feet per child*
XV	1857	St George's Sch., Battersea, London	3,200	500	6·4	Jos. Peacock		387	
XVI	1858	Sch. at Agar-town, St Pancras, London				S. S. Teulon		395	
XVII	1859	National Sch., Clerkenwell, London		300		W. P. Griffith		677	
XVIII	1860	St Mary-the-Less Sch., Lambeth, London	3,365	700	4·8	J. L. Pearson	496	497	8·6
		National Sch., St Giles in the Fields, Bloomsbury, London		1,500 (?)		E. M. Barry	818	819	5·2 (?)
XX	1862	St Paul's Sch., Clerkenwell, London		480		Roger Smith		7	
		Collyer Memorial Sch., Peckham	1,500			J. G. Stapleton		293	
XXI	1863	Holy Trinity, Hoxton	1,687	600	2·8	Mr Ashpitel		909	
XXII	1864	Parochial Sch., Milborne Port				Henry Hall		792	
		Parish Sch., St George the Martyr, Queen Square, London	2,800			S. S. Teulon	793	793	
XXIII	1865	Sch. in North-umberland St., Poplar, London	3,687	900	4·0	Messrs Francis	431	431	7·2
XXIV	1866	Congregational Sch., Liscard, nr. Liverpool	1,200	250	4·8	H. Vale	14	14	8·5
XXV	1867	Parish Sch., St Saviour's, Paddington, London	5,000	300	16·7	Edw. Roberts	212	212	12·2
XXVII	1869	Parish Sch., St Mary's, Leicester	1,950			Jos. Goddard	846	847	

Appendix 3

(A) Middle-class schools illustrated in *The Builder* before 1870

(The numbers given in the last three columns are the pages of the annual volumes of *The Builder*.)

Volume	*Year*	*Name of school*	*Architect*	*Plan*	*Elev-ation*	*Description*
VIII	1850	Friends' School, Bristol	W. Armstrong		91	91
IX	1851	Grammar School Tamworth, Staffs.	Sydney Smirke		547	546
XI	1853	Grammar School, Swansea, Glam.	Thomas Taylor	72	73	72
XIV	1856	Wellington College, Sandhurst, Berks.	John Shaw	86	87	85–6; also in 1859 vol., pp. 55–7
		Grammar School of St Olave's and St John's, Southwark	Allen, Snooke and Stock	118	119	117
XV	1857	Philological School, New Road, Marylebone	W. G. & E. Habershon	594	595	594
XVI	1858	Landsdowne Proprietary College, Bath	James Wilson		195	194
XVII	1859	Congregational School, Eccles, Lancs.	Poulton & Woodman		821	820
XVIII	1860	St Cuthbert's College, & St Aloysius' R.C. School, Ushaw, Durham	E. W. Pugin	152	153	152

Volume	*Year*	*Name of school*	*Architect*	*Plan*	*Elevation*	*Description*
XIX	1861	Godolphin School, Hammersmith	C. H. Cooke	548	549	548
		St Lawrence's College, Ampleforth, N. Yorks.	J. A. Hansom		789	791
XX	1862	St Mary's College, Harlow, Essex	R. J. Withers	28	29	28
XXII	1864	Framlingham College, Suffolk	Frederick Peck		81	80–3
		Fettes College, Edinburgh	David Bryce	846	847	845–6
XXIII	1865	Malvern Proprietary College, Worcs.	C. F. Hansom	448	47 & 449	46–8
XXV	1867	Lower Middle Class Schools, Ardingly, Sussex	Slater & Carpenter	836	837	835–6
XXVI	1868	College of God's Gift, Dulwich	Charles Barry	530	531	521–2
		College Chapel, St Mary & St Nicholas, Lancing, Sussex	R. H. Carpenter	944	945	602–3
XXVII	1869	Grammar School, Louth, Lincs.	James Fowler	86	86	85
		West of England Dissenters' College, Taunton, Somerset	Joseph James	186	187	189
		Bedfordshire Middle Class School, Bedford	F. Peck	766	767	765–6
XXVIII	1870	Great Hall, Dulwich College	Charles Barry		307	304
		Charterhouse School, Godalming, Surrey	P. C. Hardwick		567	566

(B) Middle-class schools illustrated in *The Building News* before 1870

(The numbers given in the last three columns are the pages of the annual or biannual volumes of *The Building News*.)

Volume	*Year*	*Name of school*	*Architect*	*Plan*	*Elev-ation*	*Description*
IV	1858	Sudbury Grammar School, Suffolk	Robert Pope	1,102	1,103	1,102
V	1859	Leeds Grammar School, W. Yorks.	E. M. Barry	1,014	1,015	625
VII	1861	Clifton College, Bristol	C. Hansom		856	
		Christ's College, Finchley	Edward Roberts		479	471–2
X	1863	Vaughan Library, Harrow, Middlesex	G. Gilbert Scott		669	668
XI	1864	Albert Middle Class College, Framlingham, Suffolk	Frederick Peck		904	902
XII	1865	Wesleyan College, Belfast	W. Fogerty		533	
XIII	1866	Hallfield School, Bradford, W. Yorks.	T. C. Hope	392	395	392
XV	1868	Middle-class College, Bedford	Frederick Peck	47	47	49

County list

A list of places with schools mentioned in the text, arranged by County (see Index for page references)

[*Note*: Schools and colleges which are better known by name of founder etc. will also be found in the Index under their own names.]

BEDFORDSHIRE
Bedford

BERKSHIRE
Abingdon
Bradfield
Crowthorne
Newbury
Radley
Reading
Shinfield
Uffington
Windsor

BUCKINGHAMSHIRE
Buckingham
Eton
High Wycombe
Linford, Great
Marlow, Great
Wolverton

CAMBRIDGESHIRE
Barrington
Bottisham
Burrough Green
Cambridge
Chippenham
Elsworth
Ely
Gamlingay
Heydon
Wisbech

CHESHIRE
Carrington
Chester
Church Coppenhall
Compstall
Crewe
Macclesfield

CORNWALL
Truro

CUMBERLAND
St Bees

DERBYSHIRE
Ashbourne
Chesterfield
Long Eaton

Repton
Risley
Spinkhill
Staveley
Wirksworth

DEVONSHIRE
Buckland, West
Chawleigh
Cruwys Morchard
Exeter
Kentisbeare
Lamerton
Lustleigh
Milton Abbot
Ottery St Mary
Sandford
Sydenham Damerel
Tiverton

DORSET
Dorchester
Osmington
Sherborne
Wimborne

DURHAM
Durham
Ushaw

ESSEX
Bentley, Little
Boreham
Chigwell
Childerditch
Coopersale
Felsted
Foxearth
Harlow
Leigh
Leyton
Romford
Saffron Walden
West Ham

GLOUCESTERSHIRE
Bristol
Cheltenham
Clifton
Gloucester
Kingswood
Lowbands (formerly Worcs.)
Snig's End

HAMPSHIRE
Basingstoke
Highclere
Meon, West
Portsmouth
Winchester

HEREFORDSHIRE
Cradley
Hereford
Kington
Lucton
Mansel Lacy
Ross-on-Wye
Weobley

HERTFORDSHIRE
Amwell, Little
Berkhamsted
Bishop's Stortford
Hatfield
Hertford
Hoddesdon
St Albans
Stevenage
Ware
Wheathampstead

HUNTINGDONSHIRE
Huntingdon

KENT (excluding former County of London)
Brabourne
Canterbury
Hythe
Ightham
Lydd
Maidstone
Margate
Monk's Horton
Orpington

Ramsgate
Sittingbourne
Tonbridge
Willesborough

LANCASHIRE
Blackburn
Bolton
Burnley
Bury
Cheapside
Colne
Eccles
Farington
Fleetwood
Habergham
Haslingden
Hawkshead
Lancaster
Liverpool
Manchester
Oldham
Stonyhurst
Warthfold

LEICESTERSHIRE (*See also* Appendix 1)
Appleby
Ashby-de-la-Zouch
Barkestone
Billesdon
Bowden, Great
Burton Overy
Claybrooke
Coalville
Congerstone
Enderby
Frisby
Harby
Husband's Bosworth
Ibstock
Kibworth Beauchamp
Knipton
Leicester
Long Clawson
Loughborough
Market Bosworth
Market Harborough
Medbourne
Melton Mowbray
Nailstone
Newtown Linford
Osgathorpe
Queniborough
Quorn
Ratcliffe-on-the-Wreake
Rothley
Sapcote
Sheepy Magna
Sibson
Snarestone
Theddingworth
Thrussington
Thurcaston
Thurlaston
Thurmaston
Thurnby
Twyford
Wigston Magna
Woodhouse
Worthington
Wymondham

LINCOLNSHIRE
Boston
Corby Glen
Denton
Grantham
Keelby
Lincoln
Louth
Stamford
Wainfleet

LONDON (former County of London)
For London schools see index under:
Battersea
Bermondsey
Camberwell
Chelsea
Deptford
Finsbury
Fulham
Hammersmith
Hampstead
Holborn
Islington

Kensington
Lambeth
Lewisham
London (City)
Paddington
Poplar
St Marylebone
St Pancras
Shoreditch
Southwark
Stepney
Wandsworth
Westminster

MIDDLESEX (excluding former County of London)
Enfield
Finchley
Harrow
Isleworth
Mill Hill
Northwood
Stanmore
Stanwell
Tottenham
Willesden

NORFOLK
Creake, North
Elmham, North
Norwich
Overstrand
Salthouse
Yarmouth, Great

NORTHAMPTONSHIRE
Abthorpe
Ashton
Aynho
Barnwell St Andrews
Brigstock
Burton Latimer
Clipston
Corby
Cottesbrooke
Courteenhall
Culworth
Daventry
Ecton
Finedon
Gretton
Guilsborough
Hanging Houghton
Higham Ferrers
Kettering
King's Cliffe
Lowick
Luddington
Northampton
Paulerspury
Peterborough
Weekley
Wellingborough
Yelvertoft

NORTHUMBERLAND
Berwick-on-Tweed
Ford
Morpeth
Newcastle upon Tyne
Scremerston

NOTTINGHAMSHIRE
Barnby-in-the-Willows
Bulwell
Bunny
Cuckney
Haughton
Newark-on-Trent
Nottingham
Southwell
Tuxford
Worksop

OXFORDSHIRE
Clifton Hampden
Ewelme
Oxford
Thame
Witney

RUTLAND
Casterton, Little
Oakham
Tinwell
Uppingham

SHROPSHIRE
Ludlow
Shrewsbury

SOMERSET
Bath
Bruton
Frome
Ilminster
Milborne Port
Sidcot
Stratton-on-the-Fosse
Taunton
Wells

STAFFORDSHIRE
Tamworth
Tettenhall
Wolverhampton

SUFFOLK
Beccles
Bury St Edmunds
Framlingham
Ipswich
Long Melford
Sudbury
Walsham le Willows

SURREY (excluding former County of London)
Barnes
Caterham
Cheam
Croydon
Ewell
Godalming
Guildford
Wimbledon
Wormley

SUSSEX
Angmering
Ardingly
Battle
Brighton
Buxted
Cowfold
Eastbourne
Horsham
Hurstpierpoint
Lancing
Lewes
Midhurst
Rye
Shoreham, New

WARWICKSHIRE
Birmingham
Coventry
Rugby
Stratford-upon-Avon

WILTSHIRE
Corsham
Crudwell
Farley
Marlborough
Mere
Mildenhall

WORCESTERSHIRE
Broadway
King's Norton (now part of Birmingham)
Lowbands (now Glos.)
Malvern
Wolverley

YORKSHIRE
Ackworth
Ampleforth
Apperley Bridge
Arksey
Bradford
Burnsall
Chapeltown
Cliffe
Doncaster
Drax
Drighlington
Fulneck
Halton Gill
Handsworth
Hull
Ilkley
Kirkleatham
Laughton-en-le-Morthen

Leeds
Leyburn
Malham
Otley
Redcar
Richmond
Rotherham
Saltaire
Scorton
Sedbergh
Sheffield
Shelf
Silcoates
Threshfield
Wakefield
York

NORTHERN IRELAND
Belfast

SCOTLAND
Lanarkshire
Glasgow
New Lanark
Midlothian
Edinburgh

WALES
Caernarvonshire
Bangor
Flintshire
Penley
Glamorgan
Dowlais
Swansea
Monmouthshire
Monmouth

Index

Plate 1 An English fourteenth-century school

Plate 2 Boy being 'handed', *c.* 1350

Plate 3 A fifteenth-century school

Plate 4 Schoolmaster and pupils, early sixteenth century

Plate 5 Winchester College, Hants., 1382 and later

Plate 6 Winchester, window-seats in original schoolroom, 1387–94; fireplace later

Plate 7 Eton College, Bucks., original schoolroom 1479–88; pillars later

Plate 8 Higham Ferrers, Northants., 1422

Plate 9 Stratford-upon-Avon, Warwicks., schoolroom, 1427; furniture later

Plate 10 Ewelme, Oxon., 1437–50

Plate 11 King's Norton, Warwicks., fifteenth century

Plate 12 Westminster, monks' dormitory, built *c.* 1090, used as schoolroom from 1602

Plate 13 Norwich, carnary, built fourteenth century, used as schoolroom from 1553

Plate 14 Tudor schoolmaster

Plate 15 Blackburn, Lancs., school seal, 1567

Plate 16 Louth, Lincs., school seal, 1552

Plate 17 Ipswich, Suffolk, Wolsey's Gate, *c.* 1530

Plate 18
Berkhamsted, Herts., *c.* 1541

Plate 19 Guildford, Surrey, 1557–86

Plate 20 Guildford, library, 1586; rearranged 1962

Plate 21 Ashbourne, Derbs., 1585–1603

Plate 22 Enfield, Middx, *c.* 1586

Plate 23 Felsted, Essex, pre-1564

Plate 24 Coventry, Warwicks., Bablake School, pre-1560

Plate 25 Uppingham, Rutland, 1584

Plate 26 Uppingham, inscription, 1584

Plate 27 Hawkshead, Lancs., 1585

Plate 28 Hawkshead interior, 1585; inscription later

Plate 29
Uppingham, school seal, 1584

Plate 30
An 'English' schoolmaster

Plate 31 Cheltenham, Glos., Pate's School, 1586

Plate 32 Rye, Sussex, Peacock's School, 1636

Plate 33 Wymondham, Leics., school (L.) built in churchyard, 1637

Plate 34 Medbourne, Leics., north transept adapted as school *c.* 1650

Plate 35 Uffington, Berks., c. 1617

Plate 36 Ilkley, Yorks., 1637

Plate 37 Market Harborough, Leics., 1614

Plate 38 Weobley, Herefs., pre-1653

Plate 39
Tiverton, Devon, Chilcot's School, 1611

Plate 40
Weekley, Northants., Latham's School, 1624

Plate 41 Marlow, Bucks., Sir William Borlase's School, 1624

Plate 42 Burnsall, Yorks., Sir William Craven's School, *c.* 1605

Plate 43 Burton Latimer, Northants., 1622

Plate 44 Stanwell, Middx, Lord Knyvett's School, 1624

Plate 45 Beccles, Suffolk, Sir John Leman's School, 1631

Plate 46 Charterhouse, Finsbury, London, gown boys' hall, sixteenth–seventeenth century

Plate 47 Chigwell, Essex, 1629, and later wing

Plate 48 Tiverton, Devon, Blundell's School, 1604

Plate 49 Blundell's School, interior, 1604

Plate 50 Shrewsbury School, 1595–1630

Plate 51 Shrewsbury, 'Top Schools'

Plate 52 Shrewsbury, figures over archway, 1630

Plate 53 Schoolmaster, 1631

Plate 54 A Winchester 'scob'

Plate 55 Harrow, Middx, 1615, original school (L.), altered and extended (R.) in 1819

Plate 56 Harrow, interior, 1615 and later

Plate 57 Witney, Oxon., 1660

Plate 58 Guilsborough, Northants., 1668

Plate 59 Tuxford, Notts., Read's School, 1668–9

Plate 60 Corby Glen, Lincs., Read's School, 1668–9

Plate 61 Corsham, Wilts., school and hospital, 1668

Plate 62 Clipston, Northants., school and hospital, 1667

Plate 63 Winchester, new schoolroom, 1683–7

Plate 64 Winchester, new schoolroom, interior

Plate 65 Eton, Upper School from Lupton's Tower, 1688–91

Plate 66 Eton, Upper School, interior

Plate 67 Christ's Hospital, London, rebuilding of 1682

Plate 68 Christ's Hospital, Sir John Moore's Writing School, 1695, now demolished

Plate 69 Sir John Moore's Writing School, interior

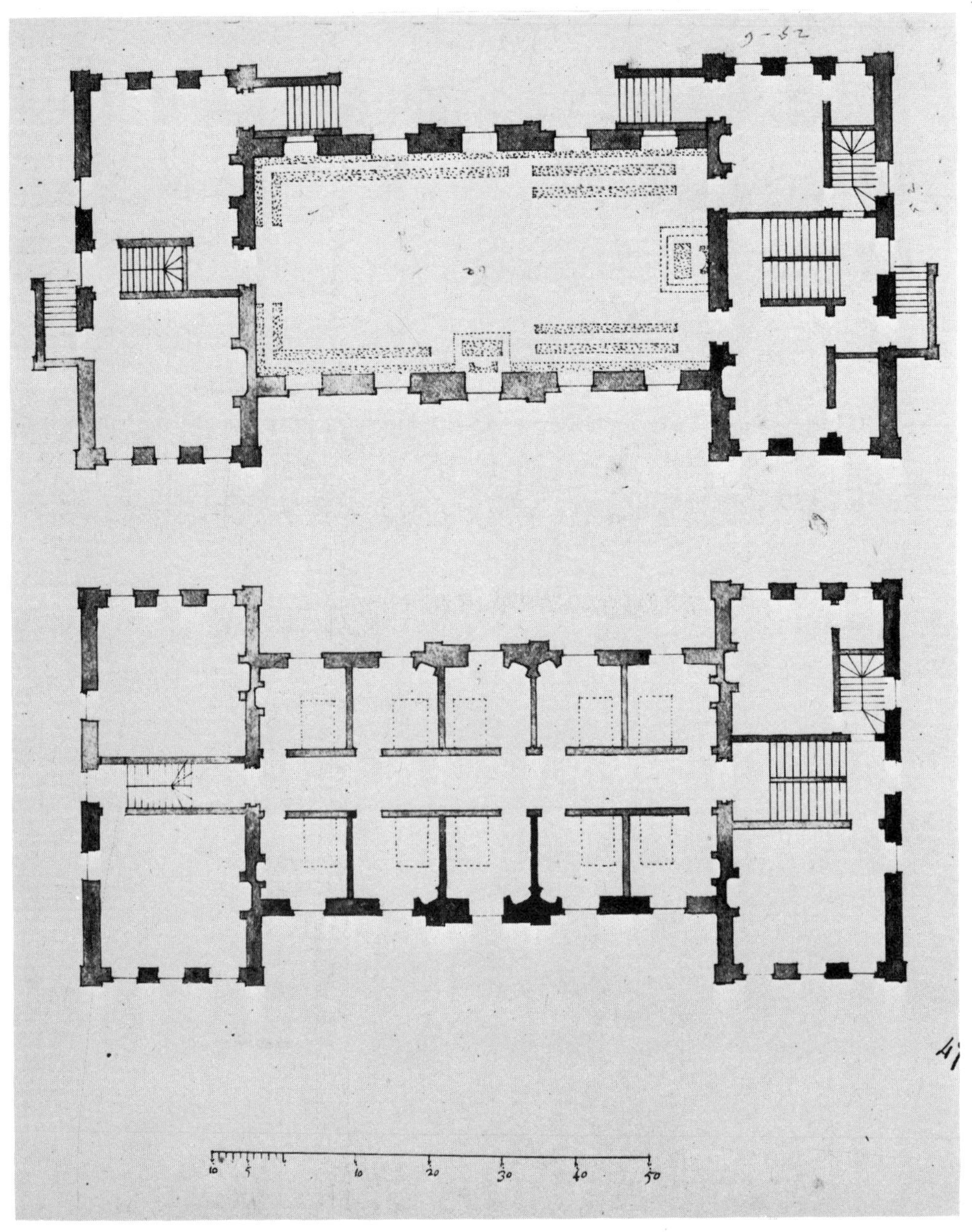

Plate 70 Wren's design for Sir John Moore's School, Appleby Magna, Leics.

Plate 71 Appleby Magna, Sir John Moore's School, 1693–7

Plate 72 Statue of Sir John Moore in Appleby School

Plate 73 Archbishop James Margetson, founder of Drighlington School, Yorks., 1671

Plate 74   A school interior, 1672

Plate 75   Courteenhall, Northants., original schoolroom, 1680

Plate 76 Eton, library, 1726–9, before restoration

Plate 77 Westminster, Little Dean's Yard and school gateway, 1734

Plate 78 Westminster, Scholars' dormitory, 1722; restored 1947

Plate 79 Westminster, dormitory, interior before remodelling

Plate 80 Scorton, Yorks., school (L.) and master's house (R.), *c.* 1720

Plate 81 Kibworth Beauchamp, Leics., school (R.) and master's house (L.), 1725

Plate 82 Kirkleatham, Yorks., Sir William Turner's School, 1709

Plate 83 Lucton, Herefs., Sir John Pierrepont's School, 1708

Plate 84 Risley, Derbs., 1706

Plate 85 Sedbergh, Yorks., rebuilt 1716

Plate 86 Denton, Lincs., 1720

Plate 87 Berwick-on-Tweed, Northumb., The Corporation's Academy, 1798

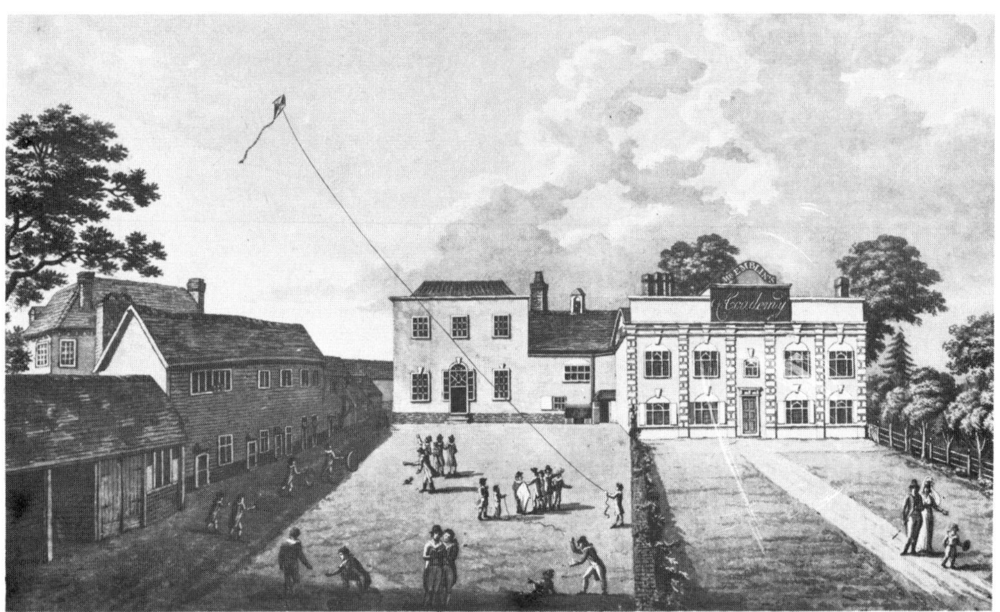

Plate 88 Leyton, Essex, Mr. Emblin's Academy, 1785

Plate 89 'The School of Deportment' by Edward Bunney, 1760–1848

Plate 90 Westminster, Blue Coat School, 1709

Plate 91 Westminster, Blue Coat School, interior

Plate 92 Westminster, Grey Coat School, 1701; restored 1955

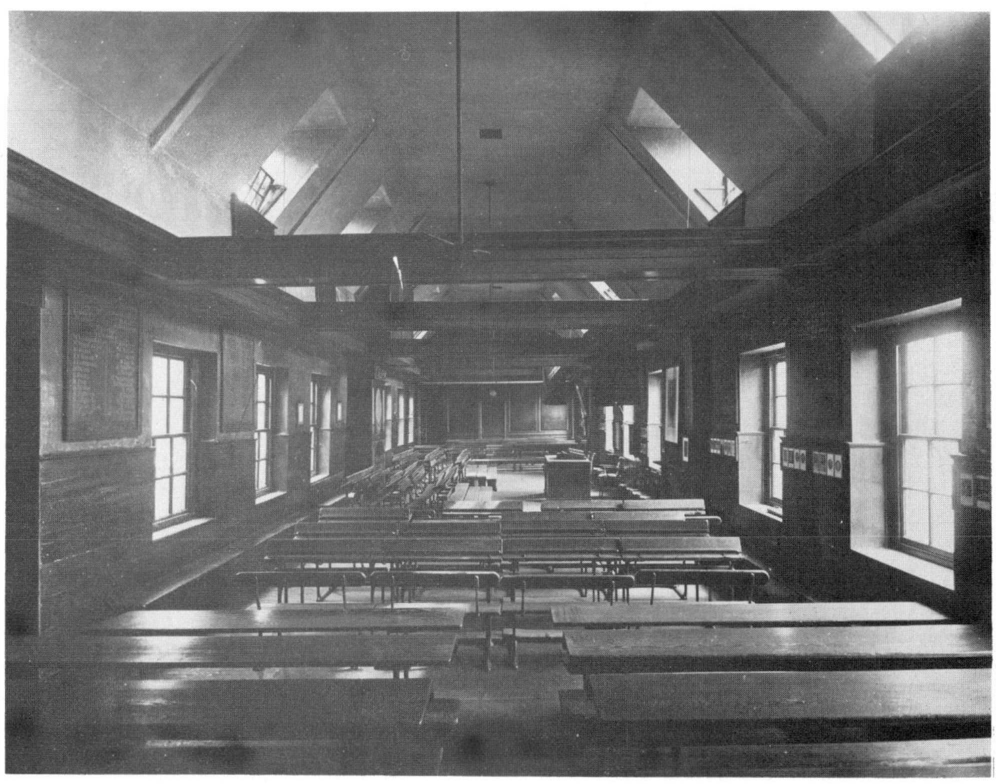

Plate 93 Westminster, Grey Coat School, hall; photo. taken in 1911

Plate 94 (*left*) Kensington, London, Charity School, 1713, now demolished

Plate 95 Kensington Charity School, sketch plan

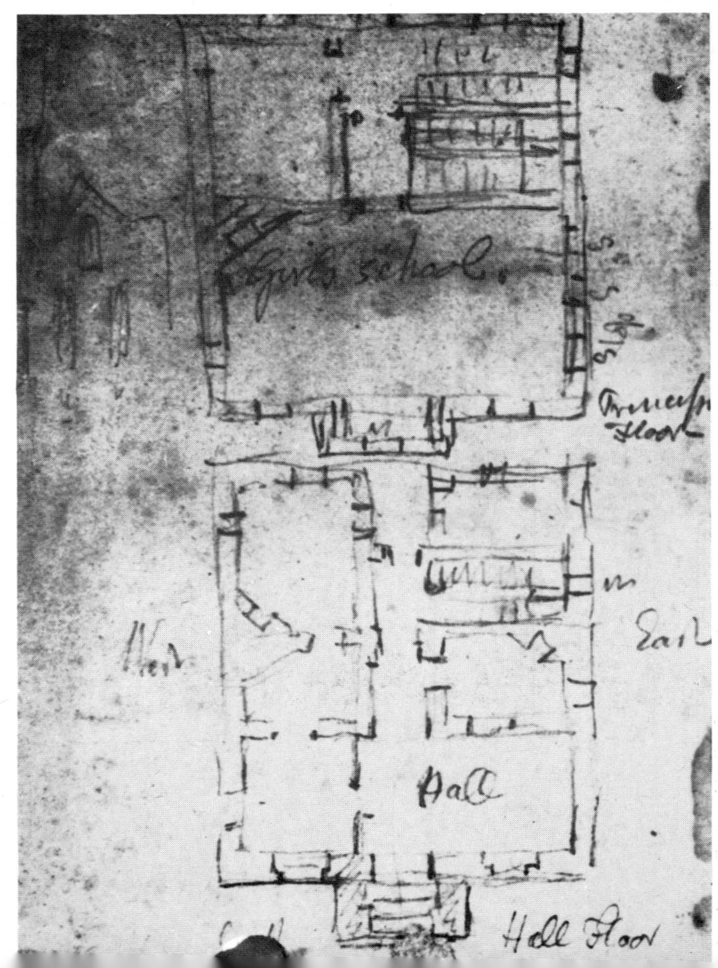

Plate 96 Bermondsey, London, Rotherhithe Charity School, 1797

Plate 97 Figure of boy from Rotherhithe School, 1742 (?)

Plate 98 Figure of girl from Rotherhithe School, 1742 (?)

Plate 99 Holborn, London, Hatton Garden Charity School, *c.* 1721; photo. taken in 1910

Plate 100 Liverpool Blue Coat School, 1716–25

Plate 101 Northampton, Monument in All Saints Church, 1747

Plate 102 Hertford, Christ's Hospital Girls' School, 1778

Plate 103 Ackworth, Yorks., school opened 1779, built as a foundling hospital, 1758

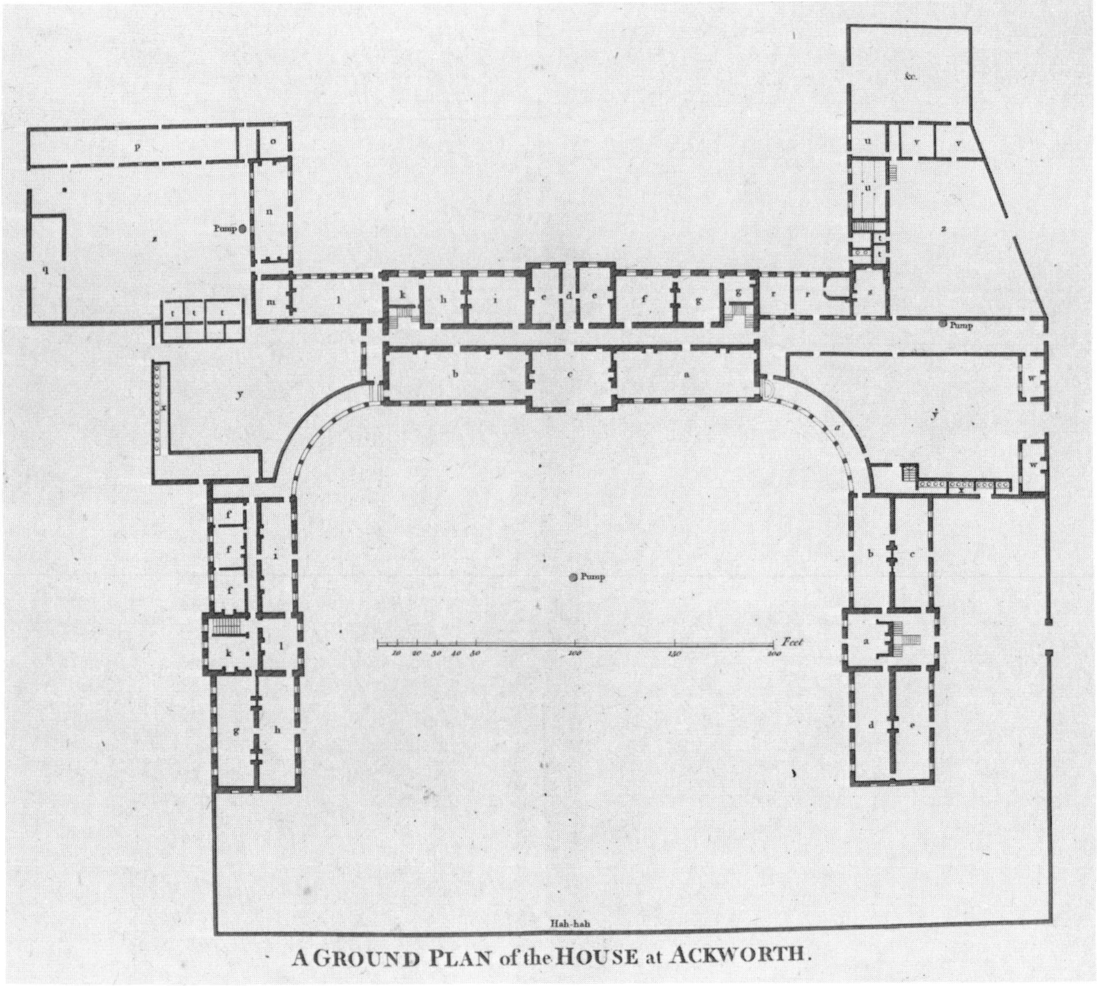

A GROUND PLAN of the HOUSE at ACKWORTH.

Plate 104 Ackworth, plan of school, *c.* 1780

Plate 105 Frome, Som., Bluecoat School and almshouse, 1728

Plate 106 Frome, Som., Stevens' Asylum at Keyford, 1798–1803; now demolished

Plate 107 King's Cliffe, Northants., master's house (L.) and boys' school (R.), 1749

Plate 108 King's Cliffe, entrance to master's house, *c.* 1752

Plate 109 Lowick, Northants., door of schoolroom, *c.* 1725

Plate 110 Shinfield, Berks., school of 1707 in centre, with extensions of 1860 (R.) and 1889 (L.)

Plate 111 Wimbledon, Surrey, octagonal school *c.* 1773

Plate 112 (*left*)
Bunny, Notts., arms and inscription, 1700

Plate 113 Thurcaston, Leics., inscription, 1715

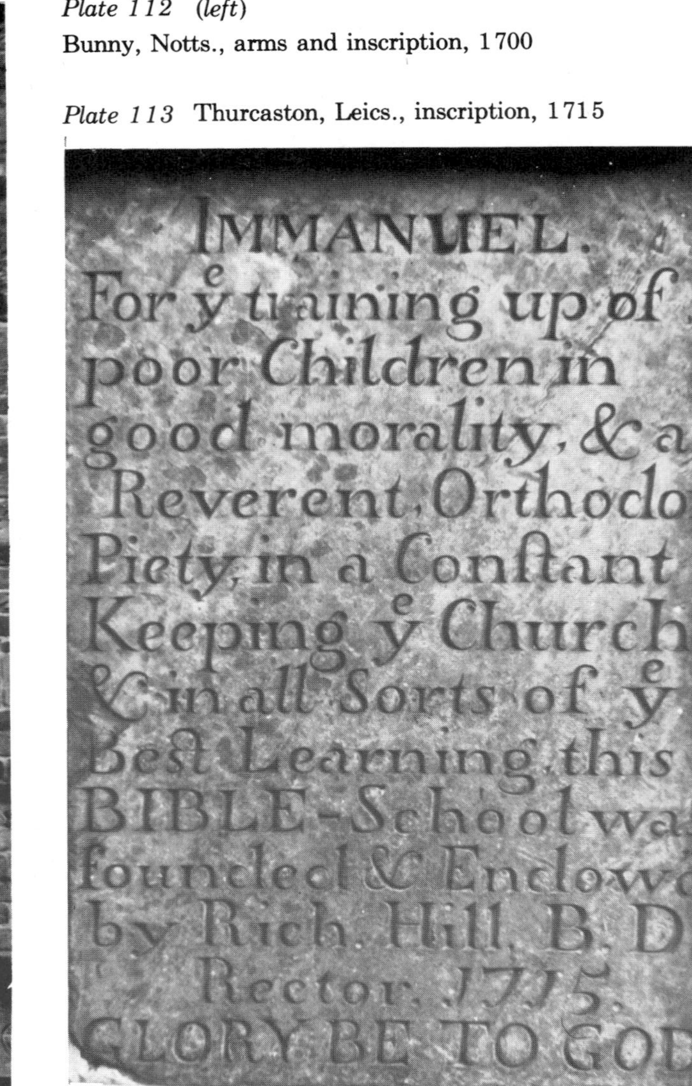

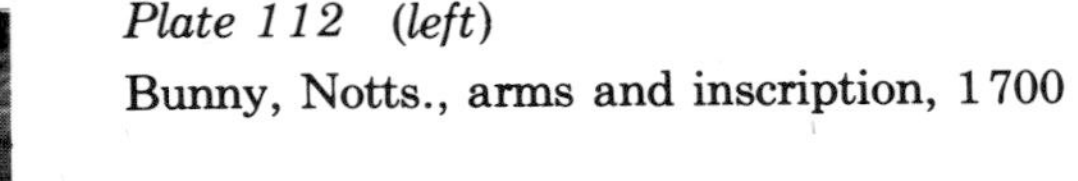

Plate 114 Chippenham, Cambs., Lord Orford's School, *c.* 1714

Plate 115 Shrewsbury, Bowdler's School, 1724

Plate 116 Rotherham, Yorks., Feoffees' School, 1776

Plate 117 Shrewsbury, Allatt's School, 1800

Plate 118 Village school interior, 1780

Plate 119 Dame school interior, 1783

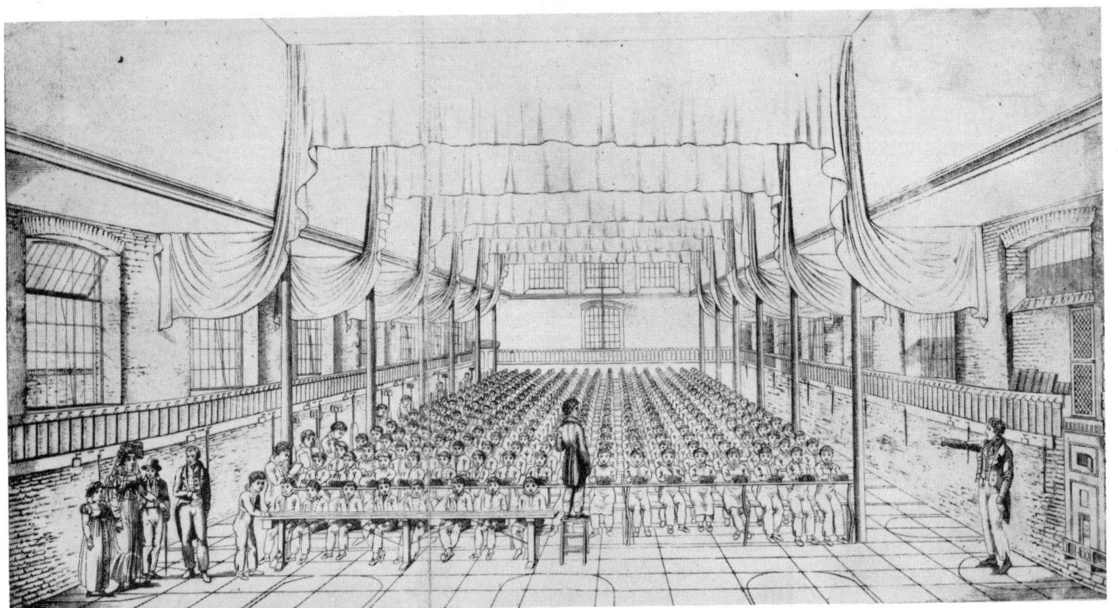

Plate 120 Southwark, London, Central School of British and Foreign School Society, Borough Road, early nineteenth century

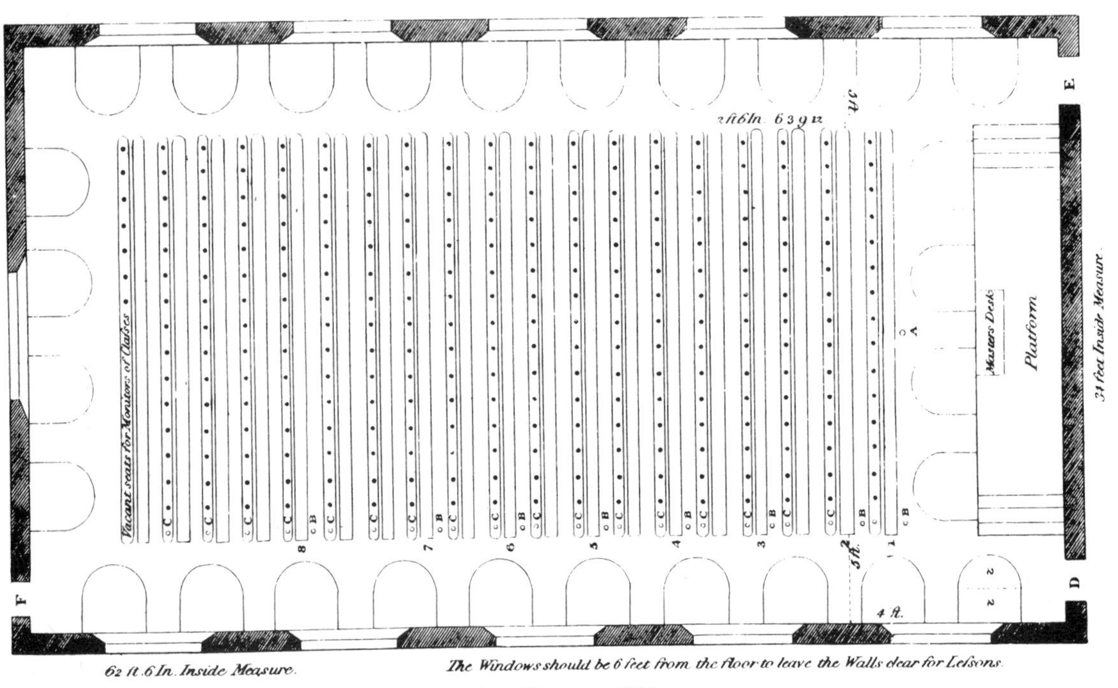

Plate 121 Plan of British school for 304 children

Plate 122 London, Central School of the National Society, Baldwin's Gardens, early nineteenth century

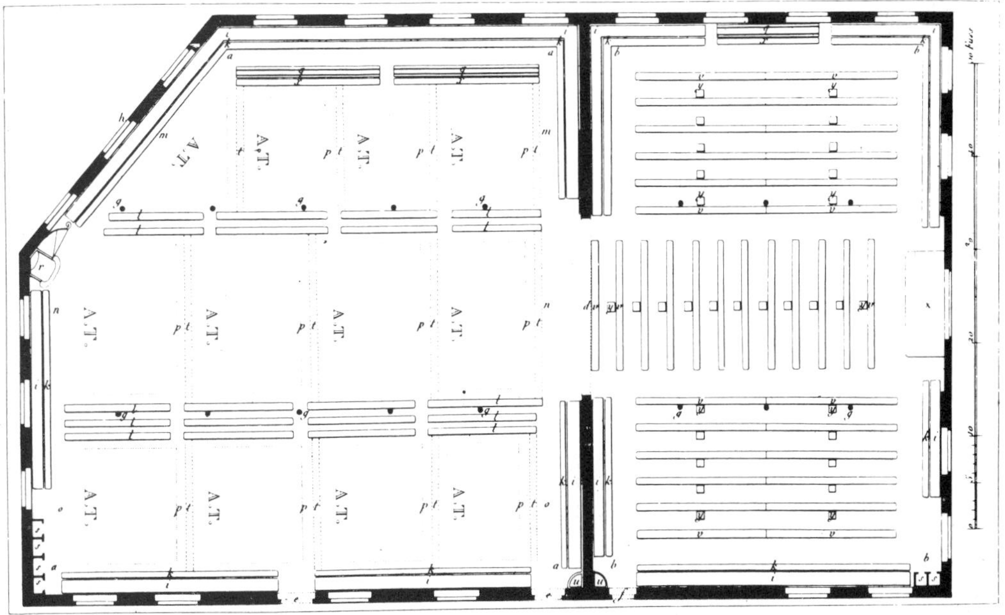

Plate 123 Plan of the above

Plate 124 Wandsworth, London, interior of Clapham Madras School, *c.* 1810

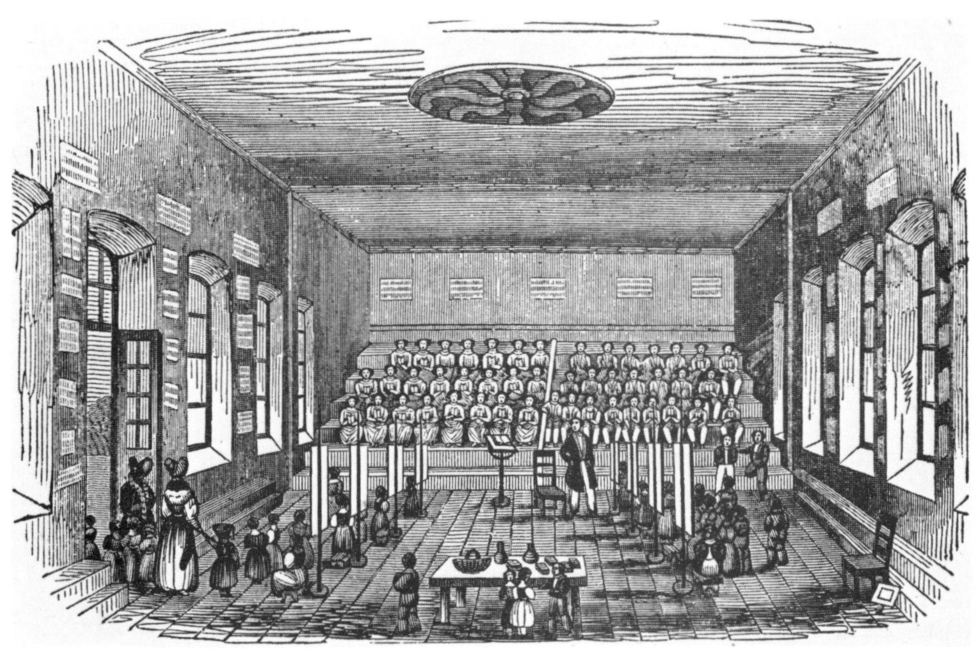

Plate 125 Stow's model infants' school, 1836

Plate 126 Handsworth, Yorks., inscription, 1800

Plate 127 Barkestone, Leics., inscription, 1814

Plate 128 Cambridge, Pound Hill, Free School, 1810

Plate 129 Penley, Flints., Madras School, 1811

Plate 130 Wakefield, Yorks., Lancasterian School, 1812

Plate 131 Wisbech, Cambs., Girls' School, 1814

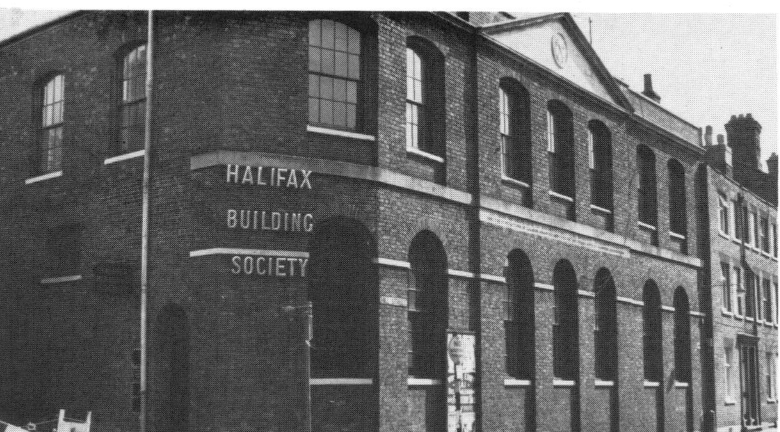

Plate 132 Shelf, Yorks., British School (L.) and teacher's house (R.), 1816

Plate 133 Daventry, Northants., interior of National School, early nineteenth century

Plate 134 St. Martin-in-the-Fields, London, National School, 1830

Plate 135 Nottingham, Barker Gate, National School, 1834

Plate 136 Ross-on-Wye, Herefs., British School, 1836

Plate 137 Finsbury, London, Clerkenwell Schools, 1828

Plate 138 Osmington, Dorset, 1835

Plate 139 Great Bowden, Leics., National School, 1839

Plate 140 Cruwys Morchard, Devon, *c.* 1840

Plate 141 Cheltenham, Glos., St. James's Square, infants' school, 1830

Plate 142 Newark-on-Trent, Notts., King Street, infants' school, 1840

Plate 143 Ashby-de-la-Zouch, Leics., Latin and English school, 1807

Plate 144 Colne, Lancs., Latin and English (?) school, 1812

Plate 145 St. Paul's School, London, rebuilt 1824; now demolished

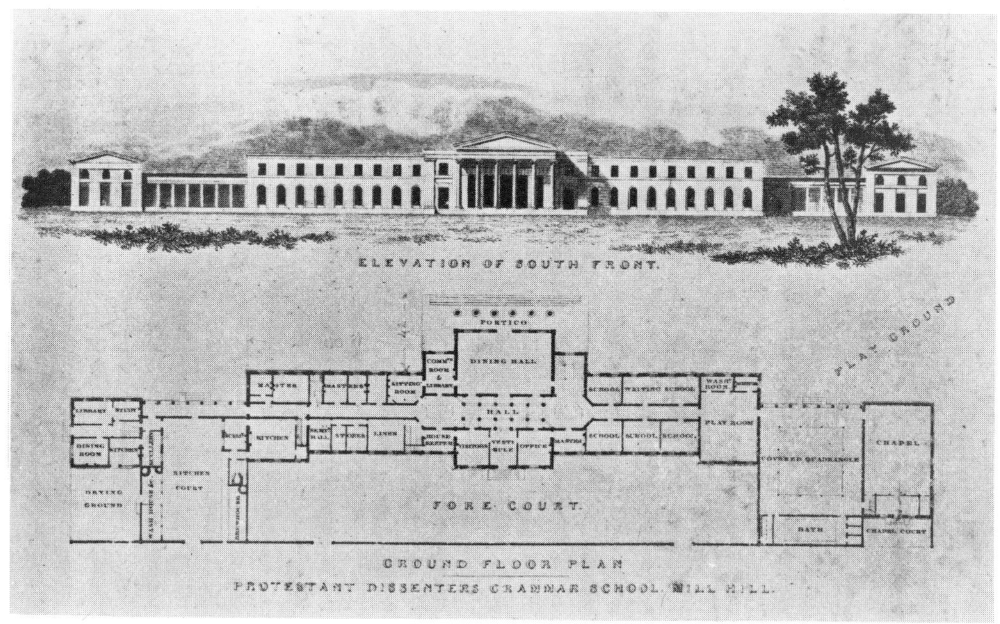

Plate 146 Mill Hill, Middx, Protestant Dissenters' Grammar School, 1825

Plate 147 Rugby, Warwicks., Schoolhouse Hall, 1816

Plate 148 Rugby, cloisters in 'Old Quad', 1816

Plate 149 Loughborough, Leics., Churchgate School, 1825

Plate 150 Market Bosworth, Leics., Dixie School, 1828

Plate 151 Wirksworth, Derbs., detail of school, 1829

Plate 152 Wolverley, Worcs., Sebright School, 1829

Plate 153 Christ's Hospital, London, Great Hall, 1829; now demolished

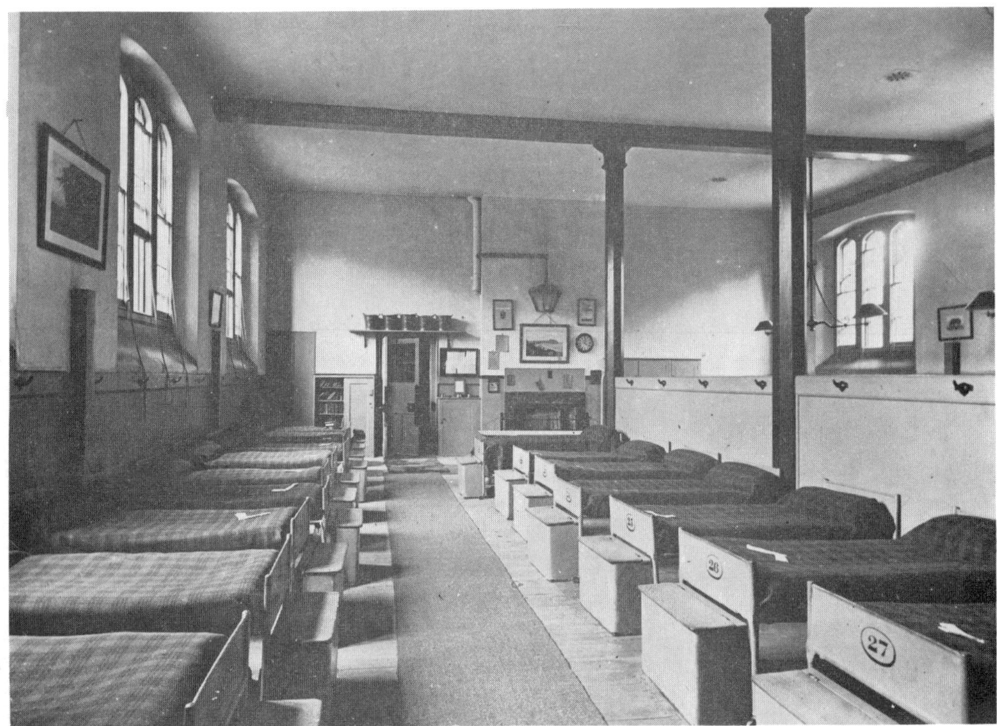

Plate 154 Christ's Hospital, dormitory, 1830; now demolished; photo. *c.* 1900

Plate 155 Bedford, schools built for Harpur Trust, 1834

Plate 156 City of London School, 1837; now demolished

Plate 157 Sheffield Collegiate School, 1836; now part of City of Sheffield College of Education

Plate 158 Leicester Proprietary School, 1837; now part of Leicester Museum

Plate 159 Birmingham, King Edward's School, the grammar schoolroom, 1838; now demolished

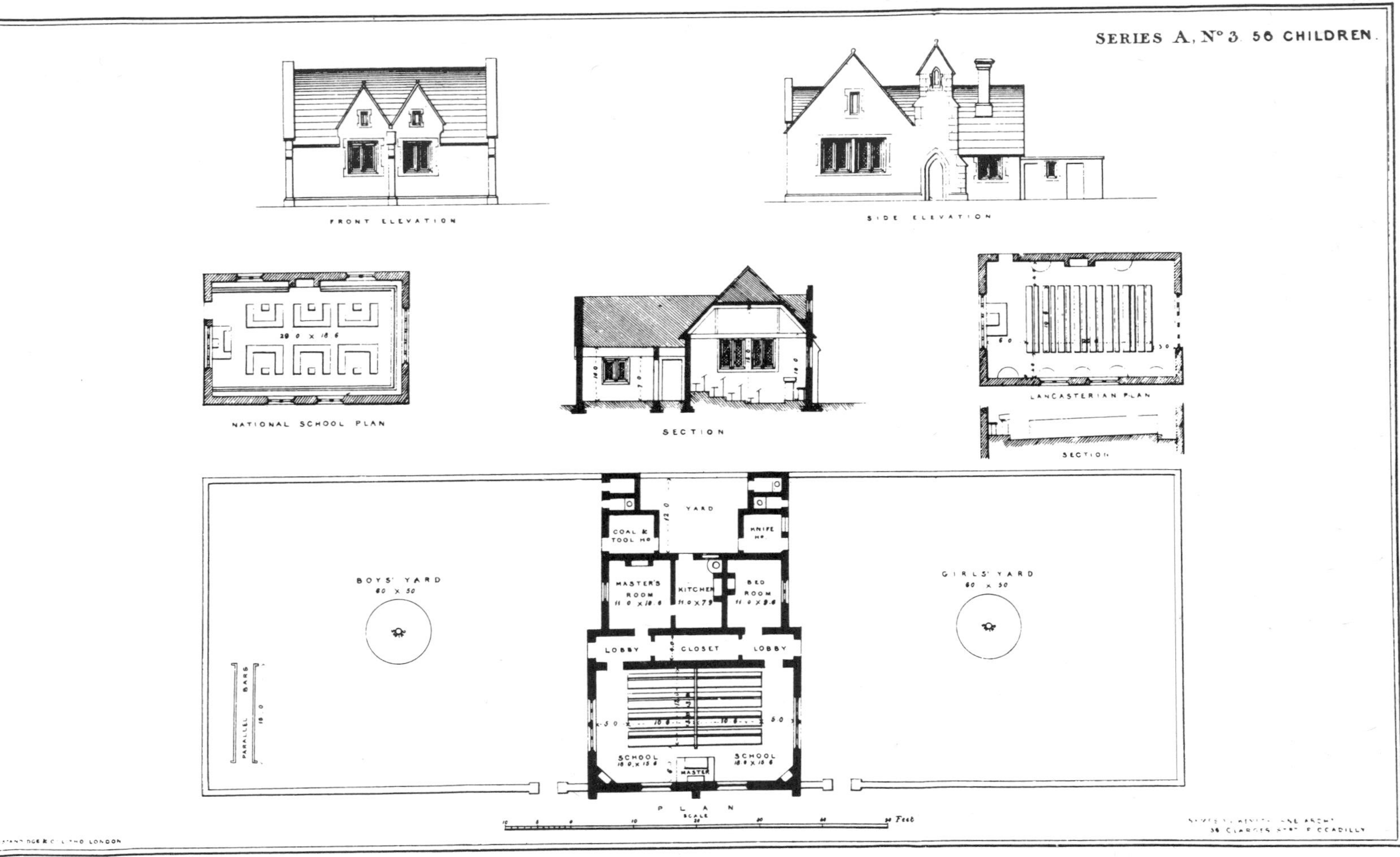

Plate 160 Committee of Council on Education, plan of school for 56 children, 1840

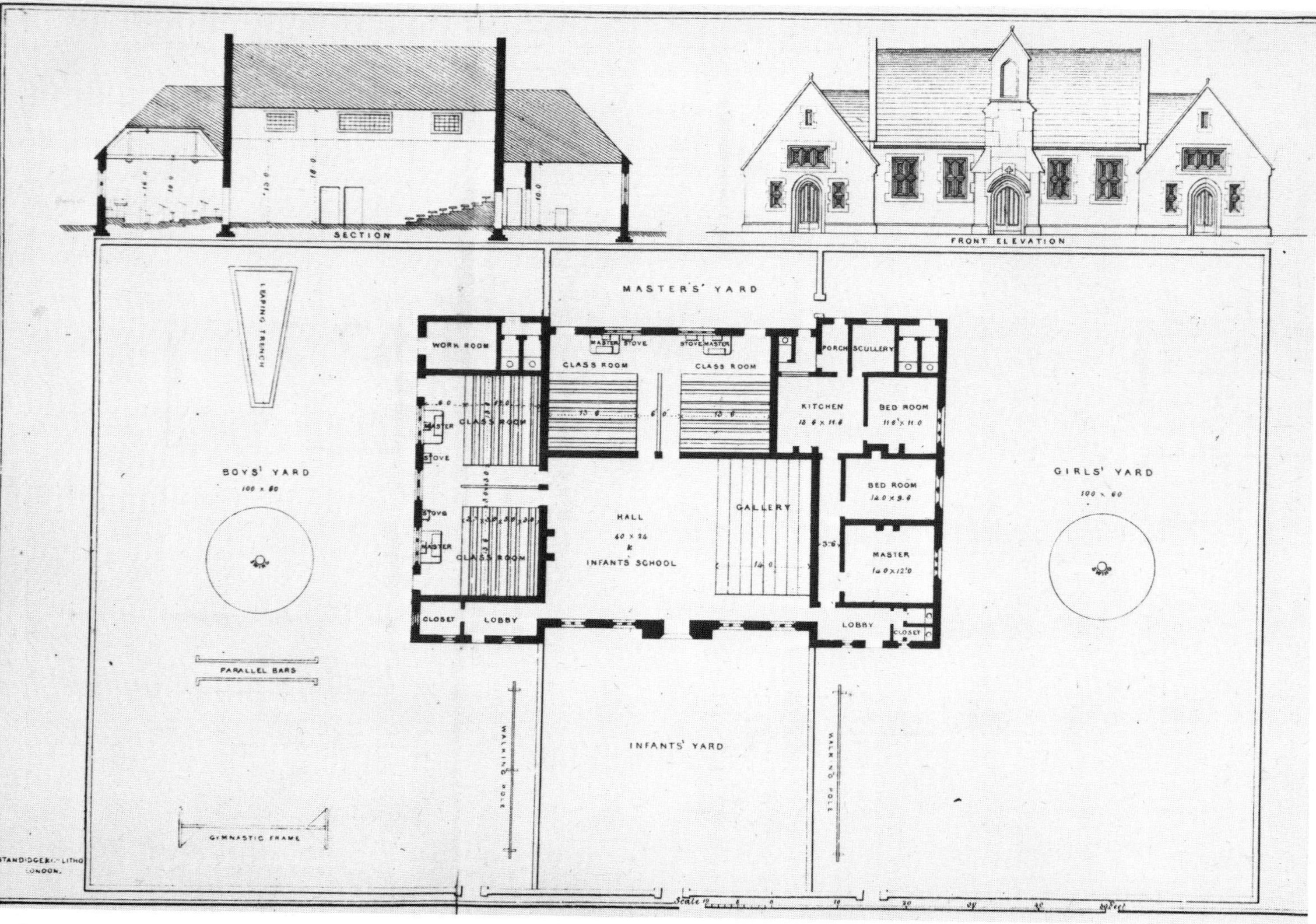

Plate 161 Committee of Council on Education, plan of school for 150 infants and 144 older children, 1840

Plate 162 Southwark, London, St. Mary Newington School, 1845 layout

Plate 163 Birmingham, Old Meeting Schools, Lancasterian layout

Plate 164 Dowlais, Glam., Guest's School, pre-1870 layout

Plate 165 London, school not known, pre-1870 layout

Plate 166 Lound, Chapeltown, Yorks., 1845, the 'ecclesiastical' style

Plate 167 Design by H. E. Kendall for a school in Early English style, 1847

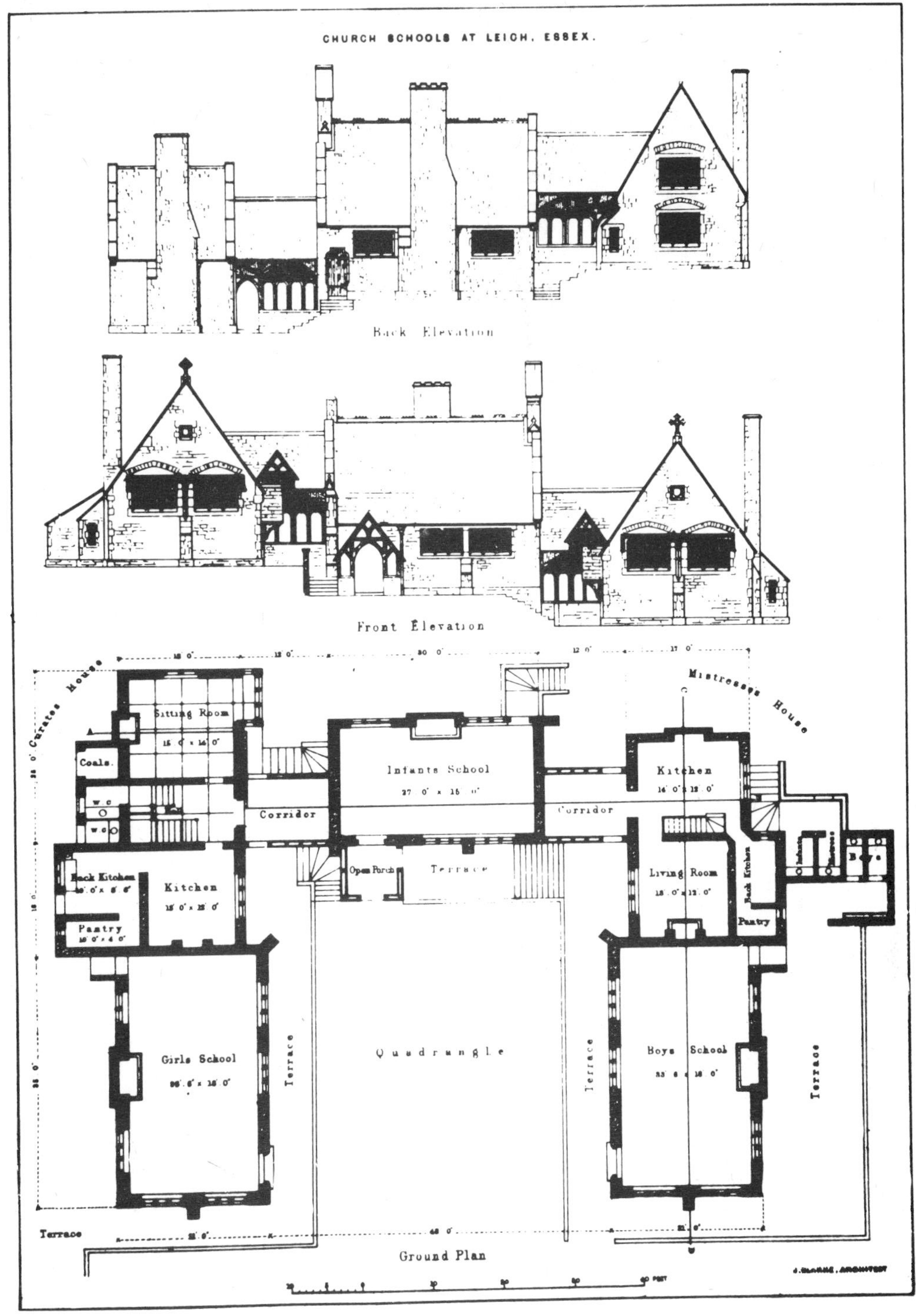

Plate 168 Design by J. Clarke for schools at Leigh, Essex, 1852

Plate 169 Berwick-on-Tweed, Northumb., National School, 1842

Plate 170 Cambridge, Russell Street, National School, 1845

Plate 171 Gretton, Northants., 1853

Plate 172 Kibworth Beauchamp, Leics., Parochial School, 1842

Plate 173 Heydon, Cambs., school (R.) and teacher's house (L.), 1846

Plate 174
Queniborough, Leics., National School, 1847

Plate 175 Habergham, Lancs., school (L.) and teacher's house (R.), 1848

Plate 176 Windsor, Berks., Queen Victoria's Schools in Windsor Great Park, 1845

Plate 177 Lowbands, Glos., Chartist Schools, 1848

Plate 178 Knipton, Leics., 1854

Plate 179 Burton Overy, Leics., 1857

Plate 180 Husband's Bosworth, Leics., 1858–60

Plate 181 Enderby, Leics., 1860

LUDLOW NATIONAL SCHOOLS.

These schools now in the course of erection, at Ludlow, are for the accommodation of 600 children—200 boys, 200 girls, and 200 infants, and have attached to them three distinct residences for a master and two mistresses. They are to be built of rubble masonry, arris pointed in blue mortar, with the windows, doors, dressings, and quoins of Bath stone. The infants' hall and school-room are to be lined with bricks. The roofs are of open timber work throughout. The design was selected in competition, and is the production of Mr. T. Nicholson, of Hereford, architect to the Hereford Diocesan Church Building Board. The builder is Mr. Coleman, of Chaxill. The cost of the whole scheme, including the purchase of the site, fencing the ground, &c. will be about 2,400*l.* towards which the Committee of Council have made a very liberal grant of 900*l.* in consideration of the efforts of the committee to raise means in the neighbourhood, and the fact that the provisions of the plan fully meet their views.

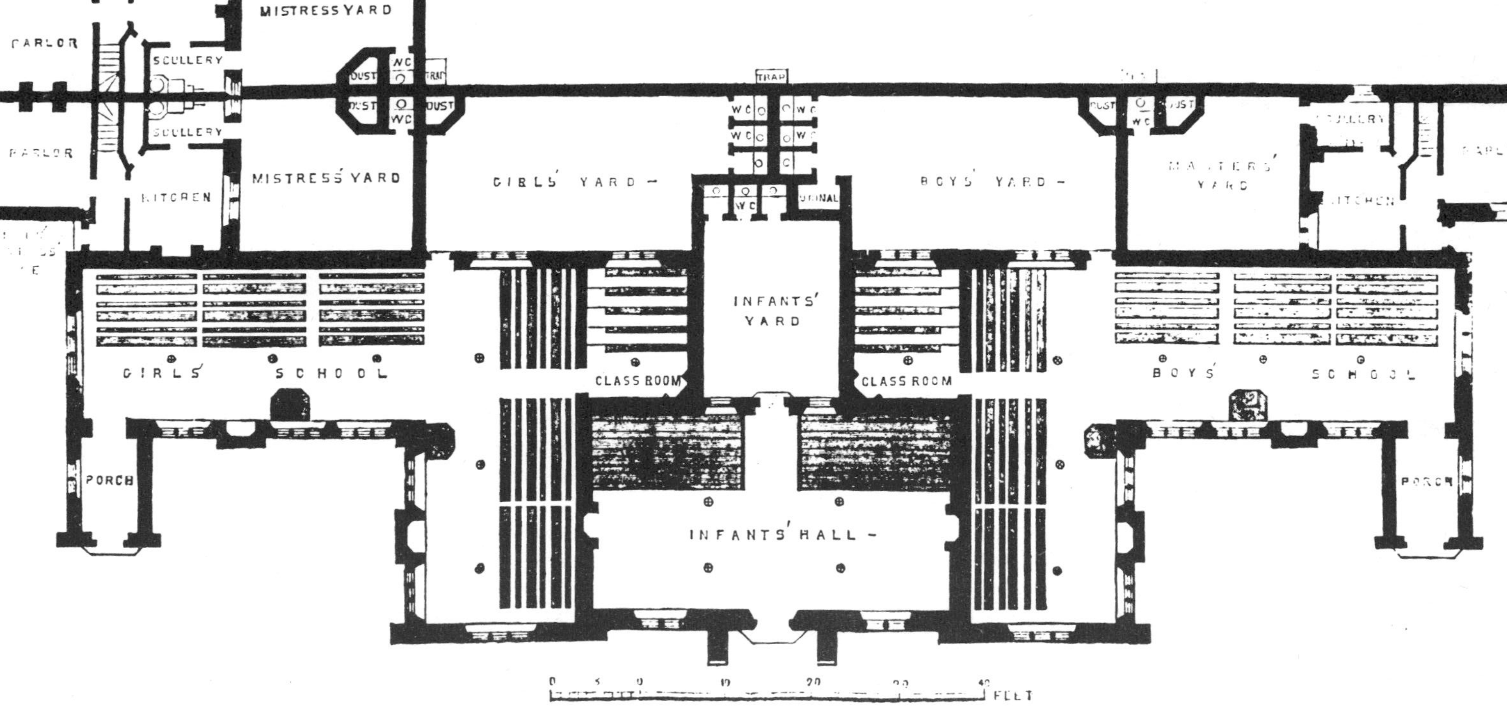

PLAN OF LUDLOW NATIONAL SCHOOLS.

Plate 182 Ludlow, Salop., plan of National Schools, 1855

Plate 183 Bristol, Redcliffe Infants' School, 1853, now demolished

Plate 184 Bloomsbury, London, Endell Street, National Schools, 1860

Plate 185 Harby, Leics., school for 100 children built for £861 in 1861

Plate 186 Brighton, Sussex, School for Blind Boys, 1861; now demolished

Plate 187 Paulerspury, Northants., pinnacle of school, 1861

Plate 188 Ely, Cambs., 'Obey them that have the rule over you', *c.* 1860

Plate 189 Northampton, Beckett and Sargeant School, figure of (eighteenth-century?) charity girl on 1862 building

Plate 190 Leicester, St. Mary's School, figure of charity boy, 1786, on 1869 building

Plate 191 Coalville, Leics., church, parsonage and school, *c.* 1840

Plate 192 Theddingworth, Leics., church, school and teacher's house, 1844

Plate 193 Ramsgate, Kent, St. Augustine's Church, School and house, 1853

Plate 194 Sheffield, Yorks., St. Vincent's School and Church, 1863

Plate 195 Cheltenham, Glos., St. Peter's School, teacher's house, 1848

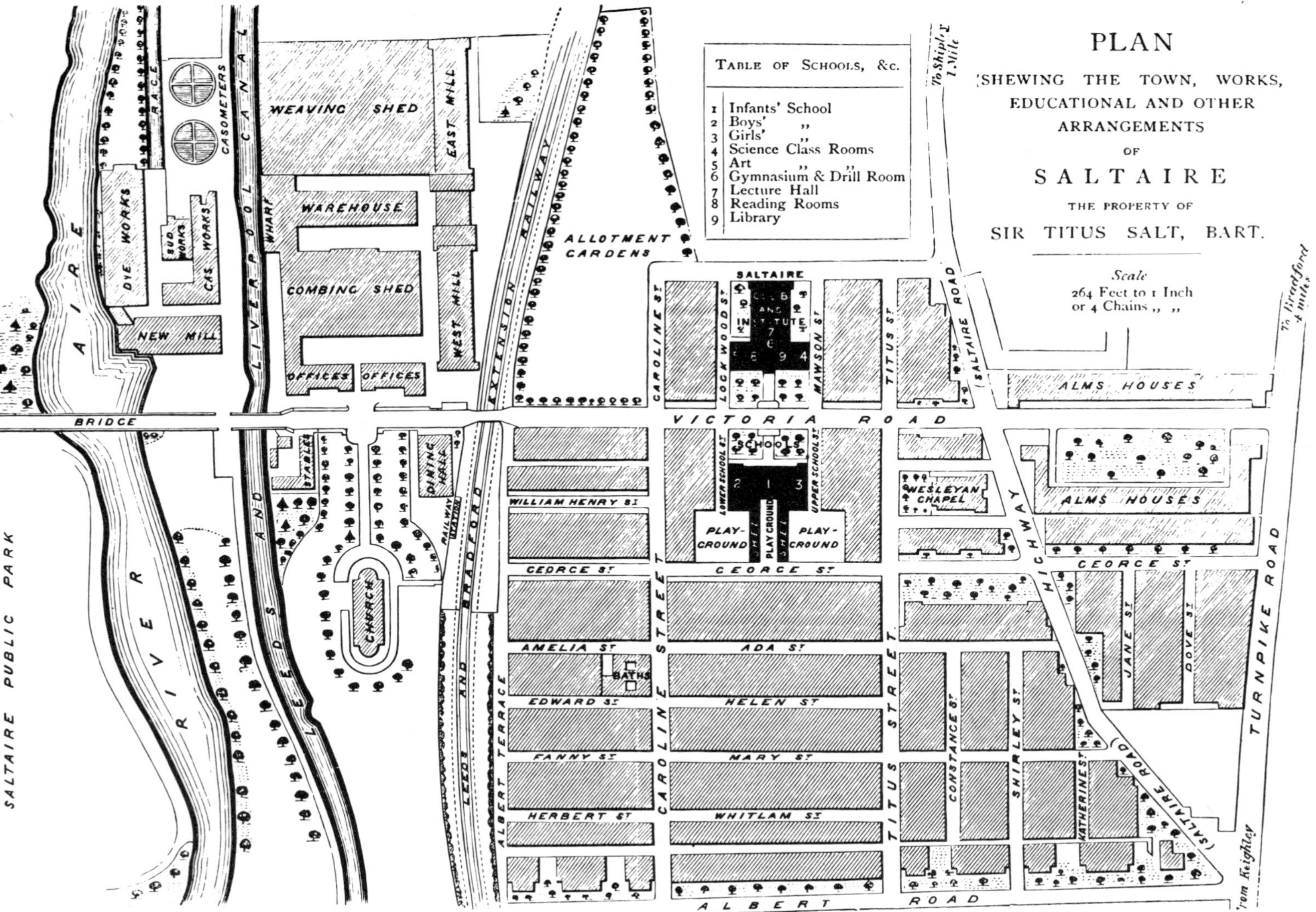

Plate 196 Saltaire, Yorks., plan of the new town, 1871

Plate 197 Saltaire, the Salt Schools, 1868

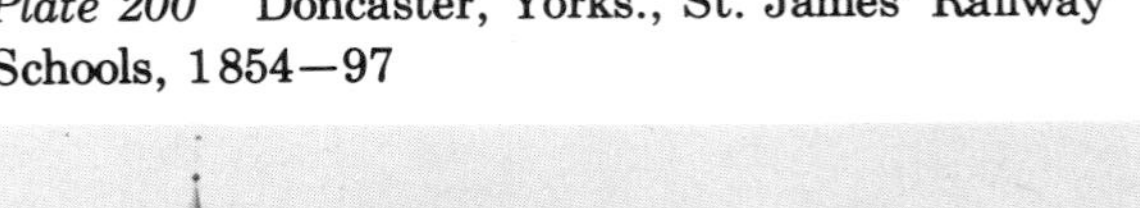

Plate 198 Detail from the Salt Schools

Plate 199 Newcastle-upon-Tyne, Northumb., Elswick Works Schools, 1866

Plate 200 Doncaster, Yorks., St. James' Railway Schools, 1854–97

Plate 201 Eton, New Buildings, 1844–46

Plate 202 Rugby, New Quad, 1867–72

Plate 203 Harrow, Vaughan Library, 1861–3

Plate 204 Liverpool Collegiate Institution, 1843

Plate 205 Cheltenham College, Glos., 1843–50

Plate 206 Marlborough College, Wilts., C-House, early eighteenth century; occupied by school in 1843

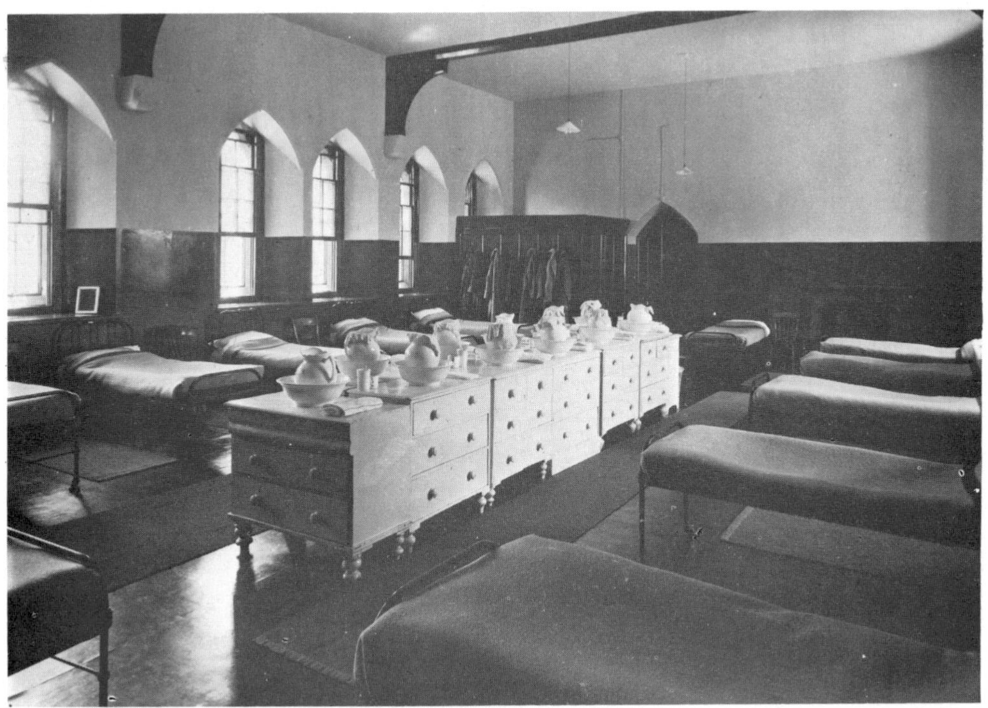

Plate 207 Brighton College, Sussex, dormitory, *c.* 1860

Plate 208 Radley College, Berks., dormitory, 1849

Plate 209 Radley College, cubicle in dormitory

Plate 210 Ratcliffe College, Leics., 1843–7

Plate 211 Taunton School, Som., 1869

Plate 212 Design for Ardingly College, Sussex, 1867

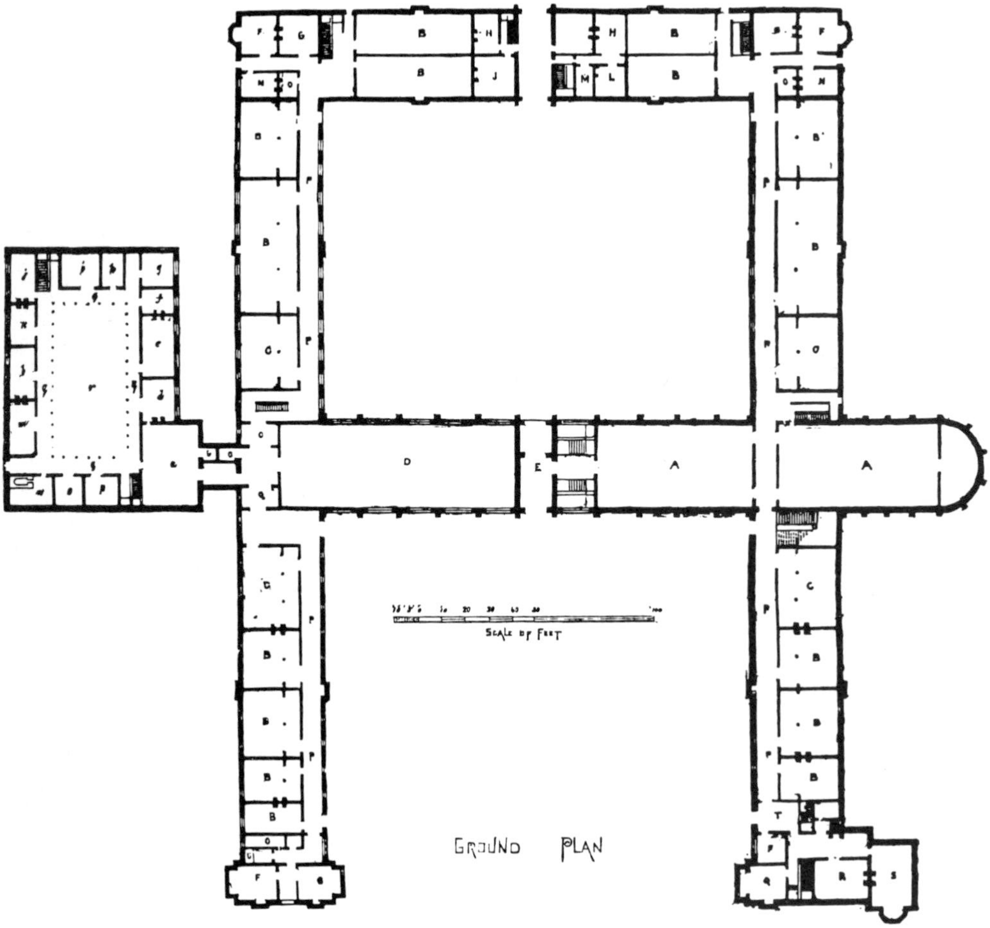

SCALE OF FEET

GROUND PLAN

Plate 213 Plan of Ardingly College, 1867

Plate 214 Lancing College, Sussex, chapel, 1868 and later

Plate 215 Wellington College, Berks., 1859

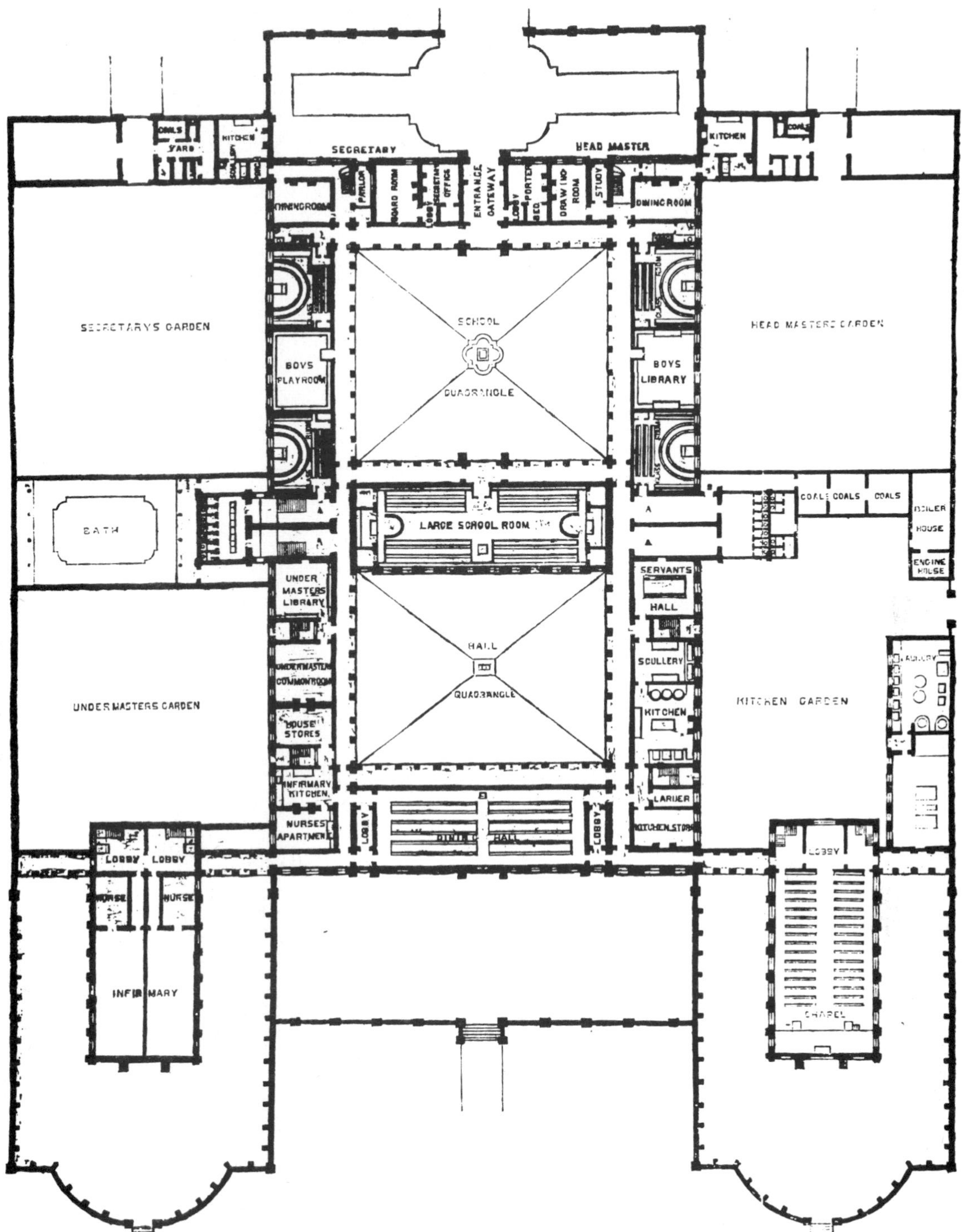

Plate 216 Wellington College, plan, 1856

Plate 217 Haileybury College, Herts., 1809; occupied by school in 1862; dome added 1876

Plate 218 Bedford, Elstow College, 1868; now demolished

Plate 219 Clifton College, Bristol, 1862 and later

Plate 220 Malvern College, Worcs., 1865 and later

Plate 221 Canterbury, Kent, King's School, delivery of speeches, 1845

Plate 222 Rotherham, Yorks., Grammar School, interior *c.* 1860

Plate 223 Wimborne, Dorset, Grammar and English School, 1851

Plate 224 Loughborough, Leics., Grammar and Commercial School, 1852

Ancient and Modern Building in Ipswich.

CONTRASTED

This shews the earnest endeavours of the Corporation to Pull down the Old Grammar School room
Erected 1351

This shews the earnest endeavours of the Corporation to Keep up the New Grammar School room
Erected 1851

To the Mayor Aldermen and Common Councilmen of the Borough
these sketches are (without permission) respectfully dedicated.

Plate 225 Ipswich, Suffolk, rebuilding the Grammar School, 1851

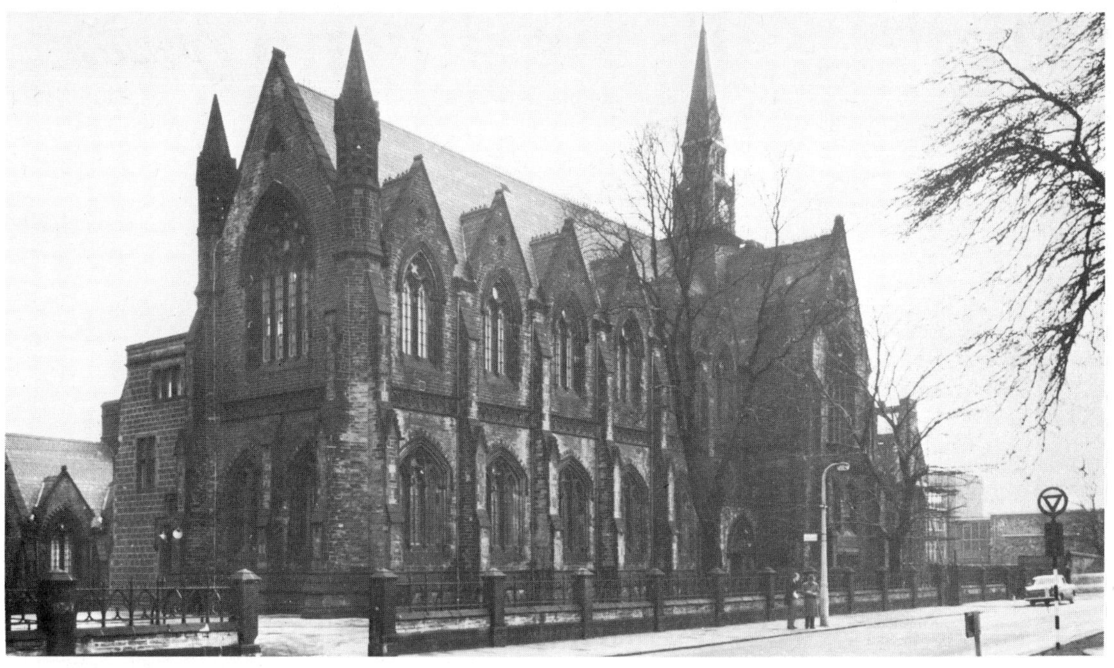

Plate 226 Leeds Grammar (Upper and Lower) School, Yorks., 1859

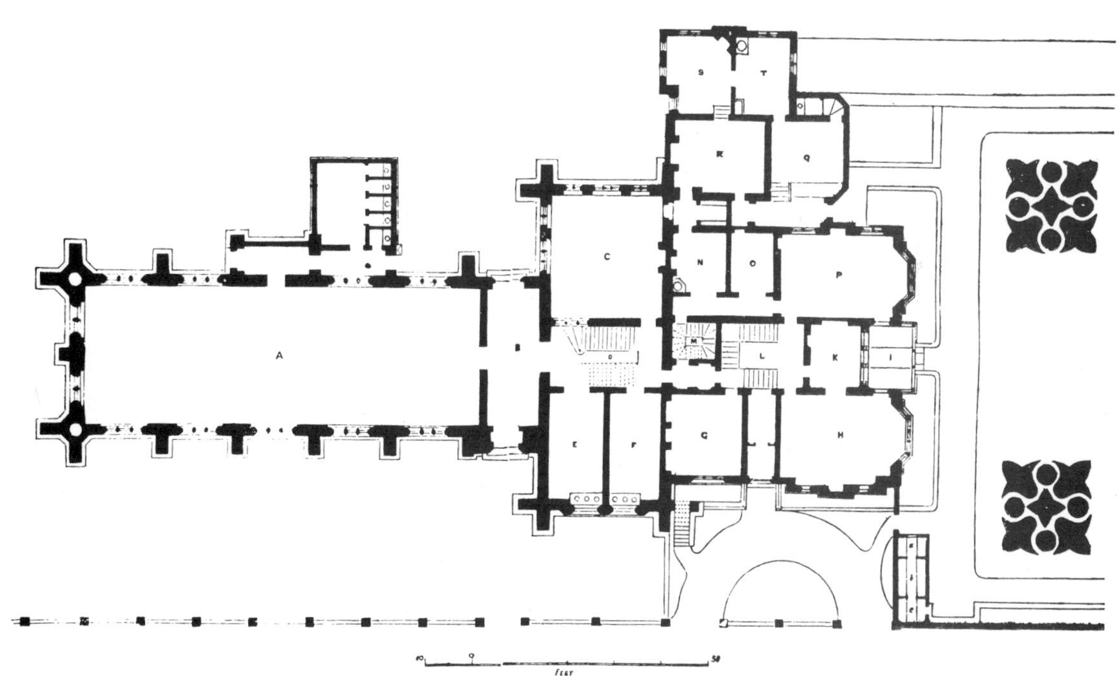

REFERENCES TO PLAN OF THE NEW GRAMMAR SCHOOL, LEEDS.

A. Lower School-room.
B. Entrance Hall.
C. Boarders' Study.
D. Boy's stairs to Upper School.
E. Cloak-room, Lower School.
F. Cloak-room, Upper School.
G. Study.
H. Drawing-room.
I. Conservatory.
K. Ante-room.
L. Principal stairs.
M. Back stairs.
N. Scullery.
O. Pantry.
P. Dining-room.
Q. Yard.
R. Kitchen.
S. Laundry.
T. Wash-house.
a. Green-house.
b. Forcing-house.
c. Potting-shed.

Plate 227 Leeds Grammar School, plan

Plate 228 Nottingham Grammar (Classical and English) School, 1868 and later

Plate 229 Doncaster Grammar School, Yorks., Big School, 1869

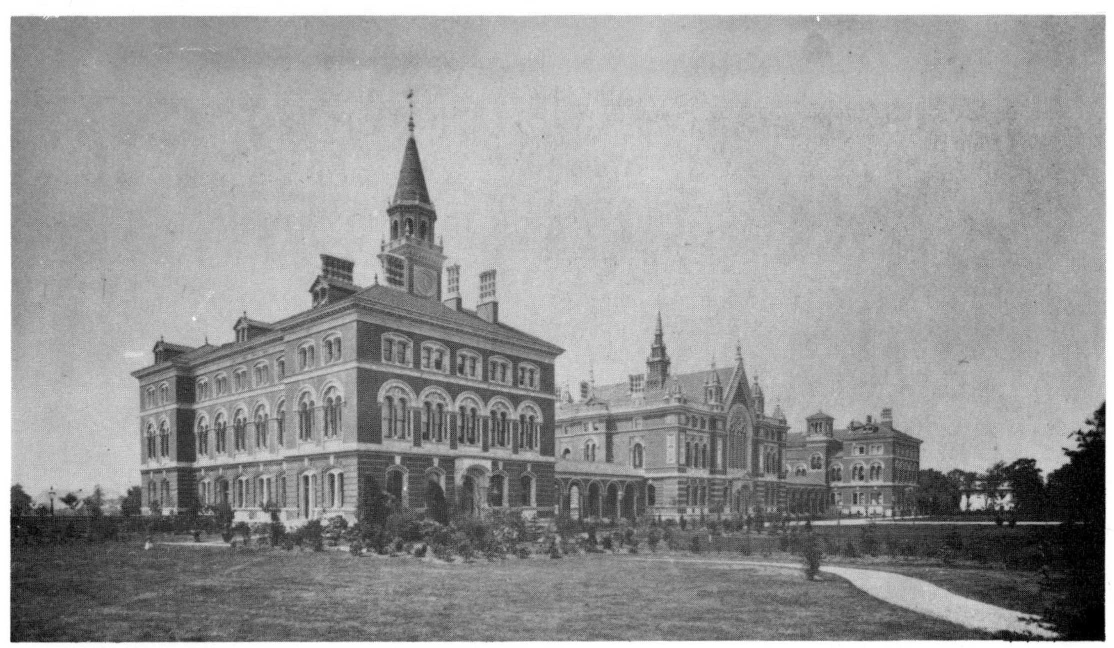

Plate 230 Dulwich College, Camberwell, London, 1866–70

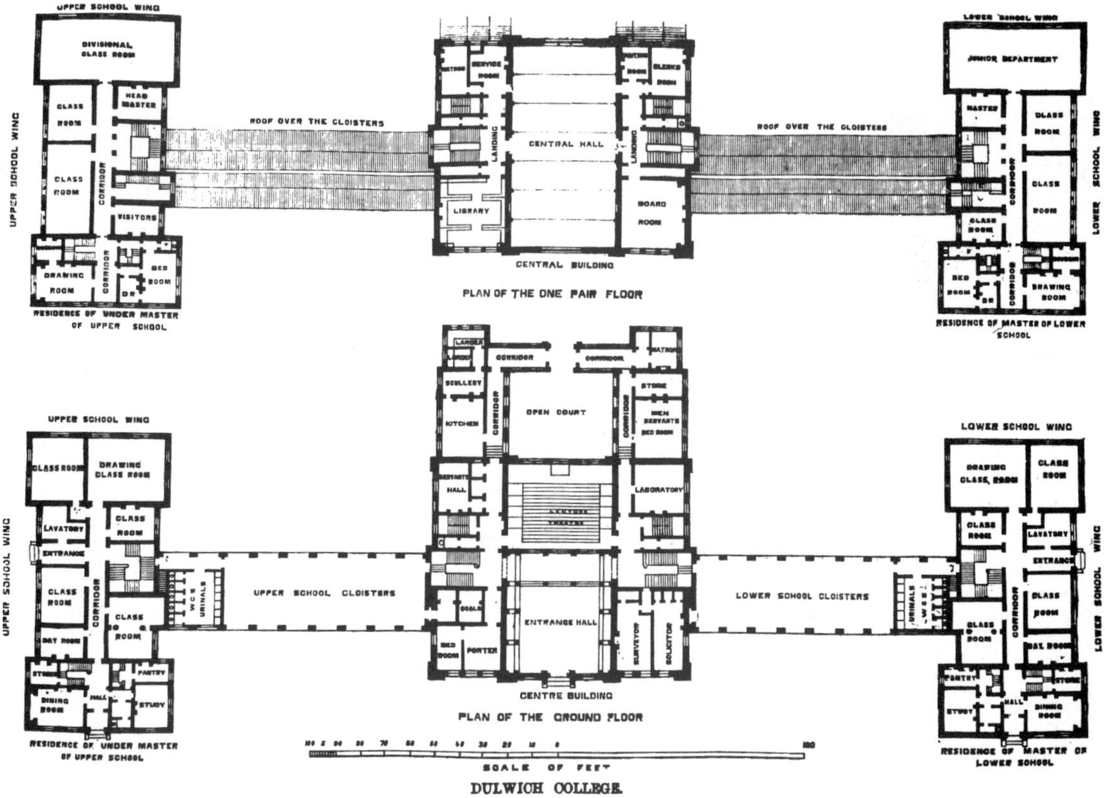

UPPER SCHOOL WING
DIVISIONAL CLASS ROOM
CLASS ROOM
HEAD MASTER
CORRIDOR
VISITORS
DRAWING ROOM
BED ROOM
RESIDENCE OF UNDER MASTER OF UPPER SCHOOL
ROOF OVER THE CLOISTERS
SERVICE ROOM
CENTRAL HALL
LANDING
LIBRARY
BOARD ROOM
CENTRAL BUILDING
PLAN OF THE ONE PAIR FLOOR
LOWER SCHOOL WING
JUNIOR DEPARTMENT
MASTER
RESIDENCE OF MASTER OF LOWER SCHOOL
CORRIDOR
SCULLERY
KITCHEN
OPEN COURT
STORE
MEN SERVANTS BED ROOM
SERVANTS HALL
LABORATORY
LECTURE THEATRE
ENTRANCE HALL
PORTER
SURVEYOR
SOLICITOR
CENTRE BUILDING
PLAN OF THE GROUND FLOOR
CLASS ROOM
DRAWING CLASS ROOM
LAVATORY
ENTRANCE
DAY ROOM
PANTRY
DINING ROOM
HALL
STUDY
W C S
URINALS
UPPER SCHOOL CLOISTERS
LOWER SCHOOL CLOISTERS
SCALE OF FEET
DULWICH COLLEGE

Plate 231 Dulwich College, plan, 1868

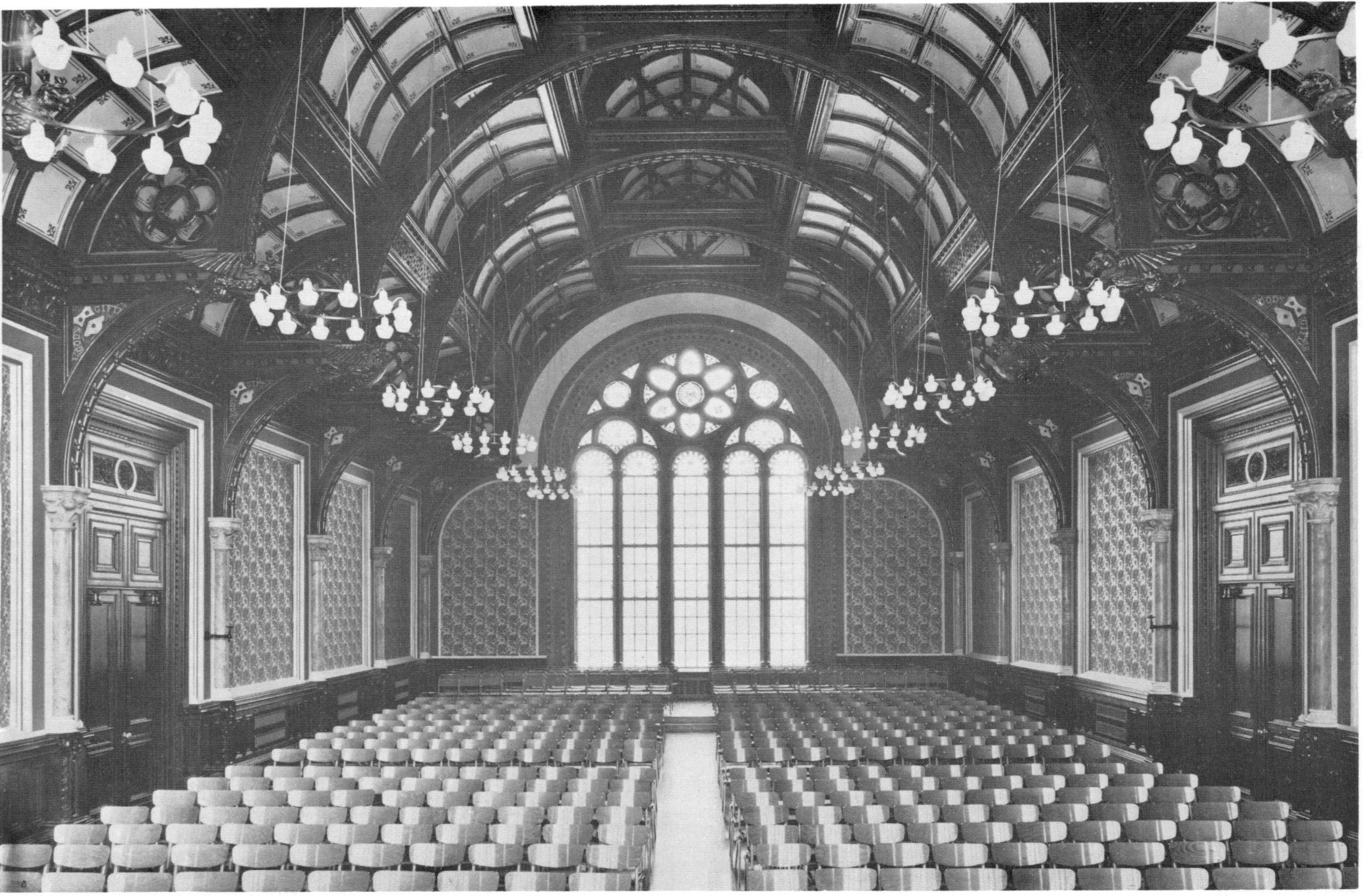

Plate 232 Dulwich College, Great Hall, 1870

Plate 233 Uppingham School, Rutland, gymnasium, 1859; photo. *c*. 1880

Plate 234 Uppingham School, chemistry laboratory, 1856(?); photo. *c*. 1880

Plate 235 Uppingham School, chapel, 1865 and later

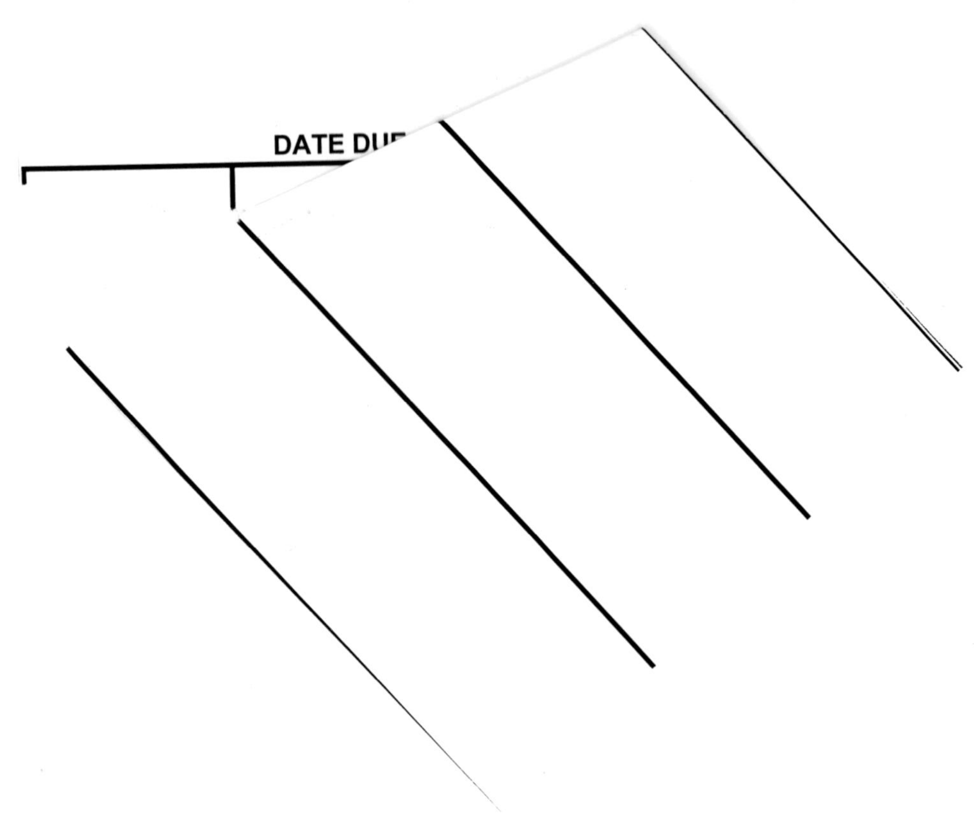
DATE DU